Central Banking

Central Banking

Theory and Practice in Sustaining Monetary and Financial Stability

THAMMARAK MOENJAK

WILEY

Cover Design: Wiley
Cover Image: © iStock.com/sebastian-julian

Copyright © 2014 by John Wiley & Sons Singapore Pte. Ltd.

Published by John Wiley & Sons Singapore Pte. Ltd.
1 Fusionopolis Walk, #07-01, Solaris South Tower, Singapore 138628
All rights reserved.

Other Wiley Editorial Offices
John Wiley & Sons, 111 River Street, Hoboken, NJ 07030, USA
John Wiley & Sons, The Atrium, Southern Gate, Chichester, West Sussex, P019 8SQ, United Kingdom
John Wiley& Sons (Canada) Ltd., 5353 Dundas Street West, Suite 400, Toronto, Ontario, M9B 6HB,
Canada
John Wiley& Sons Australia Ltd., 42 McDougall Street, Milton, Queensland 4064, Australia
Wiley-VCH, Boschstrasse 12, D-69469 Weinheim, Germany

Library of Congress Cataloging-in-Publication Data

ISBN 9781118832462 (Hardcover)
ISBN 9781118832554 (ePDF)
ISBN 9781118832578 (ePub)

Typeset in 10/12pt, Sabon Family by MPS Ltd, Chennai

To Thamrongsak and Lugsana Moenjak,
my loving parents.

Contents

Preface

This book aims to provide readers with an understanding of and insights into the roles and functions of central banks, the theories behind their thinking, and actual operational practices. In the wake of the global financial crisis of 2007–2010 there has been a renewed interest in central banking on the part of academics, practitioners, and the general public. Many believe that central banks had a leading role in contributing to the crisis, while others disagree. Most, however, agree that in the future, central banks need to play a leading role in maintaining both *monetary* and *financial* stability.

Although central banking is currently in the limelight, there are not many comprehensive books on the subject aimed at students or a general audience. Courses specifically devoted to central banking at the university level are still relatively rare. Students, investors, market and policy analysts, and even central banks' new recruits often have to search among different sources to piece together what central banks actually do and what the reasons are behind their actions. The picture they arrive at, however, can be very fragmented.

The few current books on central banking that touch on the various aspects of the subject are mainly for expert audiences, that is, interested academics and seasoned central bankers. These books often assume readers have a strong background in monetary economics, banking regulation, or other central banking operation and thus delve deeply into subtopics such as central bank independence, monetary policy transparency, or the Basel rules. This approach makes it difficult for nonexperts and novices to follow the material and put it in a proper context.

While textbooks on monetary economics can offer a very rigorous theoretical background on monetary policy, they often do not provide detailed descriptions of actual operations. In many cases, descriptions of monetary policy operations can be quite out of date. On the other hand, popular books about central banking intended for a general audience often do not offer enough theoretical background in a systematic manner for the interested reader to make sense of why central banks might choose to adopt or abandon a particular practice.

This book aims to fill in the gaps by providing an introductory overview of central banking in a manner that is systematic, up-to-date, and accessible to a general audience and students who have minimal background in macroeconomics. Theoretical reviews and examples of how theories are applied in practice are done in an easy-to-understand manner. With the background provided by the book, it is hoped that readers will be able to investigate further the topics that interest them, with the ultimate goal of helping them make informed judgments about a central bank's actions, and, hopefully, have the ability to even anticipate them in advance.

Part I provides a quick background on central banking. Chapter 1 briefly reviews the evolution of central banking and how different functions of central banks came about. Chapter 2 provides background on the international monetary system in order to provide the context in which central banks operate. Chapter 3 reviews functions of modern central banks. Although specifics do differ among modern central banks, there are commonalities as well as diversity among their functions. Chapter 4 reviews three of the most prominent mandates for modern central banks: monetary stability, financial stability, and (more controversially) full employment.

Part II focuses on *monetary stability*, the dominant central banking mandate for the past 30 years. Chapter 5 reviews the theoretical foundations of monetary policy, the policy that a central bank uses to regulate monetary conditions in the economy in order to achieve monetary stability. Chapter 6 looks at different monetary policy regimes (i.e., rules) that central banks might adopt in the pursuit of monetary stability. Chapter 7 looks at the implementation of monetary policy, which in practice is often done through operations in financial markets. Chapter 8 looks at how monetary policy can transmit across the economy and affect monetary stability as well as output and employment. Chapter 9 is devoted to the exchange rate, another key variable that central banks have to keep an eye on, as it is the price of money in terms of another currency and could also affect monetary stability as well as financial stability.

Part III focuses on *financial stability*, another key central banking mandate that started to receive attention in the 1980s and has received even more since the global financial crisis of 2007–2010. Chapter 10 reviews various definitions of financial stability, an analytical framework that could be practical for central banks' purposes, and prominent theories related to financial stability. Chapter 11 examines various tools that central banks might use to identify and monitor risks to financial stability. The review of these tools uses the analytical framework proposed in Chapter 10: the macroeconomy, financial institutions, and financial markets. Chapter 12 examines the various tools that the central bank can use against risks to financial stability.

Part IV looks at the future challenges of central banking and how central banks might prepare themselves to meet those challenges. Chapter 13 reviews the three major forces that might shape the economic and financial landscape that central banks will be operating in: the intensification of the globalization process, the continued evolution of financial activities, and unfinished business from the global financial crisis. Chapter 14 analyzes how central banks might prepare themselves to meet future challenges and deliver value to society. This analysis uses a public policy analysis framework that involves improving the analytical capacity, the operational capacity, and the political capacity of the central bank.

Ancillary materials for students and instructors can be found at wiley.com.

Acknowledgments

In writing this book I am indebted to many people and institutions, whether directly or indirectly.

At Wiley, I would like to express my gratitude to the many people who helped make the book possible, and in particular to Nick Wallwork, Jules Yap, Emilie Herman, Lia Ottaviano, Jeremy Chia, Gladys Ganaden, Chris Gage, and Tami Trask for their constant encouragement, kind help, and earnest support throughout the process.

At the Lee Kuan Yew School of Public Policy, National University of Singapore, I am grateful to the wonderful faculty, staff and fellow students, particularly my friends from the master in public management program, whose friendships are very much treasured.

I am deeply indebted to the Bank of Thailand for giving me a chance to work in many interesting jobs, tap into its vast institutional knowledge pool, and learn from my many extremely dedicated and capable friends, supervisors, and colleagues.

I am very much grateful to Charles Adams, Robert J. Dixon, Charles Goodhart, Kishore Mahbubani, Paul A. Volcker, and Christopher Worswick for kindly giving their invaluable time to review the manuscript. Any error that might appear in the book is, of course, mine.

I would like to also thank my parents, Thamrongsak and Lugsana Moenjak, whose love, support, and dedication throughout the years made this book possible.

About the Author

Thammarak Moenjak has been deeply involved with various aspects of central banking since he started working at the Bank of Thailand (BOT) in 2000.

His work experience includes modeling and forecasting, monetary policy strategy, reserves management, financial stability assessment, and corporate strategy.

Aside from being the assistant chief representative of the Bank of Thailand at its New York Representative Office in 2008–2009, Thammarak was sent by the Bank of Thailand, and contracted as an IMF expert, to help the Reserve Bank of Fiji develop its own macroeconometric model for use in the conduct of monetary policy.

Thammarak recently completed a master degree in public management at the Lee Kuan Yew School of Public Policy, the National University of Singapore, where he was on the Dean's List for Meritorious Performance, and was a Lee Kuan Yew Fellow at the John F. Kennedy School of Government, Harvard University. He has a bachelor degree in economics from the London School of Economics and a PhD in Economics from the University of Melbourne. Thammarak could be reached at thammarm@bot.or.th.

One

An Introduction to Central Banking

Part I provides background on central banking.

Chapter 1 briefly reviews the evolution of central banking since its start about 400 years ago and how different functions of central banks came about.

Chapter 2 provides background on the international monetary system. Central banking has had an international dimension since the start, and to understand central banking it is very important to know the international monetary system that central banks operate in.

Chapter 3 reviews the functions of modern central banks. Although specifics do differ among central banks, there are commonalities as well as differences among modern central bank functions.

Chapter 4 reviews modern central bank mandates, that is, their key objectives. Again, there are commonalities and differences across central banks. Three key mandates are discussed: monetary stability, financial stability, and (particularly in the case of the United States) full employment.

CHAPTER 1

A Brief Look at Central Banking History

Learning Objectives

1. Describe historical roles and functions of central banks.
2. Explain how various central banking roles and functions came about.
3. Define money and its relation to central banking.
4. Describe key commonalities and differences of modern central banks.

Historically, central banking is a relatively new phenomenon, tracing its origin to about 400 years ago. In that relatively short period of time, however, central banks have evolved to become among the most important public institutions, which profoundly affect everyone's daily life. This chapter briefly reviews the evolution of central banking in various stages, so the reader will understand the background of how central banks rose to become what they are today.

The chapter starts with the context in which the central bank was first created. Earlier roles of central banks—such as coin sorting, banknote issuance, banker to the government, and banker to banks—will first be discussed. Later, the chapter looks at newer roles of central banks, such as the lender of last resort, bank supervisor, and the conductor of monetary policy. Lastly, the chapter looks at the current stage of central banking, especially in the wake of the 2007–2010 global financial crisis that led to extensive reexamination of the role of central banks around the world.

1.1 PRIOR TO CENTRAL BANKING

Prior to the creation of central banks, societies often used precious metals such as gold or silver as the means of transaction for goods and services. In economic terms, precious metals were deemed suitable for being *money*, as they possessed three inherent characteristics. First, these metals were widely accepted as a *medium of exchange*. People were willing to trade their goods and services for precious metals, since they believed that they could use the metals to trade for other goods and services that they wanted to consume. Second, these metals were a good *store of value*. People who received these metals could keep them for future trading for what they might want to consume. Unlike grains or livestock, precious metals were not perishable, nor would they easily lose their luster. Third, they could be used as *units of account*, for they could be divided into uniform pieces according to the assigned value.

1.2 COIN SORTING AND STORING

When a society developed to a certain degree, the use of precious metals as money became more formalized and standardized. The metals were made into coins, which made them easier to transport. They were also stamped with seals or signs certifying their weight and value, which made it easier to recognize and classify them.

In Europe, by the seventeenth century, the use of coins in commerce became more cumbersome and required more effort for merchants. Different sovereigns introduced different makes of coins that were of different values and different metal content but circulated quite freely across borders. Different vintages of coins of the same nominal value from the same sovereign could also have different metal content, as sovereigns sometimes sought extra revenue by introducing coins of the same value with lighter and lighter metal content—that is, coin debasement.[1]

Furthermore, there were also risks that the coins might be worn out because of usage, such that the precious metal content became diminished, or they might be intentionally *clipped*, as people chipped out metal content from the coins.[2]

To ease the problems related to coin usage, in 1609 merchants and the city of Amsterdam, a premier global trading hub of that time, decided to set up the Bank of Amsterdam to do the tasks of sorting, classifying, and storing the coins. The success of the Bank of Amsterdam prompted other European cities and sovereigns to set up banks along the lines of the Bank of Amsterdam.[3]

1.3 BANKNOTE ISSUANCE

In 1656, the Bank of Stockholm was established in Sweden, in the fashion of the Bank of Amsterdam. At first, the bank simply took in copper coins and lent out against tangible assets such as real estate.[4] Five years later, however, as the Swedish parliament decided to reduce the amount of copper in newly minted coins, older coins of the same nominal face value became more valuable owing to their greater copper content. The public rushed to get their hands on the older coins, and the bank run threatened the Bank of Stockholm's survival.

The solution by the Bank of Stockholm to prevent the threat that it might run out of coins was to issue notes of credit (called *kreditivsedlar*) to those depositors who wanted to withdraw their copper coins. With their features of having fixed face values in round denominations, no paid interest, and being freely transferable from one holder to another, these kreditivsedlar were considered the first banknotes in the modern sense.[5] This solution was a success for about two years until the Bank of Stockholm could not redeem the notes at their face values and the government had to intervene.

In 1668, the Swedish parliament approved a new bank to replace the Bank of Stockholm. Ultimately, that new bank became the present-day Swedish central bank, the Sveriges Riksbank, currently the world's oldest central bank. (The Bank of

Amsterdam collapsed in 1819, suffering losses from their investments in the Dutch East India Company, which financed wars with England.[6])

Despite the demise of the Bank of Stockholm, the use of banknotes as a medium of exchange survived and gradually became embedded in our modern economies. As merchants who had coins deposited at the bank traded goods and services among themselves, it was clearly easier for them to transfer their coin ownerships at the bank without withdrawing those coins to settle their trades. Therefore, it was also easier for the bank to just issue notes for those who owned coins held at the bank so that they could use the notes to trade with those without accounts at the bank. In the few centuries after the pioneer banknote issuance by the Bank of Stockholm, banknote issuance became popular in many countries, but was not confined only to banks established by governments or sovereigns. In many countries, privately owned banks were also granted the right to issue their own banknotes.

1.4 BANKER TO THE GOVERNMENT

The Swedish Riksbank was chartered to not only act as a clearinghouse for merchants but also to lend funds to the government. Later on, many other central banks were also created to help finance government spending, particularly to finance wars. These included (1) the *Bank of England*, which was founded in 1694 as a joint stock company to finance the war with France and was later also given the privilege of handling the government's accounts;[7] (2) the *Bank of France*, which was created in 1800 both to help with government finances and to issue banknotes in Paris (for which it was given a monopoly), partly to help stabilize the economy after the French Revolution brought hyperinflation of paper money;[8] and (3) the *Bank of Spain*, which could trace its roots to 1782 when its predecessor was founded to finance the country's participation in the American War of Independence, although it was not until 1856 that the predecessor bank was merged with another bank to form the Bank of Spain.[9]

By helping to finance government spending and manage government finances, these early central banks enjoyed close relationships with their governments, along with good profits. As lenders to their governments, notes issued by these early central banks gained wide acceptance, since they were implicitly backed by the promise of repayment by their sovereigns. In the case of the early Bank of England, it could simply issue notes to match the sum lent to the government. In such a case, the notes (dissimilar to modern banknotes, since their face values were variable, as the amounts were handwritten by the cashier) were not backed by precious metals, but by the implicit promise of the government to pay.[10]

1.5 BANKER TO BANKS

By the nineteenth century, central banks' close ties to their governments and the wide acceptance of their banknotes (or in many cases, their monopoly on note issuance) helped induce commercial banks to also open accounts and place their deposits with the central banks, effectively becoming their clients. Consequently, the central banks became banker to the commercial banks, in addition to being banker to the government. The banker-to-banks role became more and more pronounced as the foundations of modern banking started taking shape.

In the case of nineteenth-century England, small banks proliferated in small towns doing business such as discounting merchants' bills. These small-town banks often sought out larger London commercial banks as their correspondent banks, to deposit and invest their funds and conduct other transactions. The London commercial banks, in turn, often found it easier to settle claims among themselves using Bank of England notes, as the Bank of England had a monopoly on note issuance within a 65-mile radius of London.[11]

Even more conveniently, the commercial banks could open deposit accounts at the Bank of England and use these accounts to settle claims among themselves or to keep reserves. By being the key repository and clearinghouse for commercial banks whose own networks of correspondent banks could be far-reaching, the Bank of England's function as a banker to banks became notable and helped in defining the bank as a *central* bank. The Bank of England's banker-to-banks role would become a model for many central banks to later emulate.

1.6 PROTECTOR OF THE FINANCIAL SYSTEM: LENDER OF LAST RESORT

Early banking systems were very prone to panics and bank failures. By nature, banks and other financial institutions *borrowed* funds from depositors for short maturity, and lent out those funds as loans for longer maturity. Diverse events such as bad harvests, defaults, and wars could cause bank depositors to panic and rush to withdraw their funds, putting debilitating pressures on the banks, since they might not be able to call in loans fast enough to repay the depositors.

By the early nineteenth century, it was well recognized that financial panics and resulting bank failures could be very disruptive and costly to commerce and the society at large, and not just financially ruinous to those directly involved. Successfully calming panics and rescuing banks, however, required many factors, including deep pools of financial resources, extensive networks in the financial system, operations know-how, and public confidence. This put central banks in a unique position to assume the role of protector to the financial system, owing to their close ties to their governments, large reserves, extensive networks with correspondent banks, and (in many cases) monopoly over note issuance.[12]

At first the central banks were very reluctant to lend to distressed correspondent banks, preferring to devote their efforts to the protection of their own gold reserves. Central banks still regarded themselves primarily as banks, not public institutions. Any rescue of distressed banks could thus be regarded as a rescue of competitors.[13]

With major financial panics proving detrimental to everyone, however, in the latter half of the nineteenth century the Bank of England responded to growing criticism by taking on the responsibility of *lender of last resort* to distressed banks. To protect itself from losses, and to prevent abuses by commercial banks, however, the bank would lend to troubled banks only if sound collateral was posted and would charge interest above market rates for such lending.[14]

Notably, it was also this need to have a central bank to respond to financial panics that led a revival of central banking in the United States. Prior to 1913, the United States had two central banks, which were modeled after the Bank of England—that is, the *Bank of the United States* (1791–1811) and the *Second Bank of the United States* (1816–1836)—but their charters were not renewed owing to the public's distrust of concentrated financial power. During the 80 years that the United States did not have a central bank, bank panics and bank failures were frequent. A severe banking crisis in 1907 highlighted the need for a central bank in the United States and led to the creation of the *Federal Reserve System* in 1913.[15]

1.7 BANK SUPERVISOR

By adopting the lender-of-last-resort function, central banks were taking on risks that could damage their own capital, since they might be unable to recover all the money they had put into the rescue of troubled banks. This was particularly true in cases where troubled commercial banks were facing *solvency* problems (their debts exceeded their assets and capital combined), as opposed to mere *liquidity* problems (their debts did not exceed their assets and capital combined, but they could incur losses as they tried to liquidate their assets to meet their liabilities). In practice, the fact that it was not easy for the central banks to distinguish between solvency and liquidity problems without knowing details of the troubled banks' books also made it very risky for the central banks to take on a bank rescue mission.

To guard against possible losses on their own balance sheets, it was natural that central banks would seek to assess the creditworthiness of banks they were attempting to rescue. This required *prior* familiarity with the commercial banks' operations and balance sheets. Naturally, it was also in the central banks' interests to ensure *beforehand* that all commercial banks were operated in a safe and sound manner, so that they would not easily fall into trouble.

To ensure the safety and soundness of commercial banks' operations *ex ante*, many central banks found it beneficial to have a formal authority to inspect commercial banks' operations, examine commercial banks' books, and possibly give regulatory orders to the banks when deemed fit. In other words, following the assumption of the lender-of-last-resort role, central banks started to assume formal bank regulatory and supervisory functions.

In practice, however, the bank supervisory role only became possible when the central bank came to be regarded primarily as a public institution acting in the public interest, rather than as another competitor bank acting to gain more profits. The notion that central banks were public institutions acting in the public interest only became widely accepted after 1914 in the wake of World War I, as many governments resorted to using the central banks for their wartime financial management.[16]

Even by then, however, not all central banks had embraced the bank supervisory role. In countries where bank rescues were funded primarily by taxpayer money (as opposed to the central banks' own capital), the bank supervisory role had traditionally been put under the jurisdiction of public authorities that had injected the most money; for example, the Ministry of Finance. In such countries, notably Germany, bank supervision was traditionally conducted primarily by institutions other than the central bank.[17]

CASE STUDY: The Debate on the Function of the Central Bank as a Bank Supervisor

By the late 1990s a number of central banks, including the Bank of England, the Bank of Japan, and the Reserve Bank of Australia, started to relinquish their bank supervisory role to outside agencies. Key reasons for the separation between the central bank and the role of bank supervisor included (1) changes in the financial system, partly through the liberalization process that had begun in the late 1970s, which were blurring the lines between banks and other nonbank financial institutions, and (2) the fear that the bank supervisory function would be in conflict with the central banks' other growing function, that is, that of a conductor of monetary policy.[18]

First, changes in the financial system that blurred the lines between different types of financial services—for example, banking, insurance, and fund management—suggested that bank supervision should probably be organized by the *purpose* of supervision—that is, *systemic stability* (prudential supervision) and *consumer protection*—rather than by types of market services. Therefore, bank supervision should be housed in a separate regulator that also supervised other nonbank financial institutions.[19]

Second, as a conductor of monetary policy, the central banks would have to adjust money conditions in the economy to ensure stability of the economy. With the bank supervisory function remaining at the central banks, however, it was feared that the central banks might be reluctant to adjust money conditions as required if the adjustments had the potential to jeopardize profitability and balance sheets of commercial banks under their supervision.[20]

In contrast, reasons for keeping the banking supervisory function within the central bank included (1) information sharing for the conduct of monetary policy, where microlevel information from bank supervisors could help the conductor of monetary policy understand the state of the economy better, thus making for better monetary policy decisions, and (2) information sharing with regard to payment systems and market activities, since a separate bank supervisor might find it difficult to access real-time information on the banks' payment traffic, positions with the central bank, and their standing in financial markets.[21]

The 2007–2010 global financial crisis, however, added another twist to the debate on whether the central banks should take on a bank supervisory role. In the United Kingdom, *coordination failure* among the three key regulators (the central bank, the financial supervisory agency, and the government) was cited as one reason contributing to the emergence of bank runs in the United Kingdom, as well as ineffectiveness in management of the runs. By 2011, the U.K. government decided to put supervisory function (prudential regulation) of various types of financial institutions back into the Bank of England, and create a new, separate entity responsible for consumer protection and the promotion of healthy competition among financial institutions.

1.8 CONDUCTOR OF MONETARY POLICY

Given that the early central banks already had a stronger financial status than other banks, their banknotes were very much trusted by the public. To sustain such trust, many of them embarked on the gold standard, whereby they would fix the value of their money to gold, and only issue an extra amount of money if they had gold reserves to match that extra amount of money. Afterward, however, disruptions— such as wars and the fact that the global gold supply was (and is) limited—helped force central banks off gold as a standard. By the mid-twentieth century, central banks had started to gradually learn that, in the short run, monetary policy could be used actively to affect output, inflation, and employment.

The Gold Standard and Passive Monetary Policy

Following the lead by England, by the late nineteenth century the trend among existing and emerging central banks was to adopt the *gold standard*, which meant that the central banks could issue money only according to the value of gold they held. At the time, central banks were less concerned about how the amount of money being introduced into the system might affect economic activities. The central banks *passively* varied the amount of money they printed according to the amount of gold they had, rather than *actively* printing money to stimulate economic activities. The key concern of most central banks was to keep the value of money fixed to gold at the announced level.[22]

During World War I the gold standard was practically discarded, as countries abandoned the gold peg so they could print money to finance their war efforts more freely. After World War I ended, realizing that there was not enough gold for every central bank to hold to back their domestic currencies, the international community embarked on the *gold exchange standard*. Under this system the major countries pegged the values of their currencies to gold, and smaller countries used the currencies of major countries, in addition to gold, as reserves to back their own domestic currency.

The focus on pegging the value of currency to gold remained even during the Great Depression in the 1930s. Even though by the end of World War I in 1919 central banks were already starting to be more concerned about employment, economic activity, and price levels, they still put greater focus on gold reserves.[23] At the time, understanding of the nature of the relationships between the amount of money introduced, economic activity, employment, and price levels was still relatively vague.*

Bretton Woods and the Move toward Activist Monetary Policy

By the 1950s, through the influence of John Maynard Keynes, governments and central banks became aware of the possibility of affecting economic activities through the use of *activist* fiscal and monetary policy. At that time the international community had already adopted a new international monetary framework, which came to be known as the Bretton Woods system, to replace the gold standard. Under the Bretton Woods system the United States would peg the value of its currency, the U.S. dollar, to gold at 35 U.S. dollars per ounce, and other countries would fix the value of their currencies to U.S. dollars. Effectively the Bretton Woods system was a global fixed exchange rate system, under which countries would fix their exchange rates to the U.S. dollar, whose own value was fixed to gold.

By the 1960s the use of activist monetary policy in the United States, especially to stimulate economic activity and reduce unemployment, became dominant. The

---

*Although at its start in 1913 the U.S. Federal Reserve had been given the mandate of providing a "uniform and elastic currency" (i.e., currency that could expand or contract in volume according to the demands of business)—which meant that the Fed could increase the money supply when there was an extra need for money, such as during banking panics, and reduce the money supply when conditions warranted—the Fed, for various reasons, did not seriously attempt to influence economic conditions using the money supply until at least the 1950s (Bordo 2007).

activist monetary policy, together with rising fiscal spending by the U.S. government, however, also led to accelerating inflation in the United States. Investors as well as governments of countries that pegged the value of their currency to the U.S. dollar became concerned that inflation was fast eating away the purchasing power of the U.S. dollar in terms of goods and services.

The tie between the U.S. dollar and gold also came to be questioned as the United States kept issuing more and more money, despite its fixed supply of gold. At that time, international trade and capital flow were starting to resume, as many countries completed their rebuilding efforts after World War II and started liberalizing their economies. Greater international capital movements put pressure on the currency of those countries that persistently imported more than they exported and led to speculative attacks on many of those currencies.

Taming Inflation: Money Supply Growth Targeting

By the early 1970s the Bretton Woods system became untenable. Faced with inflation pressure and attempts by many countries to exchange their U.S. dollar holdings into gold from its vault, the United States decided to delink the U.S. dollar from gold. Frequent speculative attacks also forced many countries to abandon pegging their currencies to the U.S. dollar, instead allowing their currencies to float.[24]

By the late 1970s it became increasingly recognized that the use of activist monetary policy to persistently stimulate the economy did more harm than good in the long run. Theoretical developments and experience suggested that in the conduct of monetary policy, central banks might need to follow an *explicit rule*, rather than using *pure discretion*. It was also suggested that central banks be made *operationally* independent from their governments, since elected politicians had the tendency to stimulate the economy for short-term gains rather than seeking the longer-term benefit of economic stability.[25] In being operationally independent, the central bank would still have to follow the mandates set by publicly elected officials (e.g., a country's parliament or the U.S. Congress), but once those mandates (e.g., monetary stability) were set the central bank would have the operational independence to perform operations to fulfill the mandates.

To rein in inflation expectations that had been spiraling upward since the mid-1970s, in the late 1970s and early 1980s central banks in the United States and the United Kingdom decided to sharply tighten money supplies and expressed determined commitment to follow an explicit money supply target rule. By adopting explicit money supply targets the central banks committed themselves not to *overprint* money, such that money lost its value too fast (i.e., inflation rises excessively). Despite the initial success in bringing down inflation, however, less than half a decade later money supply targeting was abandoned in both the United States and the United Kingdom, when the relationship between the money supply and real economic activity was found to be unstable.[26]

During the latter half of the 1980s it could be said that central banks were effectively in search of a nominal anchor for the conduct of monetary policy. At that time, while many small countries still chose to fix their exchange rates to the U.S. dollar and benefited from easy international trade facilitation as well as relatively low U.S. dollar inflation (which also brought about low inflation for their own currencies), macroeconomic mismanagement often later led to successive devaluations of their currencies as well as persistently high inflation.[27]

Maintaining Monetary Stability: Inflation Targeting

In New Zealand, the search for a new nominal anchor for monetary policy led to the formal adoption of inflation targeting as the monetary policy regime for the Reserve Bank of New Zealand (RBNZ) in 1989. The regime, which has since been adopted and modified by many other central banks worldwide, has three key elements: (1) an announced numerical inflation target over a time horizon, (2) an implementation of monetary policy that aims to keep inflation forecasts within the target over the time horizon, and (3) a high degree of transparency and accountability.[28]

To keep inflation within the announced target in an inflation-targeting regime, the central bank adjusts its policy interest rate over time, with the aim of influencing the cost of borrowing in the economy and thus economic activity and inflation. Inflation targeting has become popular partly because it emphasizes transparency and accountability in the conduct of monetary policy.[29] The central bank under inflation targeting will report its reasons for its decisions in the adjustments of the policy interest rate. The public can also see for itself if the central bank is able to keep inflation within the announced target or not. If the inflation target is not achieved, then the governor of the central bank might be required to explain the reason to the government or the parliament.

After RBNZ adopted inflation targeting in 1989, central banks of many advanced and emerging market countries around the world also adopted many variations of inflation targeting as their monetary policy regime. Central banks of advanced economies that have adopted inflation targeting include the Bank of England, the Reserve Bank of Australia, the Bank of Canada, and the Swedish Riksbank, among others. Among the numerous emerging-market economy central banks, such names as Czech National Bank, Bank of Brazil, Bank of Chile, Bank of Indonesia, Bank of Israel, Bank of Korea, Bank of Thailand, and South African Reserve Bank reflect a great diversity of inflation targeting countries.

After the 2007–2010 global financial crisis, the U.S. Federal Reserve and the Bank of Japan also adopted inflation targets as a guide for their monetary policies. At the moment, however, both of these central banks are still using *quantitative easing*—a nonorthodox form of monetary policy—to aid their economic recoveries. In the case of Japan, the inflation target can be seen as an *aspiration* of the country to get out of the recurring bouts of deflation that have afflicted the economy since the burst of its spectacular asset-price bubbles in the early 1990s.

Common Currency: The Creation of the Euro

In 2000, a notable development in central banks' conduct of monetary policy took place in the form of the formal introduction of a common currency, the euro, which replaced national currencies in the 11 founding-member countries of the European Union. In that year, the national central banks of the 11 founding-member countries relinquished their role as the conductor of monetary policy for their countries in favor of the European Central Bank (ECB). The ECB would now conduct monetary policy for the member countries of the euro area.[30]

1.9 THE CURRENT STAGE OF CENTRAL BANKING

Modern central banks have many commonalities, as well as differences, depending on their historical contexts and their guiding philosophies. Most modern central banks now focus on delivering low, stable inflation and financial stability, and are prohibited from directly financing government spending. To deliver low, stable inflation and financial stability, however, different central banks often take different operational approaches. Furthermore, the full-employment mandate reemphasized by the Federal Reserve in the wake of the 2007–2010 financial crisis still remains quite unique.

Commonalities in Modern Central Banking

Despite differences in the timing and circumstances of their origins, by the late 2000s it could be argued that modern central banks shared a number of underlying commonalities: (1) the focus on the maintenance of monetary stability, (2) the focus on the maintenance of financial stability, and (3) the prohibition on direct lending to the government.

First, on the *monetary stability* front, as will be discussed more in detail in later chapters, theoretical developments over the past four decades and various high-inflation experiences around the world suggest that to support *long-term* economic growth, the best thing a central bank can do is to deliver an environment of monetary stability; that is, an environment in which inflation is low and stable. In such an environment, households and firms are more likely to be able to optimize investment and consumption. This stands in contrast to the call for a central bank to always keep directly stimulating the economy. The continued stimulation of the economy is likely to result in an upward spiral of inflation, which prevents households and firms from making optimal decisions.

Second, on the *financial stability* front, experiences from various financial crises around the world (particularly the 2007–2010 global financial crisis) suggest that to ensure long-term economic growth, central banks should have a direct role in the maintenance of financial stability, and that this role should apply regardless of whether the central bank has a bank supervisory function. Central banks can help maintain financial stability, either as regulators who help to ensure that the system is resilient beforehand, or as lenders of last resort who help prevent the total collapse of the financial system. A smooth functioning financial system ensures that capital is distributed efficiently, and is thus vital to the long-term, sustainable growth of an economy.

Third, although many early central banks were originally founded to help finance their governments, *direct lending* by the central bank to the government is now often prohibited in most modern economies, as it was found to lead down the dangerous path of hyperinflation. Direct lending to the government is akin to printing money and giving it to the government so that the government can use it to finance its purchases of goods and services. Printing money and giving it directly to the government cheapens the value of money relative to other goods and services. Under the law of supply and demand, the more the central bank supplies money, the lower the price (or the value) of money will be. If done in massive amounts the purchasing power of money could fall very fast, since people will no longer trust that the money in their hands is a good store of value, which could easily result in hyperinflation.

It should also be noted that at this current time in history, *coin sorting* has largely been dissociated from modern central banking, owing to either impracticality or principles that later emerged. In most countries coins are now issued by the mint, which is a part of the treasury or the finance ministry, not the central bank. *Banknote issuance* monopoly, on the other hand, has become deeply ingrained in the psyche of the public and central banks, such that it has started to blend into the background of central banking.

Diversity in Modern Central Banking

Even after the turn of the millennium, however, as the consensus on the roles of central banks had started to coalesce around monetary and financial stability, noticeable key underlying differences remain, including (1) the actual operations in the maintenance of monetary stability, (2) the institutional setup with regard to the maintenance of financial stability, and (3) the explicit role of central banks in ensuring full employment.

First, with respect to the maintenance of monetary stability, the approaches taken by individual central banks to achieve this goal can be vastly different. As will be discussed in more detail in Chapters 6–9, central banks can choose among different monetary policy and exchange rate regimes in the maintenance of monetary stability, depending on their individual contexts and circumstances.

For example, although a growing number of central banks have begun to adopt inflation targeting as their monetary-policy framework, a number of influential central banks, including the Peoples' Bank of China (PBOC) and the ECB, remain steadfastly without an official inflation target.

Among inflation-targeting central banks, many nuances remain, including the nature of the target (e.g., the inflation target level and time horizon for achieving the target). Meanwhile, noninflation-targeting central banks of small open economies, such as the Monetary Authority of Singapore and the Hong Kong Monetary Authority, could choose to rely quite heavily on the management of the exchange rate as a way to maintain monetary stability.

Second, on the financial stability front, there is a divergence with regard to bank supervisory function. In the 1990s a number of central banks, including the Bank of England, the Bank of Japan, and the Reserve Bank of Australia, delegated their bank supervisory function to an outside regulatory agency. As discussed earlier, however, the Bank of England, after the 2007–2010 global financial crisis, absorbed back its (enhanced) supervisory function, a function which more than a decade earlier had been delegated to an outside regulatory agency.

The ECB, on the other hand, did not have a supervisory function until 2014, since after the creation of the euro the national central banks of E.U. member countries had retained that function. Only in 2013, after the height of the euro area crisis in the early 2010s, did the push for the ECB to assume supervisory function responsibilities get passed.[31] A large number of central banks, including the Federal Reserve, meanwhile have always retained their bank supervisory function (although in case of the United States, bank supervisory function is also done by other regulatory agencies, including the Office of the Comptroller of the Currency, and the Federal Deposit Insurance Corporation).

Third, as will be discussed in Chapter 4 in more detail, the Federal Reserve has full employment as a legal mandate, which is quite a notable distinction among modern central banks. Prior to the 2007–2010 global financial crisis, the Federal Reserve tended to tone down in its communications with regard to its role in ensuring full employment, possibly for fear that it might confuse the public, since in the short run there is a *tradeoff* between employment and inflation. To push unemployment down, the central bank might need to allow inflation to go up in the short run. However, if the central bank allows inflation to go up, it might appear that the central bank is willing to compromise on monetary stability.

To avoid such confusion, many central banks prefer to frame full employment as being a part of long-term sustainable economic growth, which can be provided by monetary stability. In the wake of 2007–2010 global financial crisis, however, as the U.S. unemployment rate went up and the economy faced the threat of deflation rather than inflation, the Federal Reserve again emphasized its full-employment mandate when it needed to employ an unconventional monetary policy by injecting massive amounts of money into the economy through quantitative-easing measures.

Self-Reexamination after the 2007–2010 Global Financial Crisis

The global financial crisis that transpired from 2007–2010 came as a shock to most central banks. (The details of the 2007–2010 financial crisis will be reviewed briefly in Chapter 2.) The crisis jolted the central banks to again reexamine their roles and functions.

Many central banks whose countries were worst hit by the crisis, including the Federal Reserve, the Bank of England, and the ECB, had all resorted to unconventional monetary-policy measures, such as the purchase of government securities and massive liquidity injections. In the United States and the United Kingdom, unconventional monetary policy was used by the central banks to help prevent their economies from falling into a deflationary spiral. In the case of the ECB, unconventional monetary policy was used not only to help alleviate the economic plight of some of their member countries, but also to preserve the existence of the euro system itself.

With the global financial crisis, the central banks' roles with respect to financial stability are also being reexamined in depth by various stakeholders. A consensus has seemed to emerge that central banks need to take a more active role in dealing with financial stability. Relying on market forces to regulate themselves has already proved to be quite futile, as short-term incentives of market players might be misaligned with the society's long-term interests.

There are also issues of practicality with respect to the institutional setup of central banks. As will be discussed in later chapters in more detail, coordination difficulties during the crisis prompted the U.K. government to return the bank supervisory role to the Bank of England, after the role had earlier been carved out in the 1990s.

Even half a decade after the crisis first started, the global economy is still trying to find its footing. Reexaminations of central banking roles are still ongoing, and reforms are still being debated worldwide (see details in Chapter 14). In the next chapter, to provide a broad background on the context in which modern central banks are operating in, we will review the evolution of the international monetary system. Functions of modern central banks will then be discussed in Chapter 3.

SUMMARY

Central banking has evolved considerably since its start about 400 years ago. Starting with coin sorting and storing, and in certain cases war financing, central banks have taken on the functions of banknote issuers, banker to the government, banker to banks, protector of the financial system, bank supervisor, as well as conductor of monetary policy.

Currently, there are commonalities as well as diversity in modern central banking. Commonalities include (1) the focus on monetary stability, (2) the focus on financial stability, and (3) the prohibition on direct lending to the government. Differences include (1) operational differences in the pursuit of monetary stability, (2) the institutional setup with regard to the maintenance of financial stability, and (3) the explicit role of central bank in ensuring full employment.

KEY TERMS

activist monetary policy	inflation targeting
bank supervisor	lender of last resort
banker to banks	medium of exchange
banker to the government	monetary stability
banknote issuance	money supply growth targeting
financial stability	operational independence
full employment	passive monetary policy
gold exchange standard	store of value
gold standard	units of account

QUESTIONS

1. What are the key characteristics of money?
2. What were the problems with the use of coins as a means of payment in seventeenth-century Amsterdam?
3. How did banknote issuance first come about as a central banking role, particularly in the case of the Bank of Stockholm?
4. What are key characteristics of banknotes, as compared to other IOUs?
5. What might be key advantages for early central banks in acting as bankers to their governments?
6. Why might central banks be in a unique position to become protectors of the financial system?
7. Why might a central bank emerge as a banker to commercial banks?
8. Why should a central bank supervise commercial banks?
9. Why should a central bank not supervise commercial banks?
10. Why might we perceive central banks in the gold standard era as pursuing *passive* monetary policy?
11. What might *activist* monetary policy try to achieve?
12. What could be the reasons preventing modern central banks from directly financing government debt?

13. Why might we want central banks to be operationally independent from the government?
14. What are key characteristics of inflation-targeting central banks?
15. What are some commonalities of modern central banks?
16. What are some of the key differences among modern central banks?
17. Why might we not consider livestock as money, even if it could be used to trade for goods and services in agrarian economies?
18. The government is seeking to directly borrow money from the central bank in order to invest in a large infrastructure project that could help improve the livelihood of its citizens. Should the central bank agree to lend to the government? Why or why not?

CHAPTER 2

A Brief Overview of the International Monetary System

Learning Objectives

1. Describe key features and explain limitations of the gold standard.
2. Describe key features and explain limitations of the gold exchange standard.
3. Describe key features and explain limitations of the Bretton Woods system.
4. Describe key features of the international monetary system after the collapse of the Bretton Woods system.
5. Explain plausible causes of the global financial crisis of 2007–2010.

In Chapter 1 we reviewed a brief history of central banking. In this chapter we will take a brief look at the evolution of the international monetary system to better understand the context in which central banking practices have evolved. International elements have always been present in the history of central banking, since the day that the Bank of Amsterdam was set up to sort out coins of different makes by different sovereigns. With the advent of the gold standard, central banks pegged the value of their currencies to the value of gold. As the global economy evolves, central banking practices continue to evolve along with it.

This chapter divides the history of the international monetary system into four sections. The first section covers the historical period before the end of World War II, and includes specifically the *gold standard*, the *gold exchange standard*, and the global financial turmoil of the early twentieth century resulting from World War I and World War II.

The second section covers the period after World War II to the early 1970s (i.e., the period of the *Bretton Woods system*). Despite its demise in the early 1970s, the Bretton Woods system was the start of the modern international monetary system as we know it today. Two global institutions that were initiated during the creation of the Bretton Woods system, the International Monetary Fund (IMF) and the World Bank, are still at work and remain influential in the global economic and financial environment today.

The third section covers the period after the breakdown of the Bretton Woods system. Here the highlights will be (1) the *global inflation problem* in the 1970s which led to a rethinking of the ultimate goal in monetary policy and the role of central banks in managing the economy; (2) the *speculative attacks on emerging-market currencies* in the 1990s, which led to the abandonment of fixed exchange rate regimes in many countries; (3) the *introduction of the euro* in 2000, which became another popular currency for international trade and finance; and (4) the *global financial crisis of 2007–2010* that still has ongoing effects.

2.1 EVOLUTION OF THE INTERNATIONAL MONETARY SYSTEM: BEFORE THE END OF WORLD WAR II

From the eighteenth century to the onset of World War I in 1914 the international monetary system was based largely on the gold standard. World War I prompted many countries to abandon the gold standard so that they could effectively finance their wartime expenditures. After World War I the attempts to return to the gold standard had never really succeeded.

The Gold Standard

From the eighteenth century and the onset of World War I in 1914, the influence of the Bank of England on the global financial system rose with the premiere status of the British Empire. During that period, the Bank of England pegged the value of the pound sterling to that of gold, prompting other nations—including Germany and Japan—to emulate it. The system whereby countries peg the value of their currencies to gold is known as the *gold standard*.[1]

Under the gold standard, central banks have the mandate of keeping their currencies at announced values in terms of gold. In such a system, the amount of money in circulation is dictated by the amount of gold the central bank has at its disposal. The central bank can only print more money if it has enough gold to back up that extra amount of money. It is worth noting that under the gold standard, the amount of gold the central bank has depends in part on the size of the balance of payment deficit or the surplus that the country is running. A country with a balance of payment deficit has to pay out of its gold holdings, while a country with a balance of payment surplus would receive gold payments.

The Gold Exchange Standard

During World War I many countries abandoned their gold peg and resorted to funding their war expenditures by printing money. This printing of money, together with the scarcity resulting from war damages—whether in terms of manpower, factories and equipment, raw materials, or reduced production capabilities—pushed inflation up rapidly by the time the war ended in 1918.[2]

At the International Economic Conference held in Genoa, Italy, in 1922, many countries showed a willingness to return to the gold standard. However, since there was not enough gold for every central bank in the world to hold as reserves, it was agreed that the smaller economies would hold currencies of the major economies as reserves, while the major economies would hold gold against their issued currencies. The system under which smaller countries held currencies of the major economies partially as reserves became known as the *gold exchange standard*.[3]

The Great Depression and the 1930s: Turmoil in the International Financial System

In 1919, even before the Genoa Conference in 1922, the United States had already returned to the gold standard by pegging the value of its currency to gold. In 1925 England followed suit, fixing the value of its pound sterling to gold at the level it had held prior to World War I. The decision to fix gold at the level that existed prior to World War I was made on the basis that it would help the credibility of British financial institutions, which were leaders during the gold standard era. By 1925, however, prices of goods and services in England were already at levels higher than prior to the war. The Bank of England thus had to tighten its monetary policy to push the sterling value of the gold peg up to the prewar level. The tightening of monetary policy severely pushed up British unemployment, hurt the British economy, and undermined confidence of other countries in holding their reserves in the form of deposits in London banks.[4]

In 1929, the global economy started to edge into a decade-long decline that became known as the *Great Depression*. Recent research shows that the gold standard was a key contributing factor to the starting, the severity, and the spreading of the Great Depression. By that time, most trading economies had already returned to the gold standard. With the U.S. central bank tightening its monetary policy in order to slow down its overheating economy, large amounts of gold started to flow into the United States. In order to preserve their own gold reserves, other countries also had to tighten their monetary policies and raise interest rates. This led to a worldwide contraction of monetary policy, which also brought about a sustained contraction in economic activity and a sustained reduction in the general price level (i.e., deflation).[5]

The global economic decline also led to failures of a large number of financial institutions worldwide, which deepened and widened economic contractions further. The confidence in the gold exchange standard also declined. As countries started to convert their pound sterling holdings into gold, Britain was forced to again abandon the gold standard in 1931. The decision by many countries to abandon the gold standard during the Great Depression badly affected countries that chose to keep the value of their currencies fixed to gold. This also helped generate animosity among countries, since many countries that dropped the gold standard also devalued their currencies to curb imports and protect domestic employment. The competitive devaluation of currencies, also known as a *beggar-thy-neighbor* policy, often prompted retaliations from those affected, frequently via trade barriers. During this turmoil, exchange rate volatility, trade restrictions, and deflation in the major economies in North America and Europe pushed Latin American countries to repudiate their foreign debts. The failure of the international financial system in the 1930s was something that the designers of the global financial system after World War II kept in mind.[6]

2.2 EVOLUTION OF THE INTERNATIONAL MONETARY SYSTEM: THE BRETTON WOODS SYSTEM

After World War II, the international community agreed to embark on a new international monetary system, that is, the Bretton Woods system, which was named after the place where the agreement initially took place. Under this system, the United States would hold gold as reserves and fix the value of the dollar at $35 per 1 ounce of gold. As the U.S. government started incurring heavy deficits, partly to finance the Vietnam War, the pressures on the system mounted and the Bretton Woods system was abandoned by the early 1970s.

The Bretton Woods System

In July 1944, delegates from 44 countries convened in Bretton Woods, New Hampshire, to design a new international monetary system. The aim of the design was to prevent the mistakes of the 1930s from recurring. Lessons from the 1930s suggested that to prevent future international financial turmoil, the new international monetary system should help countries sustain low inflation while also allowing them to achieve their goals with respect to balance of payments stability and full employment without the need to resort to trade protectionism.[7]

Under this new system, the value of all other currencies would be pegged to the U.S. dollar, the currency of the most powerful country to emerge from World War II, and also a country with long records of low inflation. The value of the U.S. dollar itself would be pegged to gold, at 35 U.S. dollars per ounce. Members of the system could hold reserves in terms of gold or in terms of U.S. dollar-denominated assets. Member countries had the right to sell U.S. dollar assets to the U.S. central bank (the Federal Reserve) and receive payments in gold at the announced exchange rate. In other words, under this new system all other countries would peg their currencies to the U.S. dollar, while the value of the U.S. dollar would be pegged to gold.

To help ensure long-term stability in the global economy, two new international institutions were also proposed for creation during the Bretton Woods meeting. The International Monetary Fund (IMF) was created to help member countries cope with their domestic employment problems without resorting to trade protectionism. The World Bank was created to help with the long-term development of less advanced countries.[8]

The International Monetary Fund

Experiences from the Great Depression and the turmoil in the international monetary system in the 1930s showed that ultimately governments often put more emphasis on holding down domestic unemployment than keeping their exchange rates at the announced fixed level. When domestic unemployment rose, countries often resorted to trade protectionism and competitive devaluations of their currencies, which threaten global economic stability. The goal of the IMF was to help member countries cope with their domestic unemployment problems, without resorting to trade protectionism and competitive devaluations of their currencies.[9]

To achieve its goal, the IMF relied on two main mechanisms. First, the IMF would raise funds from the member countries in the form of currencies and gold, so that the IMF could lend to member countries facing balance of payment problems. Second, although exchange rates of the member countries were pegged to U.S. dollars at certain levels, if necessary the IMF might consent to adjustments in the exchange rates. The IMF's consent to exchange rate adjustments, however, would be given only when exchange rates were deemed inconsistent with long-term fundamentals. For example, consent might be given when the global demand for a country's goods and services was deemed to be permanently reduced and the country was facing persistent serious unemployment and balance of payment deficit problems.[10]

Under the IMF agreement, when countries were ready they would also start to let their currencies be freely converted to other currencies. After World War II, however, most countries were still worried about the prospects of capital outflows, and thus restrictions were often imposed on the convertibility of their currencies. In 1945 only the United States and Canada allowed their currencies to be fully convertible. The early free convertibility of the U.S. dollar, along with the U.S. dollar's unique characteristics in the Bretton Woods system, helped the popularity of the U.S. dollar as a medium of exchange in international trade and finance.[11]

Pressures on the Bretton Woods System

With foreign exchange rates being anchored to the U.S. dollar and the value of the U.S. dollar itself pegged to gold, the Bretton Woods system helped provide much needed global economic stability from the late 1940s to the early 1960s, when countries were rebuilding their economies after World War II. By the late 1960s, however, three major forces were already putting strain on the system: (1) freer flows of international capital and balance of payment crises; (2) the U.S. macroeconomic policy package of 1965–1968, which led to high U.S. budget deficits and inflation, and; (3) the availability of gold to back the value of U.S. dollar.[12]

Freer Flows of International Capital and Balance of Payment Crises
As countries reduced their restrictions on international capital flows and moved toward free convertibility of their currencies, balance of payment crises became more acute and frequent. Under the Bretton Woods system global exchange rates were fixed, so the currency of a country with persistent current account deficits could be deemed as being out of line with long-term fundamentals, and the exchange rate might be overvalued.[13]

To protect their purchasing power from being reduced by a possible currency devaluation, investors often rushed to convert their assets from the currency of a country that had persistent current account deficits. Speculators might also choose to join in by borrowing in that currency and converting the borrowed money into another currency, waiting for the borrowed currency to be devalued so they could pocket the difference.

Under the Bretton Woods system, the central bank of the troubled country was obliged to pay the investors and speculators wishing to convert out of the currency by using the central bank's international reserves, in order to keep the exchange rate fixed at the announced level. A severe rundown in the central bank's international reserves, however, could threaten the country's ability to pay for imports and foreign debt obligations, causing a balance of payment crisis.

By the early 1960s balance of payment crises became acute and frequent, especially among Europeans who had allowed freer flows of capital and moved toward free convertibility of their currencies. Even mere prospects of currency devaluation could lead to speculative attacks on the currency and tip the country into a balance of payment crisis. In 1964 a recorded level of the United Kingdom's trade deficit prompted waves of speculative attacks on the pound sterling. In 1967 the United Kingdom had to seek IMF assistance. Meanwhile, France also had to devalue its currency (the franc), while Germany had to revalue its currency (the deutsche mark).[14]

The U.S. Macroeconomic Policy Package of 1965–1968 It has been argued that the U.S. macroeconomic policy package of 1965–1968 introduced considerable pressures that led to the collapse of the Bretton Woods system. In 1965 the U.S. government ramped up its military purchases as the Vietnam War widened, while it also increased spending on social programs without raising taxes. Initially the Federal Reserve tightened monetary policy as output expanded, but it had to reverse course in 1967 and 1968 as the resulting high interest rates hurt the construction industry. Given the rising budget deficit and expansionary monetary policy, inflation in the United States had risen to almost 6 percent a year by the end of the decade.[15]

With a rising budget deficit and inflation in the United States, there were concerns that the real value of the U.S. dollar in terms of gold was below the announced official rate of 35 U.S. dollars per ounce of gold. As U.S. inflation rose, the U.S. dollar lost its purchasing power for goods and services, which meant that the U.S. dollar had also lost its value relative to other currencies as well as to gold.

Countries that pegged their exchange rates to the U.S. dollar that wanted to retain their exchange rates at the announced pegged levels had to buy U.S. dollars to prop up the value of the U.S. dollar. The purchase of the U.S. dollars, however, raised their domestic money supplies, as they needed to use their own domestic currencies to buy up U.S. dollars. In such a situation, the rise in these countries' domestic money supply resulted in increased inflationary pressures in their domestic economies.

Sensing that the U.S. dollar needed to be devalued, speculators started to buy up gold in the late 1967 and early 1968, which prompted massive gold sales by the Federal Reserve and European central banks, draining official gold reserves in these countries. The central banks then decided to create a *two-tier market* for gold, with one tier being private and another tier being official. The price of gold in the private tier would be determined by market forces, but in the official tier central banks would trade gold among themselves at $35 per ounce.

The Availability of Gold to Back the Value of the U.S. Dollar: The Triffin Dilemma By the late 1960s, as the U.S. dollar became increasingly overvalued owing to rising inflation, the U.S. current account position increasingly worsened. As U.S. balance of payment deficits started to grow, there was also concern whether the U.S. would have enough gold to back the value of the U.S. dollar. Apart from speculative attacks on currencies, the Bretton Woods system also faced pressure from factors relating to the U.S. dollar's unique status as the world's reserve currency. While other countries pegged their currencies to the U.S. dollar, the U.S. pegged the value of its dollar to gold, at 35 U.S. dollars per ounce of gold.

In theory, the amount of U.S. gold holdings should have prevented the U.S. from running excessive balance of payment deficits, since other countries could choose to sell their U.S. dollar assets for gold from U.S. gold holdings. In practice, however, despite growing U.S. deficits, other governments were willing to hold their wealth in their international reserves in the form of U.S. dollar assets.

As the international reserves of these countries continued to grow over time, there was a possibility that the combined U.S. dollar reserves of these other countries would exceed U.S. total gold holdings. In such a case, if all countries decided to convert their U.S. dollar reserves into gold at the same time, the United States would be unable to fulfill its pledge to convert U.S. dollars into gold at 35 U.S. dollars per ounce. This situation was pointed out in 1960 by Robert Triffin, an economist at Yale University, and the conflict described became known as the Triffin dilemma.[16]

The Demise of the Bretton Woods System

With the U.S. dollar still pegged to gold at $35 per ounce, rising inflation meant that the U.S. exports kept losing their price competitiveness, which hurt the U.S. economy further as it entered a recession in 1970.[17] The United States, however, could not devalue its currency against all other currencies on its own, since under the Bretton Woods system other countries pegged their currencies to the U.S. dollar rather than the other way around. If the United States wanted to devalue its currency, *all other countries* would have to agree to revalue their own currencies.[18]

On August 15, 1971, to solve this problem, President Richard M. Nixon decided to close the U.S. gold window—that is, stop the automatic selling of U.S. dollars for conversion into gold by foreign central banks—and impose a 10 percent tax on all imports to the United States until U.S. trading partners agreed to revalue their currencies against the U.S. dollar. In December of that year an international agreement was reached at the Smithsonian Institution in Washington, DC, whereby the U.S. dollar would be devalued to $38 per ounce of gold, which effectively implied that the U.S. dollar was devalued against other currencies by about 8 percent. The 10 percent tax on imports to the United States was also eliminated.

Despite the realignment of the U.S. dollar, speculative attacks on currencies remained rampant, such that on March 19, 1973, Japan and many advanced European countries decided to let the value of their currencies *float* against the U.S. dollar. By letting their currencies float, these countries were allowing the value of their currencies to be determined by the forces of demand and supply in the financial market instead of by governments.[19]

In a world of floating exchange rates, central banks still held international reserves in the form of gold and currencies of the major economies, especially the U.S. dollar. International reserves were used for intervention in the currency market so that movement of the exchange rate would not be too volatile. Initially, a policy of floating exchange rates was deemed to be a temporary emergency response to massive speculative attacks. As time passed, however, it was almost impossible to repeg the currencies. The advanced economies thus have let their currencies float against the U.S. dollar since then.[20]

2.3 AFTER BRETTON WOODS

Since the abandonment of the Bretton Woods system in 1973, the global financial system has evolved remarkably. Since that time, there have been at least four major developments or turning points worth mentioning. First is the *global inflation problem* in the 1970s, which, beginning in the early 1980s, led to the growing acceptance of price stability as the key goal of monetary policy and the acknowledgment that central banks needed to follow a rule in their conduct of monetary policy. Second are the waves of *speculative attacks on the currencies of emerging-market economies* in the 1990s that prompted many emerging-market economies to float their currencies. Third is the attempt of European countries to create a monetary union, which ultimately led to the *introduction of the euro*, and the European Central Bank. And fourth is the *global financial crisis of 2007–2010*, which was the most severe since the Great Depression, and that is likely to change the global financial landscape ahead.

The Great Inflation of the 1970s

In the 1970s there were two oil crises, one in 1973 and another in 1979. Rising oil prices during a crisis was considered a supply shock, which threatened a slow-down in the global economy.[21] During those crises of the 1970s, central banks often deemed it necessary that monetary policy be accommodative, as a reaction to rising unemployment and to alleviate the negative effects of an economic slowdown.

As the events turned out, however, accommodative monetary policy did not successfully stimulate the economy and bring down unemployment, but instead led to fast-rising inflation. This situation, in which the economy contracted yet inflation also rose, became known as *stagflation*—a combination of the words *stagnate* and *inflation*.

Rising inflation can raise uncertainty in the economy, since businesses might try to mark up the prices of their goods and services in anticipation of inflation to protect the purchasing power of their profits. Workers, on the other hand, might try to negotiate for hikes in wages to protect against rising costs of living. The pricing behavior of firms, and wage hikes, can prompt inflation to actually rise immediately in response to anticipated inflation. Such a situation can feed on itself, and is known as a *wage-price spiral*.

As the rise in prices of goods and services becomes faster, interest rates can start to rise quickly as well, since lenders may reset their lending rates to take account of the fast decline in the purchasing power of interest income. Fast-rising interest rates can create uncertainty in the economy and distort consumption and investment decisions.

As the U.S. economy became seriously choked by the wage-price spiral, high unemployment, and high inflation, the U.S. central bank, under the leadership of Paul A. Volcker, decided that accommodative monetary policy was indeed hurting the economy. Monetary policy stance was thus reversed to be sharply contractionary in October 1979, with the Federal Reserve hiking interest rates sharply and tightening the money supply. The switch to a sharply contractionary monetary policy helped push the U.S. economy into violent recessions in the 1980s but also helped kill the wage-price spiral and successfully brought down inflation expectations.

A lesson that central banks learned from the inflation problem of the late 1970s was that during a supply shock an accommodative monetary policy might be unable to successfully stimulate the economy, and could indeed worsen the situation by introducing more inflationary pressures and uncertainty into the economy. Once an accommodative monetary stance has been taken to deal with a supply shock, it may be that to prevent inflation from spiraling out of control and to get the economy out of stagflation the central bank may subsequently need to sharply contract its monetary policy, putting even more severe stress on the economy.

After the experiences of the late 1970s to early 1980s, central banks often became more cautious in using an accommodative policy stance to deal with a supply shock. Indeed, central banks increasingly started to ponder the use of a monetary policy rule as a tool to keep inflation low and stable. In the United States, along with the tightening of monetary conditions, the Federal Reserve, under Paul Volcker, also showed a commitment to low and stable inflation through its emphasis on the adoption of money supply growth targeting as its monetary policy rule. Theoretically, by keeping money supply growth at a rate consistent with economic growth, there would be no excess money that could lead to inflationary pressures in the long run (see Chapter 6 for more details).

By the late 1980s, however, the use of monetary supply growth targeting had practically been abandoned in both the United States and the United Kingdom. As it happened, the relationship between money growth and economic growth became unstable, such that the money supply growth target often was inconsistent with the growth in economic activity.[22]

Speculative Attacks on Advanced European and Emerging-Market Currencies in the 1990s

Although major advanced economies had floated their currencies against the U.S. dollar in the early 1970s, which ended the Bretton Woods system, attempts to fix exchange rates persisted in both advanced and emerging-market economies throughout the 1970s and 1980s. By the early 1990s, however, the liberalization process that had started in the advanced economies since the late 1970s started to take hold across the world. Freer international capital mobility that came with the liberalization process made it much more difficult for countries to maintain their exchange rate pegs, as ultimately reflected in waves of successful *speculative attacks* on currencies of advanced and emerging-market economies throughout the 1990s.

Speculative Attacks on Currencies in Advanced European Economies Speculative attacks against advanced economies were felt the most in European countries within the European Monetary System (EMS) in the early 1990s. At the time the countries in the EMS operated on a formal network of mutually pegged exchange rates, such that the exchange rates of these countries would be kept within specified fluctuation margins. By 1992, the reunification of western and eastern Germany that started in 1990 had already led to an economic boom and higher inflation in Germany, which prompted Germany's central bank, the Bundesbank, to raise interest rates.[23]

With Germany—the largest EMS economy—raising interest rates, other EMS countries faced a dilemma. On the one hand, unless other EMS countries also raised interest rates, the economic boom and high interest rates in Germany would keep drawing capital out of other EMS countries into Germany, which would put depreciation pressure on the currencies of these other EMS countries. On the other hand, if they raised interest rates to match the German rate hikes they might put further negative pressure on their already-weak domestic economies.[24]

Speculators, sensing that the other EMS countries would not be able to tolerate high domestic interest rates, started speculative attacks on a number of EMS countries, which forced the United Kingdom and Italy out of the EMS in 1992, and forced the EMS to widen its exchange rate bands to +/− 15 percent in 1993 from +/− 2.25 percent for certain member countries and +/− 15 for other member countries. Speculative attacks during the same period also forced a devaluation of Finnish and Swedish currencies against the European Currency Unit (ECU), the precursor to the euro.[25,26] (See Concept: Speculative Attacks: Underlying Causes, Anatomy, and Defense for more details on how speculative attacks are done.)

Speculative Attacks on Emerging-Market Currencies   In the mid-1990s, a large number of emerging-market economies still pegged their currencies to the U.S. dollar. The maintenance of the peg was in part due to (1) the fact that a fixed exchange rate could help facilitate international trade and investment, and (2) confidence that inflation rates of countries with currencies pegged to the U.S. dollar would be more or less in line with that of the United States, and thereby benefiting from the U.S. central bank's commitment to low and stable inflation.[27] While inflationary pressures in the United States could sometimes be a problem, the United States never really experienced the kind of extreme inflation that occurred rather frequently in emerging economies that lost their fiscal and monetary discipline and deliberately printed money to finance their deficits.

Many emerging economies in the 1980s, even when faced with balance of payment crises, often resorted to currency devaluation rather than floating their exchange rates. With currency devaluation troubled countries would retain the peg to the U.S. dollar, but at a depreciated exchange rate. Later, to better reflect their increasingly diversified international trade patterns, many emerging-market countries chose to peg their exchange rates to the value of a basket of currencies (a portfolio of selected currencies, possibly comprising those of each country's major trading partners), rather than to the U.S. dollar alone. In the 1980s and the 1990s, with the United States being the far dominant global export market, however, the weight of U.S. dollar normally dominated the currency baskets.

With international liberalization measures yet to take full effect, the fixed exchange rate regime in emerging markets remained robust. As the process of globalization gathered momentum and countries started to open up their markets, more international capital started to flow in and out of these economies more freely. At first, the greater flows of capital helped finance development of the countries, particularly in export-led manufacturing industries. As more capital flowed in, however, parts of the capital also seeped into unproductive investments, including asset-price speculation. Finally, as exports to advanced economies slowed, emerging-market economies started to run into large current account deficits.

The deficits, together with asset-price bubbles, prompted international investors to speculate whether the emerging economies would be able to service their foreign debt. With the fixed exchange rate regime, emerging economies would have to repay their foreign debts out of their international reserves. In many cases, since foreign debt had already been used to finance assets that were overvalued or investments that were unproductive, investors deemed that repayments would be difficult or impossible, and that the countries would eventually have to devalue their currencies.

With prospects of currency devaluation becoming more likely, speculative attacks on the currencies took place (see Concept: Speculative Attacks for details). Such attacks led to a currency crisis in Mexico in 1994 and in East Asian countries in 1997 and 1998, which prompted many of the attacked countries to abandon their fixed exchange rate regime. Later a combination of factors, including contagion effects from the Asian financial crisis, also led to financial crises in Russia in 1998, Brazil in 1999, and Argentina in 2002. (The Asian financial crisis is discussed in more detail in Chapter 9.)

CONCEPT: SPECULATIVE ATTACKS

Speculative attacks are typically carried out against a country with a fixed exchange rate regime. Here we discuss the underlying causes and anatomy of speculative attacks, as well as defense against them, referencing the speculative attacks on advanced European economies and emerging-market economies in the 1990s.

Underlying Causes

With a fixed exchange rate regime, the central bank of a country is effectively promising to convert the domestic currency to a foreign currency at a specified exchange rate using its foreign reserves. Consequently, the country is prone to a speculative attack if (1) it is in a markedly different economic cycle from that of the country it fixes its exchange rate to (e.g., EMS countries that fixed their exchange rates with Germany in the early 1990s), or (2) it runs a persistently large current account deficit (e.g., emerging-market economies in the mid- and late 1990s).

If a country is in a different cycle from the country that it fixes its exchange rate to, then that country would face a choice between using monetary policy to address its domestic conditions or using its monetary policy to keep the exchange rate fixed at the announced target. For example, if the country is in a recession, the central bank might want to lower interest rates to help stimulate its domestic economy. If the central bank decides to lower interest rates, however, investors might move funds abroad to receive higher interest rates elsewhere. When investors move funds out of the country, they effectively sell the domestic currency, which puts depreciation pressure on the exchange rate. If enough investors sell the domestic currency, the central bank might indeed have to devalue the exchange rate.

A large and persistent current account deficit, on the other hand, suggests that the country has already been routinely paying out its foreign reserves to pay for imports of goods and services from abroad. Since the amount of a central bank's foreign reserves is finite, such a persistent drain means that the central bank might not be able to allow conversion of the domestic currency into a foreign currency at the promised rate. More likely, the central bank might need to devalue the domestic currency—that is, the public would need a greater amount of the domestic currency in order to convert the domestic currency into a given amount of foreign currency.

If a currency devaluation occurs, those with domestic currency would lose while those with foreign currency would gain. Therefore, investors would try to

(Continued)

(*Continued*)

convert their holdings of domestic currency into foreign currency if they think that a devaluation of the domestic currency is imminent. Speculators, meanwhile, might force the central bank to devalue its currency through speculative attacks.

Anatomy of a Speculative Attack

In a speculative attack, speculators effectively borrow large amounts of the domestic currency, and then use those borrowed amounts of the domestic currency to seek conversion into a foreign currency from the central bank. If the amounts of the domestic currency that speculators use to seek conversion are so large that the central bank does not have enough foreign reserves to allow conversion at the fixed exchange rate, the central bank would need to devalue the currency, or allow the exchange rate to float.

If the central bank is forced to devalue the domestic currency or allow the exchange rate to float, speculators would gain since they would have already obtained some foreign currency from the central bank. That foreign currency would have appreciated in value relative to the domestic currency. Since the speculators' borrowings are denominated in the domestic currency, which has by then lost in value, the speculators could convert the obtained foreign currency at a more favorable rate to repay for their domestic currency debts. The difference between the gain in the foreign currency obtained and their domestic currency debt repayments would be profit to the speculators.

In the attack on the British pound in 1992, Quantum Fund, a hedge fund run by George Soros (a large speculator based in the United States), borrowed and sold $10 billion worth of the British currency, around two and a half times the fund's capital. In the first two weeks of September 1992, the Bank of England spent $27 billion worth of reserves to fend off Soros and other speculators. Finally, when the United Kingdom left the EMS, the pound fell around 14 percent against the deutsche mark, and Soros's fund earned over $1 billion worth of profits.[28]

Defense against a Speculative Attack

To counter a speculative attack, the central bank might choose to raise domestic interest rates to push up the speculators' costs for domestic-currency borrowing, and at the same time keep selling foreign currencies to the speculators (and thus buy up domestic currency) at the announced exchange rates.

In a world of *limited* capital mobility, the combination of high domestic interest rates and the ability of the central bank to keep selling foreign currencies at the announced exchange rate might deter or even squeeze speculators out of their speculative positions on the domestic currency. Speculators would have to pay high interest rates on their domestic-currency borrowing, while the likelihood that the central bank would run out of reserves would be low, since in the world of limited capital mobility, the speculators cannot easily come in and borrow so much domestic currency.

In a world of *free* capital mobility, however, speculators can more easily borrow money and get hold of as much of the domestic currency as they can.

Consequently—as the Quantum Fund's attack on the British currency in 1992 and the later attacks on emerging-market economy currencies have shown—herds of large speculators can easily raise funds that match or even dwarf a central bank's entire foreign reserves and thus overcome the central bank's ability to defend its exchange rate peg.

Ultimately, if the central bank deems that it still wants to defend the exchange rate peg, it must be noted that the central bank also has the option to introduce capital controls to prevent easy conversion of currencies by nonresidents, that is, to put limits on capital mobility. The imposition of capital controls, however, also has its own costs, since it might impede access to foreign capital that might be necessary for funding of domestic investments.

The Introduction of the Euro

After World War II, countries in Europe tried to put more emphasis on political and economic cooperation. A long history of wars, including the two world wars, had proved to be very destructive. The European effort toward integration was first reflected in the Treaty of Rome, which created the *European Economic Community* (EEC) allowing free trade without tariffs among member countries, which ultimately was transformed into the *European Union* (EU) with a much broader political and economic integration mandate. Although a currency union was probably not on the minds of the signatories of the Treaty of Rome, after the creation of the EEC member countries realized that trade among themselves would be even easier if they used a common currency.[29]

Up to the late 1960s, the fixed exchange rate regime offered by the Bretton Woods system had helped facilitate international trade and finance for European countries without much worry about exchange rate volatility. With the demise of the Bretton Woods system, however, many European countries had to abandon their fixed exchange rate regimes, and the benefits of a common currency became clearer. With many stops and detours along the way, a common currency, the euro, was introduced among a core group of European Union members in 1999.[30]

Despite various obstacles, in 1999 11 advanced European countries were able to join in the creation of the euro as their common currency. These countries replaced their old national currencies with the euro. In this newly created euro area, responsibility for the conduct of monetary policy was transferred from the national central banks (NCBs) of each member country to the newly created European Central Bank (ECB), a supranational agency that put higher priority on the euro area rather than any individual country. From the start, the key goal of the ECB has been the maintenance of price stability for the euro area as a whole. With the monetary policy responsibility largely taken away, the NCBs, in turn, would focus on the regulation of their domestic banking sector.[31,*] By the middle of the first decade of the

---

*Following the European sovereign debt crisis of in the early 2010s, however, it was deemed important that the ECB should also take on banking supervision for the member countries. Starting in 2014 the ECB is to also assume banking supervisory functions over large credit institutions within the euro area.

twenty-first century, the euro had rapidly become another popular currency of international trade and finance. This owed partly to the fact that (1) the euro area includes many large, advanced economies such as Germany, France, Italy, and Spain, as well as a number of other medium-sized advanced economies, which has made the euro area a large and important block of countries, and (2) many smaller Eastern European economies were expected to join the euro area once they passed the tough admissions criteria, which would strengthen the euro area even further. In the process, the ECB became another powerful central bank whose monetary policy could significantly affect the international monetary system.[32]

The Global Financial Crisis of 2007–2010

The global financial crisis of 2007–2010 showed how the international monetary system has become globalized in nature. Although the crisis turned out to have hit the advanced economies the hardest, it also severely disrupted global trade, brought about a global recession, and threatened to bring down the whole global financial system—which had by then become inextricably intertwined across boundaries.

To understand the global financial crisis more easily, it might help to break down the complexity relating to it by focusing on the U.S. subprime crisis, which was not only central to the story, but was also echoed by similar situations in a number of European countries during that same period. Although the U.S. subprime crisis did not become full blown until late 2008, we use the term global financial crisis of 2007–2010 to also encompass the U.S. subprime crisis, because by then the cracks in the global financial system had already shown up on both sides of the Atlantic: that is, a run on banks in the United Kingdom in 2007 and high profile failures of hedge funds associated with the global securities firm Bear Stearns in the United States. In the latter part of this section, we will also discuss the European sovereign debt crisis, a related but distinct crisis that came on the heels of the U.S. subprime crisis.

The U.S. Subprime Crisis: The Run-Up   By many accounts, the U.S. subprime crisis was caused by a combination of factors, including (1) the low interest rates that had been kept at low levels for too long and resulted in a housing price bubble, (2) the deterioration in lending standards that resulted in loans being made to borrowers with poor credit quality, and (3) amplified risks due to the opacity surrounding the use of new financial innovations and products.[33]

Low Interest Rates   Although the United States suffered a recession in the early 1990s, by the late 1990s the U.S. economy had sustained an almost decade-long boom that came partly because of the productivity gains from the Internet revolution, as well as a stable macroeconomic environment. Inflation had stayed low since the mid-1980s, while the growing budget deficit that had been a problem in the 1980s and early 1990s had reversed into a surplus by the end of the decade. The growth in productivity and the stable macroeconomic environment helped contribute to a boom in stock prices, particularly those of Internet-related (*dot-com*) companies. The spectacular rise in the stock market in the late 1990s became known as the dot-com bubble.

By early 2001, however, the dot-com bubble in the U.S. stock market had burst, wiping out a lot of U.S. household wealth and severely weakening the U.S. corporate sector. Later that year, terrorist attacks in the U.S. caused worldwide financial panics. In response to these events, by the end of 2001 the U.S. central bank had lowered its policy interest rate (the federal funds rate) to 1.75 percent, down from 6.5 percent a year earlier.

Despite lower interest rates, the weakness in the U.S. economy, together with other global factors—including the SARS virus scare of 2002 and 2003 and cheap imports from China that started to flood the global economy after China had joined WTO in 2001—helped to keep U.S. inflation down. By December 2003, the U.S. inflation rate had fallen below 1 percent, which prompted fears of deflation.[34]

The deflationary scare made the Federal Reserve more cautious about subsequent hikes in interest rates, and it nudged the fed funds rate upward by only 0.25 percent at a time[35] until it reached 5.25 percent in June 2006. The low interest rates in the first years after 2000 were deemed a key factor that helped contribute to the boom in the U.S. housing market, which subsequently resulted in the global financial crisis of 2007–2010.

Between 2000 and 2006, U.S. housing prices rose by more than 80 percent.[36] Low interest rates helped contribute to the boom in housing prices in a self-reinforcing way because (1) low interest rates kept borrowing costs down, enabling people to buy houses more easily; (2) low interest rates pushed people to seek investments in assets that would yield higher returns than bank deposits, that is, stocks (which yielded dividends as well as capital gains), housing (which could yield rents as well as capital gains); and (3) as housing and stock prices started to rise rapidly, they also raised U.S. household wealth, enabling and inducing households to borrow more in order to invest in a second or third home.

Deterioration in Lending Standards At first, financial institutions lent primarily to borrowers with good credit quality (i.e., those who were more likely to be able to repay their loans). As the pool of borrowers with good credit quality started to become exhausted, however, lenders started to target their lending to borrowers of lower credit quality (termed *subprime* borrowers). In the more notorious cases, loans were made to borrowers without documentation requirements for income, jobs, or assets (the so-called NINJA loans). In other cases lenders lured subprime borrowers with complicated loans such as option-ARMs (adjustable rate mortgages that in the initial years allowed borrowers to pay below the monthly payment owed, only to add back the difference to the balance of the loan, and thus, through compound interest, increasing the amount that borrowers owed once the initial years had passed).[37]

The deterioration in lending standards came about partly because of changes in banks' business models as well as financial innovations that were deemed to be able to tame risks associated with lending. By the mid-2000s many banks in the United States and the United Kingdom had embraced securitization as a key driver in their business models. (Details on securitization are in the next section, which covers financial innovations.) Rather than making loans and holding them on their books, many banks made loans, bundled them, and sold them as a package, thereby removing the loans from their balance sheets. Since the loans were removed from their balance sheets, the banks had less incentive to be careful about the loans they made and were tempted to make as many loans as possible to gain lending fees and commissions from packaging and selling those loans. In many cases lending standards were not strictly adhered to.[38]

Opacity Surrounding New Financial Innovations   By the middle of the first decade of the twenty-first century, new financial innovations helped make the U.S. housing boom a global phenomenon. Securitization allowed banks to package individual housing loans in a pool and sell securities backed by that pool of housing loans to investors in the United States as well as abroad. The securities paid interest to investors based on interest income pooled from individual housing loans. By putting housing loans from diverse geographical areas into a single pool, the risk from a default on any individual loan had been somewhat diversified away, since all borrowers were not expected to default at the same time. Consequently, securitization helped encourage banks to push for more lending, even to those who might have poor credit history, since it would seem that the risk of such lending could be contained and managed.

Securitized U.S. mortgages (housing loans) became very popular among investors both in the U.S. and abroad because the pool of housing loans could be further sliced into different tranches (related securities offered as part of the same transaction) that bore different levels of risk. If any housing borrower did default, the buyers of the most junior tranche of the pool of housing loans would be the first to absorb the loss. In return, to compensate for such losses, the buyers of the most junior tranche would receive the highest interest rate from that pool of housing loans.

The higher interest rates that could be earned from securitized mortgages were deemed very attractive by investors when compared to interest rates earned on normal bank deposits. The opacity surrounding the securitization process of the pooling and slicing of housing loans made it very difficult for investors to accurately gauge the risks they were taking in compensation for the higher returns.

With securitization, even securities made from a pool of housing loans made to borrowers with poor credit quality (i.e., subprime loans) were deemed rather safe for investors, partly because credit rating agencies that were hired by the bank to rate these securities would often rate them as being investment grade based on the historical rise in housing prices. As demand from investors for securitized mortgages rose, banks were induced to make loans by fees that they could earn from packaging and selling the loans, and they became less cautious in making those loans.[39]

The U.S. Subprime Crisis: The Outcome   The U.S. housing bubble finally became untenable when inflationary pressures started to pick up, partly because of fast-rising oil prices, and it was deemed that the Federal Reserve would need to raise interest rates further. By the time the federal fund rate reached 5.25 percent in 2006, the U.S. housing boom had already turned into a full-blown bubble. There were fears, which later became justified, that once mortgage interest rates started to rise, subprime borrowers would be unable to repay their loans and would have to default.

By 2007 there were already signs that the global financial system was about to crack. In June 2007, two hedge funds linked to Bear Stearns (a global securities firm) appeared in news headlines, as they needed to be rescued following sharp falls in the value of their investments in securitized loans. In September 2007, Northern Rock (a British bank that had relied on fees from securitization as a part of funding) found itself in difficulties as demand for securitized loans dried up. As the news spread, Northern Rock depositors rushed to demand their money from the bank, resulting in a bank run.[40]

By 2008 the crisis had become truly global: as housing bubbles in the United States and many European countries started to burst, banks that were involved in lending to the housing and real estate sectors suffered large losses. Uncertainty surrounding the health of financial institutions also made it very difficult for banks to get funding through borrowing in the financial markets. In March 2008 the Federal Reserve had to facilitate the purchase of Bear Stearns by JPMorgan Chase, a large U.S. bank, to prevent Bear Stearns from falling into bankruptcy.

The crisis reached its peak when the U.S. government decided to let Lehman Brothers, a global securities firm, file for bankruptcy on September 15, 2008. The failure of Lehman Brother caused panic worldwide, since Lehman Brothers was a global financial firm and counterparty to a worldwide web of global financial institutions. By September 19, 2008, with the threat that a domino effect of bank failures would bring a total collapse to the whole financial system, the U.S. government decided to reverse its stance and helped rescue a number of large banks, financial securities firms, money market mutual funds, and a large insurance company (AIG). By mid-October 2008, the governments of Ireland, Britain, France, Germany, Spain, the Netherlands, and Austria also had to step in to rescue their own ailing banking systems.[41]

CASE STUDY: The European Sovereign Debt Crisis

The European sovereign debt crisis came on the heels of the global financial crisis. Despite the euro system's early success, by the later years of the first decade of the twenty-first century cracks began to appear as a number of weaker member countries were hard hit by the global financial crisis. In Ireland, which suffered from the burst of its own property bubble, the government's decision to bail out the whole banking system through the guarantee of all banking sector liabilities effectively turned private debt into public debt.[42] The unsustainable public-debt load ultimately pushed the Irish government to seek outside assistance.

In Greece and Portugal, the fall in GDP growth and government revenue prompted their fiscal deficits to rise and their already-high ratios of public debt to GDP to look unsustainable, making it difficult for the governments of these two countries to refinance their debts. Although Spain initially did not have a high public debt-to-GDP ratio, when the global financial crisis started in 2007 the country subsequently severely suffered from a burst in its own housing bubble, such that a sharp fall in GDP combined with government spending to help alleviate a sharp spike in the unemployment rate made public debt triple to more than 90 percent of GDP by 2013.[43]

Since euro-area members were required by their euro agreement to keep their fiscal deficits below 3 percent of GDP, the euro governments were required to cut spending, which hurt already-weak economic activity even further. Without fiscal spending, these troubled euro countries had no tools to help stimulate their economies during a downturn, since their conduct of monetary policy had been handed over to the ECB, which focused primarily on the euro-wide perspective. Furthermore, in having a common currency troubled euro economies did not have the choice of a currency devaluation, which might otherwise have helped cheapen their export prices and stimulate external demand for their goods and services.

With their economies struggling, the risk that the governments of these countries might be unable to repay their public debts started to rise. To compensate for the risk, investors started asking for higher interest rates on bonds from these governments. Higher interest rates further weakened the ability of these governments to repay their debts, and also weakened the European banking sector, since many European banks held bonds of troubled euro governments as assets on their books. By 2012, the governments of Ireland, Greece, Portugal, and Spain all had to seek financial assistance from the so-called troika—the IMF, the European Union, and the ECB.

2.4 GOING FORWARD

As of 2014, the fallout from the global financial crisis of 2007–2010 was still very much present in the global monetary system. In response to the crisis, central banks in major advanced economies—such as the Federal Reserve, the ECB, the Bank of Japan, and the Bank of England—lowered their interest rates to nearly 0 percent and engaged in quantitative easing (i.e., the purchase of government securities from the financial market) in one form or another.

One of the side effects of the low interest rate policy and the quantitative easing programs in the advanced economies was a large influx of capital flows into emerging-market economies. Quantitative easing programs were, in effect, injections of money into the system, as the central banks that engaged in such programs would be paying money to purchase government securities from private holders of the securities. The extra injections of money from the quantitative easing programs and the low interest rates in the advanced economies nudged investors to search for higher investment returns in countries whose growth had been less affected by the crisis. The inflow of international capital into emerging economies has caused the currencies of emerging-market economies to appreciate in value across the board since 2010.

Another related side effect of the low interest rate policy and quantitative easing programs was the increasing volatility of international capital flows. Given that the advanced economies still remained rather weak, the quantitative easing programs were perceived more or less as a life support system, whose removal could cause a scare and much volatility and panic in global financial markets. In mid-2013, for example, when the Federal Reserve announced that it might *taper* its purchases of government securities in the near future, stock markets dropped across the globe. Investors rushed to draw back their capital from emerging-market economies. The reversal of capital flows caused the exchange rates of many emerging-market economies to experience a sharp drop. Only when the Federal Reserve reversed its position and announced that tapering might not occur until sometime in the future did the stock markets rise again, and capital outflows from emerging-market economies slowed or reversed.

Going forward, the international monetary system that central banks will be operating in would likely be affected by three important forces: (1) intensification of the globalization process, (2) continued evolution in financial activities, and (3) unfinished businesses from global financial crisis. How these forces might interact to shape the international monetary system and how central banks might adapt to meet challenges that these forces might pose will be discussed in more detail in Part IV of the book.

SUMMARY

International elements have always been present in central banking, ever since the Bank of Amsterdam started sorting and storing the coins of different sovereigns. In the centuries that followed, the international monetary system that central banks operate has also evolved.

When the gold standard was in place, central banks pegged the value of their currencies to gold. The main aim was to keep the value of money at the announced peg level. The gold standard broke down during World War I, as countries abandoned their pegs so they could print more money to finance the war.

After World War I, countries adopted the gold exchange standard, whereby the major countries would still peg their currencies to gold and hold gold as reserves. Smaller countries, however, would hold the currencies of the major countries as reserves instead, since there was not enough gold for all countries to hold as reserves.

In the 1930s the Great Depression emerged; as economic activities declined, a large number of banks failed worldwide, and deflation lasted for a decade. The Great Depression was partly attributable to the focus of central banks on maintaining their gold pegs, which led to contractionary monetary policies worldwide.

Turmoil in the international financial system also occurred in the 1930s as countries resorted to competitive devaluation of their currencies as well as trade protectionism to protect employment.

In July 1944, delegates from 44 countries decided to adopt a new international monetary system, the Bretton Woods system. Under this system the United States would fix the value of the U.S. dollar to gold at $35 per ounce, while other countries would fix the value of their currencies to the U.S. dollar. The IMF was also created to help countries deal with balance of payment and unemployment problems without having to resort to competitive devaluation and trade protectionism.

With freer international capital flows, the macroeconomic policy package in the United States that led to a budget deficit and high inflation, and the limitation of gold availability to back the U.S. dollar, the pressures on the Bretton Woods system became untenable. At first the United States stopped automatic convertibility of the U.S. dollar into gold and devalued the U.S. dollar. With a balance of payments crisis and speculative attacks raging on currencies, many advanced economies decided to allow their currencies to float against the U.S. dollar.

In the 1970s, the two oil shocks and accommodative fiscal and monetary policies led to the Great Inflation problem. As inflation expectations started to spiral out of control while the economy stagnated, many academics and central bankers started to ponder the use of a monetary policy rule to ensure price stability. In 1979 the Federal Reserve decided to bring down inflation expectations by tightening monetary policy sharply, and emphasized its commitments to money supply growth targeting as its monetary policy rule. By the late 1980s, however, money supply targeting had been practically abandoned, since the relationship between money and output proved unstable.

In the 1990s, liberalization led to large inflows of capital into emerging-market economies. As inflows started to seep into asset-price speculation, and emerging-market economies started to run large current account deficits, speculative attacks forced many of the emerging economies to devalue or float their currencies.

Since the early 1990s, many central banks in both advanced and emerging-market economies have started to adopt a monetary policy regime known as inflation targeting.

In 2000, a number of European countries decided to adopt a common currency, the euro. The European Central Bank (ECB) was created to conduct monetary policy for member countries of the euro area.

Between 2007 and 2010 a global financial crisis occurred, stemming from the subprime crisis in the United States. As of this writing, the global economy has not yet fully recovered from the global financial crisis.

KEY TERMS

balance of payments crisis

Bretton Woods system

European sovereign debt crisis

global financial crisis

gold standard

gold exchange standard

the Great Depression

the Great Inflation

inflation targeting

money supply growth targeting

speculative attacks

stagflation

subprime crisis

Triffin dilemma

wage-price spiral

QUESTIONS

1. What were the key features of the gold standard?
2. Why did the gold standard break down?
3. What could be key reasons preventing countries from returning to the gold standard?
4. What were the key features of the gold exchange standard?
5. Why did the gold exchange standard break down?
6. What were the key features of the Bretton Woods system?
7. Why did the Bretton Woods system break down?
8. Why did stagflation occur in the 1970s?
9. What did the Federal Reserve do to help end stagflation in the United States?
10. Why might emerging-market economies maintain their fixed exchange rates with major currencies, such as the U.S. dollar, after the breakdown of the Bretton Woods system?
11. What were the causes of speculative attacks on emerging-market currencies in the 1990s?
12. Explain intuitively how speculative attacks on currencies could be done.
13. How might low interest rates in the United States have contributed to the subprime crisis?
14. What were the key factors contributing to the U.S. subprime crisis?
15. In the euro area, what are the main responsibilities of the ECB?
16. In the euro area, what are the main responsibilities of the NCBs?
17. What might be possible causes of the European sovereign debt crisis?

CHAPTER 3

Modern Central Banking Roles and Functions

What Exactly Is a Central Bank?

Learning Objectives

1. Describe various roles and functions of modern central banks.
2. Describe the money creation process.
3. Explain the use of monetary policy to regulate monetary conditions in the economy.
4. Explain the role of central banks in payment systems oversight and provision.
5. Explain the role of central banks as lenders of last resort.
6. Explain the role of central banks as bank supervisors.

In Chapters 1 and 2, we briefly reviewed the evolution of central banking functions over the centuries and the background on international monetary systems so we could understand the context in which central banks have become what they are today. In this chapter we will review the main functions of modern-day central banks. As discussed in Chapter 1, modern central banks do have both commonalities and diversity, and thus their functions and details of institutional designs do differ. The review presented here is thus at an overview level, where broad rationales and mechanics of the functions are discussed, so the reader can see a broader picture of how a modern central bank might look.

This chapter starts with an overview of modern central banking. We then review five key functions of modern central banks: (1) money issuance, (2) the conduct of monetary policy, (3) payment systems regulation and provision, (4) lender of last resort, and (5) banking supervision. When reviewing each of these functions, the chapter explains what the functions mean in the modern context and describe relevant basic concepts, such as the money creation process, so the novice reader understands the mechanics of how money issued by the central bank might circulate and expand into other forms of money.

3.1 MODERN CENTRAL BANKING: AN OVERVIEW OF ROLES AND FUNCTIONS

Central banking today has evolved noticeably from its origins, owing to changes in the economic and financial environment that central banks operate in and the resultant changes in the roles of central banks. After many experiences and lessons learned along the way (e.g., the Great Depression of the 1930s, the Great Inflation of the 1970s, and the global financial crisis of 2007–2010 that were discussed in Chapters 1 and 2), it has become generally accepted that the key role of a modern central bank is to provide a sound and stable macroeconomic environment such that long-term sustainable growth of the economy can be achieved.

A modern central bank can deliver a sound and stable economic environment through (1) *monetary stability*, or safeguarding the value of the currency, whether in terms of low domestic inflation or stability of the exchange rate; and (2) *financial stability*, or helping the financial system to function smoothly and efficiently in the allocation of resources in the economy.

With stability in the value of the currency and smooth and effective functioning of the financial system, it is believed that the private sector (households and firms) will be able to make optimal consumption and investment decisions, which are fundamental to the long-term growth of the economy.

Over time, to suit the modern roles of central banking, a number of the central bank functions discussed in Chapter 2 have been dropped, and the rest have been modified. Most notably, most central banks these days are no longer coin sorters, nor financiers to the government. The conduct of monetary policy to achieve economic goals has now become a key focus for most central banks. In the wake of the global financial crisis of 2007–2010, the role of a central bank as a guardian to the financial system has also again been a key focus.

In general, it could be said that a typical modern central bank has five key functions: (1) issuance of money, (2) conduct of monetary policy, (3) payment systems facilitation, (4) lender of last resort, and (5) banking supervision. Some of the central banks might not have all five functions (e.g., some might not have the bank supervision function), and details of the workings of the functions might differ from one central bank to another. Still, these five key functions represent what a typical modern central bank does. Table 3.1 illustrates how these five *functions* might fit with the *roles* of a modern central bank.

In this chapter we briefly review what these functions are, and their underlying mechanics. In Chapter 4 we will examine the goals, or mandates, of modern central banks, which may include monetary stability, financial stability, and full employment, and which determine the specific functions performed by modern central banks.

The Ultimate Creator of Money: Money Issuance

In most countries these days, banknotes are issued by the central bank. Often, a modern banknote is printed with countersignatures of the governor or the chairman of the country's central bank and the finance minister (or the treasury secretary in the United States and the chancellor of the exchequer in the United Kingdom). The

TABLE 3.1   Roles and Functions of a Modern Central Bank: How They Fit

	Monetary Stability	Financial Stability
Roles	Maintain stable value of the currency	Maintain smooth and effective functioning of the financial system and guard against financial imbalances in the economy
Functions	1. Money issuance	1. Payment systems supervision and oversight
	2. Regulation of money conditions (i.e., the conduct of monetary policy) ◀▬▬▶	2. Lender of last resort 3. Banking supervision*

*A number of modern central banks currently do not have the banking supervision function, while others do.

countersignatures reflect the fact that the banknotes issued by the central bank has the backing of the sovereign.*

In this electronic age, not only can the issuance of money be done by the central bank through banknote issuance, it can also be done through electronic means. The central bank can choose to issue money by electronically crediting a commercial bank's account held at the central bank, possibly as a payment on the central bank's purchase of government securities from the commercial bank. In this case, the central bank is issuing money in electronic form, and is not printing banknotes to pay for the government securities that it bought from the commercial bank. That electronic form of money, however, could always be converted into banknotes from the central bank if the commercial bank so desires.

Whether the central bank issues money in electronic form or in the form of banknotes, that money goes through a process called the *money creation process* when it circulates in the economy. The money creation process multiplies the initial amount of money issued by the central bank, which results in a much larger amount. The final amount of money that comes out of the money creation process constitutes money supply. (See Concept: The Money Creation Process for more details.)

The Money Creation Process and Its Influences on Economic Activity and Price Levels   The stylized money creation process described in Concept: The Money Creation Process

---

*In a modern economy coins are often issued by the mint, which is likely to be under the finance ministry, not the central bank. Since in modern times banknotes account for a much larger proportion of the money supply than coins, it is reasonable to say that it is the central bank that is the ultimate creator of money.

CONCEPT: THE MONEY CREATION PROCESS

Banknotes and coins constitute *currency*. Currency plus commercial banks' deposits in their accounts at the central bank constitute *base money*. Base money is multiplied through the money creation process as it circulates through the banking system in multiple rounds. The money creation process is essentially a system of double-entry accounting.

The money creation process can be presented by the following stylized example. In Figure 3.1, when the central bank prints new banknotes and issues them into the system, the newly issued banknotes are considered claims on the central bank and will be recorded as *liabilities* on the central bank's balance sheet.

To balance the central bank's balance sheet, the new liabilities must be supported by new *assets*. In the modern day, the central bank might support the increase in banknotes (or liabilities) on its balance sheet by using those banknotes to purchase new assets, such as government securities (e.g., Treasury bills or government bonds), foreign currencies, foreign government securities, or even gold.

Figure 3.1 illustrates a case in which the central bank prints and issues new banknotes worth $100 to purchase government bonds worth $100 from Commercial Bank A. Accordingly, the amount of money in the system first rises by $100.

On Commercial Bank A's balance sheet, the increase in banknotes received from the central bank will appear on the asset side, offsetting the decrease in government bond holdings. Since banknotes, unlike government bonds, do not earn interest, ideally Commercial Bank A would not want to let these banknotes sit idle in its vault. Commercial Bank A would actively seek to lend out those banknotes.

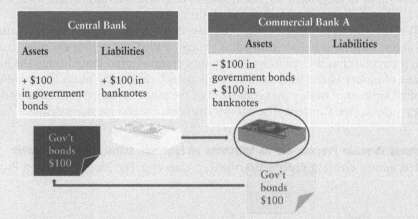

The central bank prints $100 worth of banknotes to purchase government bonds from Commercial Bank A. At the end of this stage, the amount of money in the economy rises by $100, as reflected by banknotes held by Commercial Bank A.

FIGURE 3.1 Stylized Money Creation Process: Step 1

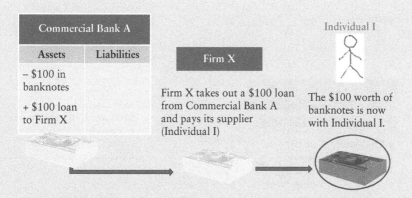

Commercial Bank A loans out $100 worth of banknotes to Firm X in order
to earn interest from the loan. To keep Commercial Bank A's balance sheet
balanced, $100 worth of banknotes is deducted from the assets side of
Commercial Bank A's balance sheet, while the $100 from the loan made
to Firm X would be added to the same side of the balance sheet.

FIGURE 3.2   Stylized Money Creation Process: Step 2

Figure 3.2 illustrates a case in which Commercial Bank A lends out $100
worth of banknotes to a borrower called firm X, who then uses the banknotes
to pay its supplier called Individual I. On the asset side of Commercial Bank
A's balance sheet, that lending of $100 worth of banknotes will be recorded as
a decrease of $100 worth of banknotes, and matched by an increase of $100
on a loan made to Firm X.

When Individual I receives the $100 worth of banknotes from Firm X, if
he still does not have an urgent use for that money, then he is likely to put that
amount of money back into his bank account, possibly for safety reasons, and
possibly to also earn interest income from that money.

Figure 3.3 illustrates the case where Individual I deposits $100 worth of
banknotes that he received from Firm X into his account at Commercial Bank B.
Here, on Commercial Bank B's balance sheet, the $100 that Individual I
deposited into his account at Commercial Bank B would be recorded as an
increase in Commercial Bank B's liabilities. To match the increase in liabilities,
Commercial Bank B would actively seek to lend out those banknotes to earn
interest on them.

In Figure 3.3, as Commercial Bank B lends to Individual II, the loan made
to Individual II would be recorded as an increase in assets on the balance sheet
of Commercial Bank B. At this point, note that while the central bank originally issued only $100 worth of banknotes, the total amount of money by this
time has already doubled to $200, since $100 in Individual I's deposit account
at Commercial Bank B would also be counted as money.

This process of money creation is likely to continue, since individuals or
firms will keep cash on hand only up to a certain level. Any extra cash beyond
that level would be invested or deposited to earn interest income. Once the extra

(Continued)

(*Continued*)

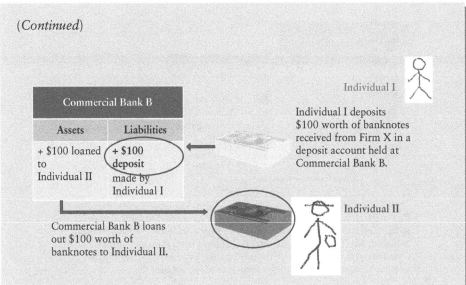

At this point, the amount of money in the system has doubled to $200 (the $100 deposited in the account of Individual I plus the $100 worth of banknotes lent out to Individual II).

FIGURE 3.3   Stylized Money Creation Process: Step 3

cash is deposited with a commercial bank, the bank would have an incentive to lend the extra cash out, so it can generate interest income from that lending. The rise in the liabilities on the bank's balance sheet in terms of an increase in deposits would amount to an increase in the amount of money in the economy, even though the cash is already lent out and is no longer with the bank.

In Figure 3.4, as Individual II used the borrowed money to buy gadgets from Merchant I, and Merchant I deposited that money into his account at Commercial Bank C, the total amount of money rises to $300 from the initial $100 that the central bank first issued. The $300 includes the $100 worth of banknotes that are still circulating within the economy, the $100 deposit of Individual I at Commercial Bank B, and the $100 deposit of Merchant I at Commercial Bank C.

From the stylized process described above, we can see that the central bank is indeed very powerful with respect to money creation. Even at this stage, the $100 worth of banknotes initially introduced by the central bank can turn into $300 worth of money in the system, with the potential of going much further as long as the process keeps repeating.

Reserves, Money Multiplier, and Money Supply

In theory, the process described could keep on repeating and thus there are no bounds on how many times the initial $100 could be multiplied. In practice, however, the amount of money created through this process would be limited by the fact that (1) banks might need to keep some cash on hand or in the

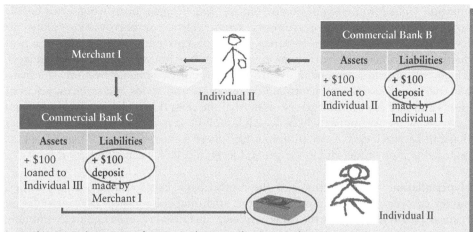

At this point, the amount of money in the system has increased to $300 (the $100 deposit at Commercial Bank B plus the $100 deposit at Commercial Bank C plus the $100 worth of banknotes at Individual III).

FIGURE 3.4   Stylized Money Creation Process: Step 4

vaults, or keep some money in their deposit accounts at the central bank, to meet withdrawal demand from depositors or other urgencies, and (2) the number of borrowers worth lending to is limited.

The money that banks keep on hand or in the vaults and in their accounts at the central bank constitutes what is known as bank *reserves*. In many countries, the central bank also sets legal *reserve requirements*, specifying the ratio of reserves to deposits that the banks are legally required to maintain.

When commercial banks keep a part of deposits on hand or in the accounts held with the central bank as reserves it is called *fractional reserve banking*. In a fractional reserve banking system, if all commercial banks hold, for example, 5 percent of deposits on hand, then the money creation process has the potential to multiply the initial amount of base money by $1/0.05 = 20$ times. If the initial base money is $100, and commercial banks hold 5 percent of deposits as reserves, then potentially the maximum amount of the *money supply* that can be created from the initial $100 is $100 \times 20 = \$2,000$. Here, 20 is called the *money multiplier*. More generically, the money multiplier is 1/(reserve ratio), where the *reserve ratio* is the ratio of reserves to deposits.[1]

suggests that money creation has a vast potential to affect economic activity. Given that the economy is initially in equilibrium, when new money issued by the central bank finds its way into a commercial bank's balance sheet, the commercial bank will actively seek to lend out that money so that it can earn interest on the loans. Money sitting idle in the vault is costly to banks, whether in terms of storage, interest that must be paid out to depositors, or foregone interest income that might be earned from lending the money out. The more money that is introduced into the system, the more banks will aggressively loan out the money. As more money is introduced into the system, banks become more willing to lend it out at lower interest and less stringent terms.

Inflation   The lower costs of borrowing and less stringent borrowing terms enable borrowers to engage in more economic activity. Firms can borrow more money to buy raw materials, build new factories, hire employees, and generally engage in production. Individuals can borrow more money to buy houses, cars, or other gadgets, which will, in turn, prompt more production and investments by firms. As firms and individuals use the money to bid up resources and goods and services, prices of goods and services will start to rise. Indeed, if the central bank keeps on printing and issuing new money, money will be worth less and less in terms of goods and services that can be purchased. A situation in which there is a continuous and sustained (as opposed to a one-time) rise in the general level of prices is called *inflation*.

Hyperinflation   At the extreme, if the central bank keeps issuing a lot of money, money can very rapidly diminish in value, such that the problem of *hyperinflation* ensues. With hyperinflation, the value of money can fall so fast, even minute-by-minute, that it is not a good store of value. People in a country with hyperinflation would rather use the money to buy goods and services right away once they get the money. With hyperinflation, people are not able to make optimal investment decisions since they can't reasonably predict investment costs and revenues even in the short term.

Recession   In contrast, if too little amount of money is introduced into the system, economic activity could very well slow down or even fall, tipping the economy into a *recession*. With a scarcity of money to lend out, banks will charge higher interest rates and impose more stringent terms on their loans. Firms will find it hard to borrow to buy raw materials, invest in new factories, hire employees, or expand their production. Individuals will find it hard to borrow money to finance their purchases of goods and services, which also affects the firms that provide those goods and services. Indeed, as money in the system becomes scarcer, and demand for goods and services falls, firms might have to cut their prices. As firms are unable make profits, they might have to also cut down on their number of workers, which would further reduce aggregate demand in the economy.

Deflation   At the extreme, if money is really scarce, economic activity could fall so much so that a large number of firms will fail, resulting in high unemployment. Surviving firms, meanwhile, might be forced to keep cutting prices to attract customers. The number of the firms' customers, meanwhile, could keep dwindling as more people lose their jobs. The situation where the general price level continuously falls is known as *deflation*.

Since the amount of money that the central bank introduces into an economy can seriously affect economic conditions, it is very important that the amount of money the central bank issues into the economy is *appropriate* for economic conditions. The central bank might also need to regulate the money creation process and money conditions in the economy through other means, a subject that we will explore in more detail in the next section.

The Regulation of Money Conditions: The Conduct of Monetary Policy

Since the central bank is the ultimate money creator and often has the power over the setting of reserve requirements, it falls on the central bank to be the one regulating the *flow* and the *amount* of money in the economy. In modern terms, it is said that the central bank is responsible for the conduct of monetary policy. As discussed before, when a lot of money is available in the economy at low cost— possibly through high money issuance, or from a reduction in reserve requirements, or from cuts in interest rates—then households and firms are likely to be stimulated to engage in more consumption and production.

When there is insufficient money in the economy or when the costs of money are high, on the other hand, households will be less able to borrow to consume, while firms will be less able to borrow to invest, expand production, or hire workers. Making sure that there is just the right amount of money available at the right cost to households and firms is something that the central bank has always aspired to as the regulator of money.

Money Supply versus Reserve Requirements versus Policy Interest Rate In a modern, complex economy, the way the central bank regulates money has become more sophisticated and *indirect*. As will be discussed in Part II of this book in more detail, most modern central banks no longer attempt to set a target for the money supply in the economy, since the relationship between the level of base money and the total level of the money supply in the economy could be very unstable. The central bank, unless it's operating a tightly controlled system, also often refrains from frequently adjusting reserve requirements (the percentage of deposits that banks can't loan out), since it might hamper the smooth functioning of the economy. For example, if the central bank raises reserve requirements in order to slow down economic activity and the banking system previously had been in equilibrium in the sense that there was no existing excess reserves, commercial banks might need to call in loans from borrowers in order to meet the new reserve requirements. Calling in loans can be very costly to the banks and their borrowers, and very disruptive to economic activity.

Instead of adjusting reserve requirements, modern central banks often attempt to regulate money conditions in the economy via the use of a *policy interest rate* and *financial market operations*. A policy interest rate is a short-term interest rate that a central bank chooses to directly influence, which gives a signal to the public as to what it sees in terms of future economic conditions and future price levels. By raising the policy interest rate, the central bank signals to the public that it wants to tone down the acceleration of economic activity and tame the rise in the general price level. By lowering the policy interest rate, the central bank signals to the public that it wants economic activity to pick up and that it wants to allow a rise in the general price level. By keeping the policy interest rate at a particular level, the central bank signals to the public that money conditions in the economy are appropriate for a favorable outlook of economic activity and the general price level. Financial market operations, on the other hand, help ensure that the policy interest rate stays at or near the level that the central bank wants to keep.

The Use of Policy Interest Rate and Financial Market Operations to Regulate Monetary Conditions in the Economy In a modern financial system, if the central bank deems that money conditions are too loose (i.e., too much money is available at too low a cost), the central bank might raise the policy interest rate. By raising the policy interest rate, the opportunity cost of money will increase, and thus lenders will be more discrete in their lending. In a modern system where news and information are available on a real-time basis, once the central bank announces the hike in the policy interest rate it is conceivable that lenders will adjust their lending behavior right away, raising the cost of their loans.

However, in the case where there is already too much money in the system, the central bank might back up the announcement of the policy interest rate hike with open market operations, whereby the central bank itself takes out money from the system by selling government bonds in the financial market. By selling government bonds in the financial market, the central bank is effectively draining money from the system, since payments for the bonds are made using money. Money that buyers of bonds pay to the central bank will effectively be out of circulation.

In contrast, when the central bank deems that money conditions are too tight (i.e., too little money is available at too high a cost), the central bank might lower the policy interest rate. With a lower policy interest rate, the opportunity cost of money will be lower and lenders will be more willing to lend. As with the hike in the policy interest rate, news and information is available on a real-time basis and so the mere announcement of a cut in the policy interest rate will lead to an adjustment in the behavior of lenders right away.

Still, if the central bank deems it necessary, it could also back up the announcement of the cut in the policy interest rate with operations in the financial market. Most likely the central bank will decide to buy government bonds in the financial market. By buying government bonds in the financial market the central bank will effectively be injecting money into the system, since the government will have to pay money to market participants for the bonds that it purchased.

The central bank's role as a regulator of money (i.e., the conductor of monetary policy), has become a key feature accorded much attention by the public in the past four decades. Changes in money conditions potentially affect everyone in the economy. After many trials and errors, and a number of theoretical and practical breakthroughs, the conduct of monetary policy is now widely viewed as a composition of both art and science. We will examine the theoretical foundations and the practice of monetary policy in more detail in Part II of the book.

Payment Systems Oversight and Provision

Even in the earlier days of central banking, commercial banks often held accounts at the central bank. The banks would use the accounts at the central bank to clear transactions among themselves. This practice was quite logical for at least two reasons. First, as commercial banks themselves often competed in the same line of business, it was rare that they would hold accounts with their competitors. As central banks started to take on the role of a public institution rather than a profit-making entity, they became less commercial in nature and were not deemed competitors by the commercial banks. Second, with the central bank being the ultimate money creator with close ties to the sovereign, the central bank was deemed to be safer and more reliable for the commercial banks' accounts. When commercial banks transacted among themselves, it became easier for them to settle with each other via their accounts held at the central bank. Accordingly, the central bank acted a banker to commercial banks by taking in deposits and clearing funds for them.[2]

At present, instead of simply clearing funds for commercial banks, the modern central bank now often takes on a more active role in national payment systems. With regard to payments systems, the modern central bank often actively participates as (1) a regulator that ensures smooth functioning of the country's payment systems, and (2) a service provider of national payment systems.[3]

Payment Systems Oversight   As a payment systems regulator, the central bank sets rules and guidelines regarding payment systems. The central bank's main aims in setting rules, arguably, are to (1) reduce the probability of a payment systems failure, (2) improve efficiency in payment systems, and (3) ensure fairness and equity in the use of payment systems.[4]

Payment system failures can cause ripple effects through the financial system and the economy, as participants might rely on payments to meet their own liquidity obligations. In extreme cases, liquidity shortages resulting from payment system failures could cause financial panics and bank runs. Consequently, failures in payment systems have the potential to disrupt economic activity and cause financial instability. It thus is in the central bank's interest to reduce the probability of such failures, which could lead to instability in both the financial system and the economy.

Apart from reducing systemic risks, the central bank also regulates the payment system for efficiency reasons. New technology often brings improved efficiency. In many cases, however, the private sector might not have the incentive to move to newer technology, as it often requires major investments. To help prod the private sector along, the mantle often falls on the public sector, particularly the central bank, to issue guidelines and regulations to help coordinate players in the private sector to move to the new technology on an appropriate timeline.[5]

Efficient payment systems are also integral to efficient monetary policy operations. Efficient payment systems can help the central bank inject and absorb liquidity more quickly. Likewise, efficient payment systems will allow commercial banks to efficiently manage their reserves. Commercial banks can borrow and lend more quickly as needed. Consequently, to ensure maximum efficiency in monetary operations it is also in the interest of the central bank, as the conductor of monetary policy, to get involved in designing and regulating payment systems.[6]

Furthermore, since payment systems are often a public good with positive externalities, the central bank might want to set rules that ensure equity and fairness in the economy. The infrastructure of a payment system network often has economies of scale and requires large investments that can only be made by the public sector or large players in the private sector. When the private sector is the one making the necessary investments, it might be beneficial that smaller players also be able to access the network at a price that is affordable to them, yet fair to those large players that made the investments.

Payment Systems Provision   The modern central bank is often the key service provider for the large-value fund (wholesale) transfer system in the economy. For interbank fund transfer payments, it is often most efficient for commercial banks to use a single integrated central system, rather than relying on different, fragmented systems. Such a single integrated central system, however, is a public good. Without public intervention, commercial banks that initially invested in such an infrastructure are unlikely to allow other commercial banks to join in (or free ride) the network. To get around this problem, most central banks often become key service providers of wholesale payments themselves. For small-value (retail) fund transfer payments, however, central banks often get involved as a service provider only with certain types of instruments, notably check clearing. Central banks would be unlikely to be involved with credit card clearing, however, since private sector service providers already provide extensive services in this area.[7]

Lender of Last Resort

As discussed in Chapter 1, historically it became natural for a bank in trouble to look to the central bank for help, if all else failed, since the central bank was the ultimate creator of money with close ties to the sovereign, and a banker to banks.[8] Prior to the recent global financial crisis, however, the modern central bank often played down this function for fear of the so-called moral hazard problem.[9]

Moral Hazard   In a banking context, the *moral hazard* problem suggests that if banks know that they can always seek assistance from the central bank, they will be more reckless in their behavior. Banks might lend to risky projects without adequately preparing for the risks they are taking on and always assume that help will be at hand. To discipline banks against the moral hazard problem, the central bank often urges the banks to find other means of assistance before coming to the central bank.[10] Often, the central bank will also make clear that it will not rescue any single bank unless it would jeopardize the whole system (i.e., too-big-to-fail).

In the wake of the recent global financial crisis and the subsequent euro crisis that threatened to destabilize the global economy, however, many central banks had to again embrace the lender-of-last-resort function in a very significant manner. Major central banks, including the Federal Reserve, the ECB, and the Bank of England, all became lenders of last resort to prevent the crises from destabilizing the financial system and the economy even more severely than it already had.

Forms of Lender-of-Last-Resort Function   Theoretically, the central bank can assume the lender-of-last-resort function in three main forms. First, it can lend *liquidity* to *individual banks*. Second, it can lend *liquidity* to the *market*, rather than to specific individual financial institutions. Third, it can inject *risk capital* into troubled banks, which effectively also implies a takeover of the banks by the government.[11]

In the first form of the lender-of-last-resort function, the central bank could provide short-term loans, possibly against collateral such as government securities, directly to a troubled bank so that it could meet its short-term obligations first. Once the troubled bank met its short-term obligations, it could return to normal functioning and would be expected to repay the borrowed funds to the central bank. The fact that the bank could return to normal functioning after meeting its short-term obligations suggest that the bank was merely facing a *liquidity problem* rather than a *solvency problem*.* In the second form of the lender-of-last-resort function, the central bank could lend out liquidity to the market, rather than to specific individual financial

---

*A liquidity problem suggests that an entity might not be able to liquidate its assets in a timely manner without incurring losses from the liquidation, and that those losses might hamper the entity's ability to meet its short-term obligations in full. If the liquidity problem is addressed in a timely manner, the losses might not be so severe and could be covered by the entity's existing capital. In such a case, if the liquidity problem is addressed in a timely manner the entity is likely to be able to return to normal functioning. A solvency problem, however, suggests that the entity might not have enough current assets to meet its current liabilities, and the entity might need to draw down a substantial portion (or all) of its capital to meet liabilities. With a solvency problem, the entity thus might not be able to return to normal functioning without a capital injection.

institutions, to reduce liquidity shortages that occur across the financial system in times of extreme stress. Examples from the global financial crisis of 2007–2010 include the Federal Reserve's Primary Dealer Credit Facility, which was set up to ease up liquidity conditions in the repo (repurchase) market,[12] as well as the Federal Reserve's Commercial Paper Funding Facility, which was created to ease liquidity conditions in commercial paper market.[13] In both cases the Federal Reserve was willing to lend to nonbank financial institutions as well as nonfinancial firms (in many cases against illiquid collateral) to help alleviate liquidity shortages in these markets.

With extra liquidity from the central bank, financial institutions or firms are able to meet their short-term obligations better. The lending can also help bring down the general level of short-term interest rates or prevent them from rising further. If short-term interest rates are low, financial institutions will be more willing to lend and borrow both among themselves and with other customers, which will help ease general tightness in liquidity and allow economic activity to continue.

The third form of the lender-of-last-resort function applies to cases in which the bank is unlikely to be able to return to normal functioning even after meeting its short-term obligations (i.e., the bank is facing a solvency problem). In such cases the central bank might need to inject risk capital into the bank and take over the management of that bank. Through injecting capital the central bank would take ownership of the bank (as opposed to merely lending) and would work to find a suitable resolution to the problem. In a way, we could view injection of risk capital into banks as a special resolution for troubled banks, which will be discussed later in this chapter.

Bank Supervisor

As discussed in Chapter 2, if the role of lender of last resort is placed upon the central bank, it is only fair that the central bank should be able to regularly assess the health of commercial banks, since if any of the banks get into trouble the central bank would have to decide if it is worth helping, and if so, pay for such help.[14] In many countries such a role has since evolved into banking supervision, under which the central bank not only has a formal duty to inspect the soundness of commercial banks' operations but also to issue regulations that will ensure such soundness.

In practice, modern central banks have a number of related but diverse tasks as bank supervisors. These tasks might include (1) licensing of new banks, (2) examination and monitoring of banks' operations, (3) setting regulatory requirements for banks, (4) enforcement of regulations to ensure corrective action, and (5) providing resolution for troubled financial institutions when necessary.[15] The aim of these tasks is to reduce risk with respect to *individual* financial institutions as well as to the *system as a whole*.

Licensing of New Banks   Many central banks undertake the task of new bank licensing to ensure that banks under its supervision will start with a sound framework.* Organizers of a new commercial bank have to submit an application to the central

---

*Note that in the United States, the Federal Reserve does not provide banking licenses. Rather, states grant banking license to state banks and the Office of the Comptroller of the Currency grants licenses to national banks. (Board of Governors of the Federal Reserve System 2005)

bank for approval. Normally, the central bank will examine the soundness of the business plan to see if the new bank will be profitable after a certain period of time. Individuals proposed for the board of directors and management of the bank will also be examined to see if they are fit and proper (i.e., they are honest and trustworthy, they have never declared bankruptcy, and they have not been directors or managers of another bank that failed).[16]

Apart from ensuring the safety and soundness of a new bank through its policy on new bank licensing, the central bank can also shape the financial landscape under its jurisdiction in such a way that systemic risks are reduced and innovation and competition are encouraged. For example, if the central bank deems existing competition among commercial banks to be already healthy and sufficient, and that more entrants will bring in *excessive* competition such that the commercial banks might have to resort to riskier activities to achieve acceptable returns, then the central bank might decide to delay new licensing. In contrast, if the central bank deems current competition and innovation to be insufficient in supporting economic activity, then the central bank can give licenses to new players or allow banks to provide a wider range of financial products.

Examination and Monitoring of Commercial Banks' Operations   Bank examination is a basic foundation of the bank supervisory process. It is done to assess the soundness of commercial banks' operations, and to ensure that that commercial banks comply with rules and regulatory requirements. In these modern days, bank examination consists of two complementary tasks, namely on-site supervision and off-site monitoring. *On-site examination* refers to a situation in which the central bank sends its staff to inspect the bank on site, at the bank's offices. Off-site monitoring is done in the period in the supervisory cycle between on-site examinations, and involves the central bank monitoring and analyzing the commercial bank's performance using data from on-site examination and other relevant sources to determine the safety and soundness of the bank's condition and performance.[17]

CONCEPT: BANK EXAMINATION

Bank examination has always been a foundation of the bank supervisory process. Modern bank examination is often composed of two main elements: on-site examination and off-site monitoring. These two elements are complementary in nature.

On-Site Examination

In a typical on-site examination, bank examiners sent by the central bank will interview the bank's management, inspect the bank's written policies and procedures, determine the degree to which the policies and procedures are actually followed, evaluate the adequacy of the bank's capital, check the accuracy of accounting records, check the adequacy of internal controls and the audit function, and check for compliance with laws and regulations. (See Table 3.2.)

Apart from being written up, results of an on-site examination are also often summarized into a single composite number in what is known as the *CAMELS* rating system (or its variants), where C stands for capital adequacy, A stands for asset quality, M stands for management (which includes internal

TABLE 3.2 CAMELS Rating Components

CAMELS Rating System	
C	Capital adequacy
A	Asset quality
M	Management
E	Earnings
L	Liquidity
S	Sensitivity to market risk

Source: Adapted from Board of Governor of the Federal Reserve System, The Federal Reserve System: Purposes and Functions (Washington, DC: Board of Governors of the Federal Reserve System, 2005).

controls, corporate governance, and audit), *E* stands for earnings (which reflects profitability), *L* stands for liquidity (the ability to convert assets into cash to meet unexpected temporary excess withdrawals), and *S* stands for sensitivity to market risk (the sensitivity of the bank's capital or profitability to changes in interest rates, foreign exchange rates, or share prices, and the bank's measures to mitigate those risks).[18]

The weight given to each CAMELS component can vary, but often the most weight is given to management. The central bank expresses its opinion about the safety and soundness of the examined bank through the CAMELS rating and the analysis contained in its report.[19]

Off-Site Monitoring

In practice, it is not cost-effective or convenient for central banks (and commercial banks) to have bank examiners on-site in each bank at all times. The supervisory central bank would thus use off-site monitoring to cover the period in the supervisory cycle between on-site examinations. During off-site monitoring, the supervisory central bank will check for correction of the financial problems revealed at the last on-site examination; plan ahead to identify areas of emerging risk to focus on in the next examination; and analyze current conditions and performance of the bank based on regulatory reports, reports of the examiners, and publicly available information about the bank, such that, if necessary, changes to the CAMELS rating, a targeted examination, or a full-scope examination that takes place earlier than scheduled can be made.[20]

Setting Regulatory Requirements for Commercial Banks The supervisory central bank has the power to set rules and guidelines for commercial banks to ensure that they operate in a safe and sound manner. Such regulations might range from the banks' corporate governance and risk management practices to capital and reserve adequacy requirements. For a central bank, *capital requirements* (the minimum capital that each bank needs to have to buffer against unexpected losses) and *reserve requirements* (the minimum reserves that each bank needs to hold against deposits to meet liquidity demand) are among the key regulations it can use to ensure the safety and soundness of commercial banks' operations.

CASE STUDY: Capital Requirements and Reserve Requirements

Capital requirements and reserve requirements are among key regulations that the central bank can use to ensure safety and soundness of banks under its supervision.

Capital Requirements

Since 1988, many central banks have adopted the capital requirement guidelines known as Basel I, which were issued by the Basel Committee on Banking Supervision, an international body based in the town of Basel, Switzerland. Basel I suggested how much capital banks should hold against different types of assets to compensate for credit risk (risk that the bank's debtors might be unable to repay their debts). A central bank that had adopted Basel I would make sure that the banks under its supervision would comply with the rules.

In 2004, the Basel Committee introduced a new version of capital guidelines called Basel II. Basel II took account of liquidity and operation risks, in addition to credit risk, which was the focus of Basel I. In addition, Basel II also aimed to adjust the practice of bank supervision by giving more emphasis to off-site supervision, whereby the bank supervisor would focus less on examining the banks' transactions and more on the banks' risk-management practices. Although Basel II had not yet been widely adopted when the global financial crisis came in 2007, the crisis made its shortcomings apparent. The Basel Committee went back to work and introduced Basel III at the end of 2010. The details of Basel I, II, and III are discussed in Chapter 12.

Reserve Requirements

While capital requirements are primarily meant to ensure that banks have enough capital to prevent unexpected losses in the value of their assets from directly affecting the banks' depositors, reserve requirements are meant to ensure that the banks have enough liquidity to meet liquidity demand.[21] Reserves are traditionally held in the form of cash, or deposits at the central bank, and thus banks can easily turn to them to meet liquidity demand. Historically, reserve requirements have also been used as a tool of monetary policy.[22] When reserve requirements are raised, banks have to keep more reserves as cash or deposits at the central bank rather than lending them out as loans. With fewer loans being provided in the economy—all other things being equal—economic activity will slow down. When reserve requirements are lowered, banks are able to provide more loans, as they are required to hold less cash and deposits at the central bank as reserves.

In modern times, not many central banks use reserve requirements as a tool of monetary policy since frequent adjustments in reserves can entail substantial costs for both banks and customers. For example, if the central bank decides to raise reserve requirements, then a commercial bank that already has its reserves at the previous minimum required levels might need to convert extra assets into cash. If the bank does not have extra assets that can be easily converted into cash, then it might need to call in loans from customers that had previously been extended.

A small number of central banks have decided to forego reserve requirements altogether.[23] Reserves can be considered extra costs imposed on banks. Cash kept as reserves do not provide returns, and can incur a cost of safekeeping. Deposits held at the central bank might also not earn interest or earn considerably less than could be gained from lending to customers. Most modern central banks, however, still deem reserve requirements to be a crucial regulation to ensure commercial banks' liquidity, and thus keep it as a regulatory tool.

Enforcement of Laws and Regulations to Ensure Compliance To make sure that commercial banks comply with laws and regulations, the central bank is often endowed with enforcement power over banks. If banks are found not to be in compliance with laws and regulations, the central bank has the power to ensure compliance from the banks using various kinds of measures, from mild to drastic, to ensure that the banks pursue corrective actions.[24]

Milder measures include moral persuasion, whereby the central bank has discussions with the management of a commercial bank to persuade it to alter its gray area actions. More drastic measures that the central bank might use to ensure compliance with laws and regulations can include removal of directors or managers of banks for negligence or misconduct and installation of a temporary administration, as well as a recommendation of a forced sale or liquidation of the bank.[25]

Resolutions for Troubled Financial Institutions   Although the central bank may set various rules and regulations and examine commercial banks' operations in minute detail, there is always a possibility that some banks might still run into trouble. To ensure that these troubled banks do not fail in a disorderly manner, the central bank and relevant authorities might need to impose special resolutions on these troubled banks.

Key types of such resolutions are (1) *liquidation*, or the closing of banks whereby the banks' assets are liquidated in order to repay the banks' liabilities; (2) *conservatorship*, or temporary administration of the banks; (3) *purchase and assumption*, under which a healthy bank purchases some or all of a failed bank's assets and assumes some or all of the failed bank's liabilities; and (4) *nationalization*, under which the government takes over a failed bank and assumes the bank's assets and liabilities.[26]

3.2 TO SUPERVISE BANKS OR NOT?

The global financial crisis of 2007–2010 brought a reexamination of the modern central bank's role as bank supervisor. In the 1990s and 2000s, many governments decided to carve the bank supervisory role out of the central bank and give the role to a specially created financial regulatory body. One rationale was that the central bank's supervisory role was inherently in conflict with its role as the conductor of monetary policy. As a bank supervisor, the central bank knew the detailed financial condition of banks under its supervision. As a conductor of monetary policy, the central bank had the obligation to tighten monetary conditions if it saw inflationary pressures building up. By tightening monetary conditions, however, business activities could slow, and firms with outsized debts might fail. Banks might have to write down loans, making the banks' own financial situations more precarious. Because of its bank supervisor role, if the central bank was aware that monetary tightening might lead to a deterioration of the banks' balance sheets then it might hesitate to tighten monetary conditions, even if inflationary pressures warranted a contraction. Consequently, by the middle of the first decade of the twenty-first century a number of central banks had already shed their bank supervisory role and relegated it to a financial services authority, also known as a financial supervisory authority (FSA).

As the global crisis struck in 2007, the reexamination of whether the central bank should delegate its bank supervisory role became particularly notable in the case of the Bank of England. Without detailed knowledge of the banking sector balance sheets, the Bank of England was caught largely unaware of financial problems in the banking sector. When bank failures threatened to become systemic, poor coordination among the FSA, the Treasury, and the Bank of England was cited as a cause. After all, the FSA, which had details on the banks' situations, did not have the money or the authority to help the banks financially. The Bank of England, which had the means to help the banks, however, did not have the details to help effectively. As the crisis unfolded, the British government decided to eliminate the FSA and place the bank supervisory role back with the Bank of England.

3.3 SO WHAT EXACTLY IS A MODERN CENTRAL BANK AFTER ALL?

From the discussion above, the modern central bank has retained and modified many of the functions discussed in Chapter 2. In general, it could be said that the modern central bank issues money, conducts monetary policy, and regulates and provides payment systems services. When required, the modern central bank also acts as a lender of last resort, although it often tries to play down this function for fear of moral hazard. In many countries, the modern central bank also supervises commercial banks (i.e., it issues new bank licenses, sets regulatory standards for banks, examines and monitors bank operations, and enforces laws and regulations to ensure that banks operate in a safe and sound manner).

The functions of the modern central bank discussed above can be grouped into two broad categories that align with two of the key modern central bank mandates, that is, monetary stability and financial stability. Those central bank functions relating to issuance of money and the conduct of monetary policy are done in such a way that monetary stability is ensured (i.e., keeping inflation low and stable). Those functions relating to payment systems regulation and provision, lender of last resort, and bank supervision, on the other hand, are all done to ensure financial stability (i.e., the smooth functioning of the financial system).

In practice, many modern central banks arrange their internal organizational structure broadly along the lines of these two mandates, with one wing dealing with monetary stability and the other dealing with financial stability.* In the wake of the 2007–2010 global financial crisis, however, it has become increasingly recognized that monetary stability and financial stability are intertwined, and one cannot exist without the other. Central banks have since put increasingly more emphasis into effective coordination between these two wings. In the next chapters, we will discuss why monetary stability and financial stability have become key mandates for the modern central bank, and how the central bank can act to fulfill these two mandates in practice.

---

*Organizationally, the banknote issuance department is often not put under the monetary stability wing, although determining the number of banknotes to issue is often done in consultation with the monetary policy department. Operationally, the banknote issuance function involves management of the printing press, distribution centers, and so on, which makes it too cumbersome to place it under the monetary stability wing.

SUMMARY

Modern central banking functions include money issuance, the conduct of monetary policy, payment systems oversight and provision, lender of last resort, and banking supervision.

In modern times, the central bank issues money in the form of banknotes, as well as in an electronic form. Money issued by the central bank goes through the money creation process, which essentially constitutes a double-entry accounting process as it circulates through the system. The final amount of money that comes out of the money creation process is the money supply.

Modern central banks also aim to regulate money conditions, since the money creation process has the potential to affect economic activity and price levels. Theoretically the central bank can regulate money conditions through the conduct of monetary policy, using reserve requirements, changing the policy interest rate, and carrying out open market operations. In practice, modern central banks often avoid using reserve requirements as a monetary policy tool, but instead use the policy interest rate and open market operations to regulate money conditions.

Modern central banks often also perform payment systems oversight and provision functions. The central bank might want to perform payment systems oversight to ensure a low probability of payment systems failure, to improve efficiency of the payment systems, and to ensure equity and fairness in the use of payments systems. The central bank is also often the provider of the wholesale payment system for the economy.

The lender-of-last-resort role can take three key forms: (1) liquidity provision to individual banks, (2) liquidity provision to the market as a whole, and (3) injection of risk capital into troubled financial institutions.

Banking supervision is not a universal function for all central banks. For those central banks that have a banking supervision function, the tasks might include licensing of new banks, bank examination, setting regulatory requirements, enforcement of laws and regulations to ensure compliance, and providing resolutions for troubled financial institutions.

In the wake of the 2007–2010 global financial crisis, there has increasingly been a reexamination of the debate about whether a central bank should perform a banking supervision function.

KEY TERMS

banking supervision	money creation process
base money	money multiplier
CAMELS	money supply
capital requirement	off-site monitoring
deflation	on-site examination
hyperinflation	open market operations
inflation	payment systems oversight
lender of last resort	payment systems provision
liquidity problem	policy interest rate

recession   reserves

reserve ratio   solvency problem

reserve requirements

QUESTIONS

1. What are main functions of modern central banks?
2. What are the key roles of modern central banks?
3. What is base money?
4. What is currency?
5. What is a money multiplier?
6. What is a reserve ratio?
7. Why does money issued by the central bank appear on the liability side of the central bank's balance sheet?
8. Loans made by a commercial bank would be recorded on which side of the commercial bank's balance sheet?
9. If a central bank issues money to a commercial bank, what does it usually take in return?
10. If a central bank issues $100 worth of new money, and takes in $100 worth of government securities in return, what will happen to the central bank's balance sheet?
11. If a central bank issues $100 of new money to a commercial bank, and the reserve requirement on banks is 10 percent, what is the maximum change in the amount of money in the system after the completion of the money creation process?
12. In Question 11, if the reserve requirement is reduced to 8 percent, what is likely to happen to the amount of money in the system?
13. What could happen if there is too little money in the system? How could the central bank help solve this problem?
14. What would happen if there is too much money in the system? How could the central bank help solve this problem?
15. Why might a central bank not use reserve requirements as a tool of monetary policy?
16. What do we mean by *policy interest rate*?
17. How can open market operations be used in conjunction with the policy interest rate in the conduct of monetary policy?
18. What could be key objectives of the central bank in payment systems oversight?
19. How did the payment system provision function historically come about for central banks?
20. Why might a central bank still need to provide payment systems infrastructure for the banking system?
21. Explain different types of actions that a central bank might perform when implementing the lender-of-last-resort function.
22. What are the goals of bank licensing?

23. What are the key differences between a liquidity problem and a solvency problem?
24. What are key differences between capital requirements and reserve requirements?
25. How are on-site examination and off-site monitoring complementary?
26. In a banking examination, the CAMELS system or one of its variants is often used. What are the key features of the CAMELS system?
27. Under the CAMELS system, which indicator indicates that a commercial bank is profitable?
28. To ensure compliance of commercial banks to banking laws and regulations, what kinds of measures can a supervisory central bank use?

CHAPTER 4

A Brief Review of Modern Central Banking Mandates

What Are the Goals That Modern Central Banks Try to Achieve?

Learning Objectives

1. Identify and distinguish different mandates of modern central banks.
2. Describe the monetary stability mandate.
3. Describe the financial stability mandate.
4. Describe the full employment mandate.
5. Explain the interlinkages among monetary, financial stability, and employment mandates in the short and long run.

In Chapter 3 we reviewed the five key functions of the modern central bank: money creation, the conduct of monetary policy, payment systems oversight and provision, lender of last resort, and banking supervision. We examined how these functions fit into two key roles of modern central banks, that is, the safeguarding of monetary stability and the safeguarding of financial stability.

In Chapter 4 we will look at the key roles, or mandates, of modern central banks in more detail. First, we will look at monetary stability and financial stability, the two key mandates common to many modern central banks. Then, we will also look at the full employment mandate of the U.S. central bank, which has regained much attention after the recent global crisis.

4.1 AN OVERVIEW OF MODERN CENTRAL BANKING MANDATES

Before going into detail on each of the mandates, however, there are two things to note about them. First, central banks' roles or mandates do evolve following changes in the economic, political, and ideological environment. Since these roles evolve over time, not every central bank, even those in the advanced economies, are on the same page with regard to each these roles, not the least in terms of explicit legal mandates.

The Evolving Nature of Mandates

As discussed in Chapter 1, central banks' roles in the economy evolved over time. Although many of the earliest central banks started with a coin sorting and storing function, or with war financing, in modern times such functions no longer belong to a central bank. After the breakdown of the Bretton Woods system, the conduct of monetary policy, a relatively new function, took center stage.

Only after the long accumulation of knowledge and hard experience—including the Great Depression, hyperinflation episodes, and the Great Inflation—have central bankers and economists come to believe that *monetary stability* (as defined by low and stable inflation and confidence in the currency) should be the goal of monetary policy, since it is believed to be a necessary ingredient for *full employment* in the long run.

Meanwhile, functions such as lender of last resort, payment systems oversight, and (in many cases) bank supervision, also put the central banks at the forefront in preventing and dealing with a crisis. Even before the wake of the recent 2007–2010 global financial crisis, many countries had already put greater focus on the concept of *financial stability*.

Monetary Stability and Price Stability   A better understanding of how a central bank can use monetary policy to contribute to long-term sustainable economic growth has led many countries over the past four decades to include *monetary stability* or *price stability* as mandates for their central banks. In this book, the terms monetary stability and price stability are used interchangeably. It is worth noting that the Bank of England has monetary stability (defined as "stable prices and confidence in the currency") as one of its core purposes (stable prices are defined by its inflation target).[1] The U.S. Federal Reserve Act has also set stable prices as an objective for the Federal Reserve to achieve since the late 1970s, with the term *stable prices* often being expressed as the *price stability objective*.[2] The European Central Bank (ECB) and the Bank of Japan also have price stability as one of their objectives.[3]

Financial Stability   Meanwhile, since most central banks do have traditional functions such as payment system oversight and lender of last resort, which are broadly aimed to help safeguard stability of the financial system, it could be said that central banks also have an inherent *financial stability* mandate. This inherent financial stability mandate often holds even if the definition of financial stability varies among central banks, or if the central bank lacks a bank supervisory function, or even if financial stability is not explicitly stated as a legislative mandate.

For example, while it is often recognized that the Federal Reserve has had an explicit dual mandate of price stability and full employment since the 1970s, it is also often argued that the Federal Reserve has always had an inherent financial stability mandate as well.[4] The Federal Reserve's financial stability mandate is further evidenced by its actions as a lender of last resort during the global financial crisis of 2007–2010.[5]

Maximum or Full Employment   In the wake of the recent global financial crisis, however, it is worth noting that the full employment mandate, particularly that of the Federal Reserve, has again come into the spotlight. Although the Federal Reserve

TABLE 4.1   Key Central Bank Mandates

Monetary Stability	Financial Stability	Full Employment
▪ Refers to stability of the value of the currency, whether in terms of domestic or overseas purchasing power. ▪ Thus encompasses price stability, and can be used interchangeably in certain contexts.	▪ Still no universally agreed-upon definition, but often refers to smooth functioning of the financial system and robustness against shocks. ▪ Thus encompasses many of the traditional central banking functions, such as payment system oversight, lender of last resort, and banking supervision.	▪ Quite uniquely, the Federal Reserve has "price stability and full employment" as its mandate. ▪ Until recently, the Federal Reserve has underplayed the full employment mandate, preferring to suggest that full employment can be achieved through price stability.

has been given a legal dual mandate of price stability and full employment since the late 1970s, it seems to have been quite reluctant to mention full employment as a separate mandate, preferring to state that maximum employment could be achieved through the achievement of price stability.[6] With the global financial crisis pushing unemployment up to record highs while inflation remained low, however, the Federal Reserve noted again in 2008 that its goals were "maximum employment and price stability."[7] (See Table 4.1.)

The Intertwining Nature of Mandates

The second thing to note about central banking mandates before we discuss them in more detail is that the three key mandates (monetary stability, financial stability, and full employment) listed above are intertwined by nature. There could be conflicts or complementarity among the mandates, depending on *time horizon* and *context*.

Short-Run Tradeoffs, Long-Run Synergy   With respect to time horizon, in the *short run* the monetary stability mandate might be in conflict with the full employment mandate. Sometimes, to maintain monetary or price stability, the central bank might need to tighten money conditions, possibly by raising the policy interest rate, which could temporarily slow down economic growth and have negative impacts on employment. In the *long run*, however, the conflict between monetary stability and full employment might not exist. If anything, to the extent that monetary stability helps economic agents plan their investment and consumption decisions more optimally, there might be synergy between the monetary stability and full employment mandates. Monetary stability could help bring about full employment in the long run.

Over the long run a violation of one of the mandates can also upset the ability of the central bank to achieve the other two mandates.[8] For example, if the central bank's financial stability mandate is compromised, a resultant financial crisis, if severe enough, could drag the economy into a deflationary spiral in which prices of goods and services keep falling, resulting in monetary instability. In such a case, a severe unemployment problem could result.

In practice, mindful of the intertwining nature of mandates, modern central banks often need to balance their actions in achieving each of them. In general, for monetary policy actions the overriding mandate being served is often price stability, for reasons that will be discussed in more detail in later chapters. In recent years, central banks have also become more mindful of the fact that monetary policy decisions might need to take account of longer-term financial stability issues.

Lessons from the recent global financial crisis suggest that if the central bank keeps interest rates low for too long because it believes that price stability, as signified by low and stable *consumer price* inflation, has been achieved, then low interest rates might encourage economic agents to engage in speculative activities.[9] Large asset price bubbles could build up, and once they burst could threaten financial stability, as well as longer-term monetary stability and, for that matter, economic growth and employment.

A Note on the Full Employment Mandate

The full employment mandate of the Federal Reserve can be considered quite controversial. Upon reviewing statements by Federal Open Market Committee (FOMC)—the committee that determines the monetary policy of the Federal Reserve—Daniel Thornton of the Federal Reserve Bank of St. Louis suggested that before the global financial crisis, even the FOMC had been very reluctant to state that maximum employment was a part of its dual mandate (the second part of the mandate being price stability).[10]

According to Thornton, research may suggest that although it is widely agreed that monetary policy can directly affect economic growth the direct relationship between monetary policy and unemployment is elusive.[11] Also, there is a hypothesis that the central bank might not be able to push unemployment down beyond a certain point without triggering inflation.* That theory was partly confirmed by the stagflation experience in the late 1970s and early 1980s, which suggested that by focusing on achieving maximum employment in the short run, the central bank can fail to satisfy both the monetary stability and full employment mandates in the longer run. Furthermore, the equilibrium unemployment rate can also shift over time, making it difficult to specify what full employment might look like.[12]

Among central banks of major advanced economies, only the Federal Reserve has emphasized full employment as its legal mandate. The Federal Reserve's full employment mandate dates back to a time when many mainstream economists still believed in the power of public institutions to actively manage macroeconomic policies and stagflation had not occurred. In the wake of the stagflation experience and more recent theoretical developments, mainstream economists and central banks have argued for central banks to focus their monetary actions on the maintenance of monetary stability rather than full employment. With monetary stability maintained, it's believed that the private sector can allocate resources more efficiently, which would result in economic and employment growth.

In the wake of the subprime crisis in 2007–2010, however, the full employment mandate regained much attention, since the severity of the crisis was so grave that

---

*This is the natural rate of employment hypothesis, which is discussed in the Chapter 6.

the U.S. economy was on the verge of falling into another Great Depression, and unemployment reached record highs. With expectations that inflation would remain low after the nadir of the crisis had passed and financial stability had been restored, the Federal Reserve cited the full employment mandate when embarking on novel measures of monetary policy, such as massive liquidity injections.[13]

Still, regardless of whether they have a full employment mandate, in practice central banks often do have to take the employment situation into consideration when carrying out policy actions, since central bank monetary policy actions normally have an impact on employment and thus the general welfare of the public.

4.2 MONETARY STABILITY

The term monetary stability describes a situation in which the value of money does not fluctuate too much, that is, money doesn't lose or gain in value too quickly. If money loses or gains in value too quickly, households and firms are unable to make optimal consumption and investment decisions. When money loses its purchasing power, we need more money just to buy the same amount of goods and services: in other words, the price of goods and services is rising. A situation in which there is a general rise in prices of goods and services is called inflation.

In contrast, when money gains in purchasing power, it means we need less money to buy the same amount of goods and services. Prices of goods and services, we could say, are falling. The general fall in prices of goods and services is called deflation. At first glance, we as consumers might seem to benefit from such a situation, since we can buy more goods and services with less money. In the longer run, if the situation persists, however, we as employees or owners or firms that sell goods and services would also lose. With falling prices, firms would make less profit, have less money to pay employees and suppliers, and have less money to repay their debts. Economic activity could slow down, affecting our income and employment.

Whether money would gain or lose in value depends, at least partly, on the central bank's actions. At the simplest level, if the central bank, the creator and regulator of money, decides to loosen monetary conditions, making money more immediately available, then money would lose its value relative to other goods and services. Goods and services will become more expensive. In other words, prices of goods and services will rise. In contrast, when the central bank tightens monetary conditions, making money scarcer, then money gains in value relative to other goods and services. Goods and services will become cheaper, and their prices will fall. If money gains or loses value very quickly, there would be consequences on the economy, since people might be unable to adjust their behavior in a timely manner. Consumption and investment behavior could be severely distorted.

Monetary Stability versus Price Stability

The term monetary stability is very closely related to price stability. Price stability, however, implicitly refers to stability in domestic purchasing power of the currency, and thus has a narrower meaning, since the value of money can also be measured in terms of overseas purchasing power via exchange rates. Monetary stability, which refers to the stability of the value of money in general, is a broader term. As mentioned earlier, the Bank of England has *monetary stability*—defined as "stable prices and confidence in the currency"—as one of its core purposes, where stable prices are defined by its inflation target.[14] Theoretically, however, both price instability and monetary instability have the same root cause, and thus sometimes the terms are used interchangeably. In the long run, if the central bank introduces too much money into the economy, money would lose value, whether in terms of domestic or overseas purchasing power. A persistent rise in inflation (the loss of domestic purchasing power) and a weakening of the exchange rate (the loss of overseas purchasing power) often come hand in hand when too much money is introduced.

In practice, the choice of whether to use the term monetary stability or price stability depends on the surrounding context and what the central bank wants to communicate to the public. In the past two decades it has become more recognized that domestic inflation and the exchange rate are two distinct operational objectives of the central bank. For a central bank that wants to emphasize that it focuses its monetary policy actions purely on stability of domestic purchasing power of the currency without much regard for the exchange rate, the use of the term price stability might be appropriate. For a central bank that wants to emphasize the fact it also cares about the stability of the exchange rate, the use of the term monetary stability might be more apt. As will be discussed later in more detail, the choice of a monetary policy regime will also have an impact on the choice of an exchange rate regime.

Here, as noted earlier, the terms monetary stability and price stability are used interchangeably to denote a situation of low and stable inflation. A more detailed discussion of the exchange rate in the context of monetary stability takes place in Part II of this book.

Why It Is Important

Monetary stability helps enable economic agents to make their investment and consumption decisions more optimally. With inflation low and stable (and with the exchange rate not overly volatile, for that matter), firms and households are able to make plans for future investment and consumption more efficiently. The ability to make efficient future plans is quite critical for long-term economic growth. With low and stable inflation, firms and households don't have to worry that the purchasing power of their investment returns will be eaten up by hyperinflation and can make better economic decisions.

As mentioned in the previous chapter, if the central bank prints more money or loosens monetary conditions, individuals and firms will be more willing and able to pursue their consumption and investment needs. Economic activity will be stimulated. Why shouldn't the central bank set the goal of having loose monetary conditions so that the economy would be stimulated all the time, and both consumption and investment grow indefinitely? There are at least two related answers to this question. First, whether the economy can grow sustainably in the long run depends on factors other than monetary conditions. These factors, such as natural and human resources, innovation, and productivity are largely outside the central bank's purview. Second, things could really get out of hand if the central bank had such a goal as its mandate. The central bank could be overzealous in loosening monetary conditions, since it is its mandate, after all. If too much money is introduced into the system, or monetary conditions are too loose, then two bad things could happen. First is inflation. With more money readily available, people would just keep bidding up prices of goods and services, which are themselves limited by scarcity of resources. Second, as money becomes more readily and cheaply available, it could get drawn into speculative activities, as it often does under those conditions.

In contrast, if the central bank tightens money conditions, then economic activity would likely to get slower, since money would not be as readily and cheaply available. Households and firms will be less stimulated to borrow and spend, whether on consumption or investment. If money conditions get too tight, money becomes very scarce and people will be much less willing to spend it. Firms might lay off workers since there is not much prospect of selling goods and services, which means household income would be reduced, and thus result in a further reduction in demand for goods and services. In such a case, economic activity could be reduced, and the economy would contract.

From the arguments above, it is thus quite clear by logic that (1) too tight or too loose money conditions are not good for the economy, and (2) the central bank should aim to set money conditions that are just right for the economy. In practice, however, what we mean by *right* money conditions could be quite a challenge to pinpoint. Various tumultuous historical experiences have been studied and analyzed by central bankers, academia, and other commentators, and it has been determined that the right money conditions can be reflected best by stability in the prices of goods and services. The general price of goods and services should not rise or fall too quickly. In other words, the value of money should be kept relatively stable. How the central bank can keep the value of money stable, and what *stable* really means, will be discussed in detail in the Chapter 5.

4.3 FINANCIAL STABILITY

Financial stability is a relatively new concept in central banking, which began to come into focus in the 1980s; given its multifaceted nature, its definition and measures still vary.[15] At the simplest level, financial stability could be thought of as an environment in which the financial sector can perform its intermediary function smoothly and without disruption.[16,*] Disruptions, meanwhile, can come from various sources, including the failure of financial institutions to meet their obligations owing to weak financial conditions, as well as failures in the payment and settlement system.

Looking deeper into the causes of disruptions, we can say that disruptions (and thus financial *instability*) often arise with (1) severe liquidity shortages among key

---

*The financial sector is often defined as referring to banks, other financial institutions (brokerage firms and insurance companies, for example), and financial markets (the money market, the foreign exchange market, the bond market, and the equity market, for example).

players in the financial system, or (2) widespread overindebtedness and a resulting inability of economic agents to repay their debt obligations, or both.[17]

Liquidity Shortages

Severe liquidity shortages among key players in the financial system suggest that these players might fail to meet their short-term financial obligations. When news emerges that a financial institution is facing a severe liquidity shortage and might have trouble meeting its short-term financial obligations, often other financial institutions will refuse to continue to lend to that financial institution, which will make it even more certain that the particular financial institution will fail to meet its short-term obligations. Depositors of that financial institution are also likely to withdraw their deposits. The failure of the financial institution in question to meet its short-term obligations can cause it to fail.

In a highly connected world, however, the failure of one particular institution can also cause ripple effects that could bring the whole system down. If one financial institution fails to meet its short-term obligations to other financial institutions, those other financial institutions would also face losses, and possibly a liquidity shortage. And if a liquidity shortage occurs across the system, those other financial institutions might be unable to meet their own obligations. Meanwhile, depositors might be queuing up to demand their deposits back from these other financial institutions at the same time, compounding the problem further.

Overindebtedness of Economic Agents

Digging deeper, we might trace liquidity shortages, and instability in the financial system overall, to asset price bubbles and overindebtedness of agents in the economy (e.g., households, firms, and the government).[18] When households or firms take out loans from financial institutions to buy assets that are fast rising in price (e.g., housing, real estate, and stocks), the loans could look very safe as long as the prices of those assets are rising. Once the bubble bursts borrowers are saddled with assets that have a lower value than the loans that they took out to purchase them. With economic activity likely to fall after the burst of the bubble, borrowers would find it increasingly difficult to repay their loans.

With borrowers unable to repay their loans, lenders would also find themselves in trouble. As will be discussed in more detail in Chapter 12, with borrowers defaulting on their loans, financial institutions would have to write down the value of these bad loans, which would thereby reduce their capital. With reduced capital, financial institutions would be much more reluctant to extend new loans and might also call in some existing loans, especially short-term ones. As more and more financial institutions become reluctant to extend new loans and instead call in existing loans, liquidity shortages could arise, resulting in the disruption described above.

Furthermore, in cases in which depositors sense that a bank might not have enough capital to cushion the writing down of bad loans, there might be a run on that bank. And such a run could be quite widespread if the public perceives that the bad debt problem is not limited to a single institution. Runs on financial institutions are indeed considered a major disruption, not just to the financial sector, but also to the economy.

CASE STUDY: Dealing with Financial Stability *Ex Post* and *Ex Ante*

Even before the concept of financial stability rose into prominence in the 1980s, central banks always had a role in maintaining financial stability. This is reflected by central banks' bank supervisory and lender-of-last-resort functions. Before the global financial crisis of 2007–2010, however, the framework that central banks normally adopted to deal with financial stability put more focus on dealing with financial stability *ex post*—that is, cleaning up after bubbles that had already burst—rather than *ex ante*—that is, preventing bubbles and overindebtedness of economic agents in the first place.[19] Before the global financial crisis, one reason for central banks' hesitance to preempt the buildup of overindebtedness was the fact that it was very difficult to identify the threshold beyond which overindebtedness violated economic fundamentals ex ante. The same applied to asset price increases.[20]

After the global financial crisis of 2007–2010, however, it was increasingly recognized that in order to sustain financial stability central banks might need to step in *ex ante* and preempt overindebtedness and asset price bubbles from turning into disruptions that cause financial instability.[21]

Why It Is Important

Financial stability is important for at least three reasons. First, financial stability is needed to ensure efficient allocation of funds within the economy. A smooth functioning of the financial system is needed in order to channel excess funds from savers to borrowers efficiently. Second, in the long run, financial stability is inextricably intertwined with monetary stability. An economy facing financial instability can slip into a deflationary spiral, as happened during the Great Depression in the 1930s and has been true of the Japanese experience from the 1990s through the first decade of the twenty-first century. Third, traditional central banking functions such as payment systems oversight and supervision, lender of last resort, and banking supervision already have financial stability aspects embedded in them.

The attention on the financial stability mandate began to take hold in the 1980s as frequent financial crises in both advanced and emerging market economies brought large economic costs.[22] Since then, two episodes of financial instability in major advanced economies have reaffirmed the need for central banks to seriously focus on their financial stability mandate: (1) the bursting of the Japanese real estate and stock bubbles in the early 1990s that tipped Japan's economy into deflation for more than two decades, and (2) the global financial crisis of 2007–2010.

In the case of Japan, when massive real estate and stock market bubbles burst in the early 1990s, banks took a large hit and the country later fell into a period of long and painful deflation, during which prices of goods and services fell for many consecutive years.[23] Postmortem analyses suggested that the central bank of Japan had allowed money conditions to be too loose, allowing massive bubbles to arise.[24] At the time, however, the Bank of Japan was willing to run a loose monetary policy because inflation appeared to be low enough.[25] As events turned out, financial instability later turned into monetary instability and Japan fell into what became known as the Japanese lost decades, during which the economy struggled unsuccessfully to climb out of a deflationary spiral for over 20 years.

If anything, the global financial crisis of 2007–2010 also confirmed that letting asset price bubbles to grow unchecked (in this case housing price bubbles in the United States and in Europe) can result in financial instability that can be very costly to society.[26] With the Japanese experience and the global financial crisis of 2007–2010 fresh in mind, central banks are starting to take a more proactive role in the maintenance of financial stability. As bank regulators and supervisors, central banks now monitor risk exposures of banks from a more forward-looking perspective, and focus more on the interlinkages among banks as well as other institutions and players.[27]

4.4 FULL EMPLOYMENT

Unlike monetary stability or financial stability, full employment is not a popular mandate for central banks, at least for advanced economy central banks. Yet it is a mandate for the most powerful central bank in the world, the Federal Reserve, so it is worth examining in a little bit of detail. The Federal Reserve's full employment mandate, like that of other central banks, has been evolving through time.[28]

The current mandate of the Federal Reserve, which dates from 1977 when the Congress amended the Federal Reserve Act, states that the Federal Reserve "shall maintain long run growth of the monetary and credit aggregates commensurate with the economy's long run potential to increase production, so as to promote effectively the goals of maximum employment, stable prices, and moderate long-term interest rates."[29] Since in periods of high inflation nominal interest rates often became high, we could infer that both the terms *stable prices* and *moderate long-term interest rates* reflect a focus on price or monetary stability. *Maximum employment*, then, would be another mandate of the Federal Reserve. Note that maximum employment as a monetary policy mandate has been considered quite controversial.[30] On one side, many argue that tasking the central bank with a maximum employment mandate will bias central bankers toward providing easy money conditions. Easy money conditions, however, as argued above, might not necessarily provide the maximum employment hoped for in the long run. In the long run, production and employment growth depends on the capacity of the economy to generate economic activity. That capacity depends, many argue, on things such as technology, research and development, and the rule of law—things that are largely outside the direct influence of money conditions.[31]

If the central bank is too intent on easing money conditions in the hope of achieving maximum employment, however, inflation is likely to prevail but maximum employment likely not to be attained. Lessons from the Great Inflation in the 1970s (discussed in Chapter 2) showed that without a brake, once inflation rises it can spiral out of control, which creates uncertainty in the economy. Household consumption and saving decisions will also be distorted since households will be unable to discern accurately what the price of goods and services will be in the future. Firms will be unable to make proper investment decisions, since they might not be able to estimate profits correctly. If anything, the argument goes, if the central bank is biased toward easy money conditions, in the long run the maximum employment mandate will be self-defeating.

In practice, economists and central bankers often use the term *full employment* rather than *maximum employment* when referring to this particular mandate. The full employment concept corresponds to the fact the authorities can never (and should never) aim for zero unemployment. For a start, at any given time there is bound to be *transitory unemployment*, as fresh graduates start to look for jobs or women start to get back into the job market as their children grow up. In practice, full employment can be expressed as the unemployment rate that corresponds to the economy's natural rate of unemployment, or nonaccelerating inflation rate of unemployment (NAIRU), which will be discussed in more detail in the Chapter 5.

Why It Is Important

The other side of the preceding argument is that without the employment mandate, the central bank will aim only for stable prices and sacrifice other important economic objectives. Absent acknowledgement of the employment aspect of the dual mandate, many argue, the Federal Reserve might overlook the importance of economic stability and employment, which at times might not correspond to low inflation.[32]

In the wake of the global financial crisis of 2007–2010, the importance of the Federal Reserve's employment mandate also became clearer. In December 2008, after previous hesitance until that time, the Federal Reserve explicitly communicated its maximum employment mandate to the public in its statement of monetary policy.[33] Given the severity of the crisis, it was understandable that the Federal Reserve wanted to make sure that the public understood that it would not sit on its hands just because inflation had been very low.

If anything, by emphasizing the maximum employment mandate after the crisis hit, the Federal Reserve seemed to want to communicate to the public that it was committed to prevent the economy from falling into a deflationary trap. The Federal Reserve was, indeed, willing to stimulate and stabilize the economy in the face of the crisis. That commitment was later evidenced by first introducing quantitative easing measures, which were introduced while inflation remained very low and unemployment approached 10 percent (a post–World War II high). Those measures were followed by a subsequent series of quantitative measures in the next few years as unemployment remained high.

By December 2012 the full employment mandate had become an explicit part of U.S. monetary policy along with price stability, with the Federal Reserve adopting the unemployment rate as one the key *forward guidance* indicators of its monetary policy.[34] Specifically, the Federal Reserve announced in December 2012 that it would keep the federal funds rate between 0 and 0.25 percent as long as (1) the unemployment rate remained above 6.5 percent, (2) inflation between one and two years ahead was projected to be no more than 0.5 percentage points above the 2 percent longer run goal, and (3) longer-term inflation expectations continued to be well anchored.[35]

4.5 BALANCING AMONG THE THREE MANDATES

In practice, modern central banks do not focus on just a single mandate. Rather, they try to achieve all three mandates even without explicitly saying so. For example, while the Federal Reserve is officially tasked with a dual mandate of price stability and full employment, it also plays a key role in sustaining financial stability, as demonstrated by the recent crisis. While other central banks might not have an explicit full employment mandate, it has often been argued that the pursuit of monetary stability will allow economic agents to behave optimally, which is essential for full employment in the long run.

Stylizing the Central Bank's Monetary Policy Actions: The Taylor Rule

While central banks often do not explicitly say exactly how they attempt to balance price stability and employment objectives when making monetary policy, studies along the line of one from Stanford University's John B. Taylor in 1993 suggested that they do, whether intentionally or not. By statistically estimating what the level of the Federal Reserve's policy interest rate should be were the Fed to give equal weight to having both (1) inflation close to the target that reflected long-run price stability and (2) output of the economy that is consistent with full employment, Taylor found that, at least during the period of the study, the estimated policy interest rate was reasonably close to the actual policy interest rate.[36]

In other words, Taylor's study suggests that we can reasonably approximate the Federal Reserve's policy interest rate decision by assuming that the Federal Reserve wants to achieve *both* actual inflation rate that is consistent with long-term price stability and actual output growth rate that is consistent with the economy's potential (and thus full employment).

On the one hand, if actual inflation rate is higher than the rate that the Federal Reserve deems to represent long-term price stability, then the Federal Reserve is likely to raise the policy interest rate to slow down inflation. On the other hand, if the actual output growth of the economy, as represented by actual GDP growth rate, is higher than the rate of output growth that the Federal Reserve deems consistent with the potential of the economy (and thus full employment), then the Federal Reserve is also likely to raise the policy interest rate.

On the occasion where inflation and output growth move in opposite directions, Taylor's study implies that the Federal Reserve would try to balance between the price stability and output (or employment) objectives. An example of such a situation is when an oil shock pushes inflation beyond the rate that the Federal Reserve deems consistent with long-term price stability, but pushes economic activity down such that output growth is below potential (and thus employment falls below full employment). Here, the Federal Reserve is likely to take both price stability and output (and, implicitly, employment) objectives into consideration when making monetary policy decisions.

Taylor's results suggested that the Federal Reserve did indeed take both price stability and employment objectives into consideration when making monetary policy. Later studies along this line also found that the so-called *Taylor rule*, which states that central banks are supposed to care for both price stability and employment, could explain monetary policy decisions of many other central banks, whether those central banks had an explicit employment mandate or not.[37] Specifics of the Taylor rule are discussed in Chapter 6.

Pursuit of the Different Mandates

In practice, regardless of whether they are official mandates, central banks normally take monetary stability, financial stability, and employment objectives into considerations when making and coordinating their policies. The way that central banks pursue these different mandates, however, differs from one central bank to another, depending on their context. For example, central banks that do not have a bank supervisory function would perform their financial stability role differently than those central banks that do have a bank supervisory role. Despite the differences, however, there seems to be an underlying trend with respect to how central banks pursue the different mandates, a trend that has evolved with the arrival of the global financial crisis in 2007–2010.[38]

Prior to the Global Financial Crisis Even before global financial crisis, it was not uncommon for a central bank to have one arm pursuing monetary stability (which is supposed also to result in full employment over the long run, if monetary stability is achieved),[39] and another arm pursuing financial stability (although how work related to achieving financial stability is defined could vary noticeably among different central banks).[40] The arm dealing with monetary stability was responsible for the conduct of monetary policy, that is, regulating money conditions in the economy. The arm dealing with financial stability, meanwhile, dealt with the regulation of banks, and also the supervision of banks if the central bank was a bank supervisor, as well as payment systems.[41]

These two arms of a central bank would normally use different sets of tools to achieve their goals. Although some of the tools can be used for multiple purposes, prior to the global financial crisis there was normally a distinction between tools used to fulfill the monetary stability mandate and the financial stability mandate.

The arm that dealt with monetary stability tried to influence money conditions through tools such as interest rates, operations in financial markets, exchange rates, and reserve requirements. The use of these tools of monetary policy affect money conditions in general, and thus potentially everyone, through changes in the value of money. Although monetary policy tools can also be used for financial stability purposes ex ante (e.g., tightening money conditions to prevent the private sector from overborrowing), central banks often were reluctant to do so.[42]

The arm that dealt with financial stability, on the other hand, normally had rules and regulations that they could set for banks as its set of policy tools, assuming the central bank was a bank supervisor. These rules and regulations set for banks were more *bottom-up* in nature, meaning the focus was on the safety and soundness of individual banks, with less focus on how the banking system as a whole might be affected by developments in the macroeconomy.[43]

For central banks that were not bank supervisors, while the financial stability arm might not have direct access to rules and regulations as policy tools, there was the option of focusing more on monitoring conditions in the financial sector and coordinating with relevant financial sector regulators as well as with the monetary stability arm and providing input to the monetary stability arm. Examples of this model include the Reserve Bank of Australia and, prior to the global financial crisis, the Bank of England.

After the Global Financial Crisis In the wake of the global financial crisis, there seems to be a rethinking of how central banks pursue their different mandates in terms of coordination across the two arms, the use of policy tools for different purposes, as well as communication with the public.

Specifically, there is increasing agreement that (1) the use of monetary policy should also take financial stability into account;[44] (2) there needs to be a set of *macroprudential* tools to help address financial stability using a more top-down approach, in addition to the microprudential tools that were the primary tools before the global financial crisis;[45] and (3) the communication on the Federal Reserve's employment mandate might be warranted.[46]

The Use of Monetary Policy to Achieve Monetary and Financial Stability With respect to the global financial crisis of 2007–2010, a lesson learned is that monetary instability in one period can lead to financial instability in the next, if the central bank becomes too complacent. Although inflation may appear low, if money conditions are too loose, then firms and households may overborrow, which can lead to asset price bubbles and financial instability.[47] And if financial instability is serious enough (possibly because money conditions have been too loose for too long), then the risk of deflation (i.e., monetary *instability*) will rise as the bubbles burst.[48] Accordingly, it can be argued that financial stability and monetary stability are ultimately linked over the long run and that central banks might need to take a longer run view in their conduct of monetary policy. Central banks need to ensure that even when inflation is low, money conditions are not so loose that financial instability later arises and comes back to affect monetary stability afterward.[49]

The Use of Macroprudential Tools to Help Achieve Financial Stability Prior to the global financial crisis, central banks had just begun to shift the focus of their bank supervisory function from the so-called *microprudential* framework toward a more *top-down* macroprudential framework.[50] In the macroprudential framework, instead of focusing on the regulatory compliance of individual banks the focus is on taming the buildup of risk in the system, whereby interlinkages among financial institutions, markets, and borrowers are taken into account. The set of tools that can be used to tame the risks of overborrowing in particular markets, such as housing or real estate, are called macroprudential tools.[51]

The specifics of macroprudential tools will be discussed in more detail in Part III of this book. At this stage, however, suffice it to say that macroprudential tools can supplement, or at times, substitute for monetary policy tools in the pursuit of financial stability. Monetary policy tools, such as interest rate levels, reserve requirements, and exchange rates, are broad based in the sense that their use could potentially affect everyone in the economy directly. With a tightening of monetary policy, for example, costs of funds are likely to rise for all individuals and firms. If overborrowing and risk buildups are occurring in only a specific market within the economy, say housing, the central bank might be hesitant to tighten overall money conditions using monetary policy, since everyone else outside the housing market might also be affected. As such the central bank might use macroprudential tools on banks under its supervision to specifically squeeze lending in the housing market.

The Communication of the Employment Mandate While full employment is still quite controversial as an explicit mandate for most central banks, unemployment has always been a factor that modern central banks at least implicitly consider when pursuing their monetary stability mandate. Unemployment can be affected by money conditions, at least indirectly in the short run, through economic growth.[52] (See the discussion on the relationship between economic growth and employment in "Case Study: The Relationship between Unemployment and Output: Okun's Law and the Output Gap" in Chapter 5.) Consequently, central banks whose monetary policy decisions could be approximated by the Taylor rule are also in effect taking employment into account in their monetary policy decisions.[53]

With respect to communication, however, it is still quite a delicate matter for central banks to acknowledge full employment as an explicit mandate, since it could create confusion among the public. In the short run, it might appear that the central bank has the ability to choose between higher inflation and higher unemployment in its use of monetary policy. Easy monetary conditions are likely to encourage more economic activity, lower unemployment, and higher prices in the short run. In the long run, however, historical experience and theoretical developments would suggest that there is actually no tradeoff between inflation and unemployment. The central bank that actively pursues lower unemployment over time might end up with both higher inflation and higher unemployment. (The theoretical foundations of monetary policy will be discussed in Chapter 5.)

Given the nuances inherent in the relationship between monetary policy and unemployment, even the Federal Reserve, which has had an employment mandate since 1977, chose to avoid explicitly communicating its mandate to consider employment in its monetary policy decisions until December 2008, after the full extent of the global financial crisis had been felt and the country was threatened with a deflationary situation.[54] In this particular case, the explicit communication of the full employment mandate and the use of the unemployment number in its forward guidance at least helped reassure the public that the Federal Reserve intended to use an exceptionally easy monetary policy only temporarily until unemployment came down to a more normal level.

SUMMARY

Key mandates for modern central banks include monetary stability, financial stability, and full employment. While most central banks have monetary stability and financial stability mandates, the Federal Reserve is rather unique in having full employment also as another explicit mandate.

These three key mandates are intertwined and might conflict as well as have synergy, depending on the time horizon and context. In the short run, monetary stability might appear to be in conflict with full employment, but in the long run monetary stability might be the foundation for full employment. Also, in the long run, monetary stability cannot exist without financial stability.

Monetary stability often refers to low and stable inflation and can be used interchangeably with price stability, although monetary stability might also suggest "confidence in the currency," as stated in the Bank of England's mandate. Monetary stability is important, since it allows for optimal investment and consumption decisions by economic agents.

Financial stability refers to conditions in which the financial system can perform its function of allocating funds within the economy efficiently and smoothly. For central banks, financial stability is important since (1) it is essential for effective allocation of funds; (2) it is intertwined with monetary stability; and (3) it is embedded into many of the traditional central banking functions such as payment systems oversight and provision, lender of last resort, and banking supervision.

The explicit full employment mandate is rather unique to the Federal Reserve, which has the explicit dual mandate of price stability and full employment. Prior to the 2007–2010 crisis the Federal Reserve did not emphasize its full employment mandate, partly because it might have created public confusion, since in the short run there might be tradeoffs between inflation and unemployment. The emphasis on the full employment mandate since then, however, provided assurance that the Federal Reserve did not focus on price stability at the expense of other important economic goals.

Since the 2007–2010 crisis there has been a rethinking of how central banks might pursue the different mandates. First, it has been acknowledged that the conduct of monetary policy might need to take account of financial stability in addition to monetary stability. Second, macroprudential tools might be used to complement monetary policy in sustaining financial stability. Third, with respect to the Federal Reserve, communication on the full employment mandate might be warranted.

KEY TERMS

financial stability	microprudential
full employment	monetary stability
macroprudential	price stability
maximum employment	transitory unemployment

QUESTIONS

1. What does monetary stability mean? Is it different from price stability?
2. Why is monetary stability an important mandate for central banks?
3. How might we quantitatively measure monetary stability?
4. What could reflect the situation of financial instability?
5. Although there are many definitions of financial stability, describe key elements that are embedded in these definitions.
6. Why is financial stability an important mandate for central banks?
7. Why might a central bank be considered to have an inherent financial stability mandate, even though that central bank is not a bank supervisor?
8. What is the Federal Reserve's dual mandate?
9. How might we quantitatively represent the concept of full employment?
10. Why might have the Federal Reserve underemphasized the full employment mandate to the public until the global financial crisis of 2007–2010?
11. How might a single focus on fulfilling the monetary stability mandate result in financial instability in the long run?
12. Why, especially prior to the global financial crisis of 2007–2010, might a central bank hesitate to prevent the buildup of financial imbalances and asset price bubbles?
13. In the long run, is it possible to sustain monetary stability by neglecting the financial stability mandate? Why or why not?
14. How might the focus on achieving maximum employment result in monetary instability in the long run?
15. Why might we say that the Taylor rule was a good approximation of the Federal Reserve's dual mandate even in the 1980s and 1990s?
16. According to the Taylor rule, if the rate of economy's output growth is beyond the economy's potential output growth rate, while inflation is above target, what would the central bank likely do?
17. What is the forward guidance strategy of monetary policy that was used by the Federal Reserve in the recovery period after the global financial crisis of 2007–2010?
18. What are the key characteristics of a macroprudential framework?
19. Why might central banks be hesitant to tighten monetary conditions to help sustain financial stability?
20. How can macroprudential tools be used to help sustain financial stability?

TWO

Monetary Stability

Part II examines various aspects of monetary stability, the dominant central banking mandate for the past 30 years.

Chapter 5 reviews the theoretical foundations of monetary policy, the policy that a central bank uses in regulating monetary conditions in the economy in order to achieve monetary stability.

Chapter 6 looks at different monetary policy regimes (i.e., rules) that central banks might adopt in the pursuit of monetary stability.

Chapter 7 looks at monetary policy implementation, which is often done through operations in financial markets.

Chapter 8 looks at how monetary policy transmits across the economy and affects monetary stability as well as output and employment.

Chapter 9 is devoted to the exchange rate, another key variable that central banks have to watch, given that it is the price of money and that it can affect monetary stability as well as financial stability.

CHAPTER **5**

Theoretical Foundations of the Practice of Modern Monetary Policy

Learning Objectives

1. Describe theories that are foundational to the modern practice of monetary policy.
2. Define and graph the short-run Phillips curve.
3. Describe the natural rate of unemployment.
4. Describe output gap.
5. Distinguish between adaptive and rational expectations.
6. Explain why operational independence of a central bank is important.

This chapter briefly reviews five theoretical developments that guide the modern practice of central banks in their pursuit of the monetary stability mandate. Specifically, these five theoretical developments, when considered together, suggest that central banks should conduct monetary policy by following a credible rule that aims for a low and stable inflation environment. A credible rule for the central bank's conduct of monetary policy helps manage public expectations that the central bank will use monetary policy to achieve only what it does best, that is, ensure long-term price stability, as opposed to trying to push unemployment below the natural rate.

5.1 AN OVERVIEW OF THEORETICAL FOUNDATIONS

Five of the most influential theoretical developments that are foundational to the practice of monetary policy as we know it today are (1) the quantity theory of money, (2) the Phillips curve, (3) the natural rate of unemployment, (4) the rational expectations hypothesis, and (5) the time inconsistency problem. These five developments led to five propositions on the design and conduct of monetary policy. These five key theoretical developments and their propositions are described next.

1. **The Quantity Theory of Money:** In the long run, monetary policy can only influence *prices* of goods and services in the economy and cannot influence

77

quantity of output or *level* of economic activity directly. The effort by the central bank to stimulate the economy by printing money will only result in rising prices and inflation in the long run.

2. **The Phillips Curve:** There is a short-run inverse relationship between inflation and the unemployment rate. When the inflation rate goes up, the unemployment rate goes down, and vice versa. The central bank can attempt to use monetary policy to fine-tune the economy by influencing these two variables.

3. **The Natural Rate of Unemployment:** In the long run, the inverse relationship between inflation and unemployment disappears. There exists a rate of unemployment that corresponds to an economy's potential, that is, the natural rate of unemployment. If the central bank tries to push unemployment below that natural rate, then in the long run, after prices and inflation expectations have fully adjusted, not only inflation but also unemployment will rise.

4. **The Rational Expectations Hypothesis:** Public expectations matter in the effectiveness of economic policies. The public is rational enough to incorporate their expectations of policy outcomes into their current behavior. Accordingly, an expansionary monetary policy that leads to a rise in inflation expectations could lead to an upward spiral in wages and prices. For monetary policy to be effective in maintaining price stability, the central bank must manage the inflation expectations of the public.

5. **The Time Inconsistency Problem:** Letting the central bank use pure discretion in the conduct of monetary policy, as opposed to following an explicit rule, could be counterproductive. Policy makers, even with the best of intentions, have an incentive to backtrack on their policies if they believe they can improve the welfare of the public. The backtracking, however, will defeat the future credibility and effectiveness of policies, thereby reducing the welfare of the public instead. For a central bank, credibility is critical if monetary policy is to work effectively in keeping inflation low and stable.

These five theoretical developments and propositions together led to the current mainstream belief among academics and central bankers that the conduct of monetary policy should follow a credible rule that aims for a low and stable inflation environment. A credible rule for the conduct of monetary policy helps manage public expectations that the central bank will use monetary policy in the pursuit of monetary stability, rather than trying to push unemployment below the natural rate.

5.2 THE QUANTITY THEORY OF MONEY

The quantity theory of money describes the relationship between money, economic activity, and the general price level in the long run. Basically, what the theory suggests is that in the long run, the total output of an economy will depend on nonmonetary factors such as capital (factories, roads, infrastructure, etc.), labor input, and technology. The attempt to stimulate economic activity through money creation will be ineffective and only result in rising prices (inflation) in the long run.[1]

The quantity theory of money is represented by one of the most famous equations in macroeconomics, the *equation of exchange*, proposed by Irving Fisher in 1911.[2] The equation can be expressed as

$$M \times V = P \times Q$$

where M stands for the quantity of money in the economy, V is the velocity of circulation of the money, P is the general price level in the economy, and Q is the quantity of products sold in the economy. In effect, we can think of the right side of the equation ($P \times Q$) as the economy's nominal GDP, since P (the general price level in the economy) is being multiplied by Q (the quantity of products sold in the economy in a given period).

Taken together, the quantity theory equation states that the amount of money (M) would have to circulate V times to finance the nominal economy (or the total volume of transactions within the economy) in a given period.

Under the quantity theory, the velocity of the circulation of money (V) is assumed to depend on forces outside the equation, such as how advanced payments technology is. The quantity of products sold is also assumed to be dependent on forces outside the equation, namely, the quantity and quality of labor, capital, and technology. Accordingly, both V and Q are assumed to be constants and not determined by any other variables in the equation.[3]

Under this theory an increase in the amount of money (M) leads to an increase in the general price level (P) in the long run, since in the long run the amount of money *does not* determine the quantity and quality of labor, capital, or technology.[4] Ostensibly money can be printed relatively easily, and the increase in the paper amount of money will debase the value of money relative to that of other goods and services in the economy, which is called inflation. The increase and improvement in labor, capital (e.g., machines and computers), and technology cannot be directly induced, in the long run, by an increase in paper money, or, for that matter, the increase in money in bank accounts, or even the increase in precious metals held by the central bank, such as gold.

The Quantity Theory of Money and Hyperinflation

In reality, numerous occasions of hyperinflation throughout modern economic history have confirmed the hypothesis of the quantity theory of money. One of the most famous episodes of hyperinflation was that in post-World War I Germany. Unable to raise enough taxes or borrow to finance efforts to rebuild the economy and pay for war reparations, the German government resorted to printing money to pay for such endeavors.

As time passed, the flood of money did not raise output or economic activity, but instead quickly cheapened the value of German currency. Between 1919 and 1923, as money quickly lost value, prices of goods and services rose by multiples of billions, the German people were unwilling to hold money for more than a few hours, instead searching for something to purchase right away. The aggressive money printing caused much disruption in the German economy before the German government decided to undertake monetary reform, negotiate for a cut in war reparations, and aim for a balanced budget.[5]

The German hyperinflation experience is often cited as strong proof of the quantity theory of money. The quantity theory of money, backed by lessons learned from hyperinflation experiences worldwide, is one key theoretical foundation against excessively easy monetary policy and excessive money printing by central banks.[6]

5.3 THE PHILLIPS CURVE

While the quantity theory of money suggests that monetary policy *cannot* be used to directly influence economic activity and output in the *long run*, the Phillips curve suggests that monetary policy *could* be used to directly influence economic activity and output in the *short run*. By the 1950s, with greater availability of macroeconomic data, economists were starting to notice an inverse relationship between unemployment and inflation. When the inflation rate was found to be low, the unemployment rate was found to be high, and vice versa. This inverse relationship between inflation and unemployment is known as the Phillips curve, named for A. W. Phillips, an economist who in late 1958 first noticed the relationship in British economic data.[7] Figure 5.1 illustrates a stylized Phillips curve.

The presence of a Phillips curve suggests that the central bank can attempt to lower the *unemployment rate* by allowing *inflation* to go up. The central bank could, for example, ease money conditions to stimulate aggregate demand and economic activity. When money conditions become easier, households and firms can borrow more to consume or invest. With greater economic activity, firms are willing to hire more labor, and thus the unemployment rate will go down. Meanwhile, with greater demand for goods and services, prices and inflation will start to rise.

The Phillips curve also suggests that the central bank can also attempt to lower inflation by allowing the unemployment rate to go up. To accomplish this, the central bank might tighten money conditions, making money scarcer, which would slow down aggregate demand and economic activity. Households and firms would find it harder to borrow to consume or invest. With lower economic activity, firms would be less willing to hire more labor, and indeed, could shed existing workers, making the unemployment rate higher. Meanwhile, with lower demand for goods and services, prices and inflation would fall.

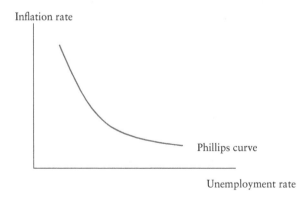

FIGURE 5.1   The Phillips Curve: Short-Run Trade-Off between Inflation and Unemployment

The Phillips Curve and Economic Fine-Tuning

Given the Phillips curve, there appears to be an opportunity for the central bank to use monetary policy to help *fine-tune* the economy. Whenever unemployment is too high and there is not much inflationary pressure, the central bank might choose to ride along the Phillips curve by easing its monetary policy stance, stimulating economic activity, and letting inflation pick up a bit. On the other hand, whenever inflation is too high and unemployment is not much of a problem, the central bank might choose to tighten its monetary policy stance, which will slow down economic activity and dampen inflationary pressures.[8]

As much as the quantity theory of money is a key theoretical reason for a central bank to resist the temptation to overprint money, the Phillips curve is a key reason for the central banks to use monetary policy to help fine-tune the economy. But why should monetary policy be able to influence economic activity and output in the short run (as suggested by the presence of a Phillips curve) but not the long run (as suggested by the quantity theory of money)? Economists only learned to reconcile the quantity theory of money and the Phillips curve in the late 1960s, with the introduction of the natural rate of unemployment concept.

5.4 THE NATURAL RATE OF UNEMPLOYMENT

By the mid-1960s, as more data became available, the inverse relationship between inflation and unemployment rate seemed to weaken. Examining inflation and unemployment data in more detail and taking into account the role of expectations, economists—notably, Edmund Phelps in 1967[9] and Milton Friedman in 1968[10]—proposed a concept that came to be known as the *natural rate of unemployment*. According to this theory, for any economy there is a rate of unemployment corresponding to the fundamentals of that economy in such a way that when unemployment is at that particular rate, the inflation rate will not change. That rate of unemployment at which inflation will not change became known as the natural rate of unemployment.

Nonaccelerating Inflation Rate of Unemployment (NAIRU)

At the natural rate of unemployment, the economy is supposed to be running at its full capacity, given the labor, capital, and technology it has. Any unemployment that exists at this natural rate of unemployment is likely to be *transitory* unemployment—for example, batches of fresh graduates and recently arrived migrants in the process of a job search, or women who are just recently returning to the job market after their children have grown up. The formal name of that natural unemployment rate (the unemployment rate for the economy at which inflation will not rise) is the nonaccelerating inflation rate of unemployment (NAIRU).

The concept of NAIRU became popular not only because it was theoretically neat (it described the state of an economy in equilibrium) but because the ability of governments and central banks to actively exploit the inverse relationship between inflation and unemployment as represented by the Phillips curve seemed to have been lost by the late 1970s. When oil shocks hit the global economy in the 1970s, governments and central banks tried to limit possible negative effects on the economy and unemployment by using stimulus policies. As time passed, however, not only did stimulus policies prove unable to bring the unemployment rate down, but inflation also rose uncontrollably.

NAIRU and the Vertical Long-Run Phillips Curve

As lessons from the 1970s became clearer, economists were able to piece together and synthesize the theories of the Phillips curve and NAIRU. The synthesized concept is that as prices and inflation expectations adjust in the long run, the short-run Phillips curve shifts up vertically, making the long-run Phillips curve vertical at the natural rate of unemployment.[11] (See Figure 5.2.)

In Figure 5.2, at point *a* on short-run Phillips curve 1, unemployment remains at the natural rate U^* as long as there are no shocks from either supply or demand. If the central bank chooses to stimulate the economy further, at first the economy might move from point *a* to point *b*, that is, the unemployment rate would fall below U^* while the inflation rate would pick up.

As inflation rate and wages start to pick up, firms and households would start to adjust their inflation expectations upward. The change in inflation expectations would build into consumption and investment decisions of firms and households, prompting core inflation to rise, and the short-run Phillips curve to shift upward. With the shift in inflation expectations, the inflation rate would rise, and the economy would now be at point *c* on the new short-run Phillips curve, Phillips curve 2. In the longer run, however, since the economy cannot run beyond its full potential unemployment would drift back to the natural rate U^*.

At point *d*, which is the new equilibrium point for the economy, notice that inflation is already above the inflation level of point *a*, the old equilibrium point. Had the central bank kept on stimulating the economy, in the longer run inflation expectations would keep rising, and the short-run Phillips curve would keep shifting upward. Inflation would keep on rising, while unemployment would not remain under the natural rate for long.

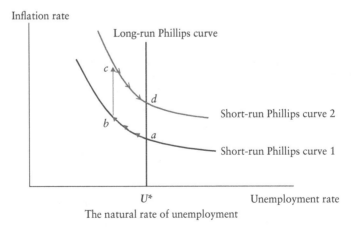

FIGURE 5.2 Long-Run Phillips Curve: There Is No Trade-Off between Inflation and Unemployment in the Long Run

CASE STUDY: How Can Unemployment Go Below the Natural Rate? The Role of Real Wages, Incomplete Information, and Expectations

From the discussion of the long-run vertical Phillips curve framework, an interesting key question arises: how can the economy actually run beyond its full capacity? At NAIRU, the economy is supposed to be already running at its full potential, and labor is already willing to work at maximum hours, given prevailing real wages. Plausible reasons why the economy might be running beyond its full potential include incomplete information, expectations, and real wages.[12]

First, let us assume that if the central bank decided to ease monetary policy further when the economy was running at its full potential, aggregate demand for goods and services would rise, and firms would need more labor input to increase their production. To get more labor firms would have to raise nominal wages. At first, labor would be willing to work longer hours than before. However, as aggregate demand for goods and services in the economy rose (as a result of the easier monetary policy), prices of goods and services would also rise. Soon enough, workers would realize that their *real* wages had not increased despite the rise in their nominal wages. Once the workers realized that their real wages did not actually rise, they would *not* supply labor beyond the level they had found to be consistent with their earlier choice, that is, at NAIRU.

How could the workers not realize earlier that their real wages had not actually increased? Information in the economy at any point in time would often be incomplete. It would normally take time to transmit information across the economy, and it would also take time for receivers of the information to digest the information and correctly arrive at its implications. When money conditions became easy and economic activity started to pick up, both employers and workers might mistakenly translate the increase in demand for their goods and services as being unique to them rather than being a part of the general trend of an increase in demand for all goods and services for the whole economy. This would not be too difficult to imagine, given that the firms might actually receive more orders for their products during periods of rising economic activity.

Once the employers and workers realized that the extra hours they put in had not actually raised their purchasing power, they would, respectively, raise the prices of their products and their wages even higher, in anticipation of rising prices of other goods and services in the economy. With everyone anticipating rising prices, and protecting their purchasing power by preemptively raising the prices of their own goods and services as well as wages, inflation would start to accelerate, even without any further increase in production or reduction in unemployment.

Note in the short run, the economy could have been running above capacity for some time. Given that technology has not changed, factories would be operating for longer hours than would be optimal. The same goes for labor. This cannot be sustained over the long run. At some point, the economy has to go back to its capacity, and the unemployment rate will have go back to its natural level, that is, at NAIRU. By that point, however, inflation would already be stuck at a higher level. Inflation, indeed, has accelerated.

Shifting NAIRU

The natural rate of unemployment is supposed to be the one that corresponds to long-run equilibrium in the economy, given existing capital, labor, and technology input. (See Case Study: The Relationship between Unemployment and Output below for more details.)

In practice, however, economists have come to believe that the natural rate of unemployment, or NAIRU, can change as the economy evolves over time. We might note here that in economics, the term *long run* simply refers to the horizon of time in which prices (as well as wages) adjust to clear markets. Over a longer horizon and in a broader context, however, the economy can evolve, with both quantity and quality of capital, labor, and technology changing over time.[13]

The idea of a shifting NAIRU came into focus in the late 1990s. Following leaps in information and communication technology and the Internet revolution in the mid-1990s, which were supposed to bring great improvements in overall productivity, researchers found that unemployment in the United States could be pushed down further than in previous decades without triggering spikes in the inflation rate.[14]

By the early 2010s, however, follow-on effects from the global financial crisis seemed to have affected the fundamentals of the U.S. economy in such a way that rising job vacancies were not matched by a similar decline in unemployment. As such, there have been discussions that NAIRU might have shifted up. Possible reasons for the mismatch in labor demand and supply include the likelihood that skills of those that were unemployed for a long time after the crisis hit might have deteriorated so much that they did not fit the requirements of employers emerging from the crisis.[15]

Figure 5.3 illustrates the possible shifts of NAIRU between the 1980s and the 2010s.

Had NAIRU in the U.S. actually shifted up after the global financial crisis, many observers deemed it important that the Federal Reserve be very vigilant in withdrawing the quantitative easing programs that it had used in fending off deflationary threats. As Figure 5.3 suggests, with a higher natural rate of unemployment, once the economy recovers and unemployment starts to go down along a new short-run Phillips curve, inflation expectations can start to rise sooner than had NAIRU been at the previous, precrisis level.

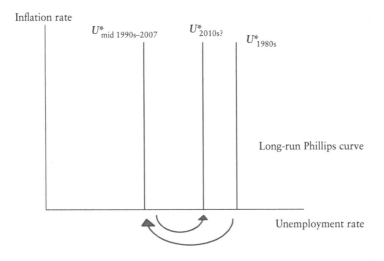

A jump in information and communications technology helped push the natural rate of unemployment in the United States down since the mid-1990s, but have structural changes following the global financial crisis pushed the rate up again?

FIGURE 5.3   Shifting NAIRU

CASE STUDY: The Relationship between Unemployment and Output: Okun's Law and the Output Gap

The concept of an *output gap* is closely related to the concept of the natural rate of unemployment and can be used more readily (or as a complement to the natural rate of unemployment concept) in monetary policy formulation.

The output gap theory can be traced back to Arthur Okun's seminal work published in early 1962.[16] In what became known as *Okun's law*, unemployment is shown to have an inverse relationship with real output.

Specifically, in the first version of Okun's law—called the *difference version*—quarterly changes in the unemployment rate, as expressed in percentage points, are related to quarterly changes in real output (GDP growth), such that greater output growth is associated with lower unemployment.[17]

Another version of Okun's law is called the *gap version*. Here we can think of an economy as having a set potential level of production—given its quantity and quality of labor, capital, and technology— known as its *potential output*.[18] At any one time, actual real output might be above, below, or at potential output. The difference between actual output and potential output is called the output gap.

$$\text{Output gap} = \text{Actual GDP} - \text{Potential GDP}$$

If actual GDP is at its potential, that is the output gap is zero, then we are likely to have "full employment" in the economy. If the calculation of the output gap equation yields a positive number, then aggregate demand has outpaced potential output, and the unemployment rate is likely to be relatively low. On the contrary, if the calculation yields a negative number, aggregate demand is still below potential output, and the unemployment rate would likely be relatively high.

In theory, we could use the concept of NAIRU to signify the natural rate of unemployment that corresponds with potential output. In such a case, if the economy is pushed to produce beyond its potential (and the unemployment rate is below NAIRU, or the output gap is positive), then aggregate demand for products is outstripping potential output, such that factories, enterprises, and labor are running overtime, resulting in accelerating inflation. In such a case the central bank might want to tighten monetary policy in order to slow down aggregate demand and dampen inflationary pressures.

If the economy is running below its potential (unemployment rate above NAIRU, or the output gap is negative, or there is a recessionary gap), there would be negative pressures on price levels and inflation. A recessionary gap is one reason for the central bank to ease money conditions in order to spur aggregate demand without having to worry too much about inflationary threats.

In practice, however, there are a number of variations of the output gap theory, and thus a number of ways to measure the output gap.[19] One way is to use an economic model to estimate the economy's production function, and derive the economy's potential GDP using data on the economy's capital stock, labor input, and technology. This, however, could be a huge task, entailing various uncertainties about the measures used, including the valuation of capital stock and the time lags that come with data gathering.

Another way is to look at the output gap as the deviation of output from its long-run underlying trend. From this perspective, the long-run underlying trend of actual GDP growth could be deemed the rate of GDP growth in the economy that is consistent with the economy's long-term *potential*. The estimation of this long-run underlying trend could be done by smoothing out cyclical movements in GDP data over a long period of time, possibly a few business cycles. The deviation of actual GDP growth for a particular time period from the potential GDP growth rate would thus represent the output gap.[20] Viewed in this way, if the actual GDP growth rate is beyond the potential GDP growth rate, there is likely to be more inflationary pressure. If the actual GDP growth rate is below the potential GDP growth rate, however, there is likely to be less inflationary pressure.

The output gap is a variable that the central bank might look at when making monetary policy decisions. Apart from looking at the current period output gap, however, the central bank might need to also look ahead into the future and project what the output gap might look like in future periods, since it often takes some time before monetary policy action can fully affect aggregate demand and inflation. However, it should also be recognized that potential output, similarly to NAIRU, could also shift over time.[21]

5.5 RATIONAL EXPECTATIONS

By the 1970s, as exemplified by what became known as the *Lucas critique*[22] and the *policy ineffectiveness proposition*,[23] economists had succeeded in formalizing the theoretical possibility that expectations might play in the effectiveness of economic policies. Prior to that, with advances in the collection of macroeconomic data and econometric techniques, policy makers had started to rely increasingly on historical relationships among economic variables when making policy decisions. For example, policy makers might rely on the historical relationship between unemployment and inflation, as reflected by the (short-run) Phillips curve, when deciding on whether to rein or stimulate aggregate demand. However, the view of many economists was that policy actions based on historical relationships might be ineffective, since the public would anticipate the consequences of such policy actions and might alter their behaviors in ways not anticipated by the policy makers.

Broadly speaking, it could be said that the *rational expectations hypothesis* was developed to address the shortcomings in economic theories (or applications of theories) that were based on *adaptive expectations*. Under an adaptive expectations framework, the expectation of the future value of an economic variable is based on its past values. For example, operating under adaptive expectations, people would assume that inflation for any one year would be the same as the previous year. If the economy indeed suffers from constantly rising inflation, then operating under adaptive expectations, people would constantly *underestimate* inflation. Assuming a framework of adaptive expectations is thus quite unrealistic, since rational people would soon notice this type of trend and take it into account in forming their expectations.

The rational expectations hypothesis addresses the shortcomings of adaptive expectations by assuming that individuals take all available information into account in forming expectations. By doing so, the hypothesis suggests that an individual's expectations are correct *on average*. Although the future is not fully predictable, by using all relevant information when forming expectations of the future values of economic variables, the individual's or the public's expectations pertaining to those variables would *not* be systematically biased.

The Lucas Critique

The rational expectations hypothesis has two important implications for the conduct of monetary policy because of the *Lucas critique* (and its close relative, *Goodhart's law*, described in the next chapter in more detail) and the *policy ineffectiveness proposition*.

The Lucas critique proposes that the effort to conduct economic policy entirely on the basis of relationships observed in highly aggregated historical data is futile, as individuals change their decisions in response to the introduction of the policy. For example, if the central bank attempts to exploit the historical inverse correlation between inflation and unemployment (as represented by the Phillips curve) by introducing policies that persistently raise inflation in the hope that unemployment will also be persistently lower, that inverse correlation between inflation and unemployment will eventually break down. Firms and individuals will raise their inflation expectations and meanwhile alter their decisions with regard to hiring and employment.

One implication of the Lucas critique is that to predict the effect of a macroeconomic policy experiment, it be better to model the parameters that govern individual behavior at the microeconomic level (as opposed to aggregated macrodata). Indeed, the latest cutting-edge macroeconomic models—such as the dynamic stochastic general equilibrium (DSGE) models—used at modern central banks for economic forecasts and monetary policy decisions these days are often built with the Lucas critique in mind. Rather than relying on the historical relationship of aggregated macrodata, these models attempt to model the behavior of a rational representative economic agent (a representative consumer, for example) at the microeconomic level.

A concept related to the Lucas critique, but which is more directly associated with the use of a monetary policy rule, is Goodhart's law, which states that "any observed statistical regularity will tend to collapse once pressure is placed upon it for control purposes."[24] Goodhart's law is often ascribed as an apt description of the breakdown of the relationship between the money supply and nominal income following the failure of money supply targeting in the United States and the United Kingdom in the early 1980s.

The Policy Ineffectiveness Proposition

The rational expectations hypothesis also had very profound implications for the conduct of monetary policy through the policy ineffectiveness proposition developed by economists Thomas Sargent and Neil Wallace in 1976 (cited earlier). The proposition suggests that if the Federal Reserve attempts to lower unemployment through an expansionary monetary policy, the effects of the change in policy stance would be fully anticipated by economic agents, who would raise their expectations of future inflation accordingly. This will counteract the expansionary effect of the change in the policy stance. At the extreme, the inflation rate will adjust but not unemployment.

The policy ineffectiveness proposition gained a lot of attention in the late 1970s and early 1980s, partly because of its neat logical deduction and probably partly because it coincided with the rise of the stagflation situation of the time. In the late 1970s the Federal Reserve had tried to cushion the effects of the second oil shock with relatively easy monetary policy, yet unemployment remained high while inflation kept rising. Since then, however, other economists have shown that if wages are sticky (i.e., nominal wage contracts do not change continuously), then macroeconomic policy will have nontrivial effects on the economy.[25] Despite the debate on the applicability of the proposition, however, it can be argued that the proposition at least made central bankers more aware of the role of expectations and the possibility of the danger of using monetary policy to actively pursue lower unemployment.

Irrationality and Other Technical Matters

While the rational expectations hypothesis has made a deep imprint on the way that policy makers have implemented macroeconomic policy since the introduction of the hypothesis in the late 1970s, it has also drawn its fair share of criticism, as with any other influential economic theory. In general, recent advances in the field of behavioral economics have suggested that, for example, individuals might not be as rational in their actions as the rational expectations hypothesis suggests. Experiments in behavioral economics have shown that rather than basing their actions purely on optimal economic outcomes, the actions of individuals can be biased by noneconomic factors, such as perception and emotion.

At a more technical level, in terms of the central banks' effort in modeling policy responses, it has been argued that the behavior of an individual representative agent does not necessarily correspond to aggregated results, owing to interactions among individuals that could lead to extreme herd behavior, such as speculation in asset prices. This implies that the sophisticated dynamic stochastic general equilibrium (DSGE) models used by central banks for economic forecasts might not be so effective, since these models often rely on modeling the behaviors of an individual representative agent.

Despite the various criticisms, however, the rational expectations hypothesis still provides useful guidelines in the formulation of monetary policy. First, the idea of rational expectations can be used to address the shortcomings of adaptive expectations when the central bank models monetary policy effects. Under the rational expectations hypothesis, economic agents are not supposed to make systemic expectational errors, thus the central bank should not expect to reliably exploit the tradeoff between inflation and employment without triggering changes in the agents' expectations.[26] Second, despite recent arguments that biases can influence rational behavior, many behavioral economists have also found that so-called irrational behaviors are actually fairly predictable, such that appropriate economic policies can be designed to take advantage of those seemingly irrational behaviors.

5.6 TIME INCONSISTENCY PROBLEM

While the NAIRU and rational expectations theories pointed out the shortcomings of using monetary policy to actively manipulate unemployment beyond the natural level, they did not exactly prescribe how the central banks should best conduct their monetary policy. A 1977 work by economists Finn Kydland and Edward Prescott[27] on the *time consistency problem* helped complete the picture by pointing out that without a binding rule, policy makers, through their best intentions for the public, would tend to retreat from their announced policies. Such retreats create a credibility problem for future policies. Once the rational public knows that the authority can always retreat from a policy, that policy and any subsequent policy change aimed to improve the public welfare will not be effective, since the public will have altered its behavior since the first policy was announced.

In terms of monetary policy, if the central bank announces that it will reduce inflation (and thus probably create unemployment along the way, given that the economy moves along a short-run Phillips curve), unless the central bank demonstrates a credible binding commitment to deliver on that announcement, the public will not trust such an announcement. The public will know that once inflation seems to have stabilized, the central bank will have many incentives to start easing its monetary policy and squeezing unemployment even further at the expense of higher inflation. (One such incentive for the central bank might simply be desire on the part of central bankers to further boost society's welfare!) Without a binding commitment against policy retreats, the central bank's announcement about reducing inflation will not be credible from the start. Inflation expectations of the public will remain high, and the central bank therefore will be unable to reduce inflation, let alone reduce unemployment.

Monetary Policy Rules

Research on the time inconsistency problem suggests that policy makers should not be allowed pure discretion in policy making. Instead, policy makers should be bound by policy rules. Policy rules make policy actions more credible and effective, since the public knows that policy makers do not have the discretion to easily retreat from their policy actions. In terms of monetary policy, the time inconsistency problem also suggests that central bankers should also be bound by rules when making policy actions. Given the current understanding of what monetary policy can actually achieve, monetary policy rules often should be those that aim to keep inflation low and stable in the long run, as opposed to getting unemployment below the natural rate.

Monetary policy rules that central banks have used to ensure price stability include exchange rate targeting, monetary targeting, and inflation targeting, as well as other implicit rules. We will look at these rules in more detail in Chapter 6. It should be noted here, however, that although monetary policy rules are meant to ensure central banks make policy actions that best support price stability, they are not necessarily straightjackets. Central banks often have a certain degree of flexibility in using discretion to act within rules. In other words, monetary policy rules help ensure that central banks act with *constrained discretion*.

The Central Bank's Operational Independence

Another important implication of the time inconsistency problem is the need for the central bank to be *operationally* independent from political interference, so it can follow its chosen monetary policy rule effectively. Politicians, concerned with short-term gains, especially reelection, often have the incentive to coerce the central bank to reduce unemployment prior to an election. As we learned from the NAIRU argument, pushing unemployment below the natural rate will allow inflation to creep up in the long run, while unemployment will move back to the natural rate. By then, politicians might have been reelected but the economy will be left with higher inflation as well as higher inflation expectations. The price stability mandate could thus be compromised along with the credibility and effectiveness of the central bank's future monetary policy actions.

To help guard the credibility and effectiveness of the central bank's monetary policy actions, and to ensure that the central bank will not easily succumb to politicians' short-term needs, it has been deemed preferable to grant the central bank operational independence. Operational independence does not mean that the central bank is accountable to no one. Rather, it means that the central bank is free to undertake monetary policy actions without undue political inference, assuming it is acting within broad guidelines to achieve operational targets approved or set by the government or the parliament, who themselves answer to the general public. Even with operational independence, the central bank can still be held accountable if it does not comply with broad guidelines or fails to achieve its approved operational targets.

5.7 TAKING THEM ALL TOGETHER

The quantity theory of money, the Phillips curve, the natural rate of unemployment, the rational expectations hypothesis, and the time consistency problem are key theoretical foundations of the modern design and practice of monetary policy and the pursuit of the monetary stability mandate by central banks, as well as the dual mandate of the Federal Reserve.

- The *quantity theory of money* explains why the central bank should refrain from overprinting the money in the *long run*. Given the economy's capital, labor, and technology input, an increase in money supply will in the long run lead to rising prices, but not output.
- The *Phillips curve* provides a basis for using monetary policy to help fine-tune the economy, or at least to trade off between inflation and unemployment in the *short run*.
- In the long run (the period over which prices and wages can fully adjust), the *natural rate of unemployment* concept and the *rational expectations hypothesis* suggest that monetary policy *cannot* be used to trade off between inflation and unemployment. Monetary policy will *not* be able to bring unemployment down below the natural rate in the long run. Were the central bank to attempt to bring unemployment down below the natural rate, in the long run, not only it will fail to bring unemployment down, but inflation would also rise.
- The *time inconsistency* concept suggests that to help the credibility and effectiveness of monetary policy, monetary policy should be conducted under an explicit rule, so that the central bank does not have the discretion to easily retreat from a monetary policy action. Furthermore, to help shield the central bank from being subjected to short-term political pressures, which could jeopardize the credibility of monetary policy, the central bank should be granted operational independence.

In Chapter 6 we will explore in more detail the rules, or regimes, of monetary policy adopted by modern central banks.

SUMMARY

Theoretical developments that have influenced the modern conduct of monetary policy include (1) the quantity theory of money, (2) the Phillips curve, (3) the natural rate of unemployment concept, (4) the rational expectations hypothesis, and (5) the time inconsistency problem.

The Quantity Theory of Money: The government should refrain from overprinting money. In the long run, monetary policy can only influence *prices* of goods and services in the economy, and cannot influence the *quantity* of output or *level* of economic activity directly. The efforts by the central bank to stimulate the economy by printing money will only result in rising prices and inflation in the long run.

The Phillips Curve: The government can attempt to fine-tune the economy in the short run by trading off unemployment and inflation. There is a short-run negative relationship between inflation and the unemployment rate. When the inflation rate goes up, the unemployment rate goes down, and vice versa.

The Natural Rate of Unemployment: The central bank should not attempt to push unemployment below the natural rate of unemployment, since this will lead to higher inflation expectations in the long run, without lowering unemployment. In the long run, the inverse relationship between inflation and unemployment disappears. There is a rate of unemployment, called the natural rate of unemployment, that corresponds to the economy's potential. In practice, the concept of an *output gap* can also be used to capture the concept of the natural rate of unemployment.

The Rational Expectations Hypothesis: Public expectations matter in the effectiveness of economic policies. The public is rational enough to incorporate their expectations of policy outcomes into their current behavior. As such, an expansionary monetary policy that leads to a rise in inflation expectations could lead to an upward spiral in wages and prices. For monetary policy to be effective in maintaining price stability, the central bank must manage the inflation expectations of the public.

The rational expectations hypothesis has important implications for the conduct of monetary policy because of the *Lucas critique* and the *policy ineffectiveness proposition*.

The Time Inconsistency Problem: To raise the credibility of the central bank with respect to its commitment to low and stable inflation, and to anchor inflation expectations, the central bank needs to conduct monetary policy by following an explicit rule rather than using pure discretion. Policy makers, even with the best of intentions, have an incentive to backtrack on their policies if they believe they can improve welfare of the public. The backtracking, however, will damage the future credibility and effectiveness of its policies, thereby reducing the welfare of the public instead. For a central bank, credibility is critical if monetary policy is to work effectively in keeping inflation low and stable.

KEY TERMS

adaptive expectations

equation of exchange

long-run Phillips curve

Lucas critique

natural rate of unemployment

nonaccelerating inflation rate of unemployment (NAIRU)

Okun's law

output gap

Phillips curve

policy ineffectiveness proposition

quantity theory of money

rational expectations

time-inconsistency problem

velocity of circulation

QUESTIONS

1. What is the equation representing the quantity theory of money?
2. What are the key assumptions used in the equation representing the quantity theory of money?
3. According to the quantity theory of money, if the amount of money in the economy rises, what would happen in the long run?
4. According to the quantity theory of money, why can't we expect monetary policy to help directly stimulate output growth in a sustainable manner in the long run?

5. Keeping in mind historical episodes of hyperinflation, is the quantity theory of money justified?

6. What is the relationship between inflation and unemployment in the short run?

7. How does the Phillips curve represent the relationship between inflation and unemployment graphically? Please draw a short-run Phillips curve.

8. If the short-run Phillips curve exists, what would happen to unemployment when the central bank attempts to reduce inflation?

9. If the short-run Phillips curve exists, what would happen to inflation when the central bank attempts to reduce unemployment?

10. What is NAIRU? Why might it represent the natural rate of unemployment?

11. How might we reconcile the Phillips curve with the concept of the natural rate of unemployment?

12. If the Phillips curve is vertical in the long run, what will happen if the central bank tries to push unemployment rate below its natural rate?

13. What are the reasons that unemployment could be pushed below its natural rate in the short run?

14. Why might the natural rate of unemployment shift over time?

15. After the global financial crisis of 2007–2010, how might the natural rate of unemployment in the U.S. have shifted, and why?

16. What might we mean by *potential GDP*?

17. What is an output gap?

18. If there is a large positive output gap, what can the central bank do using monetary policy?

19. What do we mean by adaptive expectations? With adaptive expectations, if inflation is rising, are individual's inflation expectations likely to be correct or not? Why or why not?

20. What are the key differences between adaptive expectations and rational expectations?

21. According to the policy ineffectiveness proposition, if people have rational expectations why might monetary policy be ineffective?

22. Why might the policy ineffectiveness proposition not be realized in the real world?

23. What do we often mean by the operational independence of a central bank?

24. In the world of accountability, why might one want to advocate a central bank's operational independence?

CHAPTER 6

Monetary Policy Regimes

What Monetary Policy Rules a Central Bank Can Use to Achieve Monetary Stability

Learning Objectives

1. Describe various monetary policy regimes that central banks have adopted since the end of the Bretton Woods system.
2. Explain the pros and cons of adopting an exchange rate targeting regime.
3. Explain the pros and cons of adopting a money supply targeting regime.
4. Explain the pros and cons of adopting an inflation-targeting regime.
5. Explain the pros and cons of unconventional monetary policy in the case of quantitative easing.

As discussed in Chapter 5, the concept of the time inconsistency problem suggests that without a monetary policy rule guiding how the central bank regulates money conditions in the economy, the conduct of monetary policy would not be credible nor effective. Without a monetary policy rule constraining the central bank on monetary-policy decisions, the public might not believe that the central bank would ultimately keep the promise of price stability, since there are always incentives for the central bank to backtrack on the policy and try to push unemployment down further, possibly at the cost of price stability. Without a monetary policy rule, the public's inflation expectations might thus not be properly anchored, and the central bank, for all its good intentions, might be unable to successfully control inflation and deliver price stability as promised. To effectively conduct monetary policy, the central bank thus needs to follow a monetary policy rule that will assure a rational public that a policy action will contribute positively to the overall welfare of the economy.

But exactly what monetary policy rule should the central bank follow? Theoretical developments discussed in Chapter 5, as well as historical experience discussed in earlier chapters, suggest that, in the conduct of monetary policy, the central bank should follow a monetary policy rule that ensures price (or monetary) stability. In following a particular monetary policy rule, the central bank has to design its operational processes and organizational structure to best help it achieve the objective of that rule.

6.1 AN OVERVIEW OF MONETARY POLICY RULES OR MONETARY POLICY REGIMES

In modern monetary policy jargon, to follow a particular monetary policy rule is to adopt a monetary policy *regime*. It is often called a regime because the adoption of a monetary policy rule involves various aspects of institutional design that the central bank needs in order to achieve the objectives of the rule. Specifics of modern institutional design might include *legislation* or *statute* to institutionalize and legitimize the rule and empower the monetary-policy decision-making body; the central bank's *organizational structure* that is appropriate for implementing monetary policy actions under such rule; and *other supporting infrastructures*, such as the existence of interbank markets, secondary government bond markets, relevant statistical database, and public communication tools.

Broadly speaking, given modern theoretical developments and historical experiences, a credible monetary policy rule (monetary policy regime) is one that aims to keep inflation low and stable and that provides the price and economic stability needed for long-run economic growth, rather than one that aims to reduce unemployment below the natural rate to reap short-term gains.*

In practice, the five key monetary policy rules, or monetary policy regimes, that have been used among central banks since the breakdown of the Bretton Woods system in the early 1970s include (1) *exchange rate targeting*, (2) *money growth rate targeting*, (3) the so-called *risk management approach*, (4) *inflation targeting*, and, in the wake of the recent global financial crisis, (5) *unconventional monetary policy*.[1]

The first four of these monetary policy rules, or regimes, can be thought of as being conventional monetary policy rules, which have the common goal of providing the central bank with guidance on how to conduct monetary policy to achieve monetary stability.[2] This chapter will also address unconventional monetary policy, which a number of major advanced economies decided to use as a separate regime in the wake of their crises. This chapter will review briefly the basic ideas behind all of these monetary policy regimes. In later chapters, operational details of these regimes will be discussed when appropriate.

6.2 EXCHANGE RATE TARGETING

Exchange rate targeting is a monetary policy rule under which the central bank promises to keep the exchange rate within an announced target for a given period. Under exchange rate targeting the central bank cannot change the money supply at

---

*Note here that the gold standard and the gold exchange standard are, by definition, also monetary policy rules. The gold standard, for example, was a monetary policy rule that limited the central bank to printing money only up to the amount that could be backed by the value of its gold reserves. The gold standard (as well as the gold exchange standard) as a monetary policy rule did not allow central banks to actually fine-tune the economy. To be fair, theoretical understanding at the time of the gold standard did not allow for the possibility of fine-tuning the economy (Bordo 2007).

will, lest the exchange rate move away from the announced target level.[3] Generally speaking, exchange rate targeting as a monetary policy rule can help the central bank achieve credibility and price stability if the central bank pegs the value of its currency to that of a large country that has a good record of price stability.[4]

Historically, following the breakdown of the Bretton Woods system and until the late 1990s, the currency of choice for a central bank to peg its currency to has often been the U.S. dollar for emerging-market economies and the German mark for advanced economies in Europe.[5] Despite blips during the great inflation period in the late 1970s, the United States had always had a good record of price stability, and even to this day, the U.S. dollar remains the dominant currency used in international trade and finance. Fixing the level of its exchange rate to the U.S. dollar would enable easy international transactions for the country that chooses to do so. Germany, meanwhile, after the hyperinflation episode of the 1920s, has always been very vigilant in keeping its inflation rate low. By the 1970s France and the United Kingdom had started to peg their exchange rates to the German mark as German economic prominence grew, a prelude to the creation of the euro.[6]

Later on, as countries started to diversify their trade and investment, many central banks also started to fix the value of their domestic currencies to a *basket of currencies* of their main trading partners.[7] To do this, the central bank might create an index representing the weighted value of the basket of currencies of their major trading partner countries and target the exchange rate at a certain level of the index.[8]

Also, rather than fixing the exchange rate at a particular level, the central bank could also choose to allow the exchange rate to fluctuate within a (narrow) *target band*, or to adopt a *crawling peg*—that is a system under which the exchange rate might be allowed to gradually depreciate against the pegged country, thus allowing inflation in the country in question to be higher than that in the pegged country.[9]

Whether the central bank targets the value of its currency to another currency (such as the U.S. dollar) or to a basket of currencies, or in terms of a particular exchange rate level, a target band, or a crawling peg, however, the essential mechanics can be illustrated by the following simple stylized model.

A Stylized Model of Exchange Rate Targeting

Figure 6.1 illustrates a stylized model of foreign exchange market equilibrium in a country where the central bank adopts exchange rate targeting as its monetary policy rule.

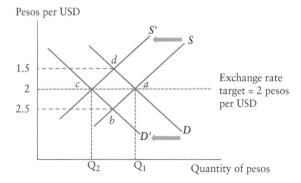

FIGURE 6.1 A Stylized Model of Exchange Rate Targeting

Initial Equilibrium   In Figure 6.1, let us say that the central bank of Country A decides to peg the value of its currency, the *peso*, at an exchange rate of 2 pesos per 1 U.S. dollar (USD). Initially, the foreign exchange market for the peso is in equilibrium at point *a*. At point *a*, demand for pesos is matched by the supply of pesos (Q_1 on the *x-axis*).

The Case of a Fall in Demand for the Domestic Currency   Assume that importers in Country A later want to convert their pesos into U.S. dollars so that they can use U.S. dollars to import goods from abroad. In that case, the demand curve for pesos would shift to the left, with point *b* potentially as the new equilibrium point.

At point *b*, however, the peso exchange rate would have dropped to 2.5 pesos per 1 U.S. dollar, which is less than the announced target level of 2 pesos per 1 U.S. dollar. To keep the exchange rate at the target level, the central bank of Country A would have to sell U.S. dollars from its foreign-exchange reserve holdings to importers and buy up pesos from them. By buying up pesos from importers, the central bank would be drawing out pesos that currently reside in private hands and in the economy at large. In effect, through its sale of U.S. dollars and purchase of pesos from importers, the central bank would be reducing the supply of pesos to match the fall in demand for pesos. The supply curve for pesos would shift to the left (from supply curve *S* to supply curve *S'*). At point *c*, which is the new equilibrium point, the exchange rate would be back at 2 pesos per dollar, the central bank's announced exchange target level.

The Case of a Rise in Demand for the Domestic Currency   In contrast to the importer example above, let us say that the initial equilibrium is at point *c*. When exporters in Country A want to convert their U.S. dollar earnings into pesos, demand for pesos rises. The demand curve for pesos would shift to the right (from demand curve *D* to demand curve *D'*), with the new equilibrium at point *d*, a point at which there are appreciation pressures on the peso. To prevent the peso from rising above the announced target level, the central bank would have to buy up U.S. dollars from exporters and sell pesos to them, thereby raising the supply of pesos in the economy. The supply curve for pesos would then shift to the right (from supply curve *S* to supply curve *S'*). To keep the exchange rate at the announced 2 pesos per dollar target, the central bank would have to expand supply of pesos until the supply curve for pesos intersects with the demand curve for pesos at point *a*, which would be the new equilibrium point.

In practice, the central bank with exchange rate targeting has to constantly adjust the money supply to meet changes in demand for the domestic currency. From the examples above, we can see that (1) demand for foreign currencies rises (and demand for domestic currency falls) when importers need foreign currencies to import goods and services from abroad, and (2) demand for foreign currencies falls (and demand for domestic currency rises) when exporters need to convert their export earnings into domestic currency. To keep the exchange rate fixed at the announced target level, the central bank has to adjust the domestic money supply to meet changes in demand for the domestic currency.

The Effects of Capital Inflows   In a country that is open to international capital flows, changes in demand for domestic currency would come not only from importers and exporters of goods and services, but also from international investors. If international investors deem that the country is a good investment prospect, then capital would flow into the domestic economy. In order to invest in the country, international investors would first have to convert their foreign currencies into the domestic currency. This would raise demand for the domestic currency. To meet the demand from international investors, and to keep the exchange rate fixed at the announced target, the central bank would have to buy up foreign currencies from international investors and supply them with domestic currency.

The Effects of Capital Outflows   In contrast, if international investors deem that the country is not a good investment prospect and want to divest from the country, then there would be a flight of capital out of the country. International investors would want to convert their domestic currency into foreign currencies. Demand for domestic currency would fall. To meet the demand of international investors and to keep the exchange rate fixed at the announced target, the central bank would have to buy up domestic currency from international investors and sell its foreign currencies to them as demanded. Through the purchase of domestic currency, the central bank would effectively be withdrawing a portion of the domestic money supply from the economy, thereby reducing the domestic money supply.

Exchange Rate Targeting in the Real World

In the real world, in a small, open economy, large and volatile flows of international capital can easily overwhelm the central bank's ability to keep the exchange rate at the fixed target. For example, if suddenly international investors no longer see the country as an investment destination and decide to convert their domestic currency holdings into foreign currencies, the central bank must have enough foreign exchange reserves in order to meet the demand of international investors if it wants to keep the exchange rate fixed at the announced target. If currency speculators deem that the central bank might not have enough foreign exchange reserves to hold the exchange rate at the announced level, they could prompt a speculative attack on the currency, forcing the central bank to devalue the currency or let the exchange rate move from the announced target. In a more globalized world, international investors and currency speculators can command larger sums of capital than the foreign exchange reserves of central banks, making it difficult for a central bank to keep its exchange rate fixed at any given level.

Exchange Rate Targeting and Monetary Policy Independence   From Figure 6.1 and the preceding discussion, we can see that the central bank does not truly have the independence to conduct monetary policy and fine-tune the economy as it sees fit. If there is a requirement to keep the exchange rate at the announced target level, the central bank will have to vary the money supply to match changes in the demand for domestic currency by importers and exporters, as well as international investors and speculators, rather than adjusting domestic money conditions to directly influence domestic aggregate demand.

An extreme form of exchange rate targeting is the use of a *currency board*, whereby the exchange rate is fixed at a particular level and the domestic currency is legally required to be fully backed up by foreign currencies held by the central bank.

The central bank is legally obliged to exchange domestic currency for a foreign currency at the specified exchange rate, and thus can only issue additional domestic currency if it has extra foreign currencies to fully back it up. A central bank in a currency board system (e.g., the Hong Kong Monetary Authority, which fixes the Hong Kong dollar at the rate of HK$ 7.8 to USD 1) cannot thus independently alter money supply as it wishes to.[10]

In general, even for those that are not on the currency board system, it could be said that the central bank under an exchange rate targeting regime must keep domestic money conditions aligned with money conditions in the country that it fixes the value of its domestic currency to. Otherwise, divergences in money conditions between the two countries will not allow the central bank to keep the exchange rate at the announced target level.

For example, let us say that Country A fixes the value of its currency to the U.S. dollar. If Country A's domestic unemployment is very high, the central bank of Country A cannot simply ease money conditions to stimulate domestic aggregate demand unless the U.S. central bank also eases U.S. money conditions. Otherwise, Country A's domestic inflation could rise much faster than that of the United States and there will be immense depreciation pressures on the value of Country A's currency. In the world of free capital flows, these depreciation pressures could simply overwhelm the ability of Country A's central bank to keep the exchange rate fixed at the target level. As will be discussed in more detail in later chapters, a currency with a higher inflation rate is likely to depreciate in value—both in terms of domestic purchasing power and overseas purchasing power—which would put downward pressure on the exchange rate.

The Impossible Trinity: Exchange Rate Targeting, Free Capital Flows, and Independent Monetary Policy   From the preceding discussion, we can see that the success of using exchange rate targeting as a monetary policy rule depends on both the degree of capital flows and the degree of monetary policy independence. The impossibility of having (1) a *fixed exchange rate*, (2) *free capital flows*, and (3) an *independent monetary policy* all at the same time is known among economists and central bankers as the *impossible trinity*. The impossible trinity has been one key reason why numerous central banks in Europe, Asia, and Latin America have been abandoning exchange rate targeting as their monetary policy rule. In a world of freer international capital flows and diverging economic cycles, many of these central banks often find it hard to maintain a fixed exchange rate and fine-tune the domestic economy at the same time. We discuss issues relating to the exchange rate in more detail in Chapters 8 to 10.

6.3 MONEY SUPPLY GROWTH TARGETING

As the name suggests, a money growth targeting rule requires that the central bank set a target rate for growth of the money supply. According to this rule, if the central bank keeps money supply growth at a target rate that is consistent with that of real economic activity, then inflation should be relatively low and stable. In the 1970s, central banks around the world had to grapple with the effects of the breakdown of the Bretton Woods system. While many central banks decided to keep their exchange rates fixed to the U.S. dollar or the German mark,[11] by the 1980s a number of advanced economy central banks, including those of the United States and Germany, had adopted money growth targets as a guide for their monetary policy actions.[12]

A Stylized Model of Money Supply Growth Targeting

Money supply growth targeting is based mainly on the quantity theory of money discussed in Chapter 5. Recall the equation of exchange

$$M \times V = P \times Q \tag{6.1}$$

where M stands for the quantity of money in the economy, V is the velocity of circulation of the money, P is the general price level in the economy, and Q is the quantity of products sold in the economy.

Rearrange to get

$$P = \frac{M \times Q}{V} \tag{6.2}$$

Given that V and Q are exogenous to the equation, and thus assumed constant, then a change in P must be equal to a change in M.

$$\frac{dP}{p} = \frac{dM}{M} \tag{6.3}$$

In differentiating with respect to time (t), changes in P over time will be equal to changes in M over time.

$$\frac{dP/P}{dt} = \frac{dM/M}{dt} \tag{6.4}$$

The preceding calculation means that the rate of change in the general price level of the economy, or the rate of inflation, is equal to the rate of change in money supply over time.

Given Equation 6.4, if the central bank allows the money supply to grow at a rate that is markedly faster than the growth rate of economic activity, inflation will accelerate. In other words, with so much money, money will soon lose its purchasing power. If the central bank pushes the money supply growth rate below the growth rate of economic activity, on the other hand, money conditions will be tight and inflation will decelerate. In extreme cases, if money becomes extremely scarce, prices of goods and services might fall, and deflation could set in.

Money Supply Growth Targeting in the Real World

In the real world, money supply growth targeting experiences are quite complicated. In the 1970s many advanced economies, including the United States, the United Kingdom, Germany, and Switzerland, adopted money supply growth targeting as their monetary policy regime, partly as a response to growing inflation, and partly because of the need to search for a nominal regime after the collapse of the Bretton Woods system.[13]

In the United States, in a response to a congressional resolution, the Federal Reserve started to publicly announce it targets for money supply growth in 1975. In practice, however, the Federal Reserve did not place high priority on meeting the supply growth target, but focused more on reducing unemployment and smoothing interest rates.[14] Without a strict commitment to money supply growth targets and with the primary focus on reducing unemployment, together with events such as oil shocks, inflation was spiraling out of control.

Only in late 1979, when the Federal Reserve (under the new leadership of Paul Volcker) decided to (1) emphasize its commitments to money supply targets (2) adjust its operating procedures to focus on setting a desired path for bank reserves and an associated range for the federal funds rate, which allowed the interest rates fluctuate more widely; and (3) push up interest rates to underscore its resolve to discourage excessive money growth, did inflation expectations started to come down.[15]

By 1982, however, the relationship between money supply growth and nominal income was found to be unstable, and the Federal Reserve began to deemphasize money supply targets.[16]

The U.S. and U.K. Experiences   Monetary growth targeting became popular as a monetary policy rule in the advanced economies including the United States, the United Kingdom, Canada, Germany, and Switzerland in the 1970s.[17] In practice, however, despite the announced money growth targets, many of these central banks also pursued other objectives, including the stability of exchange rates and the financial market. They often also attempted to fine-tune the economy based on the immediate conditions, that is, moving along the short-run Phillips curve.[18] When two major oil shocks hit the world economy in the mid- and late 1970s, central banks—notably those of the United States and the United Kingdom—tried to ease monetary conditions, and along the way overshot their money supply growth targets in order to push unemployment down.[19]

The unwillingness of U.S. and U.K. central banks to strictly adhere to their announced money supply growth targets and to actually let the targets be consistently overshot led to sharp increases in inflation.[20] As public inflation expectations rose upward in response to easy monetary policy, however, both unemployment and inflation accelerated, resulting by the late 1970s in a situation known as *stagflation* (stagnation plus inflation). As discussed in Chapter 5 in the context of the time inconsistency problem, the stagflation experience reflected the cost of using monetary policy in a discretionary manner, as opposed to following a credible monetary policy rule.

To get inflation back down, in October 1979 the Federal Reserve (under the new chairmanship of Paul A. Volcker) decided to publicly emphasize its commitments to money growth targets and allowed interest rates to shoot up to very high levels.[21] While the policy resulted in deep economic contractions in the short term, it had the effect of driving inflation expectations downward in the longer term, since it showed the willingness of the Federal Reserve to commit to price stability even at steep short-term costs. In any case, by the early 1980s both the Federal Reserve and the Bank of England ran into a technical problem in pursuing money supply growth targets: the relationship between targeted money supply growth and nominal income growth became very unstable, making it impossible to target money supply growth properly.[22] (See Case Study: The Breakdown of the Relationship between Money Supply Growth, Nominal Income, and Inflation in the United States and the United Kingdom, and the Role of Goodhart's Law for more details.)

With inflation expectations already tamped down by a tight monetary policy, the breakdown in the relationship between the growth in the money supply and nominal income growth prompted the Federal Reserve to start deemphasizing money supply growth targets by late 1982.[23] By July 1993, the Federal Reserve had completely phased out monetary targeting as a monetary policy rule, and had effectively adopted what became known as a *just-do-it*, or a *risk management*, approach to its monetary framework.[24] The United Kingdom, meanwhile, also dropped money growth targeting in the late 1980s and started pegging the value of its currency to the deutsche mark in anticipation of joining the European monetary union.[25]

The German Experience   In contrast to the U.S. and U.K. experiences, however, money supply growth targeting in Germany was quite successful from the 1970s through the 1990s.[26] Apart from using a money supply growth target as a communication tool to anchor expectations, the German central bank also announced a numerical inflation goal and used that inflation goal to calculate the necessary money supply growth rate from the quantity theory of money equation.[27] In this respect the German central bank was also flexible enough to adjust a numerical inflation goal over time to make it consistent with long-term price stability.

Furthermore, while the German central bank allowed monetary growth to sometime overshoot the target in response to shocks, it also reversed those overages later to get money supply growth back to the target over time.[28] The German's success with money supply growth targeting as monetary policy rule to maintain price stability also depended heavily on the manner in which it communicated its monetary policy strategy to the public. Although the central bank might miss its money supply growth targets by large margins, the central bank also spent a lot effort in explaining to the public how monetary policy was being directed to achieve its inflation goal.[29] This successful strategy was later adopted by the ECB through the use of the *two-pillar* strategy of monetary policy, under which ECB concerned itself with both money supply growth and inflation rates.

CASE STUDY: The Breakdown of the Relationship between Money Supply Growth, Nominal Income, and Inflation in the United States and the United Kingdom, and the Role of Goodhart's Law

By the early 1980s, as the Federal Reserve and the Bank of England had started to show more serious commitment to the rule of money supply growth targeting, the relationship between money supply, nominal income, and inflation started to break down in both the United States and the United Kingdom.[30] In terms of the quantity theory of money equation, the variable V in the $M \times V = P \times Q$ equation had become unstable, such that the central banks were having a hard time setting a growth of M variable that would rightly correspond to the growth of $P \times Q$ (or growth of nominal GDP).[31]

The instability of V could have owed to factors that altered the *cost of holding money* (including changes in inflation expectations and real interest rates), financial innovations (such as the introduction of money market accounts), and credit cards.[32] With velocity of circulation (V) being unstable, the central banks found it increasingly difficult to calibrate their money supply growth targets in a way that was consistent with nominal GDP.[33]

Goodhart's Law

This breakdown in the relationship between money and nominal income has also often been ascribed partly to *Goodhart's law*, named after the economist Charles Goodhart of the London School of Economics. The law is a close relative to the Lucas critique discussed in Chapter 5.[34] Specifically, Goodhart's law states that "any observed statistical regularity will tend to collapse once pressure is placed upon it for control purposes."[35] With money supply growth becoming a control target, this caused greater variation in nominal and real interest rates, as well as inflation, which helped increase pressure for deregulation and competition.[36] Ultimately the pressure for competition and deregulation, coupled with the speed of the evolution in information technology, helped bring about financial innovations that effectively caused instability in the velocity of circulation and destroyed the observed relationship between money and nominal income.[37]

6.4 THE RISK MANAGEMENT APPROACH

From the mid 1980s until the onset of the global financial crisis in 2007, the Federal Reserve had adopted a monetary-policy framework that became known as the just-do-it, or the risk management, approach to monetary policy.[38] In this framework, there were no announced specific targets for money supply growth or the inflation rate. Instead, the Federal Reserve closely monitored various economic data and acted in a *forward-looking* manner, in order to maintain price stability and minimize risks to employment and economic growth.[39]

Under the risk management approach, the Federal Reserve used a short-term interest rate as its policy interest rate and adjusted the policy interest rate to preempt risks that might lead to *inflation* and threaten *economic stability*. A famous example is when Alan Greenspan, then chairman of the Federal Reserve, famously tightened the Federal Reserve's monetary policy stance in 1996, explicitly to temper down "irrational exuberance" in the U.S. stock markets.[40] Despite adjusting monetary policy based on factors such as asset prices and the state of the stock market, however, when economists actually traced out monetary policy actions during the period of risk management approach, it was found that the Federal Reserve monetary-policy decisions at the time could be expressed as minimization of risks to both output growth and price stability.

A Stylized Model of the Risk Management Approach: The Taylor Rule

Despite the lack of announced monetary policy targets on the part of the Federal Reserve in the late 1980s and early 1990s, John B. Taylor, a prominent academic, deduced statistically from the Federal Reserve's monetary policy actions that the Federal Reserve had, intentionally or not, tried to keep inflation at some *equilibrium* level and the rate of GDP growth around inflation's potential growth rate.[41]

The hypothesis made by Taylor received popular attention because it seemed to approximate the Federal Reserve's monetary policy actions reasonably well. The hypothesis became known as the *Taylor rule*, which can be expressed as the formula

$$i_t = r_t^* + \pi_t + a_\pi (\pi_t - \pi_t^*) + a_y (y_t - y_t^*) \tag{6.5}$$

where i_t is the policy interest rate at time t, π_t is the inflation rate, π_t^* is the desired rate of inflation, r_t^* is the assumed equilibrium real interest rate, y_t is the actual GDP growth rate, y_t^* is the GDP growth rate at full potential, and a_π and a_y are the relative weights that the central bank assigns to keeping inflation at the target rate and getting the actual GDP growth rate to its full potential. In his 1993 paper, Taylor suggested that $a_\pi = a_y = 0.5$.

According to Equation 6.5, the Federal Reserve would raise the policy interest rate when inflation is above the desired rate or when GDP growth rate is beyond its full potential. When inflation is below the desired rate or when GDP growth rate is below its full potential, then the Federal Reserve would lower the policy interest rate. At times when inflation and output goals turn out to be in conflict—for example, when an oil shock causes inflation to rise beyond the desired rate and at the same time causes GDP growth to be below potential—the central bank might tilt the relative weights according to what it sees fit. In this case, if the central bank wants to drive down inflation expectations it might put more weight toward keeping inflation at the target rate.

The Risk Management Approach in the Real World

When the Federal Reserve quietly abandoned its money supply targeting regime in the mid-1980s it did not explicitly announce a nominal target to replace its money supply growth target. Rather, Alan Greenspan, who became the Federal Reserve chairman in 1987, conducted monetary policy by closely monitoring changes in eclectic sets of economic and financial variables and adjusting the policy interest rate to forestall inflation and prevent problems with economic stability.[42]

The Federal Reserve, under Greenspan's leadership, tried to actively conduct monetary policy to contain various shocks that risked economic and financial system stability. To mitigate the effects of the 1987 stock market crash and the 2001 terrorist attacks, the Federal Reserve injected massive amounts of liquidity into the system. The Federal Reserve also lowered interest rates markedly in response to economic slowdowns that led to recessions in the early 1990s and in the first decade of the twenty-first century.

After each recession was over, the Federal Reserve tightened its monetary policy stance by raising interest rates, notably in 1994 (which led to a crash in bond markets), 1996 (in response to "irrational exuberance" in the stock market), in the late 1990s (in response to the dot-com boom), and again in the middle of the first decade of the twenty-first century (in response to rising oil prices and inflation).

Despite the lack of a nominal target for monetary policy, monetary policy conducted under the risk management approach was approximated reasonably well by the Taylor rule from the early 1980s onwards to very early in the first decade of the twenty-first century.[43] This suggests that at the time the Federal Reserve was concerned with both inflation and unemployment, that is, the dual mandate discussed in Chapter 4.

6.5 INFLATION TARGETING

Inflation targeting is a monetary policy regime under which the central bank aims to keep the inflation rate within a specified target over a specified time frame. An inflation-targeting central bank often uses a short-term interest rate (known as the policy interest rate) as the key tool to adjust monetary conditions in the economy in a *forward-looking* manner, so that inflation, or more specifically the *forecast* for inflation, is kept within target.[44,*]

Inflation targeting as a monetary policy regime rests upon two pillars: transparency and accountability.[45] *Transparency* is conveyed through the public announcement of the inflation target that the central bank tries to achieve, as well as the reasons behind each of the central bank's monetary-policy decisions with respect to achieving the target. *Accountability* is conveyed through the fact that the central bank is accountable if the inflation target is missed.[46] With transparency and accountability, the *credibility* of the central bank in maintaining monetary stability through its conduct of monetary policy is enhanced.[47]

Note here that *unlike* money supply growth targets, an inflation target is more *transparent*, both because the inflation rate is often collected by a government agency (or agencies) outside the central bank and because the public can understand and have a feel for the implications of an inflation rate much better than for a money-supply growth rate.

Although there may be concern that an inflation-targeting central bank might be too narrowly focused on inflation, in practice inflation targeting as a monetary policy rule often allows the central bank discretion in dealing with unemployment and output, but in a more transparent and appropriate longer-term context.[48]

A Stylized Model of Inflation Targeting

Figure 6.2 illustrates a stylized model of using inflation targeting as a monetary policy rule. An inflation-targeting central bank would announce its target for inflation in advance, along with the time frame for which inflation is to remain within target.

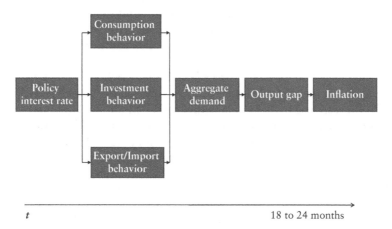

FIGURE 6.2   A Stylized Model of Inflation Targeting

---

*Technically it is more precise to say that under inflation targeting the central bank's *forecast* of inflation, rather than current actual inflation, is to be kept within target, because there is normally a time lag between a monetary policy action and a rise in prices. In the conduct of monetary policy under inflation targeting, the central bank thus acts today in response to its forecast of future inflation. In practice, however, the central bank is judged on its ability to keep actual inflation within target.

If the central bank deems that current money conditions are stimulating consumption and investment demand, as well as economic activity, too much, such that inflation may rise beyond its target in the future, the central bank might raise the policy interest rate to help tighten money conditions.

As will be discussed in more detail in later chapters, a rise in the policy interest rate could lead to a rise in other short-term and long-term interest rates and tightened money conditions, and thus a slowdown in consumption and investment demand in the economy. The slowdown in consumption and investment demand means that there would be less competition for goods and services, and thus also a slowdown in the rise in prices of goods and services in the economy; in other words, a slowdown in inflation.

It has long been recognized that before monetary policy actions can affect economic activity and inflation, however, that there would be *time lags* that are both *long* and *variable*.[49] It could take anywhere from 12 months to more than 24 months for a change in the policy interest rate to work through aggregate demand and fully affect inflation.[50] An inflation-targeting central bank would thus have to make an inflation forecast over that time horizon and adjust the policy interest rate to make sure that the inflation *forecast* would remain within target.[51] This will be a *rolling* exercise; that is, an inflation-targeting central bank would normally schedule monetary policy meetings on a regular basis (possibly every six weeks) to assess new information, make its inflation forecast two years out, and adjust its policy interest rate accordingly.

As will be discussed in later chapters in more detail, apart from affecting consumption and investment demand, a rise in short-term interest rates could also lead to appreciation pressures on the exchange rate, and thus net exports, all else being equal. With an appreciating exchange rate, the economy's exports would be priced higher in terms of a foreign currency, and thus demand for exports from the country would also fall, leading to a slowdown in domestic economic activity and lower inflationary pressures. On the other hand, with an appreciating currency, imports of foreign goods and services would be cheaper in terms of domestic currency. As such, there will be more imports to substitute for locally produced products. On the whole, a rise in short-term interest rates is likely to lead to lower *net* exports and thus a slowdown in economic activity, other things being equal. Along with weakened domestic demand, the fall in net exports would help further weaken inflationary pressures in the economy.

In contrast, if an inflation-targeting central bank deems that monetary conditions are already too tight or economic activity too slow, such that inflation might fall below its target, the central bank might choose to stimulate economic activity and demand in the economy by lowering the policy interest rate. In such a case, as other interest rates in the economy start to fall in line with the lower policy interest rate, consumption and investment demand will rise. Competing demand for goods and services will thus lead to higher inflationary pressures.

Also, as interest rates start to fall, all else being equal, the exchange rate will likely depreciate, making exports cheaper in terms of a foreign currency. Demand for the country's exports will rise, leading to more economic activity and more competition for goods and services. With a depreciating currency, imports will become more expensive in domestic currency terms and more likely to be substituted for by locally produced products. Competition for domestic resources to increase production for these import substitutions will help spur economic activity, and also inflationary pressures, going forward.

Inflation Targeting in the Real World

As discussed in Chapter 1, in 1990 the Reserve Bank of New Zealand (RBNZ) became the first central bank to adopt inflation targeting as its monetary policy regime. In designing its inflation-targeting regime, RBNZ put great emphasis on *transparency* and *accountability* in monetary-policy decisions, in line with the overall public-sector reform being carried out in New Zealand at the time. Inflation targeting emphasizes transparency in the form of a publicly announced inflation target and the reasons behind the central bank's monetary policy stance, that is, why the central bank raised, lowered, or maintained the level of the policy interest rate.[52] Accountability is conveyed through the fact that if the inflation target is missed without a good explanation, the RBNZ governor could be removed. It could be said that the emphasis on transparency and accountability helped enhance the *credibility* of RBNZ's commitment to price stability in its conduct of monetary policy in New Zealand.

Later on, when many central banks of both advanced and emerging economies were forced to find a credible monetary policy regime to replace exchange rate targeting and money supply growth targeting, inflation targeting became the regime of choice. Central banks that currently have inflation targeting as their monetary policy regimes are diverse, and include the Bank of Canada, the Bank of England, the Reserve Bank of Australia, the Bank of Korea, the Bank of Thailand, the Bank of Indonesia, the Central Bank of the Philippines, the Czech National Bank, the Central Bank of Brazil, and the Central Bank of Chile, among others.

In case of the United States, after Ben Bernanke succeeded Alan Greenspan as chairman of the Federal Reserve System, the Federal Reserve gradually modified certain procedures of their monetary policy practices so that they were more along the lines of inflation-targeting central banks. In 2009, to increase transparency the Federal Reserve started releasing its own forecast of inflation and output to the public and acknowledged that a 2 percent rise in inflation represented the Federal Reserve's definition of price stability.[53]

Later, in January 2012, the Federal Reserve officially adopted an inflation target rate, specifying that an inflation rate of 2 percent was best aligned with the mandates of price stability and full employment.[54] The Fed's announcement of an inflation target was expected to help keep longer-term inflation expectations firmly anchored, which was expected to enhance the Fed's ability to keep stimulating the economy in the wake of 2007–2010 financial crisis. The adoption of an official inflation target finally made the Federal Reserve another inflation-targeting central bank, although as of this writing the Federal Reserve is still using quantitative easing, an unorthodox monetary-policy framework that will be discussed in the next section.

CASE STUDY: Dealing with Challenges: Flexible Inflation Targeting

Despite its popularity and relative success, an inflation-targeting regime is not without challenges. Indeed, two key major challenges of an inflation-targeting regime have already actually happened: (1) the possibility that inflation might come from a *supply shock* (such as an oil shock) rather than a demand shock, and (2) the possibility that *asset-price bubbles* could occur even in a low inflation environment.[55]

Both of these challenges point favorably toward the adoption of what has become known as a *flexible* inflation regime, under which long-term price stability remains supreme but the central bank has the flexibility to deal with different sources of shocks to the economy.[56]

One of the novel approaches that a central bank with flexible inflation targeting might adopt is the Bank of Canada's program that adjusts the time horizon for it to bring inflation within target, so as to minimize the economic and financial volatility that its actions may cause. The Bank of Canada lengthens or shortens the typical two-year time horizon that it needs to bring inflation back to the target depending on the nature and persistence of the risks facing the economy. Specifically, the Bank of Canada is willing to sacrifice inflation performance over the two-year horizon if by doing so it can achieve greater economic, financial, and price stability over the longer run.[57]

Supply Shocks

In an inflation-targeting regime, the central bank is supposed to adjust the policy interest rate to influence aggregate demand in the economy. When a supply shock (such as an oil shock) occurs, economic activity can slow down owing to rising costs of production, yet inflation can also accelerate. If the central bank responds to an oil shock by being too accommodative in its monetary policy stance, then inflation expectations might rise and inflation could accelerate, as happened during the Great Inflation of the1970s. If the central bank simply raises the policy interest rate in order to bring down inflation, however, aggregate demand can weaken, hurting economic activity further.

For the central bank with flexible inflation targeting that is dealing with a supply shock, if the record of transparency, accountability, and credibility is strong (such that inflation expectations are low), then rather than quickly raising the policy interest rate and further aggravating the contraction of output, the central bank might be able to allow for a more gradual convergence of inflation with the target, given that output stabilization might also be important when facing a supply shock.

More formally, it has been suggested that the central bank with flexible inflation-targeting regime might try to minimize the *social loss function* using the equation

$$L_t = (1/2)[(\pi_t - \pi^*)^2 + \lambda x_t^2]$$

where π_t is the actual inflation rate in period t, π^* is the inflation target, x_t is the output gap in period t, and $\lambda > 0$ is the relative weight on output-gap stabilization. Rather than being entirely oblivious to output fluctuation, and given that $\lambda = 0$, inflation-targeting central banks that are not so-called inflation nutters are likely to want to give some weight (sometimes substantial) to λ.[58]

Asset-price bubbles

Even before the global financial crisis in 2007, the possibility existed that asset-price bubbles might occur in the calm environment of low *consumer* price inflation.[59] Usually, inflation-targeting central banks would use one measure or another of consumer price inflation as their inflation target, since consumer price inflation seems to best reflect the cost of living and is more readily understandable. However, the experiences from Japan in the late 1980s and the United States in the middle of the first decade of the twenty-first century suggest that asset-price bubbles can form when consumer price inflation is low.[60] Indeed, low consumer price inflation might allow asset-price bubbles to emerge, since the central bank would be more likely to keep interest rates low, making asset-price speculation easier.[61]

To deal with the possibility of asset-price bubbles, it has been suggested that an inflation-targeting central bank might need to look beyond the traditional 18-to-24-month time horizon when making monetary-policy decisions.[62] Asset-price bubbles that form during periods of low inflation might keep building up beyond the 24-month horizon, only to spectacularly burst later.[63] A notable example of a central bank using a longer horizon is the Reserve Bank of Australia, which—being cognizant of the possibility of asset-price bubbles building up and threatening price stability beyond the usual two-year forecast horizon—adopted an inflation target whose time horizon is "over the [business] cycle."[64]

More recently, central banks (whether inflation-targeting or not) have also started to look at another set of tools called macroprudential measures, to help address specific buildups of asset-price bubbles. For an inflation-targeting central bank, macroprudential measures are tools that can complement the use of the policy interest rate, since they can be applied more specifically to different areas of the economy, unlike the policy interest rate, which normally affects all sectors of the economy.[65]

6.6 UNCONVENTIONAL MONETARY POLICY

Unconventional monetary policy became the policy mode of choice among central banks of four of the major advanced economies—the United States, the euro area, the United Kingdom, and Japan—after these economies experienced a large shock in the form of a financial crisis (the global financial crisis of 2007–2010), and, for Japan, a shock in the early 1990s in the form of bursting Japanese asset-price bubbles.[66] Although the actual policy specifics differ, a common feature of the use of unconventional monetary policy is that the central bank has already pushed the policy interest rate down to zero, or almost zero, but the economy still needs further stimulus lest it fall into a deflationary spiral (or fall further into a deflationary spiral as in the case of Japan).

To complement the zero, or near-zero, interest rate policy that was implemented in response to the global financial crisis, these central banks instituted an unconventional policy response through three sets of tools, including (1) lending to financial institutions, (2) providing liquidity to key credit markets, and (3) purchasing long-term securities.[67] As noted by Ben Bernanke, the chairman of the Federal Reserve who used these tools, one common element that these tools have is that they rely on the central bank's authority to extend credit or to purchase securities.[68]

Given that the first two sets of tools (lending to financial institutions and providing liquidity to key credit markets) are more closely tied to the lender-of-last-resort function and were discontinued once the crisis was past its peak, we can consider the last set of tools (purchase of long-term securities)—which became popularly known as *quantitative easing* and was still being used as of the time of this writing in December 2013, five years after the peak of the crisis—as a form of monetary policy, albeit an unconventional one.

A Stylized Model of Quantitative Easing

After the policy interest rate is near or at 0 percent, to further stimulate the economy the central bank might choose to buy up long-term (or long-maturity, or long-dated) government securities from the private sector, with the aim of (1) *lowering long-term borrowing costs*, since government securities are often used as a benchmark for private sector lending, and (2) *restoring liquidity* to financial institutions and key credit markets so that further lending can be done to induce more economic activity.

Lowering Long-Term Borrowing Costs   Large purchases of long-maturity government securities by the central bank is often known as *quantitative easing*, or QE, since rather than purely adjusting the price of money (in terms of the policy interest rate),

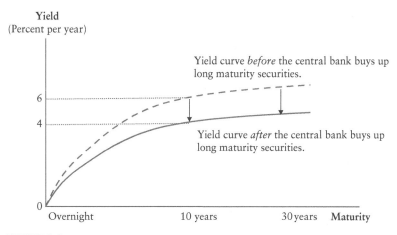

FIGURE 6.3 A Stylized Model of Unconventional Monetary Policy

the central bank is also easing shortages of liquidity in the economy by injecting a quantity of money into the hands of the private sector.

Figure 6.3 illustrates a stylized model of unconventional monetary policy in which the central bank decides to buy up long-maturity government securities from the private sector. In Figure 6.3 the horizontal axis shows the maturity of government securities (measured in time t), while the vertical axis shows the yield (interest) paid to those holding government securities (measured in percent per year). When we plot the yield of government securities at different maturities and draw a line across the plots, we have what is known as the government *yield curve*. (Details of the yield curve will be discussed in Chapter 7.)

Normally the yield curve is upward sloping, that is, yields of short-maturity securities would be lower than yields of those with a longer maturity. For example, the yield of a one-year government bond will normally be lower than the yield of a five-year government bond, the yield of a ten-year government bond will normally be lower than the yield of a thirty-year government bond, and so on. (Reasons for this will be discussed in more detail in Chapter 7.)

In practice, the private sector uses the government yield curve as a benchmark when calculating interest rates for borrowing and lending. Government securities are considered *risk-free* assets, since the government is very unlikely to default on its own securities. When the private sector lends funds among themselves, they often compare the interest from such lending with what they could get from investing in government securities (which is equivalent to lending to the government). Since lending to the government is risk free, while lending to the private sector involves risks, the lender would normally charge interest rates on private loans that are higher than yields of government securities of comparable maturities.

Figure 6.3 shows that when the central bank has already lowered its policy interest rate (a short-term interest rate, possibly an *overnight* interest rate) to zero, or near-zero, then the yield from holding government securities of overnight maturity will also be at or near zero, but the yield of government securities of longer maturity could still be much higher. For example, in Figure 6.3 the ten-year yield could still be at 6 percent per year even though the overnight yield is at 0 percent.

High long-term interest rates, however, could be a serious impediment to economic activity when the economy is already weak. Commercial loans and mortgages are often made based on long-term interest rates rather than short-term interest rates, since these loans are repaid over a long maturity. When the policy interest rate is already at or near 0 percent, to stimulate the economy further the central bank might buy up long-maturity government securities directly from the private sector in order to drive down long-term interest rates, as reflected by the yields on long-term government securities.

The *price* of a government security and the *yield* of that government security are inversely related. As the central bank starts buying up more government securities, the price of the securities rises and thus the yield of the securities falls. In Figure 6.3, as the central bank buys up more 10-year government securities, the 10-year yield falls from 6 percent to 4 percent. With the 10-year yield of government securities falling from 6 percent to 4 percent, the private sector would benchmark their interest rates for 10-year loans among themselves to this lower yield.

Restoring Liquidity   Apart from driving down long-maturity government yields, which are benchmarks for private sector lending and borrowing, the purchase of government securities from the private sector will also put more money in the hands of the private sector, especially banks. During times of crisis, private agents are often reluctant to borrow and lend among themselves. Instead, they might hoard risk-free assets, such as government securities. This leads to shortages of liquidity, which hampers economic activity.

Under quantitative easing, the central bank buys up government securities from the private sector, which amounts to putting money in the hands of the private sector, especially banks, which are often large holders of government securities. With more cash on hand, banks would have a better ability to lend to private agents and spur economic activity.

Unconventional Monetary Policy in the United States

In addition to buying up long-term government securities, which helped bring down the government yield curve and restore liquidity as described in the preceding paragraphs, the U.S. central bank also decided to buy up *private* sector securities, notably mortgage-backed securities, in its response to the global financial crisis.[69]

Credit Easing plus Quantitative Easing   The purchase of private sector securities is known as *credit easing*, to distinguish it from the purchase of government securities (quantitative easing), although both are essentially large-scale asset purchases by the central bank.[70] The purchase of mortgage-backed securities in the United States was intended to directly address problems relating to the bursting of the U.S. housing bubble, which threatened to drag the U.S. economy into a deflationary spiral. Broadly speaking, rising housing prices during the bubble buildup had helped raise household wealth and consumption spending prior to the crisis. The financial sector had helped the fast growth of housing prices by providing mortgage financing to U.S. households, and by packaging those mortgages into tradable securities known as mortgage-backed securities. When the housing bubble finally burst, the financial sector experienced great losses on unsold mortgage-backed securities that were still on their books, and had to cut down on lending. The household sector, on the other hand, faced with falling housing prices and huge mortgage debts, was experiencing a fast decline in wealth, and had to cut down on spending.

Credit Easing and the Help for the Financial Sector By buying up mortgage-backed securities, the U.S. central bank took some of the pressure off the financial sector.[71] The purchase of securities helped prevent the price of the securities held by many financial institutions from further falling and putting the financial sector at even greater losses. Indeed, by doing its job of financial intermediation by purchasing mortgage-backed securities, the U.S. central bank provided liquidity for the financial sector and helped the financial sector to regain its capacity.[72]

Credit Easing and Help for the Housing Market The purchase of mortgage-backed securities also helped alleviate pressures on the household sector. The willingness of the U.S. central bank to buy up mortgage-backed securities indirectly helped slow the fall in housing prices. The purchase of mortgage-backed securities helped prevent the price of these securities from spiraling downward. With the price of these securities stabilized and money being put back into lenders' hands, lenders were able to finance new housing purchases and thus help slow the fall in housing demand and prices, as well as household wealth.

Credit and Quantitative Easing and Help for the Labor Market Although initially the focus of credit easing and quantitative easing was primarily to ease tension in the financial sector and the housing market, as financial markets and the housing market stabilized, the Federal Reserve deemed it appropriate to use both credit easing and quantitative easing as tools to help alleviate pressures in the labor market. In September 2012, for example, the Federal Reserve announced that it would buy an additional $40 billion a month in mortgage securities and that it would reinvest principal payments of the mortgage securities it held to help put downward pressure on long-term interest rates and foster economic growth in order to help to "generate sustained improvements in labor market conditions."[73]

CASE STUDY: Dealing with the European Sovereign Debt Crisis: Not Yet a QE in 2013

In the euro area, although the ECB also engaged in lending to financial institutions and providing liquidity to key credit markets, it initially did not buy up long-term government securities in response to the global financial crisis of 2007–2010, in contrast to the Federal Reserve and the Bank of England.[74] By the early 2010s, however, as economic activity in the euro area started to slow down in wake of the global financial crisis, there were fears that governments of a number of smaller, uncompetitive euro area countries that had high levels of public debt might have troubles repaying that debt.

With the debt repayment ability of these governments in doubt, securities issued by these governments started to lose in value. International investors started demanding higher yields for holding these securities, to compensate for the risk that these governments might default on these supposedly risk-free securities. The higher yields demanded by the investors placed an additional burden on these governments to find money to pay for the higher yields demanded. The situation threatened to become self-fulfilling, since the higher yields demanded by investors would further cripple the ability of governments to repay their debt and actually push the governments into default.

Since a default by a government of a euro area member country would raise doubt on credibility of the euro as a currency and the euro area as a monetary union, the ECB announced that it was willing to buy up securities issued by governments of the troubled euro area countries. The purchase would help allay investor fears and also help bring down yields of securities issued by the troubled governments, enabling the governments in question to sort out their finances in the meantime. Also, in offering to buy up these securities, the ECB would in effect be letting the banking sector offload their vast holdings of troubled government securities from their books, limiting the chance that the sovereign debt crisis would also transform into a banking crisis.

In September 2012 Mario Draghi, the new leader of the ECB, proposed a plan to buy an unlimited amount of government securities of the member countries as a measure to stem the European sovereign debt crisis.[75] The ECB's purchase of government securities, however, would not be exactly the quantitative easing of the type conducted by the Federal Reserve or the Bank of England. Specifically, the ECB would *sterilize* its purchases of the government securities from the private sector, meaning that it would also sell its own securities to the markets to drain out the extra money it paid for the bond purchases.[76] Accordingly, government securities of the troubled economies would be replaced by ECB securities, and there would be no net effect on the quantity of money from the operation.

Challenges to Unconventional Monetary Policy

While unconventional monetary policy might have helped prevent the global economy from falling into a deflationary spiral and economic chaos, there has been criticism about the continued use of such a policy.

First, at a fundamental level, large, sustained purchases of government securities by central banks threaten to move central banks into the realm of fiscal policy. The purchase of government securities, even from the private sector, had a similar effect to that of central bank funding of government deficits. A sustained pursuit of quantitative easing could make it look like the central banks were printing money to finance government spending, which would jeopardize the central bank's credibility and political independence.

Second, a sustained pursuit of quantitative easing could end up encouraging asset-price speculation. This was partly reflected in the large run-ups in equity prices in advanced economies, even at a time that their general economic activity remained weak. The quantitative easing policy helped put liquidity into the system, but as the economies were still in the process of *deleveraging* (i.e., reducing debt overhangs from the crisis), much of the liquidity was channeled into asset markets (particularly the equity markets, but also emerging-market economies) to chase higher returns, rather than into real economic activity in the crisis-hit economies.

Third, timing the exit from quantitative easing is another challenge for central banks. If inflation starts to kick in when quantitative easing is still being used, it could make the central banks' commitment to price stability seem less credible. As such, when their economies start to recover and inflation starts to pick up, the central banks will need to sell the securities and absorb liquidity from the economy fast enough, while at the same time not creating panic in the financial markets. The timing of the exit could be quite a challenge, as demonstrated in mid-2013 when the Federal Reserve's mere announcement of the possibility of a tapering of quantitative easing policy caused so much disruption in global financial markets that the Federal Reserve had to reassure investors that the tapering would be gradual.

Fourth, the purchase of private sector securities (such as mortgage-backed securities) has been criticized on the grounds that it is "picking winners" and is "distortionary," since the central bank is effectively helping those institutions that held assets that were falling in value, while other economic sectors were left out, with no assistance from the authorities.

Despite these criticisms and challenges, however, it can be argued that the recent global financial crisis was so grave that the use of unconventional monetary policy by the central banks might have been warranted. In using unconventional monetary policy, however, central banks need to carefully assure the public that they are not becoming subordinate to their governments. Furthermore, central banks will need to be very vigilant about threats of inflation once their economies have recovered.

SUMMARY

Theoretical foundations of monetary policy conduct discussed in Chapter 5 suggested that, for monetary policy to be credible, a monetary policy rule (also called a monetary policy regime) should be adopted by the central bank.

The key monetary policy regimes that modern central banks have adopted are (1) exchange rate targeting, (2) money supply growth targeting, (3) the risk management approach, (4) inflation targeting, and (5) unconventional monetary policy.

Under an exchange rate targeting regime, the central bank aims to keep the exchange rate within the announced target. In such a regime, the exchange rate is often pegged to the currency of a large country that has a good record of monetary stability.

Under a money supply growth targeting regime, the central bank aims to keep money supply growth at a target that is consistent with nominal income growth in the economy.

Under the risk management approach, adopted by the Federal Reserve from the mid-1980s to the middle of the first decade of the twenty-first century, the central bank adjusts the policy interest rate to preempt risks that might threaten monetary and economic stability.

Under an inflation-targeting regime, the central bank adjusts the policy interest rate to keep inflation within its announced target over a prespecified time horizon. The central bank is held accountable if inflation misses the target.

Unconventional monetary policy was adopted by various central banks of advanced economies to deal with the aftermath of the 2007–2010 global financial crisis, after the policy interest rate had been reduced to or near 0 percent. At the core, such policy involves large-scale purchases of long-term securities in order to bring down long-term interest rates and ease money and credit conditions.

KEY TERMS

basket of currencies	money supply growth targeting
credit easing	quantitative easing
exchange rate targeting	risk management approach
flexible inflation targeting	the Taylor rule
Goodhart's law	unconventional monetary
inflation targeting	policy

QUESTIONS

1. What is a monetary policy regime, and why is it important?
2. How can a central bank with an exchange rate targeting regime aim to achieve price stability?
3. What is a currency board?
4. If there are large inflows of capital, what is likely to happen to the country's exchange rate? Why?
5. If there are large inflows of capital, conceptually how can the central bank under an exchange rate targeting regime keep the exchange rate within its announced target?
6. If a large number of importers need large amounts of foreign currencies to pay for their import purchases at the same time, what would happen to the exchange rate?
7. How can the central bank keep the exchange rate at the announced target if a large number of importers need large amounts of foreign currencies to pay for their import purchases at the same time?
8. What might be the reason to say that those countries that have an exchange rate targeting regime do not have monetary policy independence?
9. Why is it impossible for a central bank to achieve an exchange rate target, allow free flows of capital, and maintain monetary policy independence simultaneously in the long run?
10. What is the underlying theoretical underpinning of money supply growth targeting?
11. What are the pros of adopting money supply growth targeting as the monetary policy regime?
12. Why did the United States and United Kingdom abandon money supply growth targeting in the mid-1980s even though money supply growth targeting helped manage inflation expectations downward in the early 1980s?
13. What does Goodhart's law state and how does it apply to the practice of monetary policy?
14. In the *risk management approach* practice of monetary policy in the United States during Alan Greenspan's era, what were examples of key variables that the Federal Reserve took into consideration when making monetary-policy decisions?
15. What are the pros of the risk management approach to monetary policy?
16. What are the cons of the risk management approach to monetary policy?
17. What are the features of and rationale for inflation targeting?
18. Under inflation targeting, how do transparency, accountability, and credibility of the central bank come into play?
19. What is the key monetary policy instrument that a central bank with an inflation-targeting regime normally uses to achieve its inflation target? How can the central bank use that instrument to maintain monetary stability, if there seems to be a risk that projected inflation might overshoot its target?
20. Should an inflation-targeting central bank raise its policy interest rate if inflationary pressures come from a supply shock (e.g., an oil shock) as opposed to a demand shock?

21. Given that inflation is likely to remain low, how could an asset-price bubble be a challenge for the central bank in the conduct of monetary policy under an inflation-targeting regime?
22. What are the pros of inflation targeting?
23. What are the cons of inflation targeting?
24. How might a central bank deal with the cons of inflation targeting?
25. What are the three key elements of the policy that the Federal Reserve used to deal with the U.S. subprime crisis?
26. What might be immediate goals of quantitative easing programs?
27. In terms of their influences on the yield curve, how might quantitative easing differ from conventional monetary policy?
28. How could quantitative easing help the housing market and the labor market in the United States?
29. What are the pros of quantitative easing programs?
30. What are the cons of quantitative easing programs?

CHAPTER 7

Monetary Policy Implementation

Financial Market Operations

Learning Objectives

1. Distinguish between the financial sector and the real sector.
2. Define money market.
3. Describe how central banks can influence conditions and interest rates in the money market.
4. Explain how changes in money market interest rates can affect long-term interest rates.

Monetary policy implementation refers to ways in which the central bank could act to influence money conditions in the economy in order to achieve its mandate, whether the mandate is monetary stability, financial stability, or employment (the latter applies particularly to the case of the United States). In the previous chapter, we have discussed monetary policy rules, or monetary policy regimes, which modern central banks might choose to adopt. The regime that the central bank has chosen to adopt would dictate how the central bank might implement its monetary policy decisions in the pursuit of its mandate.

In practice, modern monetary policy is often conducted through operations in the financial markets.[1] Such operations often involve transactions with financial institutions, which will affect money conditions before affecting real economic activity such as consumption, investment, and net exports, which are components of aggregate demand. Generally speaking, changes in aggregate demand will then affect the output gap and inflation. In practice, however, changes in expectations following an announcement of the central bank's monetary policy decision might also have a prompt impact in financial markets even before the central bank embarks on any financial market operations, as market players adjust their portfolios in response to the monetary policy decision. Economic agents, meanwhile, might also adjust their economic behavior in line with changes in their expectations following the announcement of the central bank's monetary policy decisions.[2]

Figure 7.1 illustrates the link between monetary policy, the financial sector, the real sector, expectations, and inflation.

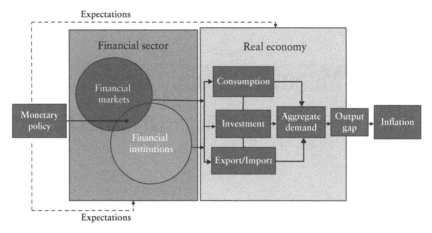

FIGURE 7.1   The Financial Sector and the Role of Expectations
The financial sector is the initial contact point of monetary policy implementation, although expectations can also have an immediate impact.

In this chapter, we will look at how monetary policy could affect the *financial sector*, which primarily is composed of financial markets and financial institutions. In particular, we will focus on central bank operations in the financial markets by looking at the nature of financial markets and the tools that the central bank can use to influence interest rates in those markets. In Chapter 8 we will look at how the effects of monetary policy on interest rates in the financial markets work their way through the *real economy* (the part of the economy concerned with producing goods and services, also termed the *real sector*) via various channels of transmission mechanisms to affect economic activity and inflation.

7.1 CENTRAL BANK OPERATIONS IN THE FINANCIAL MARKET: AN OVERVIEW

The first link between the central bank's monetary policy action and real economic activity is the financial markets. The definition of the term *financial market*, however, is often quite loose. Broadly speaking, a financial market is one in which those in need of funds and those with excess funds come to transact with each other. The transaction could be simple borrowing and lending (with or without collateral), or sales and purchases of securities or currencies. As such, the term financial market actually encompasses many markets, which are distinguished by the nature of underlying transactions.

Table 7.1 lists a number of key financial markets in which central banks often conduct their monetary policy operations.

Under normal circumstances, central banks conduct their monetary policy operations through transactions in the *money market*, the *foreign exchange market*, the *government securities (bond) market*. The preferred market(s) for operations depends on the monetary policy regime, as well as surrounding circumstances. For many central banks, the *money market*, which is the market for short-term (normally

TABLE 7.1   Key Financial Markets in Which Central Banks Conduct Their Monetary Policy Operations

Type of Financial Market	Transactions Handled	Central Bank Operations or Involvement
Money market	Short-term (less than one year) liquidity funding	Operations in the money market are done to manage the policy interest rate, which is a key reference rate for other short-term interest rates.
Foreign exchange market	Foreign exchange funding	Foreign exchange interventions are done to smooth out excess exchange rate volatility, or to keep the exchange rate within target.
Government securities market	Government funding	Transactions in the (secondary) government securities market are done to inject or absorb liquidity in the longer term.
Credit market	Corporate funding, housing market funding	Part of unconventional monetary policy used in the United States, under which the central bank targets specific liquidity shortages in the system.

less than one year) funding, is often the preferred venue for the conduct of monetary policy operations. Another main venue for monetary policy operations, especially for those central banks that are concerned with the exchange rate, is the *foreign exchange market*, which generally refers to the market for foreign exchange funding. The *government bond market*, on the other hand, is an important venue for central banks to occasionally influence longer-term interest rates.[3]

Additionally, during times of financial crisis, the central bank might extend its operations and carry out transactions in nontraditional markets such as the *credit market*.[4] The credit market is a market for debt securities and includes securities issued by banks, nonbank financial institutions, and corporations outside the financial industry. As discussed in Chapter 6, in response to the global financial crisis, the U.S. central bank decided to conduct unconventional monetary policy by buying up mortgage-backed securities and commercial paper from players in the financial market. The operations were deemed unconventional since in normal times central banks would certainly not be directly involved in corporate funding.*

It must be noted that, in a world where financial markets are closely connected, no matter what particular market the central bank chooses to operate in, the effects

---

*Another example of crisis operations would be operations of the central bank in the equity market. In the midst of the Asian financial crisis in the late 1990s, the Hong Kong Monetary Authority decided to directly purchase vast amounts of shares in the Hong Kong stock market in order to fend off foreign speculators who were trying to break its exchange rate target through short selling on the Hong Kong stock market. Such operations, however, have rarely been done even during stressful times, since they could be easily misinterpreted as central bank funding of the corporate sector.

of its operations are likely to spill out to all other markets. The magnitude of the effects in other markets, however, could vary, depending on market infrastructure as well as surrounding circumstances. By tightening conditions in the money market, for example, commercial banks would face higher short-term funding costs, which they might pass on to their operations in other markets, such as the foreign exchange market, that they themselves also operate in.

In practice, even a mere *announcement* of monetary policy operations in one market could affect conditions in other markets through the expectations effect. Players in other markets would anticipate the ultimate effects of such operations, and accordingly adjust their behavior even before the central bank actually backs up its announcement with actions. Indeed, in a world of fast information, it can be more profitable for market players to act in advance of a monetary policy announcement, such that the *anticipation* of a future policy announcement itself could drive the players' actions and actually move markets before the central bank actually does anything.

The Money Market

The money market is the market in which participants borrow or lend funds for the short term, which normally means less than one year.[5] Participants in the money market often consist of institutions that need to borrow or lend funds among themselves over the short term. At the core of the money market is interbank lending, where commercial banks lend and borrow among themselves. Also involved in the money market are nonbank financial companies and corporations outside the financial sector that come in to tap short-term funds by issuing commercial paper.[6] The government could also come in and tap short-term funding needs by issuing Treasury bills (government securities with less than one year maturity).

When the central bank conducts operations in the money market, it is effectively trying to influence the *tightness* or *looseness* of funding (i.e., borrowing and lending) conditions in the money market. By tightening lending conditions in the money market, liquidity, or availability of funds, for lending becomes scarcer. Once lending conditions in the money market become tight (as often reflected by rising money market interest rates), borrowers and lenders of funds in the money market factor in the higher opportunity costs of short-term funding into their other operations.

Tightness in short-term funding conditions could also lead to tightness in other markets and in long-term funding conditions, since borrowers could scramble to seek cheaper funding elsewhere, if possible. In the same spirit, by loosening short-term funding conditions in the money market, the central bank could also indirectly loosen funding conditions in other markets and in long-term funding.

In practice, the central bank is just another participant in the money market, but with its special status as the ultimate money creator and the setter of regulations for the banking system, the central bank has particular influences over borrowing and lending conditions in the money market. To understand how the central bank could influence the money market, it is helpful to first understand the interaction between supply and demand for funds in the money market.

Demand for Funds in the Money Market   Normally commercial banks want to hold the minimum amount of cash possible, since cash does not yield any interest, unlike loans. In practice, however, banks would not lend out all the deposits that they took in, owing to their need to hold *reserves* to meet (1) *reserve requirements*, whereby the central bank requires commercial banks to set aside a certain percentage of the deposits they took in from depositors as reserves to be held in accounts at the central bank, and (2) *contractual clearing balances*, or *settlement balances*, whereby commercial banks might keep funds in their accounts at the central bank to clear or settle transactions that are done through the central bank's payments system.[7]

Commercial banks would normally want to minimize their holdings in settlement balances and *excess reserves* (the amount of reserves over and above those required by reserve requirements or settlement balances), since money deposited at the central bank might not be paid interest, or be paid at a rate lower than the prevailing market rates.[8] If unexpected large settlement needs arise, then banks might be forced to borrow funds from the central bank at a penalty rate, or go borrow in the money market. Such a need to borrow funds constitutes a large portion of the demand for funds in the money market.[9]

Apart from banks' need for short-term funds, demand for funds in the money market could also come from nonbank private players, such as nonbank financial institutions, large corporations, and the government. These nonbank private players might have short-term funding needs, possibly for short-term financing of their investments or as working capital (to pay suppliers, or even employee payrolls). To fund their short-term financing needs, these players could issue commercial paper to tap short-term funds. Government, on the other hand, might issue government bills to tap short-term funds to finance their own short-term obligations.

Supply of Funds in the Money Market If banks find that they have been holding more reserves than would be needed to meet their reserve requirements and settlement obligations, they would normally want to lend out at least part of their excess funds in order to earn interest. The desire to lend out funds short-term would constitute the supply of funds in the money market. In practice, in places where financial markets are relatively developed, nonbank players (e.g., money market mutual funds) have also become increasingly important suppliers of funds in the money market.[10] Investors put their money into money market mutual funds, and the funds then seek to invest the money by putting it into money market securities such as commercial paper or government bills. The money invested by these mutual funds to fund commercial paper or government bills also constitute short-term lending in the money market.[11]

Theoretical Equilibrium in the Money Market In theory, at any given time, some of the players in the money market would be short of funds and need to borrow, while others would have excess funds that they want to lend out. Equilibrium in the money market would be achieved when the amount players wish to borrow matches the amount other players wish to lend. Interest rates, which are the prices of funds, help *clear* the market. If there is a large demand for funds relative to supply, interest rates would likely rise. In contrast, if there is a small demand for funds relative to supply, then interest rates would fall. In a case in which there is an unexpected demand shock such that there is net shortage of funds in the system, then interest rates could really spike up.

If the money market as a whole is extremely short of funds, however, market participants might be unable to lend among themselves and the central bank might need to step in and provide funding to market participants. In other words, sometimes movements in interest rates might be unable to clear the money market *effectively*, and the central bank, being the regulator, might need to step in and lead the market into equilibrium.

Central Bank's Influences in the Money Market

Without the central bank's presence, conditions in the money market could be quite volatile, as demand and supply of funds could be subjected to numerous external forces. The central bank's presence in the money market helps facilitate smooth functioning of the money market, not the least through its funding provision when there is a net shortage of funds in the system.

Influencing Reserve Balances   In practice, as a part of its normal monetary policy implementation, the central bank routinely uses its special position in the money market to influence money market conditions, specifically through its ability to meet demand for *reserve balances* held at the central bank by commercial banks to meet their reserve requirements or settlement obligations (as previously discussed).[12]

In the United States, when the Federal Reserve wants to ease conditions in the money market it can announce a lower target rate for the *federal funds rate*, which is the interest rate commercial banks charge one another when lending reserve balances (the funds held by commercial banks in accounts at the Federal Reserve). If there is a net shortage of reserve balances, however, commercial banks might be unwilling or unable to lend to each other at or near a rate that is consistent with this new (lower) target rate announced by the Federal Reserve. To make sure that commercial banks could and would lend at each other at the lower announced federal funds rate target rate, the Federal Reserve might back up its announcement by providing liquidity to help reduce the net shortage of reserve balances, thus enabling the banks to lend funds to each other at or near the announced federal funds target rate.[13]

Tools for Monetary Implementation   In general, we can classify tools that the central bank can use to influence conditions in the money market into four groups.

First, the central bank can use the level of the *policy interest rate* as a signal to indicate the tightness or looseness of money market conditions that it deems to be appropriate for the general economy. Second, the central bank could use *open market operations*, that is, direct transactions with money market participants to actually influence liquidity conditions in the money market. Third, the central bank can set up lending and deposit facilities (*standing facilities*) for money market participants to access, in order to help keep money market interest rates consistent with the policy interest rate without too much reliance on open market operations. Fourth, the central bank could use *reserve requirements* to directly regulate commercial banks' liquidity needs, and thus money market conditions.[14]

When used together, the first three of the channels listed above (i.e., the policy interest rate, open market operations, and standing facilities) constitute what is known as the *interest rate corridor*, which has become increasingly popular as a framework for central banks to guide money market conditions, especially in an environment in which financial markets have become liberalized and interest rates are allowed to move relatively freely. The fourth channel (reserve requirements) remains useful for central banks to regulate money market conditions, especially in cases in which financial markets have yet to be liberalized.[15]

Policy Interest Rate   The policy interest rate refers to a short term interest rate that the central bank uses to indicate its monetary policy stance. By announcing its intention to keep the policy interest rate at a particular level, the central bank can induce participants in the money market to borrow and lend among themselves at rates that are not too far off from the policy interest rate. Normally, market participants are encouraged to borrow and lend among themselves first before turning to the central bank. Competition among market participants would normally ensure that they borrow and lend among themselves at rates that are not too extreme.[16] Yet, if it seems that shortages or surpluses of funds would not be cleared easily at rates of interest near the policy interest rate, then the central bank can always step in and inject or drain out funds from market participants directly, through open market operations. With the knowledge that the central bank can always step in to ensure that rates do not go much out of line with the policy interest rate, market participants would normally borrow and lend near or at the policy rate anyhow. This, of course, is unless there is a large systemic shortage or surplus of funds that drives market participants to borrow and lend at rates far removed from the policy rate.[17]

Open Market Operations   When conducting open market operations, central bank injects or absorbs funds from the money market at the margin, so as to prevent excessive net shortages or surpluses of funds from driving a large wedge between prevailing interest rates and the policy rate.[18] Open market operations normally means purchasing and selling of securities (normally government securities and central bank bills) to market participants. With a purchase of securities, the central bank is effectively injecting funds into the system, since the central bank has to pay for those securities with money. With a sale of securities, in contrast, the central bank is effectively draining funds out of the system, as market participants who buy the securities have to pay the central bank with money.[19]

CONCEPT: VARIOUS TYPES OF OPEN MARKET OPERATIONS

Open market operations can be broadly separated into two types, according to the nature of the transaction.

Outright Transactions

The first type of transaction is the buying or selling of securities whose rights are *permanently* transferred to the buyer. In such a case, the securities are said to be bought or sold *outright*.[20]

Figure 7.2a illustrates a case in which the central bank tightens money market conditions by draining out liquidity through an outright purchase of securities from a financial institution, one of its counterparties in the money market.

In contrast, Figure 7.2b illustrates a case in which the central bank eases money market conditions by injecting liquidity through the sale of securities to a financial institution, one of its counterparties in the money market.

(Continued)

(*Continued*)

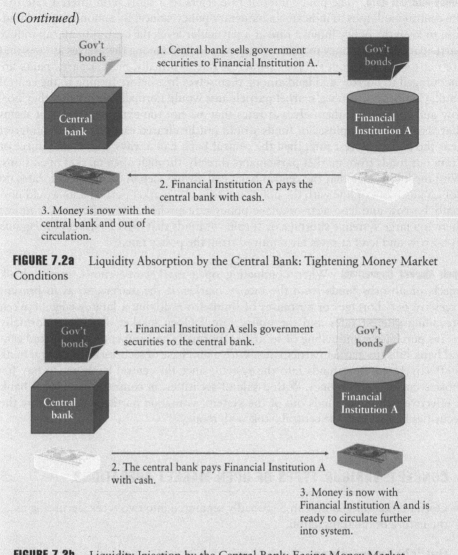

1. Central bank sells government securities to Financial Institution A.

2. Financial Institution A pays the central bank with cash.

3. Money is now with the central bank and out of circulation.

FIGURE 7.2a   Liquidity Absorption by the Central Bank: Tightening Money Market Conditions

1. Financial Institution A sells government securities to the central bank.

2. The central bank pays Financial Institution A with cash.

3. Money is now with Financial Institution A and is ready to circulate further into system.

FIGURE 7.2b   Liquidity Injection by the Central Bank: Easing Money Market Conditions

Repo and Reverse-Repo Transactions

The other main type of open market operations is the buying or selling of securities whose rights are only *temporarily* transferred to the buyer. An example of this type of transaction is a *repurchase agreement* or a *repo*, whereby the seller of securities would have to buy those securities back in a future date and at a specified price. In this case, of course, funds are drained out of the system only temporarily. If the central bank wants to inject funds into the system temporarily, on the other hand, it could do a *reverse-repo*. In this case, the central bank buys securities from a market participant with an agreement to sell back those securities to the market participant at a future date and at a specified price. In a reverse-repo, the central bank temporarily injects funds into the system.

Figures 7.3a illustrates a case in which the central bank enters into a repo transaction in order to temporarily tighten money market conditions.

Figures 7.3b illustrates a case in which the central bank enters into a reverse-repo transaction in order to temporarily ease money market conditions.

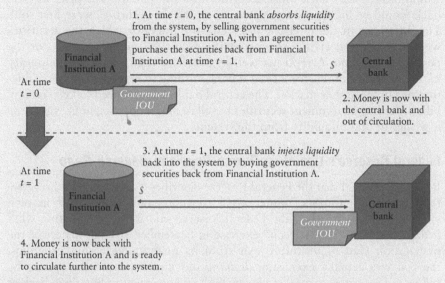

FIGURE 7.3a   Repurchase Agreement by the Central Bank: Temporarily Absorbing Liquidity

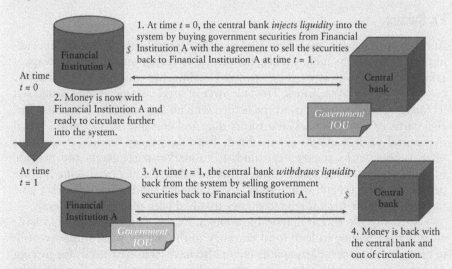

FIGURE 7.3b   Reverse Repurchase Agreement by the Central Bank: Temporarily Injecting Liquidity

(*Continued*)

(*Continued*)

A repo-type transaction is often popular in the money market, since the same securities could be used many times over. A repo could also be thought of as a loan of funds, whereby securities are used as collateral. The seller of securities would get money for her securities, with an agreement that she would have to buy back those securities in a future date. The price at buy-back would be higher than the price at which the securities were first sold. The difference in the buyback price and the price for which the securities were first sold reflects the interest charged on the lending of funds for the period of the repo. A repo (as well as a reverse-repo), with its temporary nature, is more suitable for a central bank wishing to manage temporary fluctuations in the money market. The central bank does not need to keep issuing bills or finding government securities to sell to market participants every time it wishes to drain liquidity from the system.

Federal Reserve's Use of the Terms *Repo* and *Reverse-Repo*

It should be noted that the Federal Reserve describes its own repo and reverse-repo operations from its counterparty's viewpoint rather than from its own viewpoint. As such, when the Federal Reserve said it was conducting what it described as a "reverse-repo" exercise in September 2013 as a part of the preparation plan of its future exit from its quantitative easing programs, the Fed was actually exercising *draining out* liquidity from the system by *selling* out securities to market players with an agreement to buy them back at a specified future period at a specified price.

FX Swaps

Another open market operations tool that the central bank can use in influencing conditions in the money market is foreign exchange swaps, or FX swaps.[21] Like a repo, an FX swap can be considered lending, but with foreign currency as collateral instead of securities. The borrower of local currency funds would sell its foreign currency holdings to the lender, with an agreement to buy those foreign currency holdings back at a future date and at a prespecified price. When the central bank wants to absorb funds from the money market, it can thus offer to borrow (local currency) funds from market participants and provide foreign currency as collateral on those borrowed funds. In a prespecified future period, the central bank would repay local currency funds back to market participants and take back foreign currency that had been placed as collateral.

Normally, if terms are favorable enough, market participants would have already been willing to lend local currency to the central bank this way. Still, in many cases, market participants might also have legitimate needs for foreign exchange funds, whether for their own or their customers' use. For example, corporate customers of money market participants might need to pay for imports or to repay their foreign currency debt. With the central bank willing to borrow local currency and provide foreign currency as collateral, money market participants would have another way to access foreign currencies.

On the other hand, the central bank could inject local currency funds into the money market by lending out local currency funds to market participants and take in foreign currency as collateral. In this case, market participants might be short of local currency but have a surplus of foreign currencies. This might be the case, for example, when exporters sell their export receipts to money market participants for local currency funds.

Standing Facilities Broadly speaking, standing facilities refer to facilities at which money market participants can come to borrow and lend funds directly with the central bank. While the central bank can do open market operations to drain or inject funds into the money market, these days a modern central bank often aims not to intervene in the market too often or too much. The central bank would rather have money market participants efficiently manage their own funding needs and let market forces allocate funds among the participants. In such a case, the central bank can set up standing facilities as passive tools that help smooth out volatility in money market interest rates.

When market participants are in need of short-term funds and they cannot find a lender among themselves, the participants can borrow directly from the central bank's *lending* facility. When market participants have excess funds that they cannot lend out among themselves, they can put the funds into the central bank's *deposit* facility. Of course, the central bank prefers that the interest rates money market participants charge among themselves remain in line with the announced level of policy interest rate, since the policy rate signals the central bank's monetary policy stance.[22]

Figure 7.4 provides a stylized model of how the central bank can use standing facilities to help regulate money market conditions, especially when some financial institutions might be short of funds while others have excess funds.

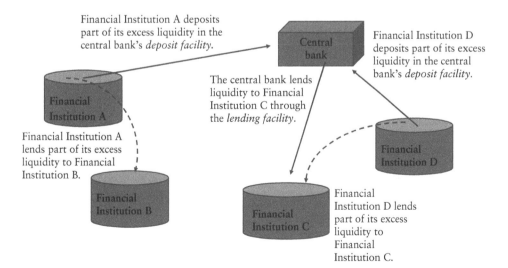

FIGURE 7.4 Use of Central Bank's Standing Facilities to Help Manage Liquidity in the Money Market

CONCEPT: THE INTEREST RATE CORRIDOR

In practice, market movements can indeed be very volatile, and net shortages or surpluses in the market can push market participants to borrow and lend among themselves at rates far different from the level of the policy interest rate. The use of *standing facilities* along with the *policy interest rate* and *open market operations* constitutes the so-called *interest rate corridor*, whereby borrowing and lending in the money market are kept within the corridor and consistent with the policy interest rate.

Lately, many central banks in advanced and emerging-market economies have decided to use an interest rate corridor system, with standing facilities that help put a ceiling and a floor on how far the rates that market participants charge among themselves can diverge from the policy interest rate. Central banks that have adopted an interest rate corridor system include the Federal Reserve, the Bank of England, the ECB, the Reserve Bank of Australia, the Reserve Bank of New Zealand, the Bank of Korea, the Bank Negara Malaysia, the Bangko Sentral ng Pilipinas, and the Bank of Thailand, among others.[23]

Figure 7.5 provides a stylized illustration of interest rate corridor mechanics.

In Figure 7.5 we can see that the interest rate that the central bank charges for its lending through the lending facility would be noticeably higher than the policy interest rate, to encourage market participants to first find lenders among themselves before turning to the central bank's lending facility. The rate charged at the central bank's lending facility, however, will not be significantly higher than the policy interest rate (usually it is the policy interest rate plus half a percentage point). This is to encourage market participants to charge each

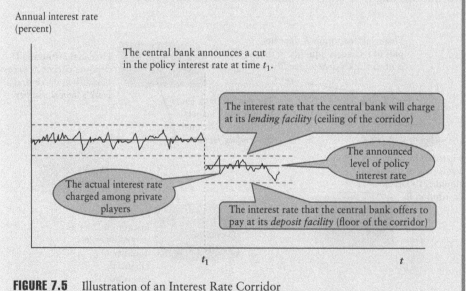

FIGURE 7.5   Illustration of an Interest Rate Corridor

other rates not much higher than the policy rate—otherwise, market participants can always turn to the central bank's lending facility. The interest rate charged at the central bank's lending facility is thus effectively the ceiling for interest rates charged by money market participants when lending and borrowing among themselves.

In contrast, when money market participants have excess short-term funds that they cannot lend among themselves, they can deposit those funds at the central bank's deposit facility. The interest rate given at the central bank's deposit facility will be noticeably lower than the policy interest rate, in order to encourage market participants to first find borrowers of funds among themselves before turning to the central bank's deposit facility. The interest rate paid at the central bank's deposit facility is unlikely to be significantly lower than the policy interest rate, however (usually the policy rate minus half a percentage point). The interest rate paid at the central bank's deposit facility is thus effectively a floor on rates in the money market.

Reserve Requirements   Theoretically, reserve requirements can be another tool that the central bank can use to influence conditions in the money market. When the central bank raises reserve requirements, banks that are money market participants have to reserve more cash per dollar they take in as deposits. With a hike in reserve requirements, conditions in the money market would be tighter since money market participants would have to designate more funds as reserves, and thus would be able to lend out less. Those who were initially short of funds would have to scramble harder to find funds to meet the stricter requirements.

In practice, however, reserve requirements are *not* very popular as an *active* tool to influence the money market in a system in which the financial market has been liberalized and interest rates are allowed to float.[24] In such a system, the central bank often prefers to have market forces allocate funds in the money market and would be more likely to use a policy interest rate to signal its monetary stance. Frequent changes in reserve requirements can have profound effects on bank credit extension.[25] Theoretically, in the case of a bank that had been efficiently lending out its deposits such that its reserves are already at the existing requirement, a hike in reserve requirements might prompt the bank to call in its callable loans from firms and households in order to meet the stricter reserve requirements. Firms and households who are denied loans or having their loans called in would have a very hard time adjusting.

In contrast, had the policy rate been used as the policy tool, a hike in the policy interest rate would only have a gradual effect on firms and households. As money market conditions are tightened, the bank might raise interest rates on its new loans or on its floating rate loans rather than calling in loans that have already been extended to meet its own reserve requirements. In such a case, firms and households would have time to adjust their behavior accordingly, which would be less traumatic than having their loans called in.

7.2 TRANSMISSION OF MONEY MARKET INTEREST RATES TO OTHER INTEREST RATES IN THE ECONOMY

The earlier discussion suggested how central banks can influence conditions in the money market and thus money market interest rates. For changes in money market conditions to affect real economic activity and price levels, however, conditions and interest rates in other segments of the financial market must first also respond to changes in money market conditions and money market interest rates. For the central bank's conduct of monetary policy to affect the real economy, interest rates charged on corporate loans, personal loans, and mortgages (which are long-term interest rates, or *long rates*), as well as deposit rates and expectations of players in the economy, must first change.

The Yield Curve

In practice, how changes in money market conditions might affect long-term interest rates are partly reflected by movements in the government bond *yield curve*. A government bond yield curve plots yields (or interest rates) on different maturities of government securities. Figure 7.6 illustrates a government bond yield curve. The vertical axis represents the yield on government securities in percentage per year. The horizontal axis represents maturity, or the time that government securities have left before they actually become due (have matured). Yields on government securities with the shortest maturities would be nearest to the vertical axis.

In Figure 7.6, the short maturity end of the yield curve at zero is overnight maturity. This represents the yield of government securities that are maturing overnight. If the policy interest rate is an overnight interest rate, then the yield of government securities maturing overnight must be equal or very close to the level of the policy interest rate. Otherwise, there could be *arbitrage* opportunities, whereby economic agents could make riskless profits by borrowing funds from a lower rate source and lending those funds at a higher rate.

For example, if the overnight yield of government securities is much higher than the policy interest rate, then market participants could borrow funds from the money market for overnight at, or very near, the policy interest rate, and invest the borrowed funds into government securities that are also maturing overnight, earning riskless profits. The opportunity to earn riskless profits will draw a large number of participants into such an activity, such that the yield will converge to the policy interest rate. In a financial market that is efficient, market forces will keep the yield of government securities at very short maturity very close to the policy interest rate.*

---

*In contrast, had the yield for overnight government securities been *much lower* than the policy interest rate, investors would dump the securities and lend overnight funds in the money market in order to earn interest very near or at the policy interest rate. The dumping of overnight securities will have the effect of pushing the price of the securities down (and the yield up). Again, in a reasonably efficient market, market forces will drive the overnight yield very close to the policy interest rate, if the policy interest rate is an overnight rate.

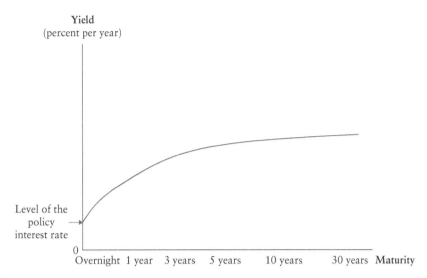

FIGURE 7.6 Illustration of a Government Bond Yield Curve

Possible Shapes of the Yield Curve In theory, although the very short end of the yield curve will be anchored by the policy interest rate, the yield curve can take any shape. Normally there are three general shapes used to describe yield curves, namely upward-sloping (normal), flat, and downward-sloping (inverted). Figure 7.7 illustrates what a normal, a flat, an inverted, and a humped yield curve might look like.

An upward sloping (normal) yield curve means that the short-term yields are lower than the longer-term yields. A flat yield curve means that the yields are equal, or almost equal, at every maturity (debt securities of shorter maturities will have lower yields than longer-term debt securities). A downward sloping (inverted) yield curve means that the short-term yields are higher than the longer-term yields (debt securities of shorter maturities will have higher yields than longer-term debt securities). An upward-then-downward (humped) yield curve means that yields of medium-term maturities are higher than those with shorter or longer maturities.

The Government Bond Yield Curve as a Benchmark for Setting Other Interest Rates Banks and other financial institutions often use the government bond yield curve as a benchmark when they set interest rates on loans and deposits. Interest rates on loans and deposits at short maturities are benchmarked against the yields of government securities with short maturities (i.e., the *short end* of the government bond yield curve). Interest rates on loans and deposits at longer maturities are benchmarked against the yields of government securities with long maturities (i.e., the *long end* of the government bond yield curve).

The reason the government bond yield curve is normally used as a benchmark is that yields on government bonds represent *risk-free* interest rates. Lending to the government is normally assumed to be risk free, particularly in terms of domestic currency lending, since the government can always impose taxes to repay its debt. When setting interest rates to be charged on corporate and household borrowers, banks and other financial institutions would thus just add a *risk premium* to risk-free

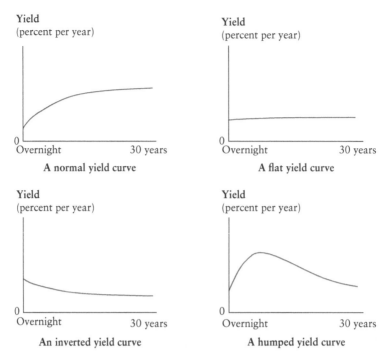

FIGURE 7.7   Illustration of Normal, Flat, Inverted, and Humped Yield Curves

rates at corresponding maturities, to compensate for the possibility that borrowers would be unable to pay back the loans.

The Central Bank's Influence on the Yield Curve   In the normal conduct of monetary policy (as opposed to the unconventional conduct of monetary policy; see Chapter 6) the central bank usually tries to influence the short end of the yield curve and let market forces determine longer-term yields and interest rates. Consequently, the reaction of long-term interest rates to changes in the policy interest rate are not so straightforward. Although the central bank can use the policy interest rate to tightly anchor interest rates at the very short end of the yield curve, long-term interest rates are generally allowed to float in places where financial markets are liberalized (see Figure 7.8). How changes in short-term interest rates might affect long-term interest rates involves many forces, and the results are indeed not entirely predictable. A hike in the policy interest rate, while likely to push up other short-term interest rates, does not necessarily always translate to a rise in long-term interest rates.

In practice, the effect of changes in short-term rates on long-term rates depends on the interplay of various factors, including the initial levels of long-term and short-term rates, expectations about future central bank actions, and liquidity conditions of players in the financial markets. The complexity of the relationship between short-term rates and long-term rates is reflected partly by the fact that there are at least three competing theories of yield curve. All of the theories are consistent with any shape of the yield curve but propose different reasons for why the yield curve might take a particular shape. The details of the theories are discussed next in Concept: Term Structure Theories and the Shape of the Yield Curve. ·

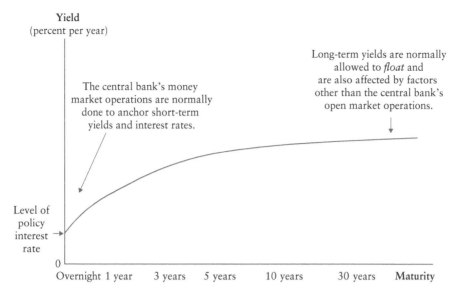

FIGURE 7.8   In Normal Times, the Central Bank Operates Primarily at the Short Maturity End of the Yield Curve

CONCEPT: TERM STRUCTURE THEORIES AND THE SHAPE OF THE YIELD CURVE

Theories of the yield curve, or theories describing the term structure of interest rates, attempt to explain the relationship between short-term interest rates and long-term interest rates, thatis, why a yield curve might take a particular shape. The three competing theories of the yield curve are (1) the *pure expectations theory*, (2) the *liquidity preference theory*, and (3) the *market segmentation theory*.[26] The fact that all of these theories could offer different explanations that are consistent with any shape of a yield curve suggests the complexity of transmission mechanisms from a change in the policy interest rate to changes in interest rates at longer maturities.

Pure Expectations Theory

The *pure expectations theory* assumes that the various maturities on the yield curve are perfect substitutes, and thus the shape of the yield curve depends on market participants' expectations of future short-term rates. According to the pure expectations theory, when short-term rates are expected to rise in the future, the yield curve would be upward sloping. When short-term rates are expected to fall, the yield curve would be downward sloping. When short-term rates are expected to remain constant, the yield curve would be flat. (See Figures 7.9a and 7.9b.)

(Continued)

(*Continued*)

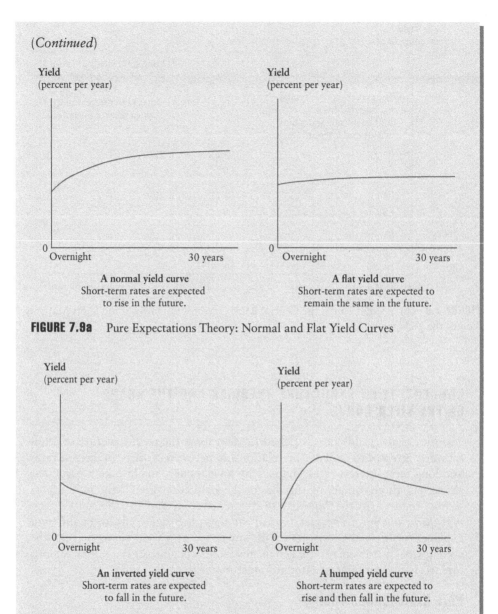

FIGURE 7.9a   Pure Expectations Theory: Normal and Flat Yield Curves

FIGURE 7.9b   Pure Expectations Theory: Inverted and Humped Yield Curves

To illustrate the point, think of the three-month rate being the *short rate*, and the three-year rate being the *long rate*. Within the space of three years, there is a series of 12 consecutive three-month rates. If the short rate (i.e., the three-month rate, is expected to rise within that three-year period, obviously the rate charged for lending long term for three years starting today would be higher than the current three-month rate. Thus when we plot the yield curve, it would be upward sloping, since the three-month rate is lower than the three-year rate.* The humped yield curve, in contrast, would occur when short rates are expected to rise, then fall.

Liquidity Preference Theory

The *liquidity preference theory* suggests that investors require additional compensation (i.e., a liquidity premium) to hold longer-term securities, and thus yields on longer-term maturity securities are higher than shorter-term maturity securities. This is because holding on to longer-term securities involve greater risk than holding on to shorter-term securities. Shorter-term securities would be redeemable for cash sooner rather than later, and thus investors will have a greater choice with what to do with the money. Holders of longer-term maturity securities will have to wait for a longer time before securities can be redeemed for cash, and in the meantime there are many things that could go wrong.

According to the *liquidity preference theory*, an upward sloping yield curve could still be consistent with expectation of declining short-term rates in the future, if the liquidity premium more than compensates for the expected fall in future short-term rates. If rates are expected to fall sharply, however, even adding in a liquidity premium would not prevent the yield curve from being downward sloping. A humped yield curve, on the other hand, could also be humped even with a liquidity premium added to yields in all maturities. (See Figures 7.10 and 7.11.)

Market Segmentation and Preferred Habitat Theories

In contrast to the *pure expectations theory*, the *market segmentation theory* suggests that the various maturities of the yield curve are not exactly close substitutes, and thus it is the supply and the demand for securities at each maturity range that determine the yields of securities within that maturity range (see Figure 7.12). According to this theory, different types of investors have different preferences for maturity range. Investors with longer-term liabilities, such as life insurance companies and pension funds, often prefer holding securities in a longer-term maturity range. Investors with shorter-term liabilities, such as commercial banks, may have a preference for holding securities with a shorter maturity. This theory fits quite well in a situation where there are legal or institutional policy restrictions that prohibit investors from purchasing securities with maturities outside a particular maturity range. Money market mutual funds, for example, are normally required to invest only in securities with maturities of less than one year.

---

*The current three-month rate would also be known as the 3-month spot rate, while the current three-year rate would also be known as three-year spot rate. The three-month rates for the subsequent periods after the initial three months are known as three-month forward rates. Note that the average (not the simple average) of the three-month rates for the three-year period would be equal to the three-year spot rate.

(Continued)

(*Continued*)

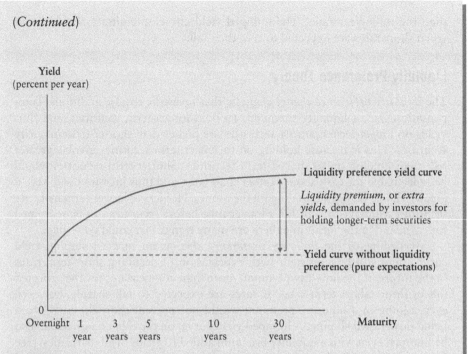

FIGURE 7.10   Liquidity Preference Theory: Liquidity Premium

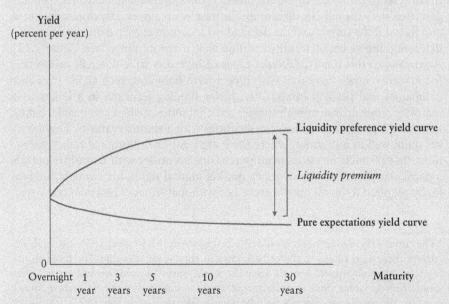

FIGURE 7.11   Reconciling Pure Expectations Theory and Liquidity Preference
Theory: Liquidity Premium Added to Decreasing Expected Rates

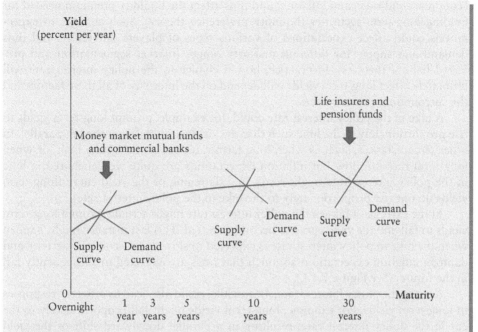

FIGURE 7.12   Market Segmentation Theory: Different Types of Players Dominate
Different Segments of the Yield Curve

A weaker form of the market segmentation theory is the *preferred habitat
theory*. According to this theory, although different types of investors have
their preferred maturity ranges for their investments, investors can still move to
other maturity ranges if the yields in those other maturity ranges are attractive
enough for them. Similar to the market segmentation theory, however, the preferred habitat theory also takes the view that yields are determined by supply
and demand for various maturity ranges.

7.3 MONETARY POLICY AND THE YIELD CURVE

As mentioned previously, the reactions of long-term yields to changes in the policy
interest rate depend on many factors. A change in the policy interest rate could
produce different results on longer-term rates depending on various factors, including the initial level of interest rates, expectations, and the interactions of different
market players.

The Effects of the Policy Interest Rate on the Long End
of the Yield Curve

Broadly speaking, changes in the policy interest rate may alter expectations for future
movements of short-term rates (pure expectations theory), as well as expectations for

economic conditions and inflation, and thus affect the liquidity premium needed for holding long-term securities (liquidity preference theory). Such changes in expectations could affect expectations of various types of players differently, and thus demand and supply for different maturity ranges (market segmentation and preferred habitat theories). In practice, how a change in the policy interest rate will ultimately affect long-term yields will depend on the interplay of all these factors and the surrounding circumstances.

A hike in the policy interest rate could, for example, prompt long-term yields to rise proportionately to the hike such that the yield curve shifts upward in parallel. In other circumstances, such as when long-term rates are already quite high, or when long-term rates are low but inflation expectations are quite well anchored, a hike in the policy interest rate might result in a flattening of the yield curve (long-term yields do not rise proportionately to the hike in the policy interest rate).

At the extreme, a hike in the policy interest rate might actually prompt long-term yields to fall and the yield curve to become inverted. This last instance might happen when the hike in policy interest rate is expected to slow down economic activity and dampen inflation expectations so much that rates are expected to subsequently fall in the future. (See Figure 7.13.)

A cut in the policy interest rate, meanwhile, could also lead to different responses in long-term yields. For example, long-term yields might fall proportionately to the cut in the policy interest rate, resulting in a parallel downward shift of the yield curve. In contrast, long-term yields might fall less than proportionately than the cut in policy interest rate, resulting in a steepened yield curve. At the extreme, long-term yields might actually rise in response to a cut in the policy interest rate, had the cut been expected to boost up economic activity so much so that long-term inflation is expected to accelerate. (See Figure 7.14.)

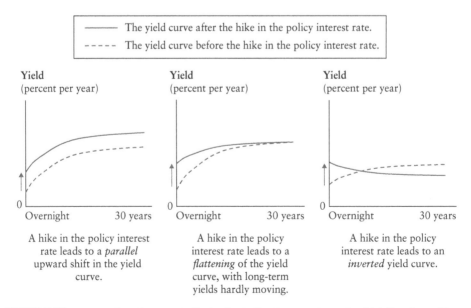

FIGURE 7.13 Examples of How a Hike in the Policy Interest Rate Could Affect Long-Term Yields in Different Ways

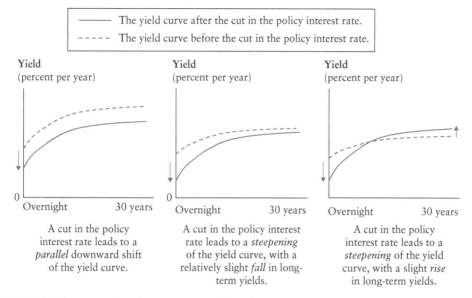

FIGURE 7.14   Examples of How a Cut in the Policy Interest Rate Could Affect Long-Term Yields in Different Ways

The Yield Curve as a Leading Economic Indicator

In practice, since the yield curve could be influenced by multitudes of forward-looking expectations, it is deemed to also contain valuable information for policy making. Modern central banks routinely monitor movements in the yield curve to gauge not only what is happening in the financial markets, but also what market players might be expecting about the general economy.

A downward-sloping, or inverted, yield curve suggests that interest rates are more likely to fall than not in the future. In the United States, since it has been found that short-term rates exceeded longer-term rates in each of seven recessions since 1970, an inverted yield curve is often deemed as a good predictor of a coming recession.[27] An economic explanation of why an inverted yield curve might be a good predictor of a recession is that an inverted yield curve suggests that economic agents do not see economic opportunities that might offer high rates of return in the future, compared to what they could earn now.

Unconventional Monetary Policy and the Yield Curve

As discussed earlier, in the normal conduct of monetary policy, the central bank tries to influence only the short end of the yield curve and lets long-term rates be determined by market forces. In the wake of the recent global financial crisis, however, many central banks of economies affected by the crisis decided to embark upon quantitative easing, which is an unconventional monetary policy. As discussed in Chapter 6, quantitative easing is done with the central bank directly purchasing long-term securities and influencing the long end of the yield curve.

The use of quantitative easing is likely to have three complementary objectives. First, by directly purchasing long-term government securities, the central bank would help push down long-term government yields. Since yields on government securities are usually used as a benchmark for private sector lending, the pushdown of long-term yields on government securities could translate into lower long-term lending (and borrowing) rates among the private sector.

Second, by purchasing other long-term securities, such as mortgage-backed securities, from market players, such as banks, the central bank would be effectively providing much needed liquidity to those players during the time of crisis. The liquidity provided will help the players meet short-term obligations, and enable financial markets to continue functioning in a smooth manner, which is essential for financial stability.

Third, with large enough purchases of securities, the central bank would in effect be injecting money into the economy. Players in the financial markets, such as banks, will have enough excess liquidity to finance economic activity by households and firms. Since the policy interest rate will normally be at or near 0 percent by the time unconventional monetary policy is used, the central bank uses the option of easing monetary conditions further through such purchases of securities.

SUMMARY

Monetary policy implementation refers to the ways in which the central bank can act to influence money conditions in the economy in order to achieve its mandate.

To influence money conditions, the central bank might operate in various types of financial markets, including (among others) the *money market*, the *foreign exchange market*, the *government securities market*, and the *credit market*. The money market is the key market in which modern central banks operate to influence money conditions in the economy. The money market is the market in which participants borrow or lend funds for maturities of less than one year.

The central bank typically influences conditions in the money market by influencing reserve balances held by commercial banks at the central bank, using tools such as the policy interest rate, open market operations, and standing facilities. The use of the policy interest rate, open market operations, and standing facilities together constitutes the interest rate corridor system, which keeps money market interest rates near the desired policy interest rate.

Transmission of money market interest rates to other interest rates in the economy can be seen through the movements of the yield curve. The yield curve shows yields (interest rates) at different maturities; the policy interest rate (which is often an overnight interest rate) is at the very short-maturity end of the yield curve. The government yield curve, which shows yields of government securities at different maturities, is often used by financial market players to benchmark rates for risk-free lending.

The yield curve is normally upward sloping, but could also be downward sloping (inverted), as well as flat. Theories explaining the shape of the yield curve include pure expectations, liquidity preference, and the market segmentation or preferred habitat theories.

Normally, the central bank tries to influence the short end of the yield curve. In the wake of the 2007–2010 crisis, after major central banks had cut their policy interest rates to or near 0 percent, many of them decided to also use unconventional monetary policy (e.g., quantitative easing) to influence the longer end of the yield curve.

KEY TERMS

credit market	money market
deposit facility	open market operations
financial market	outright transaction
foreign exchange market	policy interest rate
FX swap	preferred habitat theory
government securities market	pure expectations theory
government securities yield curve	repos
interest rate corridor	repurchase agreement
inverted yield curve	reserve balance
lending facility	reverse repurchase agreement
liquidity preference theory	reverse-repo
liquidity premium	standing facility
market segmentation theory	yield curve

QUESTIONS

1. What are the key differences between the financial sector and the real sector?
2. Please give examples of the key financial markets in which central banks conduct their operations.
3. What is a money market?
4. How can a central bank tighten conditions in the money market?
5. How can a central bank ease conditions in the money market?
6. In open market operations, what is an *outright* transaction?
7. In open market operations, what is a *repo* transaction?
8. Does the central bank always need to conduct open market operations to influence money market interest rates? Why or why not?
9. How does an interest rate corridor system work?
10. How might reserve requirements be used to influence conditions in the money market?
11. Why might the central bank not want to use reserve requirements to influence money market conditions?
12. What is a yield curve?
13. When the central bank adjusts the policy interest rate, it is trying to directly influence which end of the yield curve?
14. According to expectations theory, why might a yield curve be upward sloping?
15. According to expectations theory, why might a yield curve be downward sloping?
16. According to expectations theory, what does a humped yield curve imply?
17. According to liquidity preference theory, why might a yield curve be upward sloping?
18. According to liquidity preference theory, could an expectation of a falling short-term interest rate be consistent with an upward sloping yield curve?
19. According to market segmentation theory, why might the yield curve be upward sloping?

20. What is the likely implication of a downward sloping yield curve on the state of the economy going forward?
21. If the central bank raises its policy interest rate, which is an overnight rate, by 0.25 percent, what is likely to happen to the 10-year yield of government securities?
22. Theoretically, is it possible that the yield curve could become inverted after a hike in the policy interest rate?
23. What is the difference between the normal conduct of monetary policy and quantitative easing in terms of the intention to influence the yield curve?

CHAPTER 8

The Monetary Policy Transmission Mechanism

How Changes in Interest Rates Affect Households, Firms, Financial Institutions, Economic Activity, and Inflation

Learning Objectives

1. Describe how changes in interest rates can affect unemployment and inflation through households' behavior.
2. Describe how changes in interest rates can affect unemployment and inflation through firms' behavior.
3. Describe how changes in interest rates can affect unemployment and inflation through behavior of financial institutions.
4. Explain why might there be uncertainty and time lags in the monetary policy transmission mechanism.

Chapter 7 discussed how the central bank's conduct of monetary policy operations could affect interest rates in the financial markets. This section will discuss how changes in interest rates might affect the behavior of households, businesses, and financial institutions, and thus aggregate demand and general price levels in the economy. The *transmission* of effects to economic activity and inflation from the implementation of monetary policy is often known as the monetary policy transmission mechanism (see Figure 8.1).

Through its conduct of monetary policy, the central bank uses the policy interest rate to signal its monetary policy stance and to try to influence interest rates and money conditions within the economy, and ultimately GDP, employment, and monetary stability. Changes in monetary conditions and interest rates will then affect lending behavior of financial institutions, as well as the spending, saving, and investment behaviors of households and businesses, which, in turn, will affect aggregate demand and inflation.

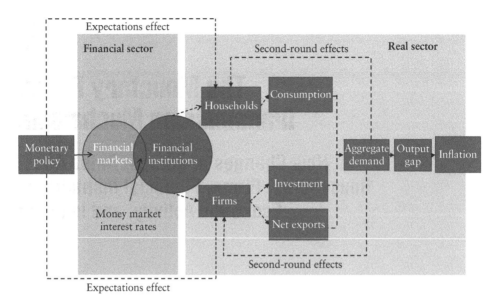

FIGURE 8.1   Transmission of Monetary Policy through Households, Firms, and Financial Institutions

This chapter will examine the monetary policy transmission mechanism by looking at how behaviors of *households*, *firms*, and *financial institutions* are likely to react to changes in money conditions, which can be typified by changes in prevailing borrowing and lending rates within the economy. It must be noted, however, that although it's called a *mechanism*, monetary policy does not necessarily transmit in a mechanistic way, and the transmission itself can be viewed from different perspectives.[1] If anything, monetary policy transmission has inherent uncertainty, whether in terms of timing or the relative importance of the different channels through which monetary policy is transmitted.[2]

CONCEPT: A NOTE ON NOMINAL AND REAL INTEREST RATES: THE FISHER EQUATION AND INFLATION EXPECTATIONS

While the central bank can directly influence short-term interest rates through adjustments in the policy interest rate through normal policy operations, and directly influence longer-term interest rates by unconventional monetary policy, such as quantitative easing, such interest rates discussed in previous chapters so far have been expressed in *nominal* terms, that is, not deflated by inflation expectations.

The Fisher Equation

Economists, however, believe that households' and firms' consumption and investment decisions are influenced by *real* interest rates, or nominal interest rates deflated by inflation expectations. This concept is expressed in what is known as the Fisher equation (named for Irving Fisher, an American economist), or

$$r = i - \pi^e$$

where r is the real interest rate, i is the nominal interest rate, and π^e are inflation expectations.

When economic agents decide to save or invest an amount of money, intuitively they compare the nominal interest rate with what they expect inflation will be over the time horizon being considered. If the nominal interest rate is below what they think inflation would be over that period (i.e., the real interest rate is negative), then they might be better off spending their money now, since they are not expecting interest earned on the money to keep up with inflation.

For our discussions on monetary transmission mechanism that follow, we are referring to *real* interest rates, although the term *real* is sometimes omitted for conciseness. Indeed, if inflation expectations are stable in the short run, we can safely say that a rise in *nominal* interest rates implies a rise in *real* short-term interest rates.

Inflation Expectations

In practice, there are three main ways that a central bank can gauge the inflation expectations of the public. First is through surveys. A typical question asked of the public in a survey might ask respondents what they think the inflation rate will be over the next year, the next 5 years, and the next 10 years. Inflation expectations for each time horizon would then be calculated from the mean value of the surveys' answers.

Second would be looking at *breakeven* inflation, which is the difference between the yield of a *nominal* government security and the yield of an *inflation-protected* government security. Unlike most government securities, which are nominal securities, inflation-protected government securities have their principal adjusted by the inflation rate.[3]

For example, if a five-year nominal government security has a yield of 5 percent, while a five-year inflation-protected government security has a yield of 2 percent, then the breakeven yield would be 3 percent. In this case, we could say that inflation expectations of the public over the five-year horizon are also 5 percent minus 2 percent = 3 percent. In other words, given the yield difference of 3 percent, the public would be indifferent between holding the five-year nominal government security and the five-year inflation-protected security.

Third, the central bank could use economic models to estimate inflation expectations.[4]

8.1 MONETARY POLICY AND HOUSEHOLDS' BEHAVIOR

Generally speaking, changes in interest rates can affect households' spending and saving decisions via six main effects, namely (1) the *intertemporal substitution effect*, (2) the *income effect*, (3) the *wealth effect*, (4) the *exchange rate effect*, (5) the *expectations effect*, and (6) *second-round effects*.

In this section, we will discuss the first four effects, namely the intertemporal substitution effect, the income effect, the wealth effect, and the exchange rate effect (see Figure 8.2). The final two effects, that is, the expectations effect and second-round effects, will be discussed later in the chapter in the context of both households' and firms' behavior.

The Intertemporal Substitution Effect: Consumption Today versus Consumption Tomorrow

The intertemporal substitution effect refers to the effect that changes in interest rates might have on the decision of households to substitute *current* consumption for *future* consumption, and vice versa. If households raise their consumption today, they will have lower savings available for consumption in the future. In contrast, if households cut their consumption today, they will have higher savings available for future consumption.

Higher interest rates imply greater opportunity costs for current consumption and thus tend to encourage households to delay their consumption into the future. With higher interest rates households can receive higher returns on their savings, and thus are likely to save more and spend less. In other words, with higher interest rates, household can have more future consumption if they delay their current consumption.[5]

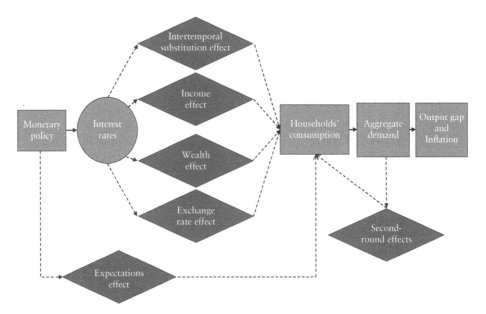

FIGURE 8.2 Effects of Changes in Interest Rates on Households' Consumption Behavior

Accordingly, with higher interest rates households are likely to substitute future consumption for current consumption. In contrast, lower interest rates imply lower opportunity costs for current consumption, which would encourage households to raise their current consumption relative to future consumption.

CONCEPT: SAVERS VERSUS BORROWERS, AND DURABLE GOODS VERSUS NONDURABLE GOODS

Intertemporal substitution works in the same way whether households are savers or borrowers. Whether consumption of a product could be very much delayed into the future, however, would also depend on the nature of the product in question.

Savers versus Borrowers

The intertemporal substitution effect works in the same way whether the households are *savers* or *borrowers*. For *savers*, higher interest rates mean that any withdrawal for spending purposes would incur higher opportunity costs owing to the higher interest income that is given up. For *borrowers*, higher interest rates mean that the funding cost of any current purchase of goods and services would be higher and thus they are more likely to be discouraged from borrowing to finance consumption.

According to the intertemporal substitution effect, then, higher interest rates tend to slow down household consumption spending whether those households are savers or borrowers. Both depositors and borrowers might delay their purchases until interest rates have come down or until they really need to make their purchases.[6]

Durable Goods, Big-Ticket Items, Nondurable Goods, Luxuries, and Essentials

The intertemporal substitution effect is especially noticeable with consumption of *durable* goods and big-ticket items.[7] Consumption of durable goods, such as cars and appliances, can be postponed relatively easily, since these goods do not need to be replaced very often. Consequently, if interest rates are rising households may find it easier to delay the purchase of such goods. Similarly, when interest rates are rising, consumption of *luxury* goods and services could also be relatively easily delayed. In contrast, purchases of nondurable goods, such as food and *essential services* (e.g., utilities), cannot be as easily delayed, and thus are less sensitive to changes in interest rates.

The Income Effect

Household consumption spending tends to rise and fall with household *disposable income*.* When disposable income is high, a household is likely to consume more,

---

*Income that is available after taxes.

and vice versa. Rising interest rates, however, could add to or subtract from household disposable income, depending on whether the household is a *net borrower*, or a *net lender*.

For a household that is a *net borrower* with an initial level of debt (which could be composed of anything from mortgages to personal loans to credit card debt), a rise in interest rates is likely to raise the household's interest burden and reduce its disposable income. There will be less flow of funds available for these households to spend on goods and services.

To maintain the old level of consumption spending, these households would either need to borrow more (and incur even more debt) or cut their spending. In contrast, for a household that is a *net saver*, rising interest rates will result in higher interest income, which will augment household disposable income, encouraging the household to consume more.[8]

Despite the opposing effects that higher interest rates might have on disposable income of net borrowers and net savers, in general the view is often that higher interest rates are more likely to *reduce* aggregate consumption. One underlying reason is that higher interest rates essentially have the effect of redistributing income from net borrowers toward net savers. In most countries, income distribution is such that there are fewer net savers than net borrowers.[9]

Furthermore, compared to net borrowers, net savers tend to have a *lower marginal propensity to consume*; that is, for every dollar increase in disposable income, a net saver tends to spend less on consumption than a net borrower. Redistributing income from net borrowers to net savers would thus suggest a fall in aggregate consumption spending.[10]

The Wealth Effect

Changes in interest rates affect asset valuation. Consumption spending also rises and falls with household wealth. With greater household wealth, a household is likely to consume more, and vice versa. Household wealth can be held in the form of *financial assets* (stocks and bonds, and also possibly pension and mutual funds) and *real assets* (particularly housing). Since rising interest rates tend to have negative effects on the valuation of both financial assets and real assets, they are likely to reduce household wealth and thus household consumption spending.[11]

When interest rates rise, financial assets tend to drop in value. *Bond prices* are inversely related to interest rates, not the least since bond coupon payments are often fixed at a nominal value. When interest rates rise compared to the fixed value coupon payments, existing bondholders are foregoing the possibility that they could actually receive higher interest rates elsewhere, or from new bonds that have yet to be issued.

Stock prices are also inversely related to interest rates. Higher interest rates mean that future income streams of businesses are discounted with a larger discount factor, making stock prices and the present value of the firms themselves lower. Furthermore, with higher interest rates feedback between consumption spending and stock prices also occurs, since firms' expected revenues (and thus stock prices) are likely to fall along with lower consumption spending.[12]

Households often also hold a significant portion of their wealth in the form of *housing*. Rising interest rates, however, tend to slow down the rise in house prices or even push prices down. With higher interest rates, the financing of a house purchase becomes more difficult, dampening demand and housing prices. As house prices fall, households may perceive themselves as being poorer and thus restrict their consumption. In the worse cases (especially after the burst of a housing bubble), since home purchases are often financed by mortgage loans, if the value of a house falls so much that it is below the value of the mortgage owed, household wealth in the form of housing could be negative, and household consumption could be seriously affected.[13]

The Exchange Rate Effect

Higher interest rates tend to strengthen the exchange rate, other things being equal. A strengthening of the exchange rate is likely to shift demand of consumers more toward imported goods and services and away from domestically produced goods and services, since imported goods and services will be cheaper than before.

Furthermore, in a country that has a significant level of household wealth held in foreign-currency denominated assets (foreign stocks and bonds, and foreign real estate, for example), an exchange rate change that is significant enough to affect net wealth could also affect household consumption.[14]

Taking the Four Effects Together: The Effect on Household Consumption and Savings

In the aggregate, other things being equal, higher interest rates are likely to *reduce* household consumption spending overall. If the exchange rate is stronger following the rise in interest rates, consumption spending will likely shift away from domestically produced goods and services and toward foreign produced goods and services. In essence, the central bank's decision to tighten its monetary policy stance is likely to reduce household consumption spending and increase imports, other things being equal. The central bank's decision to loosen its monetary policy stance, on the other hand, is likely to encourage more consumption spending and more consumption of domestically produced goods and services.[15]

8.2 MONETARY POLICY AND FIRMS' BEHAVIOR

Firms are entities created to combine labor and other inputs in a production process, such that they can sell resulting products for profit, which can then be distributed to the firms' shareholders or retained within the firms. Monetary policy could affect firms' spending, saving, and investment behavior through five key effects, namely (1) the *funding costs effect*, (2) the *asset price effect*, (3) the *exchange rate effect*, (4) the *expectations effect*, and (5) *second-round effects*.

This section will focus on how changes in money conditions and interest rates could affect firms' behavior through the first three effects, that is, the *funding costs*

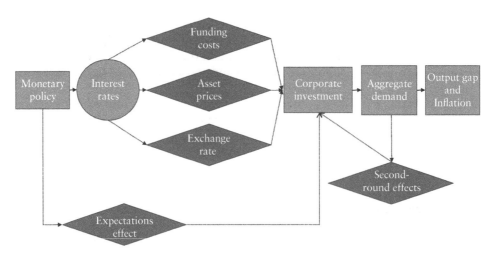

FIGURE 8.3   Effect of Changes in Interest Rates on Firms' Behavior

effect, the *asset price effect*, and the *exchange rate effect*. (See Figure 8.3.) The final two effects (the *expectations effect* and *second-round effects*) will be the focus of the next section, where we will look at expectations and second-round effects in the context of both households' and firms' behaviors.

The Funding Costs Effect

For indebted firms, higher interest rates can raise interest expenses and worsen cash flows. In response firms might attempt to cut costs or delay other expenses, for example, by cutting down workers' hours of work or delaying workforce expansion. Furthermore, since higher interest rates raise funding costs for new investment projects and make the projects less profitable, firms might also choose to delay their new investments, for example, purchases of new equipment.[16]

For firms that are debt free or have funds in the money market or bank deposit accounts, higher interest rates imply higher interest income. For these firms, higher interest income suggests greater cash flows available for new investment projects or workforce expansion. However, even if new investment projects or workforce expansion could be funded entirely by the extra interest income, firms have to take into account that higher interest rates also suggest greater opportunity costs for the use of funds, as well as a higher discount factor to be used for their new investment projects. If new investment projects cannot be entirely funded by the extra interest income then these firms will also have to take into account higher funding costs.[17]

Given the aggregate effects on both interest expenses and income, the funding costs effect suggests that higher interest rates are more likely to slow down firms' spending and investment.[18]

The Asset Price Effect

Higher interest rates lower the value of firms' assets, not the least because a higher discount factor and a lower income stream are used in the valuation of assets. In the simplest terms, the value of an asset can be approximated by the *net present value* formula

$$NPV = \sum_{t=0}^{N} \frac{R_t}{(1+i)^t}$$

where NPV is net present value of the asset, t is the time period, N is the number of periods, R_t is the difference between cash inflow and cash outflow generated by the asset at time t, and i is the discount factor. Generally, the discount factor i is correlated with the expected prevailing interest rates at time t. Accordingly, higher interest rates are likely to result in a higher discount factor, which will lower the net present value, and thus the current price, of the asset.

Lower asset prices make firms' applications for *bank credit* more difficult, since bank loans are often secured by assets that are posted as collateral. Also, with lower assets values, and thus lower net worth, publicly listed firms will find it more difficult to issue *new shares* to finance new investments. Furthermore, since the valuation of a new investment project is often done using a NPV-based formula, rising interest rates are likely to *decrease* net present value of the project, both because of the projected reduced income stream and the higher discount factor, and there is thus likely to be fewer new investment projects approved. Consequently, given the asset price effect, higher interest rates are thus also likely to reduce firms' spending on expansion and new investment projects.[19]

The Exchange Rate Effect

Higher interest rates can draw capital inflows into the domestic economy and lead to a strengthening of the exchange rate (see Chapter 9 for more details). A strengthening of the exchange rate is likely to affect both costs and revenues of domestic firms, especially those that produce exports, or those competing with imports.[20]

On the *cost* side, a strengthening of the exchange rate could raise the domestic cost of production relative to the foreign cost of production. In effect, firms that produce domestically would become less price competitive, as they would need to charge higher prices than their competitors to just break even.

On the *revenue* side, a strengthening of the exchange rate could make domestically produced products become more expensive *than before*, when compared to foreign produced products. Foreign imports would become cheaper compared to domestically produced products. Similarly, the country's exports would become more expensive compared to foreign produced products. With higher prices, customers are more likely to switch from domestically produced to foreign produced products. Revenue of firms that rely on domestic production is thus likely to decline.

With higher costs and lower revenues, firms' *profits* would tend to fall. The exchange rate effect is likely to be felt more acutely by manufacturing firms. They would be thus less likely to spend to expand their domestic workforce, and indeed might shift their plants and factories overseas. In addition to manufacturing firms, the agricultural sector and parts of the service sector (such as tourism) are also likely to be affected by the exchange rate effect.

Overall, the exchange rate effect suggests that higher interest rates will result in a *slowdown* in domestic economic activity, as domestic production of goods and services become less competitive compared to foreign production.

8.3 EXPECTATIONS AND SECOND-ROUND EFFECTS ON HOUSEHOLD AND FIRM BEHAVIOR

In this section we will discuss how changes in interest rates could affect households' and firms' behavior through the *expectations effect* and *second-round effects*. (See Figure 8.4.)

According to the expectations effect, rational and forward-looking households and firms are likely to adjust their behaviors immediately after—or even before—a change in monetary policy stance is announced, in anticipation of things to come. The expectations effect could thus affect economic activity even before a monetary policy action actually starts to affect interest rates for deposits and loans.[21]

Second-round effects, on the other hand, suggest that changes in households' and firms' spending behaviors are likely to affect aggregate demand, which, in turn, will introduce feedback loops back to household and firm spending behaviors. Second-round effects are thus likely to further amplify the initial impact of a monetary policy action on household and firm behaviors.[22]

The Expectations Effect

One significant way that a change in the central bank's monetary policy stance might affect behavior of households and firms is through expectations. A tightening of the monetary policy stance might signal that future economic activity will slow down and money might be harder to come by. Consequently, households might start to cut down their consumption (and thus raise their savings) even before they actually experience changes in their interest burden or interest income. Firms, on the other hand, anticipating slower consumption demand, might choose to slow down their activities, buy less input materials, schedule fewer hours of work, and postpone their investment plans.[23]

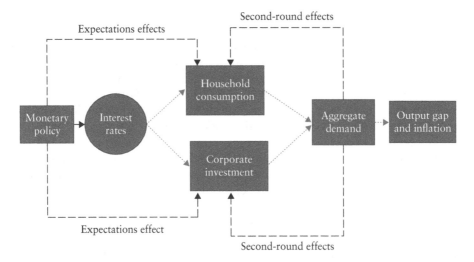

FIGURE 8.4   Expectations and Second-Round Effects on Household and Firm Behavior

The expectations effect involves a lot of uncertainty. If a significant tightening of the monetary policy stance is unexpected, for example, the response of households and firms is likely to differ quite a bit from a case in which the tightening is fully anticipated, or in the case of a less drastic tightening. The strength of the feedback loop between expectations and the actual behavior of households and firms is also very difficult to gauge, not the least because each household and each firm are different.

Second-Round Effects

Previously we discussed how changes in monetary policy stance could affect the behavior of households and firms, not the least through direct changes in households' disposable income, firms' cash flows, asset prices, the exchange rate, and expectations, and so on. In practice, however, the so-called second-round effects also play a significant role in monetary policy transmission.

Second-round effects can be thought of as a feedback loop between induced changes in aggregate demand and further changes in the spending behavior of households and firms. With greater aggregate demand, firms are more likely to expand their production. The firms' suppliers along the supply chain will also benefit. Demand for labor in the economy will rise and households' disposable income is likely to rise along with it. This would lead back to a further rise in demand for all goods and services in general. In a downturn, a fall in aggregate demand would lead to cuts in labor demand, a fall in households' disposable income, and a further fall in aggregate spending.[24]

The feedback loop of second-round effects, indeed, mimics the nature of business cycles. Once a change in monetary policy stance starts to affect households' and firms' behavior, the feedback loop kicks in. With the presence of second round-effects, indeed, a change in monetary policy stance is likely to also transmit widely throughout all sectors of the economy and affect everyone.

8.4 MONETARY POLICY AND FINANCIAL INSTITUTIONS

In the previous section we discussed the monetary policy transmission mechanism, focusing on the effects that a change in monetary policy might have on households and firms, the ultimate agents that make consumption, saving, and investment decisions. Another way to describe the monetary policy transmission mechanism is through financial intermediaries such as commercial banks, which often play important roles as conduits of monetary policy transmission, since households and firms borrow and save through them.

The ultimate effects of monetary policy transmission on output and inflation will be the same whether expressed through changes in households' and firms' behavior or through the effects on financial intermediaries. Indeed, these two channels are two sides of the same coin, as the following discussion makes clear.

Broadly speaking, we can see that monetary policy transmits through financial institutions via (1) the *credit channel*, whereby lenders pass on changes in the policy interest rate and money market rates to customers through retail deposit and lending rates, which then prompts changes in the *external* financing costs of firms and households (as opposed to *internal* costs incurred through financing spending

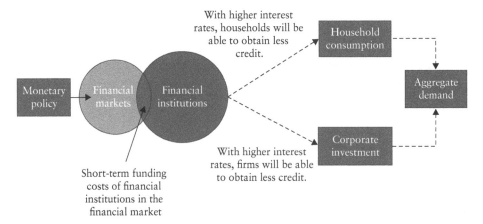

FIGURE 8.5   Credit Channel: Higher Interest Rates Make Financial Institutions More Wary in Lending to Households and Firms

using retained earnings or savings)[25] and (2) the *balance sheet channel*, whereby monetary policy affects households' and firms' balance sheets, net worth, and liquid assets, and thus the willingness of financial intermediaries to lend to them.[26] These two channels often work in tandem, and are indeed quite intertwined in certain aspects.[27]

The Credit Channel

When the policy interest rate is raised, money market interest rates are also likely to rise. Short-term funding costs of financial intermediaries will rise, and ultimately financial intermediaries are likely to pass on their higher funding costs to their borrowers through higher lending rates.

   Rising lending rates could *lower* the borrowers' ability to repay their debts (e.g., borrowers would be faced with higher monthly debt repayments while their revenue might slow in line with an economy that is facing higher interest rates). Consequently, banks and other lenders might add a higher *premium* to their lending rates to compensate for rising credit risk when interest rates are rising, or they might extend credit more cautiously in general (see Figure 8.5). On the whole, lenders might be more cautious in extending credit in an environment of rising interest rates.[28]

The Balance Sheet Channel

The balance sheet channel, on the other hand, is the corollary to wealth and asset price effects through which changes in interest rates affect households and firms. With higher interest rates, households' and firms' assets are likely to fall in value, making the assets less valuable as collateral for loans. Higher interest rates are also likely to result in lower wealth and net worth for borrowers since discount rates will now be higher for their wealth and future income. Overall, this would lower creditworthiness of households and firms, and nudge financial institutions to reduce the supply of credit to them.[29] (See Figure 8.6.) The reduced supply of credit will then help contribute to a slowdown in aggregate demand.

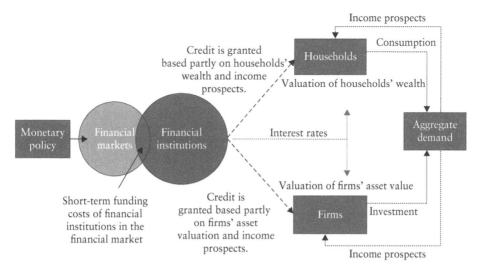

FIGURE 8.6   Balance Sheet Channel: Higher Interest Rates Lower the Collateral Value of Assets

8.5 TIME LAGS AND UNCERTAINTY IN MONETARY POLICY TRANSMISSION

From the discussions above, it can be seen that changes in monetary policy stance take some time to have their full effects play out. There are at least five identifiable steps before a change in monetary policy fully affects price levels in the economy: (1) the transmission from the implementation of monetary policy operations to money market interest rates; (2) the pass-through from money market interest rates to borrowing and lending rates for households and firms; (3) the adjustments in households' and firms' spending behavior; (4) second-round effects, which comprise feedback loops between households' and firms' spending behavior and aggregate demand; and (5) the expectations effect, which can be a wild card that hastens or slows the transmission of monetary policy. (See Figure 8.7.)

First, the change in monetary policy stance affects *money market interest rate*s. This stage is likely to be very short, since money market rates are likely to adjust immediately in response to changes in liquidity conditions. Indeed, financial asset prices could change even before there is an actual shift in the monetary policy stance if that shift is anticipated by market participants. Such changes might be reflected in changes to the shape of the yield curve.

Second, changes in money market interest rates would be translated into changes in *borrowing* and *lending rates* charged to *households* and *firms*. Changes in money market rates will likely affect financial institutions' short-term funding costs immediately, but it could take time before financial institutions adjust their retail deposit and lending rates since they will have to consider many other factors, including the shape of the government yield curve (which would partly dictate the level of longerterm interest rates), peer competition, and profit margins. Adjustments in retail interest rates are likely to be gradual and could take months. Furthermore, adjustments in

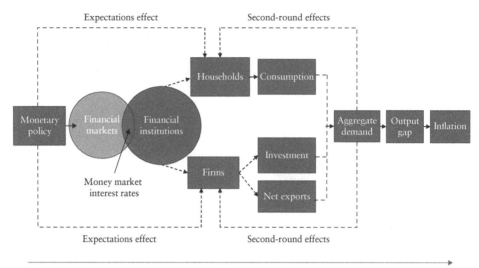

Elapsed time is between 1.5 and 2 years.

FIGURE 8.7 Time Lags and Uncertainty in Monetary Policy Transmission

lending and deposit rates might not be perfectly synchronized depending on various factors, including the initial levels of the rates, the stage of business cycles, etc.

Third, households and firms are also likely to take time to adjust their *spending behavior* in response to changes in retail borrowing and lending rates. Of course, as discussed earlier, changes in expectations could make households and firms promptly adjust their behaviors. The full effects, however, are unlikely to come from changes in expectations alone. Certain spending habits will need time to adjust. The full response of firms to changes in household spending will also take time, whether in terms of volume of production or alterations in spending for previously planned investment projects.[30]

Fourth, it will take time for *feedback loops*, or second-round effects, to take place. There will be chain reactions through firms' suppliers. These changes by firms will affect employment and income of the labor force, which would feed back into household consumption spending, all affecting aggregate output of the economy. Meanwhile, pricing of firms' goods and services will also likely change in response to changes in household demand, and the feedback loop will also lead to wage negotiations and adjustments.

Fifth, expectations of households and firms could hasten the transmission of monetary policy to changes in output and inflation, but in a nonlinear way. If households and firms expect that the central bank is fully committed to monetary stability, even a small hike in the policy interest rate might prompt them to adjust their behavior quickly. Otherwise, the central bank might need to hike the policy interest rate many times before the public adjusts their behavior.

From the outline above, we can see that changes in monetary policy stance take time to fully affect the economy's output and prices. Such time lags can be quite long, and the exact timing can vary, depending on many outside factors including expectations, confidence, the stage of business cycles, etc. Empirically, studies have shown that it could take up to a year for a change in monetary policy to reach its peak effect on demand and output, and another year for the effect on inflation to be fully realized, although estimates vary.[31]

The Conduct of Monetary Policy Given Time Lags and Uncertainty

Given the time lags and uncertainty involved with the transmission mechanism of monetary policy, the central bank needs to be quite cautious and forward-looking when considering a policy action. A change in monetary policy stance today will only be fully felt about one to two years later, and by that time surrounding circumstances might have already changed.[32] Despite the time lags and uncertainty, however, it is still the central bank's job to conduct monetary policy in such a way that stability and growth of the economy is promoted.

To do its job properly, the central bank needs to understand the intricacies of and linkages within the economy. It also needs to be adept at forecasting future economic and inflation outcomes so that it can decide on an appropriate monetary policy action today. In practice, many modern central banks rely on a suite of macroeconomic models to forecast the future outlook for the economy and inflation. Such macroeconomic models often capture key relationships and linkages within the economy.

In a modern central bank there are likely to be a number of competing macroeconomic models based on different mathematical and statistical techniques, so that the bank can cross-check the consistency of the forecasts. Such models can range from a spreadsheet model with more mechanistic linkages of macroeconomic variables to a *macroeconometric model* that relies on econometric estimates of historical macroeconomic data to the so-called *dynamic stochastic general equilibrium* (DSGE) model that is based more on theoretical microeconomic principles and interactions among key agents (such as households and firms) within the economy.

Given the time lags and uncertainty involved, the central bank will often make projections based on different possible *scenarios*. For example, the central bank might try to project GDP growth and inflation rates based on different estimates of future oil prices. The final forecasts that are used as a basis for monetary policy decisions, or *baseline* forecasts, are often expressed as the range of values (as opposed to a single value) that key economic variables (such as GDP growth and inflation rates) are most likely to be over the forecast horizon.

In practice, if inflation and GDP growth forecasts are projected to diverge much from a so-called acceptable (or target) range, it would be a signal for the central bank to reconsider its monetary policy stance. Whether the central bank will actually change monetary policy stance will also depend on the policy makers' judgment, as it is usually accepted that even the most sophisticated macroeconomic models cannot capture the full complexity of the economy, and thus forecasts from the models can have a certain degree of error.

SUMMARY

Changes in real interest rates can affect saving and investment decisions of households and firms, and thus economic activity, inflation, and employment.

Monetary policy can affect household spending and saving decisions via six main effects, namely (1) the *intertemporal substitution effect*, (2) the *income effect*,

(3) the *wealth effect*, (4) the *exchange rate effect*, (5) the *expectations effect*, and (6) *second-round effects.*

Monetary policy can affect firms' spending, saving, and investment behavior through five key effects, namely (1) the *funding costs effect*, (2) the *asset price effect*, (3) the *exchange rate effect*, (4) the *expectations effect*, and (5) *second-round effects.*

The effects of monetary policy on households' and firms' consumption and investment decisions can transmit through the *credit channel* and the *balance sheet channel*, which themselves work through financial institutions.

Since there are many steps through which monetary policy transmits through the economy, the ultimate effects on output, inflation, and employment will have long and variable *time lags.*

KEY TERMS

asset price effect of monetary policy transmission

balance sheet channel

breakeven yield

credit channel

dynamic stochastic general equilibrium model (DSGE)

exchange rate effect of monetary policy transmission

expectations effect of monetary policy transmission

feedback loop

funding costs effect of monetary policy transmission

income effect of monetary policy transmission

inflation-protected security

intertemporal substitution

macroeconometric model

nominal interest rate

real interest rate

second-round effects of monetary policy transmission

time lags of monetary policy transmission

uncertainty of monetary policy transmission

wealth effect of monetary policy transmission

QUESTIONS

1. Households' and firms' investment and savings decisions are influenced by real or nominal interest rates?
2. If the expectation is that inflation will be 2 percent per year and the nominal interest rate is 5 percent per year, what is the real interest rate?
3. If the yield on a five-year nominal government security is 5 percent and the yield on a five-year inflation-protected government security is 3 percent, what are breakeven inflation expectations and the breakeven yield?
4. How does an increase in interest rates affect aggregate household spending through the intertemporal substitution effect?
5. How might the effects of an increase in interest rates be different for wealthier households and less wealthy households?
6. Since a rise in interest rates can raise income for savers, why might we think that in the aggregate a rise in interest rates is likely to cause a fall in consumption?
7. How is an increase in interest rates likely to affect consumption of durable goods compared to nondurable goods?

8. How would an increase in interest rates be likely to affect aggregate household spending through the income effect?

9. How would an increase in interest rates be likely to affect aggregate household spending through the wealth effect?

10. Why might a household reduce its consumption even before a change in the policy interest rate actually starts to work through the intertemporal substitution, income, and wealth effects?

11. What do we mean by second-round effects of the transmission mechanism?

12. How does an increase in interest rates affect business spending through the funding cost effect?

13. How might rising interest rates affect firms' spending and investment behavior through the funding cost effect?

14. Why are rising interest rates likely to reduce the value of firms' assets?

15. How might rising interest rates affect firms' spending and investment behavior through the exchange rate effect?

16. How would a change in interest rates likely affect financial institutions?

17. How does a rise in the policy interest rate work through the credit channel?

18. How does a rise in the policy interest rate work through the balance sheet channel?

19. What are the reasons that the length of the time lag associated with the monetary policy transmission mechanism is uncertain?

20. What is the usual time lag between the time the policy interest rate is changed and the time the change has an effect on the economy's output and inflation?

21. When conducting monetary policy, how can a central bank deal with the uncertainty of the time lag for monetary policy transmission?

CHAPTER 9

The Exchange Rate and Central Banking

Learning Objectives

1. Explain how movements in the exchange rate can affect monetary stability, financial stability, and unemployment.
2. Distinguish between a rigid peg, a free-float, and a managed float exchange rate regimes.
3. Explain key theories that attempt to explain exchange rate determination.
4. Identify key factors that can affect the exchange rate.
5. Describe the way in which the central bank can influence the exchange rate.

At its core, the exchange rate is the price of money expressed in terms of another currency. Accordingly, the exchange rate is an important variable that the central bank must watch, even if the regime of that central bank does not involve exchange targeting. In Chapter 9 we will examine issues relating to the exchange rate in relation to central banking in more detail.

This chapter starts with a brief review of how the exchange rate might affect price stability, financial stability, and the real economy in theory and in practice. The chapter will then review the alternative exchange rate regimes, or frameworks, that a modern central bank can adopt. The exchange rate regimes that will be reviewed include the rigid peg regime, the free-float regime, and the managed float regime. Later on the chapter will review exchange rate theories so that the reader can see the fundamental forces that would influence the exchange rate in the absence of direct central bank intervention. The chapter will then review how the central bank can deal with the exchange rate using various instruments. Lastly, the chapter will discuss the management of official foreign reserves, which are a key tool in exchange rate management.

9.1 THE EXCHANGE RATE, MONETARY STABILITY, FINANCIAL STABILITY, AND MACROECONOMIC STABILITY

The exchange rate is an important variable that the central bank has to watch, regardless of whether the central bank uses an exchange rate targeting regime. Apart from being the price of money in terms of another currency, movements in the exchange rate can affect monetary stability as well as financial stability.

In Theory

Theoretically, movements in the exchange rate can have implications for the central bank's pursuit of *monetary stability* as well as *financial stability*. In terms of monetary stability, if a country depends heavily on energy imports, for example, a fast depreciating exchange rate implies a fast rise in energy prices in terms of the domestic currency, which could translate into a fast rise in consumer price inflation and affect inflation expectations. In such a case, if inflation expectations have not been well managed, then monetary stability could be compromised, as witnessed during the great inflation period of the 1970s, when oil shocks helped contribute to a sharp and sustained rise in inflation.

In terms of *financial stability*, if a country has a high proportion of public or private debt denominated in foreign currencies, a sharp depreciation in the exchange rate could prove troublesome. With a sharp depreciation in the value of domestic currency, debt denominated in foreign currency could balloon when measured in terms of domestic currency. If the country does not have a reliable source of foreign income, this will affect the country's ability to repay its debt, which could lead to a financial crisis, as occurred among emerging-market economies in Asia and Latin America in the 1990s.

For many emerging-market economies, an excessively volatile exchange rate could also have direct implications not only on monetary stability and financial stability, but on the *real economy*, as reflected by output and employment. For those emerging-market economies that rely heavily on exports, for example, a fast appreciating exchange rate implies a fast rise in the price of the country's exports in terms of foreign currencies. This could lead to a fast fall in demand for the country's exports and the country's domestically produced products, which could lead to a sharp fall in production and a jump in unemployment.

In Practice

In practice, how the exchange rate affects monetary stability, financial stability, and macroeconomic stability would depend on the context and could be quite complicated.

A review of research from different central banks by the Bank for International Settlements, for example, found that the *pass-through* effect on inflation by exchange rates over the 1990s was small and had declined over the period studied.[1] The decline owed partly to the greater availability of hedging instruments to deal with short-term exchange rate risks, and partly to the trend toward the adoption of more flexible exchange rate regimes, which familiarized importers with exchange rate volatility and thus prompted them to change prices less frequently.[2] Furthermore, the pass-through effects of the exchange rate on inflation also varied among different sectors of the economy, as well as among exporters and importers.[3]

These studies further showed that the effect of exchange rate movements on current account balances (as with their effects on the real economy) was also declining.

A depreciating currency, for example, was not found to always lead to an expansion in output.[4] In other cases, while the exchange rate was found to historically play a crucial role in the adjustment of current account balances, changes in the economic environment meant that this might not necessarily be the case in the future.[5]

Despite the complicated picture with regard to the effects of the exchange rate on monetary stability, financial stability, and the real economy, however, the central bank often does keep a close watch on it by the virtue of the fact that the exchange rate is the price of money in terms of another currency and that it is a key economic variable in a globalized economy. Whether the central bank does anything to influence the exchange rate, however, depends on the context and the exchange rate regime it has adopted for its currency.

9.2 EXCHANGE RATE REGIMES

An exchange rate regime refers to the operational rule and related institutional mechanisms that the central bank adopts for the management of the exchange rate of its currency. In modern times, exchange rate regimes could range from rigid exchange rate pegs to completely free-floating exchange rates.

A Spectrum of Exchange Rate Regimes

With the end of the Bretton Woods system, currencies no longer had a universal peg that tied them to the value of gold. In theory, the exchange rates of currencies were now determined by market forces. In practice, after the Bretton Woods system had ended, a number of Western European countries at first used a system of exchange rate bands and capital controls that helped limit the movement of their currencies against one another, and which was a precursor to introduction of the euro.[6] Many emerging-market countries, meanwhile, decided unilaterally to maintain their exchange rate pegs with the U.S. dollar, to facilitate international trade and investment.[7]

As time went by, the increasingly connected nature of global economies and financial markets made rigid controls over currencies untenable and countries had to seek ways to manage their exchange rates in the way that best suited their needs. In the decades after the demise of the Bretton Woods system, various exchange rate regimes have been tried, adopted, and abandoned.

In practice we might view exchange rate regimes as constituting a spectrum, with a *hard* or *rigid peg* system (e.g., with either a common currency—where an independent currency is abandoned, while some other currency is adopted—or a currency board) on one end, and a *free float* (a type of flexible exchange rate regime whereby the exchange rate is purely determined by market forces) on the other end.[8] In between these two extreme ends, there are a range of regimes under which the central bank influences the exchange rate to temper pure market forces.[9]

The differences among these exchange rate regimes range from a slight shading to stark contrast. For our purposes, it's useful to look at exchange rate regimes as being on a continuum, with a rigid peg system at one end and a free-float system at the other. Figure 9.1 presents a spectrum of exchange rate regimes.

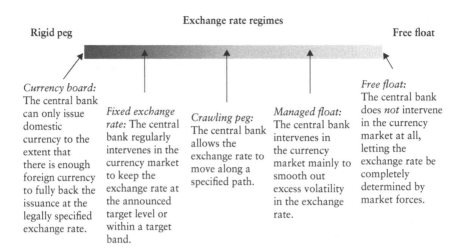

FIGURE 9.1 A Spectrum of Exchange Rate Regimes

The Rigid Peg End

Theoretically, rigid exchange rate pegs could take the form of a *common currency* or a *currency board*.[10] In a common currency area, the central bank replaces its national currency with a currency commonly used within a specified economic area (e.g., the euro in the euro area). In practice, of course, a common currency such as the euro can float against other currencies outside the common currency area.

Under a currency board system, the central bank can only issue domestic currency to the extent that it is fully backed by foreign reserves at the specified exchange rate.

A Common Currency   A common currency constitutes the most extreme form of a rigid peg system.[11] Under this system, as is the case in the euro area, member countries abandon their own currencies and adopted a common one (e.g., the euro). The euro area member countries do not have monetary policy independence; instead monetary policy is conducted by the ECB, which aims to sustain monetary stability for the euro area as a whole rather than for any individual member country.

In practice, however, as a currency the euro is classified as a *free-floating* currency by the IMF, since the ECB allows the value of the euro to be largely determined by market forces.[12]

A Currency Board   A *currency board* is another extreme form of a rigid peg system, whereby each unit of the local currency issued by the central bank is required by law to be fully backed by foreign currency reserves. Under a currency board, local currency notes and coins are fully convertible into a specified foreign currency at a specified exchange rate. Accordingly, the central bank does not have the independence to just issue whatever amount of money it sees fit for the country's prevailing economic conditions. If the central bank wants to issue an extra unit of local currency, it is legally required to have enough foreign currency to back that extra unit of local currency.

An example of a government that uses a currency board is the special administrative region of Hong Kong; the Hong Kong Monetary Authority fixes the Hong Kong dollar at the rate of HK$ 7.8 to USD 1, and cannot independently depart from that ratio even if it wishes to.[13]

The Rationale for a Rigid Peg   A country may adopt a common currency for both political and economic reasons. A common currency such as the euro is part of the larger goal of political and economic union. Having a common currency helps to eliminate exchange rate risk and encourage cross-border investment and trade among member countries.

Meanwhile, one reason a country might choose to adopt a currency board system is that it helps enhance the credibility of the local currency. Holders of local notes and coins are assured that the central bank has enough of the foreign currency to allow them to convert their local notes and coins into it at prevailing exchange rates. This guarantee of currency conversion at the prevailing exchange rates under a currency board system is particularly useful to boost confidence in the local economy, since otherwise the holders of local currency might be tempted to rush out of it at the first sign of trouble, creating a self-fulfilling prophecy.

Furthermore, as with the case of a common currency, a currency board could also be quite helpful in facilitating international trade and investment for a small open economy (or an international trading hub such as Hong Kong) since it eliminates exchange rate risk for traders and investors.

The Free-Float End

At the other end of the exchange rate spectrum from the rigid peg is the free-float regime. In contrast to an exchange rate peg, in a free-float regime the central bank allows exchange rate to be *completely* determined by market forces.

Other things being equal, whenever the demand for local currency rises the exchange rate will appreciate, and whenever the demand for local currency falls the exchange rate will depreciate. Under this regime the central bank is not supposed to intervene in the foreign exchange market, and thus movements in the exchange rate can be quite volatile, since demand and supply of a currency are normally influenced by many factors, particularly expectations of market players, which can be quite fickle.

Rationale for a Free Float   One key reason why the central bank might adopt a free-float regime is that monetary policy could then be freely used to address domestic concerns. Accordingly, we can say that a central bank that chooses to adopt a free-float regime does not see a particular need to manage the value of its currency with the exchange rate to order to achieve monetary stability.

In contrast to a rigid peg regime, under a free-float regime the central bank has the independence to freely use monetary policy to achieve a monetary stability mandate in a way that is in accord with particular conditions in the economy, without having to be too concerned about the implications for the exchange rate. For example, if the domestic economy is in a severe recession the central bank could choose to lower interest rates and ease money conditions to help decrease funding costs and boost domestic demand, even though lower interest rates and easy money conditions might put downward pressures on the exchange rate (all other things being equal).

Furthermore, in a world of greater capital flows it could be difficult for the central bank to keep the exchange rate fixed at any particular level for a sustained period of time. For the central bank to successfully resist depreciation pressures on the exchange rate, for example, it might need to have large amounts of foreign currencies on hand and use those foreign currencies to buy up domestic currency to shore up the value of the exchange rate (see the section on exchange rate targeting regimes in Chapter 6).

In any case, in a world in which economies are continually evolving, an *equilibrium exchange rate* that suits the country's economic fundamentals could be quite elusive, as will be discussed later in the chapter.[14] Consequently, the central bank might want to let the exchange rate be moved by market forces rather than attempting to keep it fixed at a particular level.

Also, for many economies, the development of financial markets is so advanced that economic agents can hedge against exchange rate volatility rather readily and cheaply. In these cases the central bank does not need to bear exchange rate risks for private agents, as private agents can already efficiently protect themselves.

In 2013 the following countries were among those classified by the IMF as having a free-floating exchange rate regime: euro area member countries, Australia, Canada, Chile, the Czech Republic, Israel, Japan, Mexico, Norway, Poland, Sweden, Israel, Japan, Mexico, Norway, Poland, Sweden, the United Kingdom, and the United States.[15]

The Middle Options

In between a rigid peg, such as the currency board system, and a free float there are exchange rate regimes under which a central bank intervenes against market forces to varying degrees. Note here that the definitions of exchange rate regimes can vary, and that what the central bank might say about its regime *de jure* might differ from what it actually practices *de facto*.

Traditional Fixed Exchange Rate   A fixed exchange rate regime traditionally refers to those that are similar to the Bretton Woods system, whereby the central bank might allow the exchange rate to fluctuate within 1 percent on either side of the announced target.[16]

Fixed Exchange Rate with a Horizontal Band   Under a fixed exchange rate system with a horizontal band, the exchange rate is allowed to fluctuate within a horizontal band around the announced exchange rate target. The width of the band could range from 2.5 to 15 percent, such as was the case under the European Monetary System that was a precursor to the euro.[17]

Crawling Peg   Under a crawling peg regime, the central bank allows the level of the exchange rate to gradually appreciate or depreciate along a controlled path that it deems consistent with the economic fundamentals of the economy. In 2013, the IMF classified China's exchange rate regime as being a *crawl-like arrangement*.[18]

Managed Float Under a managed float exchange rate regime, the central bank allows market forces to largely determine the exchange rate, but intervenes to smooth out fluctuations and excessive volatility in the exchange rate.[19]

Rationale for the Middle Options The reasons why a central bank might want to adopt an exchange rate regime that is neither a rigid peg nor a free float could depend on the circumstances that it finds itself in. For a central bank that leans more toward the fixed exchange rate regime, a key reason to adopt such a system could be that it needs to anchor the value of its currency to that of another low-inflation country in order to achieve credibility and low inflation for its own economy.

On the other hand, a central bank that chooses to adopt a crawling peg regime (or, as with China, some variation of it) may be one whose country depends heavily on international trade and investment with a financial market that is in an early stage of liberalization, meaning that private agents would not have much access to or experience with hedging instruments. In this instance, the central bank would partly bear the exchange rate risk for private agents (such as exporters) while the agents are adapting to the new economic environment.

Finally, in a country that depends a lot on exports with a financial market that has been very much liberalized with international capital flowing in and out relatively freely, a central bank might choose to adopt a managed float regime, whereby it would intervene only to smooth out excessive fluctuations in the exchange rate, rather than trying to keep the exchange rate at a particular level or on a particular path. In this case the central bank might also encourage the development of hedging instruments that private agents can readily use to hedge against exchange rate risk.

CASE STUDY: The Interesting Case of Singapore: Basket, Band, Crawl

Singapore's exchange rate management framework is an interesting case. While embracing free flows of capital, the country has used an exchange rate targeting regime since the 1980s and has successfully maintained long-term monetary stability despite its heavy dependence on the external sector.

In using the exchange rate as an instrument to sustain monetary stability, rather than adopting a rigid peg or allowing a free float, the Monetary Authority of Singapore (MAS), Singapore's central bank, has adopted a framework for exchange rate management known as *basket, band, crawl,* or BBC.

According to the 2011 MAS publication *Sustaining Stability, Serving Singapore*, the basket feature of the MAS framework refers to the fact that the MAS pegs the value of the Singapore dollar to a basket of currencies belonging to Singapore's major trading partners and competitors, thereby creating a *trade-weighted index* for the Singapore dollar. (Currencies of countries with a higher value of trade with Singapore would be given higher weights in the index.) The *band* feature refers to the fact that the MAS allows the trade-weighted Singapore dollar to float within a policy band, the width of which is undisclosed. The *crawl* feature of the framework refers to the fact that the MAS regularly reviews the exchange rate band, and adjusts the band over time to ensure that it is aligned with the underlying fundamentals of the economy. The trade-weighted Singapore dollar would thus *crawl* along the path of the exchange rate band over time.

Given the nature of the BBC regime, MAS sees itself as having three levers to adjust its monetary policy: the *slope*, the *width*, and the *level* of the band. The slope can be adjusted to allow the currency to appreciate faster or slower in response to changes in the economic situation that are expected to persist for some time. The width of the band can be widened to accommodate market-driven movements that result in the strengthening or weakening of the currency that are expected to be temporary, and narrowed after markets have stabilized. The level of the entire band can also be adjusted upward or downward in response to more significant, sharp, sustained shocks, such as a financial crisis.

At the same time, MAS sees three key reasons why the exchange rate should be used as its monetary policy tool to maintain monetary stability. First, Singapore was (and is) a small, open economy whose domestic prices are largely determined by world prices, and whose domestic prices of factor inputs (such as labor) are influenced largely by external demand. This is reflected partly in the fact that the value of both imports and exports each almost doubled Singapore's GDP.[28] Second, unlike larger economies in which investment would be sensitive to changes in interest rates, Singapore relies mainly on direct foreign investment, which is not very sensitive to Singapore's own interest rates. Third, to promote Singapore as an international financial center, MAS has allowed free flows of capital and has willingly ceded control over domestic interest rates and the money supply.

Given Singapore's heavy reliance on the external sector and the potentially huge implications of free capital flows on domestic prices, using the exchange rate to achieve monetary stability is not an easy task. According to MAS, Singapore's success in maintaining price stability using the BBC framework rests on two key unique conditions.

The first condition involves the *automatic drain* on Singapore's liquidity in the form of persistent fiscal surpluses and the mandatory contributions of firms and households to Central Provident Fund savings accounts, both of which continuously take Singapore dollars out of the system. Consequently, MAS has to keep making up for the drain on liquidity by injecting Singapore dollars into the economy, in the process buying up U.S. dollars. This has resulted in the accumulation of international reserves at MAS, which augments its ability to manage the exchange rate over time.

The second condition involves the high *credibility* of MAS in maintaining the regime, which has lessened the prospect of speculative attacks on the currency. This credibility itself rests on the huge reserves available to defend the system; the persistent fiscal surpluses that keep on draining Singapore dollar liquidity; and a flexible labor market, which implies that the labor market can clear relatively easily, meaning monetary policy can be used to maintain long-term price stability without undue strain on employment and the economy.[20]

9.3 EXCHANGE RATE THEORIES

In the previous section we saw that unless the central bank puts the exchange rate on a rigid peg, the level of the exchange rate will be determined at least partly by market forces. Even with a rigid peg exchange rate regime, however, the central bank will still need to counter market forces if it wants the exchange rate to remain pegged at the announced level. This section reviews theories that attempt to explain the forces behind exchange rate movements, so the reader can understand the context in which the central bank deals with issues relating to the exchange rate.

It should be noted, however, that at the moment there is no one single theory that can satisfactorily explain exchange rate behavior in a unified manner. One exchange rate theory that might seem to readily fit exchange rate behavior in one context might be completely irrelevant in another. To understand why the exchange rate might move in a certain manner in any given context, it is extremely useful to have at least some grasp of all key variations of exchange rate theory. Broadly speaking, exchange rate theories can be classified into four main categories, namely (1) *purchasing power parity* (PPP), (2) *monetary approach*, (3) *portfolio balance models*, and (4) *exchange rate market microstructure*.

Purchasing Power Parity

Purchasing power parity (PPP) provides a key building block in our understanding of the exchange rate. PPP is based on the notion of the law of one price, whereby if markets are perfectly efficient and goods can be transported freely at no costs, then the price of identical goods should be the same everywhere in the world, after adjusting for exchange rates.

An Illustrative Example of PPP The following is a simple but effective example that can help in the understanding of PPP. Assume that a particular make of pen is the only product in the world. If such a pen costs, say, 1.5 U.S. dollars in the United States and 1 euro in Germany, then according to PPP the exchange rate between the U.S. dollar and the euro should be 1.5 U.S. dollar per 1 euro.

If the exchange rate was not at 1.5 U.S. dollar per 1 euro, and was instead at 2 U.S. dollars per euro, then a German trader could bring 1 euro to the U.S. and exchange it for 2 U.S. dollars. He could then buy the pen at the cost of 1.5 U.S. dollars and bring the pen back to Germany in order to sell it for 1 euro. That German trader, or indeed any investor who embarks on such a scheme, would then pocket a risk-free profit of 0.5 U.S. dollars, or 0.25 euros.

In the preceding example, as long as that profit opportunity exists, profit seekers will keep exchanging euros for U.S. dollars to exploit the opportunity. As demand for the U.S. dollar rises, however, the value of the U.S. dollar cannot stay at 2 U.S. dollars per euro sustainably. The U.S. dollar exchange rate will keep strengthening against the euro until it reaches 1.5 U.S. dollars per euro, consistent with the price of the pen. In that case, there is no more riskless profit opportunity and the exchange rate reaches its equilibrium.

Absolute PPP: The Law of One Price There are two forms of the PPP concept, namely *absolute PPP* and *relative PPP*. The pen example above corresponds to absolute PPP, which corresponds directly to the law of one price. Absolute PPP suggests that a basket of identical goods will have the same price in any two countries after adjusting for the exchange rate. If the price is not the same, then the exchange rate is not in equilibrium and international investors could arbitrage in a scheme similar to the pen example above, which would then pressure the exchange rate to move to its equilibrium. In real life, given that transportation costs and obstacles in trade between countries do exist, as do differences in customs and tax rates, in the short-run, and the fact that investors cannot arbitrage between the price of certain location-specific services (e.g., the price of getting a haircut) in two countries, the exchange rate could remain quite different from the equilibrium suggested by absolute PPP.

Relative PPP: A Change in the Exchange Rate Reflects Inflation Differential Whereas the absolute PPP concept focuses on the *level* of the equilibrium exchange rate, the relative PPP concept focuses on the changes in the exchange rate. Given a basket of identical goods in two countries, if the price of the basket in country A rises faster than the price in country B, the exchange rate of country A should depreciate relative to the exchange rate of country B. Specifically, according to relative PPP, a change in the exchange rate between the currencies of two countries should equal the difference in the countries' domestic *inflation* rates.

To use our earlier pen example, if over the year the price of the pen in the United States has risen by 10 percent to 1.65 U.S. dollars while the price of the pen in Germany has remained flat at 1 euro, then the exchange rate at the end of that one year period would be 1.65 U.S. dollars per euro. Indeed, the 10 percent drop in the U.S. dollar against the euro over that one-year period would be a result of the difference between U.S. inflation (10 percent) and German inflation (0 percent) over that same period.

Usefulness of PPP as a Theory   The concept of PPP is useful in the understanding of long-run exchange rate behavior.[21] Data often show that the actual exchange rate can diverge quite a bit from the equilibrium exchange rate implied by absolute PPP, at least in the short run. The reasons why the actual exchange rate might diverge from the absolute PPP equilibrium could range from taxes and structures of the labor market to *menu costs*—costs related to the frequent changing of prices, as with printing costs for restaurant menus. Over the long run, as relevant adjustments in the economy started taking hold, the exchange rate will be more likely to behave in line with behavior described by the PPP concept.

The Big Mac Index   A well-known attempt to gauge exchange rate equilibrium as suggested by absolute PPP is the Big Mac index published annually by the *Economist* magazine. This index compares the price of a Big Mac being sold in McDonald's restaurants worldwide. A key advantage of the Big Mac index is that Big Macs are being sold globally in the same manner with largely the same ingredients, and yet are locally produced, so there is no international transportation costs involved. With such characteristics, according to absolute PPP, the price of a Big Mac should be the same anywhere, after adjusting for the exchange rate. In practice, however, this is often not the case. The reason for this could be that the cost of producing a Big Mac might not really be identical worldwide (wages and rent could be different across countries), or that the exchange rate is over- or undervalued, or both.

Uncovered Interest Parity (UIP)

Another key building block in the understanding of exchange rate behavior is the concept of *uncovered interest parity* (UIP). Unlike PPP, the concept of UIP takes into account investor expectations and the role of asset prices in the determination of exchange rates. UIP assumes that domestic and foreign assets are *perfectly* substitutable and the exchange rate would move to help equalize international investment returns such that there would be no riskless arbitrage opportunity.

An Illustrative Example of UIP   Suppose that we have an international investor who can choose between investing in a U.S. government bond or a German government bond. Let us assume that the bonds in question have the same risk profile and are of the same maturity. If the investor can switch between these two bonds promptly and seamlessly, then the only remaining differences between them are the currencies they are denominated in (U.S. dollar and the euro) and the interest rates they offer.

In order to maximize total returns on investment, the investor would thus only need to consider two factors, namely the interest rate differential between the two bonds and the likelihood of adjustments in the exchange rate between the U.S. dollar and the euro, the two currencies that these two bonds are denominated in.

For this example, at equilibrium the differential between U.S. and German interest rates would have to be matched by the expected percentage of depreciation of the U.S. dollar against the euro. This could be expressed as the equation

$$r^{us} - r^{eur} = e^s$$

where r^{us} is the interest rate on the U.S. government bond, r^{eur} is the interest rate on the German government bond, and e^s is the expected percentage of depreciation of the U.S. dollar per euro.

According to UIP, as long as the expected percentage of depreciation of the U.S. dollar relative to the euro differs from the interest differential on the otherwise identical U.S. and German government bonds, investors would expect the returns from investment from these two bonds to be different. Investors would seek to invest in the bond that is expected to provide higher total returns and shift away from investing in the bond that is expected to give lower total returns. As investors switch toward the more lucrative investment, the expected *total* returns of these two bonds would be equated.

To further illustrate this point, let's say that the annual yield on the U.S. government bond is at 10 percent and the annual yield on the German government bond is at 5 percent. If, however, the expected depreciation of the U.S. dollar per euro were only 2 percent per year, the expected return from an investment in the U.S. bond would be greater than that from the German bond. Investors would continuously switch their investments from the German bond to the U.S. bond, thereby reducing yield on the U.S. bond. Investors would stop switching between these two bonds only when the expected returns from these two bonds are equal, that is, when the interest rate differential between the U.S. and German bonds declined to 2 percent, equivalent to the expected percent of depreciation of the U.S. dollar against the euro.

Usefulness of the UIP From the illustration above we can see that UIP pins down the expected change in exchange rates, but not the level. In practice, however, while UIP provides a very important conceptual framework, accounting for the UIP relationship might be complicated by many factors.[22] The assumption of *perfect substitutability* between assets used in UIP, for example, might not necessarily always hold. Even bonds with the same credit rating might differ in terms of liquidity. Consequently, investors might not rush to switch between them as UIP would predict.

Also, investors might not be as *rational* as the theory assumes. Investors could have a bias toward investments in their home country and be less willing to switch to foreign bonds, for example. Furthermore, the long-run equilibrium exchange rate itself can change, thus affecting expected exchange rate depreciation. Despite these real-life limitations, however, UIP remains a key building block in our understanding of the exchange rate since it offers a theoretical baseline that could later be adjusted to different situations.

Portfolio Balance Models

Portfolio balance models refer to a large class of exchange rate models that attempt to address real-life limitations of the PPP and UIP concepts by taking into account relevant factors that might influence the exchange rate, including differences in the riskiness of domestic and foreign assets as well as the country's current account.[23]

Implications of Riskiness and Diversification of Bond Holdings on the Exchange Rate   In contrast to UIP, which assumes domestic and foreign assets are perfect substitutes, portfolio balance theories recognize that domestic and foreign assets are not perfect substitutes since there are often differences in their riskiness.[24] In practice, differences in the riskiness of bonds could come from many sources. For example, a country that issues a larger supply of bonds is more at risk of being unable to repay bondholders when the bonds mature, other things being equal. A country with lower productivity is also more likely to default on it bonds.[25]

Under portfolio balance theories, since domestic and foreign bonds are not perfect substitutes, investors would hold both domestic and foreign bonds to diversify their risks and maximize their investment returns.[26] Unlike the world of UIP, according to portfolio balance theories, investors will not rush to entirely switch from domestic to foreign bonds whenever the interest rate differential on the bonds does not match the expected depreciation of the exchange rate, or vice versa. Instead, investors would want to diversify their portfolios by holding both domestic and foreign bonds at the same time (but more likely in different proportions).

To compensate for holding a riskier bond, however, investors will also likely demand that the riskier bond pays a higher interest rate. In other words, a risk premium would have to be paid for investors to hold the riskier bond. According to portfolio balance theories, the interest differential on domestic and foreign bonds thus reflects not only the expected exchange rate depreciation as prescribed by UIP, but also the risk premium paid to compensate investors for holding the riskier bond. Persistent or large deviations from UIP (i.e., cases in which the interest rate differential is not matched by the expected depreciation of the exchange rate), could thus be at least partly explained by the existence of risk premiums.

Role of the Current Account   Aside from differences in the riskiness of investments, portfolio balance theories also put emphasis on the role of a country's current account as a factor determining the country's exchange rate.[27] A country's current account surplus suggests that the country exports more than it imports. Accumulation of export proceeds over import payments implies a rise in a country's foreign assets. However, since foreign and domestic assets are not perfect substitutes, and portfolio balance theories suggest that investors often want to hold both foreign and domestic assets in their portfolios, parts of the country's net export proceeds would be repatriated back to invest in domestic assets. The repatriation of those export proceeds would drive up the value of domestic currency relative to that of foreign currencies. Therefore, the country's current account could play a role in determination of the exchange rate. Over time, however, the strengthening of domestic currency could reduce the country's current account surplus since it would make the country's exports more expensive than before.

From the preceding discussion we can conclude that large and persistent deviations from UIP are thus also possible for the country's current account position. If we examine this further, then we see that since current account dynamics and the country's growth prospects are intertwined, portfolio balance theories would seem to also suggest that factors affecting the country's growth prospects would also play a role in the determination of the exchange rate. The final result, however, could be rather complex since it depends on wide-ranging factors, including the nature of factors affecting the country's growth prospects and the corresponding current account dynamics.

For example, if the country is experiencing higher productivity growth (possibly, say, from a burst of new innovations), then the higher income growth that comes with higher productivity could encourage the country to start to consume more and run current account deficits. On the other hand, the rise in productivity might enable the country to produce and export more, and run current account surpluses. Whichever path the country follows, however, the exchange rate would likely be affected. Furthermore, higher productivity and higher potential growth would likely lead to higher expected returns from investment in that country's domestic assets, which would then alter its exchange rate dynamics.

Exchange Rate Market Microstructure

The preceding exchange rate theories focus mainly on the longer-term macroeconomic determinants of exchange rate behaviors. In practice, however, it has been observed that the exchange rate can change in almost a continuous manner, even if there has not been a change in inflation, the current account, or potential growth data.* Research has thus increasingly put more focus on the interaction among players in the foreign exchange market as a key determinant of the exchange rate.[28] This focus gives rise to the microstructure theory of the exchange rate market.

Under the exchange rate microstructure theory, attention is paid to how players in the exchange rate market (individuals, firms, and financial institutions) use information available to them when trading currencies in the market. Often players have to aggregate a wide range of dispersed information, including that on macro variables such as future inflation and economic growth, as well as that on actions of other players in the market. Owing to information asymmetry and the fact that players might aggregate dispersed information differently, different players are likely to have different views on the intrinsic value of a currency.

With numerous players in the market at any given moment, and with news and information being introduced throughout the day, it is conceivable that the exchange rate would adjust almost moment-by-moment, depending on how players in the foreign exchange market decide to trade, given their interpretation of available information. Research on market microstructure is also starting to provide more insight into the understanding of how the central bank's announcement of monetary decisions might affect the exchange rate. By examining exchange rate behaviors in periods following a monetary policy announcement, researchers will be able to gauge how a hike in the policy interest rate, for example, might influence exchange rate movement.

Implications of Exchange Rate Theories for Exchange Rate Policy

Although there is no one single unified theory that can explain exchange rate behavior at all times, existing theories do offer many useful insights that are pertinent to central banking. Here we discuss four of them.

---

*For most countries, inflation data are updated monthly while current account data and economic growth projections are updated only quarterly.

First, from PPP we know that if the central bank allows inflation to rise persistently, then ultimately the exchange rate is likely to be weakened, other things being constant. Indeed, according to the concept of relative PPP, for any pair of countries, if inflation in one country rises persistently beyond that of the other, then its exchange rate would likely depreciate vis-à-vis that of the other country. If the central bank of a country runs an easy monetary policy stance, then, other things being equal, the currency of that country is likely to depreciate in the long run.

Second, from UIP we know that if a country's interest rate is higher than that of another country, then its exchange rate will have to depreciate over time such that total returns from investments in these two countries would be equal. If a country unexpectedly raises its interest rates, then its exchange rate will have to instantaneously appreciate in response so that over time the exchange rate can then depreciate, other things being equal.

Third, from the portfolio balance theory we know that assets of different countries differ in riskiness and thus are not perfectly substitutable, as UIP assumes. An interest rate differential between any pair of countries might thus not necessarily lead to pressure on the exchange rate. Furthermore, if a country's economy grows then the country might be perceived as getting stronger, and thus the perception of risk associated with investing in that country might fall. Accordingly, if monetary policy is conducted in a way that is conducive to increasing economic growth, then the exchange rate might also strengthen, other things being equal.

Fourth, from the exchange rate microstructure theory we know that the exchange rate can fluctuate on an almost continuous basis, owing to changes in expectations of players in the financial markets. Therefore, the central bank will have to take into account that their actions *and* nonactions relating to monetary policy could drive the expectations of players in the foreign exchange market, induce them to adjust their exchange rate positions, and thus affect the exchange rate.

9.4 DEALING WITH THE EXCHANGE RATE IN PRACTICE

In practice, the central bank has to deal with the exchange rate at both the macro level and at the operational level. At the macro level, the central bank would have to be aware of how its policy on the exchange rate fit with its overall monetary policy framework. The exchange rate, interest rates, and the inflation rate are inextricably intertwined in the long run, as they all represent various aspects of the cost of money.

At the operational level, the central bank would have to figure out how, if it wants to do so, to best influence the exchange rate. The central bank might want to intervene in the foreign exchange market, or to regulate flows of capital. These actions, however, do have costs that the central bank will need to consider.

Dealing with the Exchange Rate: The Macro Concepts

At the macro level (as opposed to at the operational level), the central bank has to take into account that the exchange rate, inflation, and interest rates are interrelated. The central bank's action to influence one variable could affect the other two variables.

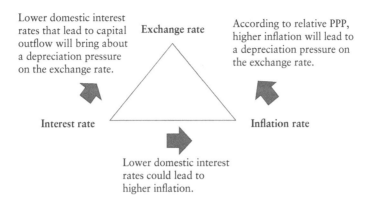

FIGURE 9.2   The Exchange Rate, Inflation, and Interest Rates Are All Intertwined

The Relationship between the Exchange Rate, Inflation, and Interest Rates   As is implicit in the various exchange rate theories discussed above, *inflation*, *interest rates*, and the *exchange rate* are related. The central bank's action to influence any one of the variables is likely to affect the other two, at least over the long run (see Figure 9.2).

For example, other things being equal, a *loosened* monetary policy stance could raise *inflation*, according to the monetary theories discussed in Chapter 5. With higher inflation, according to *relative PPP*, the exchange rate of the country with respect to an anchor country would over time depreciate proportionately in relation to the inflation differential between the two countries. On the other hand, according to *UIP*, the loosening of monetary policy that resulted in lower interest rates would also result in an exchange rate depreciation, other things being equal.

Congruence in the Central Bank's Actions toward the Three Variables   As the exchange rate, inflation, and interest rates are all intrinsically intertwined, any policy action to affect one of these three variables will affect not only the variable in question but will also indirectly affect the other two. Any attempt to move any two pairs of variables in *opposing* directions will be likely to prove unsustainable in the long run.

For example, say a central bank wants to hike interest rates to keep inflation down, but at the same time wants to keep exchange rates weak in order to stimulate exports. Specifically, let's also say that the central bank wants to *fix* the exchange rate at a level it deems favorable to the country's exports. In such a case, by raising interest rates to tame inflation but keeping the exchange rates fixed, the central bank is essentially creating a profit opportunity for investors to bring in foreign capital to invest in that country (in order to gain from interest differentials), since if the fixing of the exchange rate holds, the expected depreciation of the currency will be zero.

In other words, in this particular case, the central bank is violating UIP. Such a scheme would be self-defeating for the central bank, since the higher interest rates will attract more foreign capital, driving up the demand for domestic currency. However, since the central bank wants to fix the exchange rate, the central bank will have to intervene in the foreign exchange market by injecting money into the economy to satisfy the greater demand for domestic currency. The injection of money will, of course, defeat the initial purpose of the hike in interest rates, that is, the taming of inflation.

At the extreme, if the public realizes at the start that the central bank has both low inflation and fixed exchange rate objectives, the public might be skeptical about the effect that the hike in the policy interest rate might have on inflation. Monetary policy and the central bank itself might lose their credibility. Even without the fixed exchange rate objective, any large scale foreign exchange intervention without "sterilization" (the central bank's absorption of liquidity from the system through its selling of securities to financial market players) could jeopardize the central bank's price stability objective credibility.

In theory, the central bank has many options to deal with the exchange rate. At one extreme, it could focus solely in keeping the exchange rate at a predetermined fixed level through exchange rate targeting. At another extreme, it could choose to let the exchange rate float freely so that it is completely determined by market forces (although this is very unlikely in practice). In between these two extremes, the central bank would choose the degree of exchange flexibility that it deems most suitable to economic conditions or the central bank's objectives, or both.

CASE STUDY: Exchange Rate Policy and the Asian Financial Crisis

As discussed above, since interest rates, exchange rates, and inflation are all interrelated, any attempt to influence interest rates and inflation rates in an inconsistent way will be self-defeating. The situation can be seen most clearly in a currency crisis when a country is forced to massively devalue its currency or abruptly abandon a fixed exchange rate regime.

Fixed Exchange Rate Regime

Prior to the Asian financial crisis in the late 1990s, many of the currencies in the region were on a *de facto* fixed exchange rate regime. In such a situation, if the central bank is to maintain the fixed exchange rate regime it cannot freely implement independent monetary policy to manage domestic demand, since to keep the exchange rate fixed domestic interest rates must be in line with those of the anchor economies, predominantly the United States in this instance.

Liberalization: The Arrival of Foreign Capital

As countries such as Thailand, South Korea, and Indonesia started to liberalize their economies in the 1980s, foreign capital started to pour in, partly attracted by the high growth potential of the economies and the cheap labor that could be used for export-based manufacturing. While some of the foreign capital came in to finance export-oriented manufacturing, as the Asian economies heated up, some of the capital started to seep into asset price speculation (e.g., on stocks and real estate markets).

Note here during that time, foreign capital that poured into the Asian economy came in the form of *foreign loans* as well as *foreign direct investment* and *portfolio investment*. Foreign direct investment means that foreign investors set up their operations in the domestic economy, or buy domestic firms, or jointly invest with domestic firms. Portfolio investment means that foreign investors invest in the domestic bond and the stock markets. In this case, foreign capital also poured into Asian economies in the form of foreign loans, as foreign banks lent to Asian banks and the Asian corporate sector to take advantage of *interest rate differentials* between advanced economies and emerging-market economies.

Interest Rate Differentials and Implicit Guarantee on Exchange Rate Risk

Theoretically, domestic interest rates in Asia were kept in line with those of the anchor economies to which their exchange rates were fixed. However, given that loans in emerging economies had higher risks than loans in advanced economies, and given that there was also a huge demand for funds in Asian economies, Asian domestic interest rates were considerably higher than those in the advanced economies, in other words, owing to both the *risk premium* demanded by foreign lenders and the *demand for funds* by Asian borrowers.

Also, with their fixed exchange rate regimes, Asian central banks were essentially protecting investors and borrowers from *exchange rate risk* in such cross-border lending and borrowing transactions. Consequently, foreign commercial banks were willing to lend to Asian commercial banks and the corporate sector to take advantage of the interest rate differentials that came with an *implicit* central bank guarantee against exchange rate risk.

The Outcome

Ultimately, as Asian exports slowed in line with their advanced economy export markets, the current account deficits of many Asian economies grew larger, creating a dilemma. On the one hand, interest rate cuts by central banks could help stimulate *domestic* demand in these Asian economies and a devaluation of their currencies could help stimulate exports and reduce current account deficits. On the other hand, interest rate cuts by central banks would put pressure on the exchange rates and a devaluation of the currencies could bring financial instability, since domestic Asian banks and the corporate sector had borrowed heavily from overseas without hedging the exchange rate risk, and at the same time a huge chunk of the money had already either seeped into projects that could not be liquidated quickly or seeped into asset price speculation.

As discussed in Chapter 2, when such dilemma became apparent, international investors and speculators have incentives to engage in speculative attacks against central banks with fixed exchange rate regimes. In this case, a series of massive speculative attacks forced the Bank of Thailand to float the Thai baht on July 2, 1997, which started the Asian financial crisis since other Asian currencies (including the Korean won and the Indonesian rupiah) were also forced to float. As a result, countries around the region suffered massive economic instability. It should be noted that prior to the crisis the fixed exchange rate regime had helped push inflation expectations down and had also helped facilitate international trade and investment for many Asian countries. As the economies of these countries became liberalized and foreign capital started to pour in, however, the countries entered into an *impossible trinity* situation, since they could not independently use monetary policy to manage domestic demand in their economies and at the same time kept their exchange rates fixed.

Equilibrium Exchange Rates   When a central bank intervenes to keep exchange rates at a certain level, it is often legitimate to ask if the central bank thinks such a level is an equilibrium exchange rate for the economy. (Otherwise, why would the central bank do so?) In a world where information is incomplete and prices are inflexible, however, determining an equilibrium exchange rate is rather elusive.[29]

In practice, there have been many definitions of an equilibrium exchange rate. Some of them are (1) the exchange rate that balances the current account, (2) the *fundamental equilibrium exchange rate*, (3) the exchange rate that is consistent with PPP, (4) the exchange rate that equates one's export prices with those of the trading partners, and (5) the exchange rate that equates domestic costs to foreign costs.[30]

As we shall see, these definitions are not exactly congruent among themselves. A level of exchange rate that seems to suggest equilibrium in one sense does not necessarily suggest equilibrium in another. Table 9.1 summarizes the pros and cons of these different definitions of equilibrium exchange rate.

Exchange Rate That Balances the Current Account   In theory, a sustained balanced current account should imply that the economy has achieved equilibrium with respect to external trade. An exchange rate that balances the current account could thus be deemed an equilibrium exchange rate.

TABLE 9.1   Different Concepts of Equilibrium Rate: Examples and Their Pros and Cons

	Exchange rate that balances the current account	Exchange rate that is consistent with PPP	Exchange rate that equates export prices with those of trading partners	Exchange rate that equates domestic costs to foreign costs
Pros	A sustained current account balance implies that the economy is in equilibrium.	Popular for comparing standards of living.	Theoretically reflects the equilibrium exchange rate, if countries have the same profit margin.	Bypasses the problem of profit margin measurement that comes with the measure of export prices.
Cons	Certain stages of development may need a current account that is not balanced.	Does not reflect external balances. Not all goods and services can be traded across border.	Countries do not have the same profit margin for their exports.	Other measurement problems: goods are not identical, different labor market structures, etc.

Source: Adapted from Tony Latter, *The Choice of Exchange Rate Regime*, Handbooks in Central Banking No. 2 (London: Centre for Central Banking Studies, Bank of England, 1996).

In practice, however, there are at least two reasons that the exchange rate that ensures a balanced current account might not represent an equilibrium exchange rate. First, the feedback loop between the exchange rate and the current account is often uncertain and is subject to time lags. The balanced current account that we see today does not necessarily correspond to the exchange rate that we see today.

Second, countries in different stages of development and investment opportunities might need a current account that is not balanced, which would result in accompanying structural capital inflows or outflows. For example, a country that needs foreign investment might be better off having a current account deficit, which would be financed by capital inflows. On the other hand, a country that does not have enough local productive investment opportunities might be better off having a current account surplus and invest its surplus (capital) abroad.[31]

Fundamental Equilibrium Exchange Rate   The *fundamental equilibrium exchange rate* can be defined as one that produces the optimal current account plus normal capital flows.[32] This definition allows for the needs of a current account that is not balanced and structural net capital inflows or outflows. In practice, however, this definition also suffers from the uncertainty and time lags of the feedback loop between the exchange rate and the current account (and the accompanying capital flows). Furthermore, it is difficult to determine the optimal level for the country's current account and capital flows.

Exchange Rate That Is Consistent with PPP   The exchange rate that equates overall domestic price levels with international price levels, or the exchange rate that reflects PPP, is another candidate for the concept of an equilibrium exchange rate.[33] The PPP exchange rate would reflect the value of the domestic currency in its ability to purchase an identical basket of goods and services across borders.

In practice, however, many goods and services cannot be traded across borders, and thus arbitrage activities that are supposed to equate domestic and international prices and ensure that the exchange rate accurately reflects PPP might not exist. Furthermore, while PPP is useful in comparing international standards of living, it does not reflect the country's external balance.

Exchange Rate That Equates Export Prices with Those of Trading Partners' Another candidate for the equilibrium exchange rate is one that equates one country's export prices with those of its trading partners.[34] Theoretically, this rate should ensure a level-playing field among countries in the global market. In practice, however, the same export prices do not necessarily translate into the same profit margins in different countries. Thus, such an exchange rate would still not necessarily represent an equilibrium exchange rate.

Exchange Rate That Equates Domestic Costs to Foreign Costs Although an exchange rate that equates per unit cost of domestic goods to those of the trading partner countries could solve some of the problems associated with differences in profit margins that were a problem for the exchange rate that equates export prices, problems of measurement remain.[35] Goods that are exported from different countries are not necessarily identical, although they might be of the same type (e.g., different varieties of rice). Differences in labor market structures across countries could also complicate measurements of wage costs.

Implications of the Elusiveness of an Equilibrium Exchange Rate for the Central Bank The discussion above suggests that a universally accepted notion of equilibrium exchange rate might not exist in practice. When trying the influence the level of the exchange rate, the central bank will have to decide which concept of the equilibrium exchange rate would best fit its context.

In practice, since economic data often involve time lags, the central bank's decision to intervene in the foreign exchange market to keep the exchange rate at an equilibrium defined based on any definition discussed also risks being untimely. Owing to time lags, by the time statistics on current account data, profit margins, or labor and material costs come out, the inherent equilibrium exchange rate might have already changed.

The elusiveness of an equilibrium exchange rate is also the reason that, unless a fixed exchange rate regime is adopted, central banks in a managed float regime often choose to intervene to smooth out excess volatilities in the exchange rates rather than to intervene to sustain the exchange rate at a particular level, while those that are in a free-float regime might simply let the exchange rate be determined purely by market forces.

Dealing with the Exchange Rate: The Operations Level

At the operations level, the central bank can influence the behavior of the exchange rate in three major ways. First, the central bank's implementation of *monetary policy* could influence the exchange rate, both *indirectly* through changes in pertinent macroeconomic variables and *directly* through expectations of participants in the foreign exchange market. Second, the central bank could attempt to directly temper or alter exchange rate movements through intervention in the *foreign exchange market*. Third, the central bank could influence the exchange rate through *regulations regarding capital flows*.

The Direct and Indirect Effects of Monetary Policy From the exchange rate theories discussed above, it is possible to broadly distinguish the channels through which monetary policy affects the exchange rate into those that are long term and those that are short term. In the long term, monetary policy affects the exchange rate indirectly through changes in relevant macroeconomic variables, which might include inflation, productivity, and the current account, among others. In the short term, monetary policy can have effects on conditions and expectations in the foreign exchange market microstructure.

By affecting the behavior of inflation and growth, monetary policy can influence the exchange rate in the long run, as PPP and the portfolio balance models predict. This channel of influence would work relatively slowly, as it takes time for monetary policy to first influence macroeconomic variables, and later, for macroeconomic variables to affect the exchange rate. In the short run, monetary policy announcements can influence expectations of foreign exchange market players and thus the exchange rate right away, as UIP and the market microstructure predict.

Foreign Exchange Intervention Apart from influencing the exchange rate through the conduct of monetary policy, the central bank can directly influence the exchange rate through direct intervention in the foreign exchange market. The term *foreign exchange market intervention* often refers to the central bank's act of buying and selling foreign currencies in the foreign exchange market.[36]

By buying up foreign currencies and paying for them using domestic currency, the central bank is effectively raising the supply of domestic currency in the system, thus putting downward pressures on the price of domestic currency, (i.e., the exchange rate). In contrast, by selling out its holdings of foreign currencies and taking in domestic currency instead, the central bank is effectively draining domestic currency from the system, thus putting upward pressures on the exchange rate. If the scale of such purchases or sales of foreign currencies is large enough, the central bank can indeed directly influence the exchange rate.

Sterilized Foreign Exchange Market Intervention In the act of a foreign exchange intervention, the central bank is effectively changing the supply of domestic currency. A change in the supply of domestic currency resulting from a foreign exchange intervention, however, has the potential of introducing unwanted side effects, since such a change would directly affect money conditions in the economy. For example, an increase in the supply of domestic currency resulting from a foreign currency purchase can put downward pressures on interest rates in the domestic money market. Unless the central bank wants to also lower interest rates in the money market, the central bank would need to *sterilize* the foreign currency purchase to eliminate potential unwanted side effects on money market interest rates.

In the example above, the central bank might choose to sterilize the foreign currency purchase by absorbing the extra supply of domestic money through the sales of domestic securities, such as government bonds and securities issued by the central bank to players in the money market. By selling its government bond holdings, or issuing its own securities for sales to money market participants, the central bank is effectively draining domestic money from the system. Such acts of buying up foreign currencies and at the same time selling or issuing domestic securities to drain out the resulting extra supply of domestic currency is known as a *sterilized foreign exchange intervention*.

For an emerging-market country, a sterilized foreign exchange intervention of capital inflows could be costly to the central bank, often because the central bank would be purchasing low yielding foreign currency assets (e.g., U.S. Treasuries) while issuing higher yielding domestic securities.[37]

Regulations of Capital Flows   Another possible way to influence movement of the exchange rate is through the use of regulation on capital flows. As we discussed earlier in the section on exchange rate theories, the decision by international investors to invest or not invest in a country can affect that country's exchange rate. If international investors perceive that investment in a country would yield a good total return, they would likely pour capital into that country. As foreign capital starts to flow in, the country's exchange rate is likely to appreciate, since international investors would have to convert their foreign currencies into that country's domestic currency to make an investment.

Normally, inflows of foreign capital are often welcome in a country with an open economy, since they could be used to finance domestic investment projects. However, if many investors decide to pour capital into the country at the same time, the influx of capital could put a lot of upward pressure on the exchange rate. This is especially a problem with a small emerging-market country that does not have much capacity to accommodate large inflows of capital.

With a fast appreciating currency, the country's exports are likely to become less competitive as they become more expensive, while the domestic economy is also likely to experience many distortions, especially if its internal prices and wages cannot change quickly in response. On the other hand, if local prices and wages can respond very quickly to changes in the exchange rate, the economy would still be experiencing problems if exchange rate movements are fast or volatile.

Economic distortions resulting from capital inflows could be worse if a large portion of capital inflows is the so-called hot money that aims to capture quick returns, possibly through speculation in the stock and real estate markets. Apart from causing a fast appreciation in the exchange rate that often results in economic distortions, such flows of hot money could lead to nonproductive investments and bubbles. Since large and fast inflows of capital potentially have great adverse effects on the economy, the central bank always has an option to impose regulations to temper the magnitude and the velocity of such flows.

Regulation of capital flows, or capital controls, can take various forms. Among the best known are the *Tobin tax* and *unremunerated reserve requirements (URRs)* on capital inflows. A Tobin tax refers to a tax charged on spot foreign exchange transactions. This has the effect of imposing extra costs on currency conversion and thereby lowering potential total returns from cross-border investment. Unremunerated reserve requirements on capital inflows, on the other hand, require that a certain percentage of the capital that investors bring into the economy be deducted and held in special accounts that pay no interest for a specified period. This also has the effect of lowering potential total returns from cross-border investment.

In practice, although the central bank always has the option of imposing capital controls to temper pressures on the exchange rate, it rarely exercises such options. The introduction of regulations on capital flows could discourage all types of capital, not just hot money, since it translates into uncertainty for international investors. In the real world it is very difficult to discriminate between speculative and productive inflows. Also, over time, speculators often find loopholes even in a well-designed regulation that aims squarely at hot money.

Management of Official Foreign Reserves: The Other Side of the Central Bank's Balance Sheet

The central bank's intervention in the foreign exchange market entails selling and buying of domestic currency, which directly affects the central bank's liabilities. Such selling and buying of the domestic currency, however, would often be financed by official foreign reserves (OFRs), which are assets on the central bank's balance sheet. Accordingly, central banks often also have the duty of managing their portfolios of OFRs as a byproduct of their exchange rate management.

Official Foreign Reserves and the Exchange Rate Policy According to the IMF, official foreign exchange reserves are official public sector assets that are readily available to and controlled by the monetary authorities for a range of objectives including to "support and maintain confidence in the policies for monetary and exchange rate management, including the capacity to intervene in support of the national or union currency; limit external vulnerability by maintaining foreign currency liquidity to absorb shocks during times of crisis or when access to borrowing is curtailed, and in doing so provide a level of confidence to markets that a country can meet its external obligations; demonstrate the backing of domestic currency by external assets; assist the government in meeting its foreign exchange needs and external debt obligations; and maintain a reserve for national disasters or emergencies."[38]

In practice, OFRs could include gold, foreign currencies, foreign government securities, foreign government guaranteed securities (such as mortgage backed securities), as well as foreign corporate bonds and foreign equities, depending on the statute governing the particular central bank.

When the central bank wants to dampen exchange rate appreciation, it could intervene in the foreign exchange market by selling out domestic currency and buying up foreign currencies. The sales of domestic currency will raise supply of the domestic currency and dampen the appreciation pressures on the currency. The purchase of foreign currencies will contribute to the buildup in OFRs.

When the central bank wants to temper exchange rate depreciation, it can buy up domestic currency by selling parts of its OFRs in the foreign exchange market. The purchase of domestic currency will reduce its supply of domestic currency and temper depreciation pressures on the currency. The sales of foreign assets out of OFRs will reduce the amount of OFRs under the control of the central bank.

OFRs and the Central Bank's Balance Sheet The use of OFRs in foreign exchange market intervention will have implications for the central bank's balance sheet. OFRs can be considered *assets* on the central bank's balance sheet that are financed by *liabilities* such as domestic currency (e.g., money issued to buy up foreign currencies during foreign exchange market interventions), and central bank securities (e.g., securities issued by the central bank when sterilizing the effects of foreign currency purchases).

The purchase of foreign currencies to temper appreciation pressures on domestic currency will have the effect of enlarging the central bank's balance sheet by raising both assets and liabilities, if such a purchase is done without sterilization, or is being sterilized by the issuance of *central bank* securities. Foreign currencies purchased will now be considered as a part of OFRs and thus the central bank's assets.

If the central bank uses domestic currency to buy foreign currencies without sterilization, then the domestic currency used in that operation would contribute to the rise in the liabilities of the central bank. If the central bank uses the domestic currency to buy the foreign currencies but then sterilizes the operation by issuing *central bank* securities to drain out the extra domestic currency from the system, then OFRs (assets) would rise, while liabilities would also rise, but ultimately in the form of the central bank's issued securities, rather than the domestic currency.

If the central bank uses the domestic currency to buy foreign currencies but sterilizes the operation by selling domestic *government* securities to drain the extra domestic currency from the system, then the size of the central bank's balance sheet will remain the same as that before the purchase of foreign currencies. The composition of the asset side of the balance sheet, however, will be different from before, as the central bank would have effectively substituted its government securities holdings with the foreign currencies purchased.

Management of OFRs When the central bank buys up foreign currencies to temper appreciation pressures on the domestic currency, it normally does not want to simply keep the purchased foreign currencies in its vault. Rather, it would prefer to preserve the purchasing power of those foreign currencies it has, and possibly earn some investment returns. As such, the central bank would often diversify foreign currencies it has into various financial instruments, making it into an investment portfolio.

In managing its portfolio of OFRs, the central bank often aims for *safety*, *liquidity*, and appropriate *returns*. Traditionally, central banks invest their OFRs in safe, highly liquid instruments, such as foreign currency deposits at reputable financial institutions, as well as highly rated foreign government securities, particularly U.S. government securities.

In the past decade, however, OFRs of many emerging-market economies have grown very quickly, owing partly to the central banks' need to purchase foreign currencies in response to appreciation pressures on the domestic currency that came from the growth in their export earnings and capital inflows from advanced economies. In the wake of the 2007–2010 financial crisis, the large balances of OFRs, often financed by issuance of central bank securities, have become a concern from a balance sheet perspective.

In the wake of the crisis, returns from investment in traditional reserves assets, such as foreign currency deposits and government securities of advanced economies, fell to historical lows. Meanwhile, to sterilize their foreign currency purchases, the emerging-market central banks often had to issue securities that pay higher interest rates than could they receive on their investment in OFRs. Furthermore, as emerging-market currencies kept appreciating, emerging-market central banks were also experiencing huge valuation losses on their holdings of foreign assets when measured in terms of their domestic currencies.

In response to *carry* losses (the difference between the low yields of investment in traditional reserves assets—such as short-term deposits and advanced economies government securities—and the high interest rates that emerging-market central banks had to pay on their sterilization securities), as well as valuation losses, many emerging-market central banks started to diversify into other classes of assets. These new asset classes often included emerging-market government securities, mortgage-backed securities guaranteed by advanced market governments, corporate bonds from both advanced economies and emerging-market countries, and equities. The specific classes included in the mix depend on what the central banks' own statutes allow.

SUMMARY

The exchange rate is a key variable that the central bank must watch, since it is the price of money in terms of another currency and could affect monetary stability as well as financial stability. Exchange rate regimes can range from rigid pegs on one end of the spectrum to free floats on the other. In the middle, regimes include the traditional fixed exchange rate, the fixed exchange rate with a horizontal band, the crawling peg, and the managed float.

Major exchange rate theories include purchasing power parity, uncovered interest parity, portfolio balance models, and exchange rate market microstructure theory.

At the macro level, the central bank must be aware of the interrelationship among the exchange rate, inflation, and interest rates. Also, the central bank must be aware that a free-float exchange rate regime, free-capital flows, and an independent monetary policy cannot coexist in the long run. Furthermore, the determination of an equilibrium exchange rate can be quite elusive.

At the micro level, the central bank can influence the exchange rate by interventions in the foreign exchange market, as well as by regulations on capital flows.

Foreign exchange market intervention entails the management of official foreign reserves by the central bank.

KEY TERMS

absolute purchasing power parity

Big Mac index

common currency

crawling peg

currency board

equilibrium exchange rate

exchange rate market microstructure theory

exchange rate regime

exchange rate risk

fixed exchange rate with a horizontal band

foreign direct investment

foreign exchange intervention

foreign loans

free float

impossible trinity

managed float

official foreign reserves

portfolio balance model of the exchange rate

portfolio investment

purchasing power parity

relative purchasing power parity

rigid peg

risk premium

sterilized foreign exchange intervention

Tobin tax

traditional fixed exchange rate regime

uncovered interest parity

unremunerated reserve requirements

QUESTIONS

1. Provide an example of the way that the exchange rate can affect monetary stability.
2. Provide an example of the way that the exchange rate can affect employment.
3. Provide an example of the way that the exchange rate can affect financial stability.
4. In a rigid peg exchange rate regime, can the central bank independently print money to stimulate the economy without regard to money conditions in the country that it pegs its exchange rate to? Why or why not?
5. Why might a central bank choose a currency board for its exchange rate regime?
6. What are the drawbacks of a currency board system?
7. Why might a central bank choose to adopt a free-float exchange rate regime?
8. What are the problems with a freely floating exchange rate?
9. What are key differences between a managed float exchange rate regime and a crawling peg exchange rate regime?
10. According to relative purchasing power parity, if inflation goes up, what is likely to happen to the exchange rate?
11. Why might an exchange rate deviate from purchasing power parity in practice?
12. According to uncovered interest parity, what is the relationship between the interest rate differential between two countries and their corresponding exchange rate?
13. According to uncovered interest parity, if the interest rate in one country is hiked unexpectedly, what would happen to the exchange rate of that country? Why?
14. According to portfolio balance models of exchange rates, why might uncovered interest rate parity (UIP) not hold?
15. According to portfolio balance models of exchange rates, if a country's productivity improves what is likely to happen to the exchange rate?
16. Why might the exchange rate move continuously, almost second-by-second, given that important economic data are released only monthly or quarterly?
17. Why can't the central bank aim to have an exchange rate target, free capital mobility, and independent monetary policy at the same time? What is this concept called?
18. How useful is the concept of equilibrium exchange rates? Please discuss using at least three examples.
19. What is sterilized foreign exchange intervention?
20. Why might sterilized foreign exchange interventions be costly for emerging-market central banks to undertake?
21. What might be the reasons for the central bank to impose capital controls?
22. What might be the reasons for the central bank to not impose capital controls?

Three

Financial Stability

Part III focuses on financial stability, another key central banking mandate. The financial stability mandate started receiving attention in the 1980s but has received even more since the global financial crisis of 2007–2010.

Chapter 10 reviews various definitions of financial stability, provides an analytical framework that could be practical for central banks as they consider how to fulfill this mandate, and reviews the theoretical foundations of financial stability.

Chapter 11 examines various tools that central banks might use to identify and monitor risks to financial stability. This review is done using the analytical framework proposed in Chapter 10, and prospective tools are examined from three key overlapping areas, namely the macroeconomy, financial institutions, and financial markets.

Chapter 12 looks at various tools that the central bank could use to intervene to address risks to financial stability. Review of these tools also uses the analytical framework proposed in Chapter 10.

CHAPTER 10

Financial Stability

Definition, Analytical Framework, and Theoretical Foundation

Learning Objectives

1. Define financial stability.
2. Explain why financial stability is important as a central banking mandate.
3. Explain how weaknesses in the balance sheets of households, firms, and the government could affect financial stability.
4. Describe the risks facing a financial institution.
5. Describe the risks facing a network of financial institutions.
6. Explain why information asymmetry could lead to instability in financial markets.

As discussed in Chapter 4, financial stability has increasingly been recognized as a key mandate of central banks, in addition to monetary stability (and, in the case of the United States, full employment). Given the relative newness of the focus on financial stability, which started in the 1980s,[1] the definition, analytical framework, and operational framework for financial stability are all still very much at the early development stages when compared to monetary stability.[2]

This chapter first reviews issues surrounding the definition of financial stability. The chapter then proposes an analytical framework that a central bank could use to view financial stability from a practical perspective. The chapter ends with a review of theoretical principles that will be helpful in understanding probable causes of financial instability and how the central bank might deal with them.

10.1 DEFINITIONS OF FINANCIAL STABILITY

Among the three widely cited central bank mandates, financial stability is arguably the only one that does *not* yet have a single, quantifiable, operational definition that is widely agreed upon.[3] For price stability, one could argue that *low and stable inflation* is often the agreed-upon operational definition. For employment, despite various complications one can think of the unemployment rate as a measure that can be used, possibly against the natural rate of unemployment as a benchmark. This lack of an agreed-upon, quantifiable definition of financial stability reflects both the relative newness and the complexity of the issues involved.

Although central banks have been involved with financial stability functions since their early days,* financial liberalization in the last few decades has brought about rapid changes in the financial system globally. The complexity and interconnectedness of global financial systems have grown more than most would have expected prior to the crisis of 2007–2010. Although many central banks started to put more emphasis on developing tools and a framework for financial stability functions in the late 1990s, partly in response to the delegation of the bank supervision role to outside regulators, the framework and the tools developed for the maintenance of financial stability were still relatively immature when compared to the rapid changes in global financial systems.

The complexity of the issues involved have led to many different definitions of financial stability being proposed, oftentimes with different emphases. A 1990 paper by Ben Bernanke (now former Federal Reserve chairman) and economist Mark Gertler focused on the balance sheets of economic agents and suggested that financial stability depended on the net-worth positions of potential borrowers.[4] The paper argued that if the net-worth positions of potential borrowers were low enough, there could be collapse in investment and thus economic activity.

Meanwhile, a 2006 paper by economists Oriol Aspachs, Charles Goodhart, Miguel Segoviano, Demetrios Tsomocos, and Lea Zicchino suggested that *credit risk*—that is, the ability of borrowers to repay their debts in full—is central to financial stability, and thus low *probability of default* by borrowers is a key metric for financial stability.[5] This followed a 2005 paper by Charles Goodhart that stated, "If everyone always fully paid their debts, with certainty, there would be no credit risk, probably no money (since everyone's IOUs could be used in trade), and no need for financial intermediaries."[6]

A 2009 paper from Claudio Borio and Mathias Drehmann focused more on the performance of financial institutions, defining financial stability as the converse of financial instability, with instability occurring because of "a set of conditions that is sufficient to result in the emergence of financial distress/crises in response to normal-sized shocks."[7]

Gary Schinasi's 2004 paper looked at the broader financial system rather than financial institutions, and defined financial stability as the ability of the financial system to (1) facilitate both the efficient allocation of economic resources and the effectiveness of other economic processes, (2) assess, price, allocate, and manage financial risks, and (3) maintain its ability to perform these key function primarily through self-correcting mechanisms.[8]

These diverse emphases in defining financial stability suggest that financial stability is indeed *multifaceted* in nature, and that one has to look at the interaction of various facets to get a more complete picture.

---

*As a lender of last resort, and thus as a bank supervisor, as well as a guardian of the payment system, for example.

10.2 A PRACTICAL ANALYTICAL FRAMEWORK: THE MACROECONOMY, FINANCIAL INSTITUTIONS, AND FINANCIAL MARKETS

It might be helpful to recognize that financial stability encompasses three key interrelated elements for central banks: (1) a *macroeconomy* that is free of major financial imbalances, (2) a system of *financial institutions* that is sound and stable, and (3) *financial markets* that are smoothly functioning. These three elements of financial stability normally interact with each other in a state of flux, and the absence of *any one* element can lead to financial instability as well as the failure of the other two elements.* Figure 10.1 illustrates the overlapping dimensions of the three key elements of financial stability.

An analytical framework based on recognizing the three key elements and their interrelationships is practical from the central bank's vantage point for at least three reasons. First, it helps *disentangle* the inherent complexity of the interrelationships among the key elements of financial stability into more tractable and manageable parts. Second, it corresponds well with the *institutional setup* of most modern central banks, even those without supervisory function. Third, it corresponds well to the disparate *body of theoretical and empirical research* on the issues related to financial stability that can also be grouped roughly into these three specific areas (see Gertler's 1988 paper, for example).[9] The body of research on financial stability will be discussed in more detail later in the chapter.

The Inherent Interrelationships between the Macroeconomy, Financial Institutions, and Financial Markets

The interrelationships of the macroeconomy, financial institutions, and financial markets are inherent in nature. One can see that for financial institutions to be sound

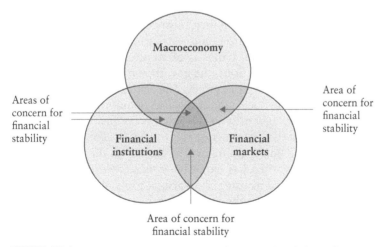

FIGURE 10.1   Overlapping Dimensions of Financial Stability: The Macroeconomy, Financial Institutions, and Financial Markets

---

*In such a framework, a stable payments system helps stitch the three elements seamlessly together.

and stable, or for financial markets to continue to function smoothly, it is often a prerequisite that the macroeconomy be free from major financial imbalances—that is, households, firms, and the government are free from excessive indebtedness.[10] If they are not free from excessive indebtedness, and their debts cannot be repaid in full, then their lenders (financial institutions), and ultimately savers in the economy, would have to bear financial losses.

If the losses of financial institutions are (or believed to be) large enough, then the financial intermediation process in the macroeconomy could be at risk (this process is described in section 10.3). Depositors could rush in to withdraw their money, while creditors of the financial institutions might call in their loans. Disruptions in investment and consumption could ensue. Furthermore, troubles among financial institutions could freeze lending in the money market and also usher in panics in other financial markets. As such, the financial system as a whole would be unstable and unable to function smoothly or effectively.

On the other hand, panics in financial markets* could bring a negative feedback loop to financial institutions and the macroeconomy. Firms that rely on financial markets might find themselves short of funds during dire times, while households could be hit with both income and financial losses (from job cuts, and the fall in the value of their financial asset holdings, for example), dampening their demand for goods and services. In the case of severe financial instability, economic activity could sharply contract and price stability would be threatened.

By grouping the issues into these three separate categories, we can often identify issues that crosscut these three key interrelated areas. Accordingly, once the issues are identified, they could be more effectively dealt with, knowing how they might fit in the big picture. Coordination using information and tools from different units of the central bank will often facilitate effective solutions to problems.

Financial Stability and the Organization of Central Banks

Through their conduct of monetary policy, most central banks already have a unit to monitor, assess, and forecast inflation and output in the macroeconomy. The monetary policy unit of these central banks is often already tasked with assessing the behavior of households, corporations, the government, and external sectors, as well as monitoring developments in asset prices. The central banks can thus easily leverage the existing capability of such a monetary policy unit to monitor and assess risks to financial stability that might arise in the macroeconomy.

Meanwhile, through their conduct of routine *financial market* operations, most central banks also have a unit that interacts actively with the financial markets. This unit of the central banks often has extensive contact with players in the financial markets and has experience in using the various tools at its disposal to influence financial markets. The central banks can thus leverage the existing capability of such a financial market operations unit to monitor and assess risks to financial stability that might arise from financial markets.

---

*Financial markets are markets where market players with excess funds and market players in need of funds transact with each other. Market players might include banks, nonbank financial institutions, and large and retail investors. The term *financial markets*, in fact, is a generic term that encompasses a great variety of specific markets, including money markets (for short-term lending), capital markets (for long-term funding, which include both equity and bond markets), and other markets, such as foreign exchange markets (for foreign exchange funding), derivatives markets (for hedging activities), etc.

As for monitoring financial institutions, those central banks that have a bank supervisory unit can use it to provide timely and detailed assessments on the banking sector's financial health. For central banks with a bank supervisory function, such a unit also often has experience and tools to influence banks on issues related to financial stability. Even central banks *without* a banking supervisory role often have a unit that assesses and monitors developments in financial institutions, and those central banks could utilize such a unit in monitoring and assessing risks that might come from financial institutions, and to coordinate with relevant banking supervisory agency outside the central banks.

In any case, it is well recognized that close coordination and data-sharing among these three units, as well as with outside agencies, is vital if a central bank is to effectively deal with financial instability risks.

10.3 FINANCIAL STABILITY: THEORETICAL FOUNDATIONS

Unlike the body of research on price stability and employment, the theoretical underpinnings of financial stability practices remained in the relatively early stages of development and are still quite fragmented. To make the review of relevant theoretical knowledge more tractable, it might be useful to group it into the three key areas of financial stability mentioned above: the macroeconomy, financial institutions, and financial markets (see Table 10.1).

TABLE 10.1 Grouping of Key Theories Relating to Financial Stability

Area of focus	Key studies and theories	Key hypotheses	Key implications
Macroeconomy	Fisher (1933), Gurley and Shaw (1955), Kindleberger (1978), Minsky (1986), Bernanke and Gertler (1990)	Financial activities and economic activities could feed on each other. The macroeconomy is thus prone toward instability.	Moderation of financial activities to prevent excessive risk buildups that could threaten the macroeconomy might be needed.
Financial institutions	Diamond and Dybvig (1983), Rochet and Tirole (1996), Allen and Gale (2000), Freixas, Paragi, and Rochet (2000)	Individual financial intermediaries are prone toward bank runs. Linkages among financial institutions also make the system prone toward instability.	Deposit insurance, effective supervision of both individual banks and the banking system as a whole, as well as resolutions to stop a run, are needed.
Financial markets	Akerloff (1970), Stiglitz and Weiss (1981)	The existence of information asymmetry in financial markets suggests that market prices do not necessarily reflect underlying risks.	Mitigation of information asymmetry and related problems (e.g., moral hazard, adverse selection, principal agent problems) will be needed to reduce unintended risk buildups.

First, at the macroeconomy level, key theories focus on interaction between *financial* activities of economic agents and their *real* economic activity. Acceleration in financial activities, as reflected by fast growth in credit and asset prices, for example, could induce more consumption and investment, which would then bring about more increases in credit and asset prices. Once the increases in credit and asset prices turned into a bubble and burst, however, the resulting declines in credit and asset prices would amplify the contraction in real economic activity. Theories focusing on this interaction were disseminated in 1933 by Irving Fisher[11], in 1955 by John Gurley and E. S. Shaw,[12] in 1986 by Hyman Minsky,[13] in 1978 by Charles Kindleberger,[14] in 1990 by Ben Bernanke and Mark Gertler,[15] and in 2004 by Claudio Borio and William White (2004).[16] Later research, including a 2002 paper by Claudio Borio and Philip Lowe[17] and a 2009 paper by Borio and Mathias Drehmann,[18] found evidence to support such theories.

Second, with respect to financial institutions, relevant theories include models of bank runs, such as those pioneered by Douglas Diamond and Philip Dybvig in 1983,[19] which suggested that financial intermediation generally has a smooth functioning equilibrium, but is also *inherently* prone to instability. Banks often make long-term, illiquid loans, using funds raised from deposits that have a short-maturity or can be called back by depositors at will. A bank run can occur whenever there is a panic among depositors, since the bank will not be able to call back loans and repay depositors as demanded. Looking at the banking system as a whole, as banks themselves are often linked with each other (whether through *direct* exposures such as interbank lending or through *indirect* exposure where they are similarly exposed to the price swings in assets that they hold, e.g. loans, and government securities), the effects of a shock to one bank would be distributed throughout the system. We can include later work related to *systemic* bank runs, such as 1996 research from J.C. Rochet and J. Tirole,[20] 2000 research from F. Allen and D. Gale[21] and research the same year from X. Freixas, B. Parigi, and J. C. Rochet,[22] and work on the resiliency and fragility of financial network, such as that from Andrew Haldane in 2009,[23] in this group of theories as well.

Third, with respect to financial markets, are theories relating to market failures based on information asymmetry, as pioneered and applied to financial markets by George Akerloff in 1970,[24] which suggested that financial markets are not completely efficient and conditions such as adverse selection can occur (e.g., see the 1981 paper by Joseph Stiglitz and Andrew Weiss, "Credit Rationing in Markets with Imperfection"[25]). With information asymmetry, prices of financial assets might not reflect the true underlying risks. With distorted risk-reward profiles, investors thus might accumulate excessive positions in certain financial assets, which could lead to financial imbalances and financial instability. Furthermore, during times of financial stress, information asymmetry might exacerbate the situation: for example, through coordination failures, whereby financial firms either refuse to lend to each other or charge prohibitively high interest rates in order to insure against risk.

The Macroeconomy: Interaction between Financial and Economic Cycles

The influence of *financial* activities (e.g., borrowing and lending) on *real* economic activity (e.g., consumption and investment) has been recognized since at least the time of the Great Depression, when Irving Fisher[26] argued that poorly performing financial markets contributed to the severity of the economic downturn (see Mark Gertler's 1988 paper[27]). Since then, studies such as one by Gurley and Shaw in 1955,[28] Kindleberger in 1978,[29] Minsky in 1986,[30] Bernanke and Gertler in 1990,[31] Borio and Lowe in 2002,[32] Borio and White in 2004,[33] and Borio and Drehman in 2009[34]—as well as papers by Borio in 2011[35] and 2012,[36] have noted how *financial* activities and *real* economic activity can interact to reinforce boom-and-bust cycles.

To make a review of theoretical foundation in this area more tractable, it might also be helpful to delineate related issues into (1) the behavior of economic agents, (2) the role of nonmoney financial assets, and (3) the behavior of financial intermediaries.

The Behavior of Economic Agents　Work along the line of the research cited above by Gurley and Shaw in 1955, Kindleberger in 1978, Minsky in 1986, and Bernanke and Gertler in 1990 pointed out that the balance sheets or net-worth positions of economic agents (e.g., households and firms) can influence their spending and investment behavior, and thus business cycles.

Theoretically, a strong net-worth position of an agent would imply greater resources available for spending or for use as collateral for borrowing. With a strong balance sheet (probably supported by a strong prices for assets), an agent can spend more (which would help generate more economic activity). Robust economic activity, meanwhile, could also support a further rise in asset prices and the agent's balance sheet in a self-reinforcing manner.

A fall in asset prices, in contrast, could weaken the balance sheet of agents and their ability to spend or borrow, which would slow down economic activity. If agents have heavy debt burdens relative to net worth, possibly as a result of prior borrowing to purchase or invest in assets when asset prices were rising, then the fall in asset prices could weaken their balance sheets and suppress their ability to spend. Note that if agents had financed asset purchases largely by using borrowed funds, then even a small fall in asset prices can severely harm their balance sheets.

If asset prices fall far enough, many agents in the economy might find their net worth to be very low or negative, which would not only affect their ability to spend and, by extension, general economic activity, but could also hamper their ability to repay their debts This could result in both a banking crisis and a collapse in general spending. Work by Borio and Lowe in 2002 and Borio and Drehmann in 2009 showed that unusually strong increases in credit and asset prices could indeed lead to banking crises in advanced as well as emerging-market economies.

Given that governments can also be considered economic agents, the strengths and weaknesses in governments' balance sheets can influence real economic activity. Using data from both advanced and emerging-market economies that spans about 200 years, in 2010 Carmen Reinhart and Kenneth Rogoff showed that countries whose governments have weak balance sheet positions (i.e., heavy debt loads that represent more than 90 percent of GDP) were likely to have lower GDP growth rates than otherwise.[37]

CONCEPT: FINANCIAL INSTABILITY IN MINSKY'S FRAMEWORK

The work of the late Hyman P. Minsky has received much attention in the wake of the 2007–2010 crisis, partly because it aptly describes how the interaction between activities in the macroeconomy and financing activities can bring about financial instability.

In his book *Stabilizing an Unstable Economy*, first published in 1986, Minsky touched on various aspects of financial instability, from macroeconomic theories to the practices of bankers.

Here we focus on how the interaction between activities in the macroeconomy and financing activities might contribute to financial instability (see Figure 10.2).

According to Minsky, financing activities can be categorized into three distinct types. The first is *hedge finance*, which dominates during an economic recovery phase. During this period lenders focus on repairing their balance sheets, and thus focus on loans to projects whose cash flows from operations are more than sufficient to meet contractual payment commitments.

Second, *speculative finance* emerges as the economy recovers and starts to grow. Lenders focus on projects that might have income shortfalls in the near term but will likely have positive returns over the long run. Examples of such projects might include capital-intensive investment projects, as well as ordinary fixed-rate mortgages.

Third, *Ponzi finance* becomes more prevalent after the economy has been in a protracted growth period. Borrowers, focusing on capital gains on assets

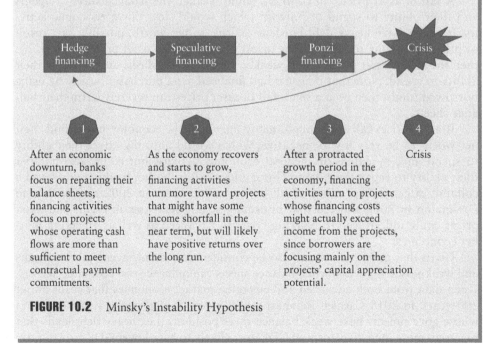

FIGURE 10.2   Minsky's Instability Hypothesis

rather than how a projects' income might cover operational and financing costs, are more willing to invest in projects whose financing costs might actually exceed total income over the life of the project. We can think of variable rate subprime mortgages as being an example of Ponzi finance.

As Ponzi finance becomes pervasive, any hiccup (e.g., rising interest rates) can lead to financial instability, since under Ponzi finance, lenders are already lending to projects that are not viable in the long run.

At any one time, the economy might have a mix of these three types of financing activities. But as the economy keeps growing, incentives in the economy lead to a transition from hedge finance to speculative finance, and then to Ponzi finance.

For example, initially after a crisis interest rates are often low and liquidity plentiful, and banks themselves might shy away from speculative and Ponzi finance. As the economy starts to recover, but short-term interest rates are still relatively low, firms and households might find it profitable to engage in speculative financing, that is, to borrow at the low short-term rates and invest in capital-intensive long-term projects that offer higher long-term yields. As the economy enters the boom phase and asset prices start to rise, then households and firms might start to engage in Ponzi finance, that is, borrowing to invest in projects for the purpose of asset price appreciation, even if cash inflows from the projects might not cover operational costs and debt repayment commitments for the projects. Adding to this, Minsky points out, are the inherent incentives of bankers to use leverage to expand their lending operations, which can easily tip the whole system into instability.[38]

The Role of *Nonmoney* Financial Assets   The research of both Gurley and Shaw in 1955[39] and Kindleberger in 1978[40] pointed toward to the importance of *nonmoney* financial assets; that is, those financial securities issued by intermediaries that can contribute to acceleration and crashes in economic activity. In their research Gurley and Shaw pointed out that if the central bank were to effectively maintain economic stability, there would be a needs for *financial control*—controls on the proliferation of *nonmoney* financial assets—in addition to *monetary control*, or control of money.

Meanwhile, Kindleberger pointed out that throughout history, booms and resulting crashes could be traced to an introduction of new asset classes, whether the asset was tulips in early sixteenth-century Holland or dot-com shares in the late twentieth-century United States.[41] Kindleberger passed away in 2003, before the global financial crisis of 2007–2010, but securities backed by subprime mortgages come to mind as another new asset class that led to a boom and a resulting crisis. The role of nonmoney financial assets in a financial crisis has gained much attention in the wake of the 2007–2010 crises, although prior to that mainstream research in macroeconomics has tended to neglect it. See "Concept: Money versus *Nonmoney* Financial Assets in Macroeconomics" for more details.

CONCEPT: MONEY VERSUS *NONMONEY* FINANCIAL ASSETS IN MACROECONOMICS

Most mainstream macroeconomic research from the 1950s to the period prior to the global financial crisis of 2007–2010 ignored the impact that financial assets could have on real economic activity and often treated financial intermediaries as *passive* agents who collected funds from lenders and distributed them to borrowers (see, for example, the work of Gertler in 1988 and Borio in 2012[42]).

According to Gertler's 1988 work,[43] the lack of emphasis on *nonmoney* financial assets and financial structures among mainstream macroeconomists was attributable to at least the three factors that follow.

1. The influence of work by Franco Modigliani and Merton Miller in 1958,[44] which "derived the formal proposition that real economic decisions were independent of financial structure," and thus it did not matter to the value of the firm whether the firm borrowed or issued equity to finance its investment.
2. The publication of Milton Friedman's and Anna Schwartz's 1963 book,[45] which emphasized the role of the money supply (as opposed to *nonmoney* financial assets) as a key contributing factors to the severity of the Great Depression.
3. The popular use of reduced-form econometric techniques, particularly vector auto regression (VAR) models that aim to capture the dynamics among key macroeconomic forces by using the fewest number of variables possible in the modeling process. As such, money often ends up being the main variable representing other (non-money) financial variables as well.

Later on, even when macroeconomists in central banks and in academia started to develop macroeconometric and general equilibrium macroeconomic models for use in monetary policy, the influence of mainstream macroeconomics and the difficulties of incorporating complex financial structures into these types of models still prompted macroeconomists to emphasize money as the only key financial variable. When financial intermediaries are treated as passive agents, the only monetary variable(s) in a macroeconomic model are interest rates (or the money supply), which do not necessarily capture developments in financial activities that might later have implications for real economic activity (see the previously cited work of Gertler in 1988 and Borio in 2011[46] and 2012 for examples).

The Behavior of Financial Intermediaries   Hyman Minsky's 1986 book emphasized that managers of financial intermediaries indeed were active profit maximizers, and that their profit maximizing behavior would lead them to fund projects that were progressively more speculative (projects that relied progressively more on capital appreciation, as opposed to income flows), driving the economy further into a boom period.[47]

To keep profits and their bonuses growing, managers of financial intermediaries will also likely need to engage in higher leveraging (i.e., borrowing more funds to invest in more projects). When the economy inevitably slows and these projects do not generate as much income as expected, the failures of the speculative projects and the highly leveraged position of financial intermediaries leads to a financial collapse.

How a financial collapse feeds back to the real economy was also captured by Ben Bernanke's 1983 work, which pointed out that the collapse of the financial system was a key determinant of the Great Depression's depth and length.[48] The breakdown of banking activity and the crisis in security markets choked off financial flows to borrowers, who did not have easy access to other forms of credit, which further weakened borrowers' balance sheets.

Financial Institutions: Intermediation, Bank Runs, and Banking System Resiliency

In their influential 1983 study, Douglas Diamond and Philip Dybvig presented a model that formalized the act of financial intermediation and how financial intermediation might inherently be prone to instability in the form of bank runs.[49] While Diamond and Dybvig focused on runs involving a single bank, later work, such as that by J.C. Rochet and J. Tirole in 1996, F. Allen and D. Gale in 2000[50] and X. Freixas, B. Paragi, and J. C. Rochet the same year,[51] investigated contagion and systemic effects of a bank run.

Financial Intermediation   According to Diamond and Dybvig, the act of intermediation can be thought of as liquidity creation by banks. Savers are often reluctant to lend directly to businesses or households, since those loans are illiquid; that is, they cannot be converted into cash quickly without incurring substantial losses. By taking in funds from savers and promising that savers can withdraw their funds easily, with very low or no costs, banks are in fact creating liquidity in the system. If savers deem liquidity to be important to them, they will be more likely to deposit some of their funds in banks. Banks then pool these funds together and lend them out to borrowers under long-term contracts. In a sense, by pooling deposits banks are providing depositors with an insurance arrangement in which depositors share the risk of liquidating an asset early at a loss.[52]

By pooling deposits from a large number of depositors who normally have uncorrelated expenditure needs, a bank needs to keep only a small fraction of funds on hand to meet demand for withdrawals at any given point in time. The bank can then lend most of the rest of the funds out to its borrowers so that the funds can earn interest. The interest earned can be applied to deposits or used to cover the bank's operating costs, and, if possible, pay dividends to the bank's shareholders. At any given point in time a bank can function smoothly as long as only a small fraction of depositors want to withdraw their deposits. Normally depositors would be expected to have uncorrelated expenditure needs and thus would be unlikely to withdraw their deposits at the same time. (See Figure 10.3.)

The Diamond-Dybvig Model: The Switch from Normal Functioning to a Bank Run   If at any given point in time the bank's depositors demand withdrawals in excess of the funds that the bank has on hand, then the bank could get into serious trouble. As Diamond and

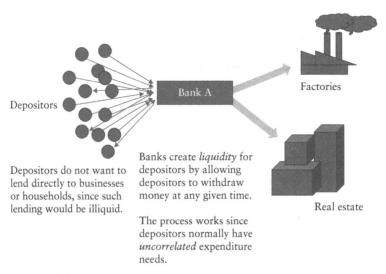

Depositors

Depositors do not want to lend directly to businesses or households, since such lending would be illiquid.

Banks create *liquidity* for depositors by allowing depositors to withdraw money at any given time.

The process works since depositors normally have *uncorrelated* expenditure needs.

Factories

Real estate

FIGURE 10.3   A Stylized Diamond-Dybvig Model: A Normal Functioning Equilibrium

Dybvig point out in their 1983 work cited above, a bank cannot easily call in their loans in order to raise funds to meet depositors' demands without incurring significant losses, since those loans are long-term.

Indeed, if a large enough portion of depositors demand withdrawal of their funds at the same time, the bank could simply run out of money and go bankrupt. Depositors would then have to litigate to recover their funds from the liquidation of the bank's assets. In practice, the recovery of funds through litigation could take a long time, and depositors would have to contend with the possibility that they might be unable to recover all their funds.

Consequently, if depositors expect that a large proportion of depositors would want to withdraw their money at the same time, it is rational for all depositors to rush in and try to withdraw their money. Depositors know that those who withdraw their money early are likely to have an advantage, since at that time, the bank might still have enough money on hand to repay depositors. This situation creates a self-fulfilling prophecy, with all depositors rushing in to be the first to withdraw. (See Figure 10.4.)

According to Diamond and Dybvig, there are thus two equilibriums in financial intermediation: one is normal functioning, and the other is a bank run. The normal functioning case would occur as long as depositors expect most other depositors to withdraw money only when they have real expenditure needs. In such a case, it is rational for all depositors to also withdraw only when they have real expenditure needs.[53]

A bank run, however, can occur whenever depositors expect most other depositors to rush in and close their accounts. In such a case, it is rational for all depositors to rush in and close their accounts. The switch from the normal functioning equilibrium to a bank run could be triggered by multitudes of tangible and intangible things, including, notably, expectations.

The Banking System as a Network   The groundbreaking model of a bank run proposed by Diamond and Dybvig in 1983 focused mainly on the case of a run on an individual

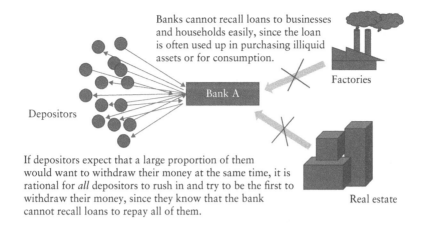

Banks cannot recall loans to businesses and households easily, since the loan is often used up in purchasing illiquid assets or for consumption.

Factories

Bank A

Depositors

If depositors expect that a large proportion of them would want to withdraw their money at the same time, it is rational for *all* depositors to rush in and try to be the first to withdraw their money, since they know that the bank cannot recall loans to repay all of them.

Real estate

Only those who come while the bank still has money on hand will likely be repaid on time and in full.

FIGURE 10.4   A Stylized Diamond-Dybvig Model: A Bank Run

bank. Later, researchers started to look at the possibility of a systemic bank run, in which distress in one bank could be transmitted to other banks through *direct* and *indirect* linkages.

Most prominent among the *direct* financial linkages are interbank loans, where banks lend to each other, possibly to meet liquidity needs. Payment systems are also direct linkages, albeit of a more physical type. With these direct linkages among banks, the banking system can be examined as a network. A hiccup that affects the ability of one bank to meet its obligations to another could lead to ripple effects through the network.

Indirect linkages are also a factor, because banks do often hold similar types of assets in their portfolios and thus the value of their portfolios will also be affected by each other's actions. For example, during a panic, once a troubled bank starts a fire sale of its short-term assets to raise funds, prices of those assets could fall very sharply, causing losses in other banks' portfolios. Other banks might then be forced to have their own fire sales, which would affect everyone further.

The work of Rochet and Tirole in 1996,[54] Allen and Gale in 2000,[55] and Freixas, Parigi, and Rochet[56] the same year examined cases where the failure of one bank or the payment systems triggered a chain of subsequent failures. In 2009, Andrew Haldane looked at how the financial network had become more fragile in the periods leading up to the 2007–2010 financial crisis.[57]

Network Resiliency and Network Fragility   Theoretically, connections between banks can make the banking network more *resilient* as well as more *fragile*, depending partly on *linkage structures*, *diversity of institutions*, and the *density of activities* or *concentration of risks* in the banking system.

According to Allen and Gale's 2000 work, in a better connected network—that is, where the interbank market is *complete*, meaning that banks of different types (e.g., commercial banks, investment banks, banks that focus on wholesale lending, and banks that focus on attracting deposits from savers) are all connected to one another—then potentially risks could be better distributed throughout the network. The proportion of the losses in one bank's portfolio can be shared by more banks through interbank agreements.[58]

In contrast, if the linkages between the banks in the network are incomplete—that is, banks of different types are *not* well linked to one another in the interbank market—the failure of a bank of one type could potentially lead to failures of banks of the same type, then those of similar types, which could trigger the failure of the entire network.

In 2009 Andrew Haldane pointed out that the *diversity* of banks had gradually declined in the decades before the 2007–2010 financial crisis, owing to the pursuit of similar business and risk management strategies.[59] With less diversity, banks are more susceptible to the same types of shocks and the banking system as a whole will be less resilient.

In the same speech Haldane also stated that global and national banking networks had been increasing in *density* prior to the 2007–2010 crisis, with large financial hubs becoming more common. With a concentration of activities in hubs, or in systemically important institutions, the system is likely to be more fragile, especially when there are shocks to the hubs or the systemically important institutions.[60]

Financial Markets: Reasons for Market Failures

In traditional economic analysis, financial markets are portrayed as having many attributes of the ideal, perfectly competitive market. Entries and exits are relatively easy, such that no single player can have sustained appreciable effects on prices, and market information can transmit quite fast and extensively.

The belief that financial markets are, to a great extent, *efficient* led regulators to take a more hands-off approach toward financial market regulations. With efficient financial markets, it was believed that market players would be able to make sound financial transactions based on their preferences and their assessment of risks as reflected by market prices.

Events relating to the global financial crisis of 2007–2010, however, suggested that financial markets were not as efficient as had previously been believed. Information asymmetry was indeed pervasive in the financial markets at all levels, and prices in the financial market therefore did not accurately reflect the underlying risks of financial market transactions. As Gertler pointed out in his 1988 work, inefficiencies in financial markets could manifest themselves in the behavior of financial markets and institutions, causing those inefficiencies to be significant factors contributing to aggregate economic activity.[61]

In the context of the 2007–2010 crisis, the presence of information asymmetry implied that risks could be underpriced, and thus market players might be accumulating excessive risks that, taken together, could threaten the stability of the system. Indeed, as the financial crisis unfolded, the inherent presence of information asymmetry in the financial markets became clearer. At the height of the crisis, the presence of information asymmetry also led to various types of failures in financial markets, such that intervention by the government was needed.

Studies on information asymmetry, which started in the 1960s, suggest at least four key problems that could be applicable in the understanding of financial

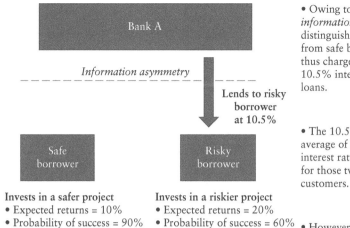

FIGURE 10.5 A Stylized Model of Adverse Selection

stability issues, including (1) adverse selection, (2) the principal-agent problem, (3) moral hazard, and (4) coordination failure. Furthermore, a fifth—externalities—which is a classic factor in market failures, was also found to be a factor in the financial crisis.

Adverse Selection Adverse selection refers to situations in which inferior products, services, or clients are more likely to be selected because buyers and sellers do not have equal relevant information. In terms of banking, this could occur when a bank cannot distinguish between safe and risky borrowers, and thus would charge them the same (average) interest rate. This would deter safer borrowers from borrowing from the bank, since that rate would be too high to make their safer projects profitable. Only risky borrowers will borrow from the bank, since, if successful, their projects could still be very profitable. Yet, since only risky borrowers would come to borrow, and still be charged an average rate rather than the higher rate commensurate with their credit risk, the bank is more exposed to risks than it should be. (See Figure 10.5.)

The Principal-Agent Problem The principal-agent problem refers to a situation in which a principal hires an agent but does not have complete information as to whether the agent will act in the best interest of the principal or in the best interest of the agent. (See Figure 10.6.)

In the wake of the 2007–2010 global financial crisis, the principal-agent problem was revealed to be prevalent in many contexts and layers throughout the financial industry. An example would be investment banks' compensation packages, under which the interests of the banks' managers were not fully aligned with those of shareholders. As is often the case, a large part of managers' and traders' compensation was bonuses paid according to the banks' financial performance for the year. With bonuses tied to yearly performance, managers and traders at investment banks

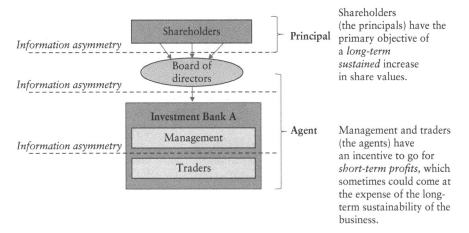

FIGURE 10.6   An Example of Principal-Agent Problem in an Investment Bank

are incentivized to focus on short-term profits instead of the long-term sustainability of the business. The drive to achieve short-term profits often encouraged the banks' managers and traders to engage in really aggressive business practices, such as proprietary trading, even though these practices might be too risky for the banks and their shareholders in the long run.

At a more micro level, Minsky's argument that bankers are profit-maximizing individuals who are under pressure to innovate and have incentives to leverage up their banks for short-term profits also resonates rather well with the events that led to the 2007–2010 crisis.[62] Since then, various authorities in several jurisdictions have attempted to introduce laws to regulate bankers' compensation in order to deincentivize bankers from undertaking undue risks, and have also introduced laws to limit banks' leverage ratio. In the last section of this chapter, when we review theories of asymmetric information, we will discuss in more detail the issue of how bankers' compensation packages might have led them to take undue risks.

Moral Hazard   Moral hazard refers to a situation in which players act more haphazardly once they are insured. Moral hazard occurs because the insurer does not have the ability to monitor or restrain the actions of the insured once the insurance contract is implicitly or explicitly made. In banking and finance, popular examples of the moral hazard problem include those related to deposit insurance and the government's implicit bailout guarantees for financial institutions. With the presence of deposit insurance or implicit bailout guarantees, depositors and investors have fewer incentives to actively seek information or ensure the soundness of the banks or financial institutions that they deposit or invest their money with. Instead, the depositors and investors will be more likely to deposit and invest their money with financial institutions that offer the highest returns, since they know that their deposits and investments will be covered by deposit insurance or by the government's implicit bailout guarantees.

Coordination Failure   The presence of information asymmetry can also lead to coordination failure in the financial markets. In the presence of greater uncertainty, the presence of information asymmetry in the financial markets might simply stop transactions among market players. Such a situation occurred and became acute at the height of the 2007–2010 financial crisis, as banks were unwilling to lend to each other because no one was certain about the financial health of their counterparties. In the presence of great uncertainty, information asymmetry means that interest rates (which reflect the prices of transactions in the financial markets) could not act as a signaling device for efficient allocation of funds in the financial markets. In that case those with excess funds to lend can choose to either keep the funds to themselves or charge prohibitively high interest rates to compensate for unknown risks.

Externalities Externalities occur when the price of a product does not reflect the social costs of producing the product. In other words, externalities occur when private costs are socialized. In the context of banking and finance, the failure of a large or systemically important financial institution (SIFI) imposes costs not only on its depositors, shareholders, employees, and its direct counterparties, but also on other financial market players and society at large.

The presence of externalities suggests that profits from the transactions of a systemically important bank accrue only to the bank's shareholders, employees, and depositors, while losses from such transactions, if large enough to threaten the bank's survival, accrue to all market players and society at large.

CASE STUDY: Information Asymmetry and the Lead-Up to the 2007–2010 Crisis

As the 2007–2010 crisis unfolded, it became clear that prices at which financial transactions had been done in the lead-up to the crisis were not based on full information. Information asymmetry was present at various levels of financial transactions, from simple subprime mortgage lending to sophisticated derivatives trading. In many ways, it could be argued that the pervasiveness of information asymmetry in various pockets of the economy helped contribute to the emergence of the crisis.

Adverse Selection

An example of adverse selection in the context of the global financial crisis is subprime mortgage lending in the United States. The term *subprime* is often used for those borrowers who do not have good credit histories, or have low debt repayment ability. Inquiries found that prior to the crisis, in order to earn more brokerage fees from mortgage lenders, mortgage brokers had willfully disregarded subprime borrowers' ability to pay, in many cases requiring no proof of income or assets from borrowers. Borrowers, in turn, were provided with mortgage loans whose terms were very disadvantageous to them and were not easy to understand. (See Figure 10.7.)

In this subprime mortgage lending situation, bad mortgage loans were selected for borrowers who had the least ability to pay. The ultimate outcome was that, as subprime borrowers started defaulting on their mortgages, mortgage lenders took large losses and many went bankrupt. Apart from illustrating a case of adverse selection, the above example also points to the principal-agent problem, another problem related to information asymmetry.

The Principal-Agent Problem

In the subprime mortgage lending example above, we can see that mortgage brokers (agents) did not act in the best interest of mortgage lenders (principals). Mortgage brokers were paid commissions by mortgage lenders if they could get borrowers to sign up for mortgage loans. Here, the mortgage brokers' interest were misaligned with the mortgage lenders' interest. Mortgage brokers' main interest was to sign up more and more borrowers so that they would get commissions from mortgage lenders.

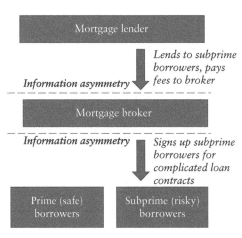

• Mortgage brokers, anxious to sign on borrowers so they can get fees, took on subprime borrowers without proper credit checks.

• Subprime borrowers, with low ability to repay, were lured by the seemingly attractive but opaque contracts, as well as by rising housing prices.

• Mortgage lenders added many more unhealthy subprime loans to their books than they should have.

FIGURE 10.7   A Stylized Adverse Selection Example: Subprime Lending

This could be done with little regard to the borrowers' debt repayment ability, as long as the commissions got paid. Mortgage lenders' main interest, on the other hand, was that borrowers be able to repay their mortgages.

Moral Hazard

The 2007–2010 crisis also highlighted the fact that investment banks' compensation packages for managers and traders were another case of the moral hazard problem. Since managers and traders' bonuses were often directly tied to profits, it made sense for managers and traders to pursue strategies that were likely to generate the most profits (e.g., buying securities backed by subprime mortgage securities), even if the strategies were extremely risky. The events before the financial crisis revealed that if the risky strategies that they pursued succeeded, managers and traders could make millions. Since the managers and traders were essentially using other people's money (the banks' balance sheets) in the pursuit of their strategies, the most they would lose would not be their own money, only their jobs, if those strategies ultimately failed. Since managers and traders were largely insulated from the financial risks they took, they were more likely to pursue riskier strategies in a blind chase for profits, which could be costly for their banks but not, essentially, for them.

Implications of Market Failures for Financial Stability   As the preceding discussions have shown, problems such as adverse selection, moral hazard, or the principal-agent problem can lead to bad outcomes in financial transactions. In the context of financial stability, it could thus be said that if the prices of financial assets do not reflect all known information, then such prices also might not accurately reflect inherent risks of the underlying assets. Owners of those financial assets might be unknowingly holding assets that are inherently too risky for them. (Think of banks owning bad mortgage loans or homeowners owning houses they can't afford, for example.) In some cases, buyers of financial assets could be just agents for the ultimate owners of those assets, and could have misaligned interest with those owners. (Think of investment banks' managers and traders as agents who bought subprime mortgages that were put on the banks' balance sheet, with the banks' shareholders as the ultimate owners of the banks, for example.)

As players in the financial system accumulate their ownership of mispriced assets, their financial positions can become extremely shaky without them realizing it. Taken in the aggregate, if the shaky financial positions of individual players becomes a big enough problem, it could become a systemic risk and a threat to the financial system. To deal with information asymmetry in the financial stability context, hence, at least three broad issues must be addressed: (1) *transparency* in financial information, (2) the *financial literacy* of the population, and (3) *alignment of incentives* to correct for potential principal-agent problems.

SUMMARY

Financial stability is a relatively new term, and as such there is not yet a single, quantifiable definition that is widely agreed upon, unlike, for example monetary stability, which could be defined as low and stable inflation.

Definitions of financial stability often encompass many elements, including the smooth and effective functioning of the financial system, the low probability of default, the absence of stress and disruptions in the financial system, and the absence of major financial imbalances in the economy.

To make the analysis more tractable, this book uses an analytical framework divided into three key interrelated areas of financial stability: the macroeconomy, financial institutions, and financial markets. Such a framework helps group fragmented theories with regard to financial stability, and also corresponds well with modern central banks' institutional setups.

Theoretically, threats to financial stability might occur in the macroeconomy through the interaction between real economic activity and financial activities. Easy money conditions could encourage more speculative activities, which can turn into asset price bubbles and economic instability. The work of Gurley and Shaw in 1995, Kindleberger in 1978, and Minsky in 1986 provides insight into this phenomenon.

According to the 1983 work of Diamond and Dybvig, a bank is inherently prone to a run, since it takes in deposits that are very liquid but lends out the funds into illiquid projects. The banking system network can promote the resiliency as well as the fragility of banks, depending on the linkage structures, the diversity of banks, and the density of banking activities (see, for example, the 2000 work of Allen and Gale, and the 2009 work of Haldane).

In theory, if financial markets function efficiently, then prices in the markets should reflect inherent risks. The inherent information asymmetry of the type pointed out by Akerloff in 1970 and Stiglitz and Weiss in 1981, however, can lead to moral hazard, adverse selection, externalities, coordination failures, and principal-agent problems, which imply that financial market prices might not reflect inherent risks.

KEY TERMS

adverse selection	externalities
asset price bubbles	financial network
bank run	financial stability
coordination failure	hedge finance
credit risk	information asymmetry

macroeconomy   principal-agent problem

moral hazard   probability of default

nonmoney financial assets   speculative finance

Ponzi finance   systemic bank run

QUESTIONS

1. Why could there be diverse views as to the definition of financial stability?
2. Give examples of different views on the definition of financial stability. What elements might be common among these views?
3. How might stability in the macroeconomy, financial institutions, and financial markets be related?
4. Does a central bank with no bank supervisory function have a role in maintaining financial stability? Why or why not?
5. How could weaknesses in households, firms, or the government's balance sheets affect stability of the macroeconomy?
6. Why might a central bank need to be mindful of the proliferation of new nonmoney financial assets?
7. What could be theoretical reasons that nudged central banks to put less focus on financial factors relative to monetary factors before the 2007–2010 global financial crisis?
8. With reference to Minsky's 1986 book, is the macroeconomy inherently stable or unstable? Why or why not?
9. Why might overindebtedness of economic agents lead to financial instability?
10. Referring to the Diamond-Dybvig model, why might a bank run be a facet of an equilibrium state of banking?
11. How might an increase in connectivity among banks *increase* resiliency of a banking system?
12. How might an increase in connectivity among banks *reduce* resiliency of a banking system?
13. In terms of interconnectedness among banks, what are *direct exposures*?
14. In terms of interconnectedness among banks, what are *indirect exposures*?
15. Why might troubled banks and firms cause stress and disruption in financial markets?
16. Give an example of the principal-agent problem in the run-up to the global financial crisis.
17. Give an example of moral hazard problem in the run-up to the global financial crisis.

CHAPTER 11

Financial Stability

Monitoring and Identifying Risks

Learning Objectives

1. Identify key indicators that central banks use in monitoring risks in the macroeconomy that are threats to financial stability.
2. Identify key indicators that central banks use in monitoring risks in the financial institutions system that are threats to financial stability.
3. Identify key indicators that central banks use in monitoring risks in financial markets that are threats to financial stability.

Successful maintenance of financial stability requires (1) monitoring and identifying risks and (2) intervening to reduce risks when necessary. In this chapter we discuss a variety of ways the central bank can monitor and identify risks to financial stability.

In line with the analytical framework discussed in Chapter 10, this chapter first reviews some of the basic tools for monitoring and identifying risks in the three interrelated areas of financial stability, namely (1) the *macroeconomy*, (2) *financial institutions*, and (3) *financial markets*. By grouping the monitoring tools into the three interrelated areas, it is hoped that readers will be able to grasp the concepts behind the tools and their interrelations more readily. In the real world, there are often multitudes of risks and contagion channels that can lead to financial instability, yet they are not easily disentangled or addressed by any one particular tool. At the end of the chapter we also look at some of the approaches in risk monitoring and risk identification that use data from the three areas of financial stability in a more integrated way.*

Note that although after the global financial crisis of 2007–2010 a lot of research effort was put into developing monitoring tools and a framework for financial

---

*It should be noted here that the discussion presented in this chapter aims to provide an overview of the tools that are relatively widely available and does not get deeply into technical details. Those interested in researching technical details can refer to the Notes section.

stability, these tools and the framework used for the identifying and monitoring of risks to financial stability are still very much a work in progress.[1] As in any human endeavor, there is still ample room for refinement and improvement.

Furthermore, it should be noted that there is no one-size-fits-all, standard tool-kit. Determining the appropriate tools to use in a particular situation depends on the circumstances of a particular economy, including its structure, stage of financial development, and regulatory regime.

11.1 MONITORING AND IDENTIFYING RISKS IN THE MACROECONOMY

As discussed in Chapter 10, events in the macroeconomy, possibly driven by the interaction between financial activities and economic activity, can lead to financial instability. As the economy enters into a protracted growth period, there is a tendency for agents, whether households or firms, to take on more debt in order to finance projects with rosy economic prospects. Heavy debt loads, however, mean that there is a greater possibility that these economic agents will be unable to repay their debts when an economic downturn arrives.

When households or firms face difficulties repaying debt, financial institutions may have to absorb losses on their balance sheets. If the losses are large (or are believed to be large) enough, then the solvency of the financial institution might come into question. This raises the possibility of a bank run, or even a systemic bank run if interbank exposures are large or when financial institutions have similar exposures. Resulting liquidity squeezes could also lead to breakdowns in financial markets.

History has also shown that heavy debt loads in government (as opposed to those of private sector agents, such as households and firms) can also lead to financial instability. When a government has difficulty repaying debt, it might be unable to finance expenditures for things like employee payrolls and procurement contracts made with private sector firms, which would have ripple effects throughout the economy. This situation could be especially acute if the government has been relying mainly on borrowing foreign currency to finance its expenditures. Figure 11.1 shows factors in the macroecomony that may affect financial stability not only in the macroeconomy itself, but also in financial institutions and financial markets through interrelated areas.

To monitor and identify financial stability risks in the macroeconomy, the central bank might want to look at the *balance sheet* of different groups of economic agents (e.g., households and firms), as well as that of the macroeconomy itself. Overindebtedness by any of the key agents of the real economy (households, firms, and the government), as well as overindebtedness of the economy as a whole to *external* creditors could lead to financial imbalances that weaken the financial sector and ultimately lead to financial instability. Although overindebtedness of agents might be difficult to identify, the central bank might also consider adopting the *gap* measurement approach advocated by Claudio Borio and Philip Lowe in two separate papers published in 2002, whereby the actual level of credit to GDP is compared to its historical trend as a rough indicator of agents' degree of indebtedness.[4]

In addition to monitoring the indebtedness of economic agents, the central bank might also want to monitor and identify risks from the asset side of the economy. Fast-rising *asset prices*, such as those in stock and real estate markets, could indicate

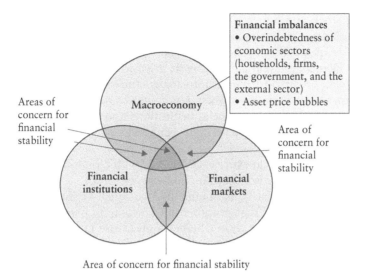

FIGURE 11.1   Financial Stability Issues in the Macroeconomy

the possibility of widespread speculation in asset prices and possible asset price bubbles. Speculation in asset prices often induce more and more players to take on heavy debt loads in order to bid for assets. If asset prices rise to levels that are far above those justified by their fundamentals, then it is also likely that buyers of those assets have taken on debt loads at levels not justified by their fundamentals. Once the economy starts to cool and asset prices start to drop, these buyers could be left with unserviceable debt loads that lead them to default.

Using data from many economies that used a variety of policy regimes, Borio and Lowe[3] and Borio and Drehmann[4] found that the coexistence of fast growth in *credit* and *asset prices* often proceeded banking crises. This suggests that the fast growth of credit will indicate a low capacity on the part of economic agents to absorb shock (i.e., a sustained rise in credit suggests that economic agents have racked up too much debt), while a fast rise in asset prices might indicate a high degree of asset price misalignment. To monitor and identify financial stability risks in the macroeconomy, the central bank thus needs to look at the possibility of overindebtedness on the part of each economic agent, the possibility of overindebtedness in the overall economy, and the movement of asset prices.

The Household Sector

At the most basic level, the central bank might want to look at the rate of growth of overall household debt and the composition of that debt (mortgage, credit card, and auto loans, for example). Data on household debt might come from various sources, including loans granted to individuals and households by financial institutions and comprehensive household surveys.

A fast rise in the level of household debt, even when accompanied by a similar rise in household income or household wealth, might warrant attention by the central bank. Experience from the global financial crisis has shown that fast-rising mortgage debt, even when accompanied by fast-rising household wealth (itself due to fast-rising stock and housing prices), can lead to financial instability when the economy slows down or when housing prices start to drop.

Financial ratios, such as household debt to GDP and household interest payments to income, as well as the growth in various types of credit extended to households (e.g., credit card loans, auto loans, and mortgages), can be useful in assessing household indebtedness. Such data might come from surveys at the micro level, coupled with data from financial institutions and macrolevel data. Although there is no hard and fast rule to determine exactly the point at which these ratios or growth rates could reflect overindebtedness, a fast rise in these measures could be a reason for concern. Historical experience coupled with cross-country analyses could also help determine if there is a cause for concern.

In addition, the central bank might also consider adopting a gap measure approach along the lines of that proposed by Borio and Lowe in 2002[5] and Borio and Drehmann in 2009[6] to analyze whether a given rise in household debt should raise concern. For example, the ratio of household debt to GDP might be compared to its historical trend; a large gap between the current ratio of household debt to GDP and the historical trend might warrant more concern. The central bank might also want to see whether the rise in *housing prices* deflated by GDP is much beyond its historical trend, in order to evaluate the degree to which the household sector might be exposed to risk accumulation in housing prices.

The Corporate Sector

Similarly to the household sector, at the most basic level the central bank needs to look at the growth rate of corporate sector debts to monitor and identify risks in the corporate sector. Pertinent data would include loans to the corporate sector by financial institutions as well as bond issuance by the corporate sector itself.

The dot-com bubble in the early years of the twenty-first century suggests that fast-rising corporate debt, even in the midst of an economic boom and rosy economic prospects, should be closely monitored. During an economic boom, firms might decide to use borrowed funds to undertake large capital investments with rosy economic prospects. Large capital investments, however, often take time to pay off, and thus once the economy slows, firms might find it difficult to repay their large debt loads.

In addition to looking at the growth rate of *corporate debts*, the central bank might find it useful to also examine the components of corporate debt, for example, whether the loans are short-term or long-term and whether they are denominated in local or foreign currencies. At a more nuanced level, the central bank might also want to look at various key financial ratios—for example, *debt-to-income, debt-to-capital*, and *interest payments-to-income*—to assess whether the corporate sector is overindebted. To have a more complete picture, such assessments would need to be done at both the micro and macro levels, and could be considered in a time-series context as well as using a cross-country comparison. The same gap measurement approach used for the household sector could also be applied to the corporate sector.

The Government Sector

At the most basic level, the central bank needs to assess the growth of public debt, or debt for which the government is liable, to monitor and identify financial stability risks from the government sector. Fast-rising public debt might threaten fiscal sustainability, that is, the ability of the government to repay debt without resorting to a debt default. A debt default by the government would have far-reaching repercussions on financial stability. Banks, pension funds, and mutual funds often hold government securities as a staple in their portfolio holdings. A default by the government would devalue portfolios of these entities considerably. Furthermore, interest rates for private sector loans are often benchmarked against the yields of so-called risk-free government debt. A debt default by the government could make interest rates in the economy become very volatile and disrupt the financial intermediation process in the economy.

In addition to public debt growth data, ratios of *public debt to GDP* and the *government debt repayments to total government expenditures* are among the most useful indicators for a fiscal sustainability assessment. Here the gap measurement approach might be used to measure how the public debt-to-GDP ratio might have deviated from its historical trend. To be comprehensive, however, the central bank might also need to examine the *composition* of public debt, such as the currency of debt denomination and debt maturity. Government debt denoted in a foreign currency requires that the government have enough of that foreign currency to repay the debt when it becomes due. Local currency denominated debt, however, is easier to roll over, or refinance, by new debt issuance.

In certain cases, the central bank might also need to look at the growth of the government's *contingent liabilities*, that is, those liabilities that might not currently be on the government's balance sheet but ultimately must be financed by the government when the need arises. Examples of contingent liabilities include everything from future public healthcare liabilities to the debt of government-owned enterprises.

In addition to balance sheet data, it might also be useful to look at the country's *sovereign debt ratings*, as well as the difference (or *spreads*) between the yield of securities issued by the government and the yields of those issued by another country whose bonds are used as an international benchmark (such as the yields of securities issued by the U.S. and the German governments, which are considered international risk-free, or safe-haven, rates). The experience of the European sovereign debt crisis in the early 2010s showed that when fiscal sustainability is in doubt, a drop in the country's sovereign rating combined with a rise in the *spread* between the government yield and the yield of a safe-haven benchmark can make refinancing of existing government debt very difficult, making an actual government debt default more likely. Another key variable that might warrant being closely monitored is the movement in the yields of *credit-default swaps* (CDS) of the country's sovereign debt, which are essentially an insurance premium on the government securities of the country.

The External Sector

A fast rise in debt owed to external creditors can also represent a grave threat to financial stability. The experiences of the 1990s in Asia and Latin America have shown that a fast rise in external debt (as also reflected in a fast rise in capital inflows) could ultimately lead to concurrent currency and banking crises. Fast rising capital inflows can easily find their way into stock market and real estate speculation, fueling asset price bubbles. When asset price bubbles start to burst, capital flights can occur promptly, putting tremendous downward pressure on domestic currency. In a fixed exchange rate regime, if the central bank does not have enough reserves to satisfy those wishing to pull their capital out, then it might be forced to allow the currency to be devalued. The currency devaluation could cripple the ability of agents in the economy to repay their foreign currency debts, especially if the agents' income was mainly from domestic sources. Meanwhile, the domestic banking sector would also likely be suffering from their exposures to asset price bubbles.

To monitor and identify financial stability risks in the external sector, the central bank will need to look at both the growth and level of external debt incurred by various agents of the economy, as well as the currency and maturity profiles of that debt. Capital flows data will also need to be closely monitored. Useful indicators for assessing the sustainability of foreign debt would include the ratio of *short-term debt to international reserves holdings*, the *degree of currency mismatch* of the debt and the source of income to finance that debt, the *degree of maturity mismatch* of the debt (are short-term foreign currency debts being incurred to finance long-term local projects?), as well as the *net open currency positions* of the debt (the degree of foreign currency debt not being hedged for currency risk).[7]

Asset Price Bubbles

Apart from the overindebtedness of economic agents, financial stability concerns can be indicated on the other side of the economy's balance sheets by fast-rising *asset prices*. Fast-rising asset prices, such as those for real estate or stocks, could indicate that speculative activities are ongoing and becoming prevalent. A prevalence of speculative activities could reflect inherent instability in the financial system, since speculation often involves borrowing to invest in assets with the expectation of fast capital gains. (The fast rise in prices does not necessarily reflect the fundamental value of the assets.) Once the asset prices drop back to reflect their fundamental values, those who borrowed to invest in the assets could face an overindebtedness problem, since the value of the assets might be lower than the debt that they incurred when purchasing the assets.

At the most basic level, the central bank needs to look at the growth rate of real estate and stock market prices, as they are easily subject to speculation. In monitoring and identifying financial stability risks from asset prices the increase in loans related to these markets also needs to be closely monitored. Although it is very difficult to judge *ex ante* whether prices in these markets have risen much beyond fundamentals and are exhibiting signs of bubbles, comparisons with historical averages and across countries could provide some useful hints. As noted previously, Borio and Lowe[8] and Borio and Drehmann[9] have suggested using the gap approach by comparing the real (i.e., inflation adjusted) asset price to its historical trend (possibly as represented by a statistically smoothed long-term trend line, such as the Hodrick-Prescott filter whereby the short-term cyclical fluctuations are removed from a time series data, leaving only the long-term trend line of the variable).

For the real estate market, one might also need to look at different segments of the market separately, as speculation might be concentrated primarily in particular types of real estate (e.g., housing versus commercial real estate, luxury condominiums versus stand-alone houses, etc.), or in particular geographic areas. For the stock market, key indicators other than prices include *price-earnings* (*P/E*) ratios, for the market as a whole as well as for different segments of the market.

The Link between the Macroeconomy and Financial Stability

Historically, experiences worldwide have shown that if any of the aforementioned sectors in the real economy experience difficulties in debt repayment, or when asset price bubbles started to burst, the financial sector will often also find itself in trouble. Financial institutions that lent to those troubled sectors will have to absorb losses as default rates rise. They might also need to cut back on lending and call in existing loans. Meanwhile, activity in the financial markets could stop, as financial institutions are often the key players in the financial markets. As financial institutions cut back on lending and liquidity in the financial markets dries up, economic activity could contract or slow down, which would weaken debt repayment ability in the economy further.

Papers by Borio and Lowe[10] and Borio and Drehmann[11] have shown empirically that strong increases in credit and asset prices have tended to precede banking crises. Strong increases in credit and asset prices can signal accumulation of risks in the system. Strong credit growth can indicate that economic agents are heavily indebted and thus have low capacity to absorb shocks, while strong growth in asset prices can reflect a greater degree of price misalignment. In such a situation, a shock to asset prices could propel the system into a crisis.

11.2 MONITORING AND IDENTIFYING RISKS TO FINANCIAL INSTITUTIONS

In monitoring and identifying financial stability risks that might arise from financial institutions, one must look at both individual institutions and the financial institutions system as a whole. In a world in which financial institutions are increasingly connected with each other through both direct and indirect exposures, contagion among financial institutions and systemic bank runs are very possible. Figure 11.2 shows factors relating to financial institutions that may affect financial stability not only in the institutions themselves, but also in the macroeconomy and financial markets through interrelated areas.

Key Types of Risks to Individual Financial Institutions: Credit, Market, Liquidity, and Operational

As discussed earlier, if agents in the macroeconomy are already overindebted and finding it difficult to repay their loans, financial institutions might have to absorb losses. If the losses are believed to be so large that they threaten to wipe out a large part of the bank's capital, then the bank's financial position could be seriously jeopardized, and there could be a run on the bank. The risk that the bank's debtors or counterparties might be unable to repay their debts in the manner specified in the loan contracts, or fulfill their obligations to the bank, is part of what is known as *credit risk*.

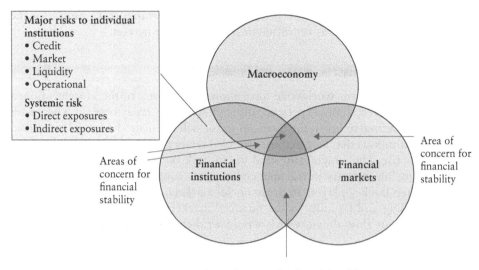

Major risks to individual institutions
• Credit
• Market
• Liquidity
• Operational

Systemic risk
• Direct exposures
• Indirect exposures

Macroeconomy

Financial institutions

Financial markets

Areas of concern for financial stability

Area of concern for financial stability

Area of concern for financial stability

FIGURE 11.2   Financial Stability Issues among Financial Institutions

Risks to financial institutions, however, can come not only in terms of credit risk, but also in many other forms, including market risk, liquidity risk, and operational risk. *Market risk* arises when movements in market rates and prices (such as interest rates, foreign exchange rates, and equity prices) adversely affect the institution's financial position. *Liquidity risk* arises from the possibility that an institution would not be able to meet its obligations as they come due (possibly because it cannot liquidate assets or obtain adequate funding), as well as the possibility that an institution would not be able to unload its holdings without significantly lowering the market prices of the assets and incur large losses, owing to the dearth of market players during market disruptions. *Operational risk* arises from the possibility that operational problems (e.g., breaches in internal controls, fraud, or unforeseen catastrophes) will lead to unexpected losses for an institution.[12]

Assessing Individual Institutions' Risks

Traditionally regulatory authorities have assessed individual institutions' safety and soundness by examining the institutions' CAMELS (as discussed in Chapter 3, CAMELS stands for capital adequacy, asset quality, management, earnings, liquidity, and sensitivity to market risk). As banking activities and financial institutions became more complex (for example, through the addition of overseas subsidiaries and branches as well as a more prevalent use of complex derivatives), however, regulatory authorities recognized that examinations of financial institutions must place greater emphasis on the institutions' risk management practices and internal controls. At the same time it should be noted that the failure of a single or even a couple of financial institutions may not necessarily cause serious threats to the stability of the system as a whole, provided the failed institutions are not large or systemically important. Indeed, in the United States many small banks are allowed to fail each year and are not rescued by the government.

Monitoring and Identifying Risks in the Financial Institutions System

The recent financial crisis has reemphasized the need for the monitoring and identi-fication of risks inherent in the *system* of financial institutions, in addition to those related to *individual* institutions.[13] This is partly due to the *fallacy of composition* problem: the seemingly robust health of individual financial institutions might not reflect the true health and resiliency of the system as a whole, owing to complexities of interrelationships, processes, and interactions among the individual institutions themselves.

For example, while each individual financial institutions might seem to have a high enough capital buffer to deal with shocks in normal times, when panic actually arises it might be rational for these individual institutions to stop lending and bor-rowing activities among themselves, which, in turn, would heighten credit and liquid-ity risks for the system as a whole. The problem could easily be exacerbated when, in response to the heightened risks, all institutions might at the same time attempt to do a fire sale of their assets (to preempt or to arrest *marked-to-market* losses or to raise capital), thereby lowering the prices of everyone's assets.

The techniques for monitoring and identifying systemic risk in the financial system are still in the early stages of development. Among the approaches that have gained attention in the wake of the recent global financial crisis are those that target *risk dis-tribution* within the financial network, and *risk concentration* in systemically impor-tant financial institutions (SIFIs). (See for example, the 2009 work of Segoviano and Goodhart,[14] the 2011 work of Minoiu and Reyes,[15] the 2010 work of Chan-Lau,[16] and the 2011 and 2012 reports from the Basel Committee on Banking Supervision.[17])

Risk Distribution within the Financial Network

The financial system can be seen as a type of network, where financial institutions (banks and nonbanks) interact by borrowing and lending among themselves. The network can help promote resiliency of individual institutions by enabling those short of liquidity to tap funds from those with excess liquidity.[18] As discussed in the previous chapter, however, the network can also lead to risk contagion across institu-tions, whether through direct balance sheet exposure or through indirect exposure, such as through common types of assets in portfolio holdings.

As the 2007–2010 financial crisis has shown, as the network becomes more complex, risk contagion can come through multiple channels, including breakdowns in interbank lending and the fire sale of assets that lead to more losses on the banks' portfolio holdings. Opacity of information regarding linkages within the network tend also exacerbate the problem, since it makes it difficult for financial institutions and regulatory authorities to locate exactly where the risks actually lie and who is severely exposed, and thus makes it difficult to contain the problem.

To gain a more complete picture of how risks are distributed within the financial system, network analysis techniques have increasingly been applied to the finan-cial system. It is believed that network analysis, which has previously been done in fields as diverse as medicine (disease contagion), ecology (ecological systems), and engineering (electrical power grids), can help in identifying and mapping the linkages (direct and indirect) among various financial institutions within the network.[19]

By constantly monitoring (direct and indirect) linkages and financial institutions within the financial network, it is expected that the authorities would be able to better understand risk propagation and distribution within the financial system. Currently, developments in this area are still in an early stage, as the researchers and regulatory authorities are still grappling with issues related to the data that will provide a more complete picture of the system's linkages and how risks might proliferate among financial institutions in the system. (See, for example, the 2009 paper from Segoviano and Goodhart.[20])

Risk Concentration: Systemically Important Financial Institutions (SIFIs)

Complementing the network analysis approach whereby risk distribution within the financial system can be mapped out, the authorities also need to assess the *systemic importance* of each individual financial institution (banks and nonbanks). Since the failure of a systemically important financial institution (SIFI) could threaten the whole system, it could be said that systemic risk is inherent to and concentrated in risks to individual SIFIs. To monitor and identify system risk, the authorities thus need to monitor and identify risks exposure in SIFIs.

Prior to the failure of Lehman Brothers in 2008, the notion of risk concentration in the banking system was deemed to be largely typified by the concept of *too-big-to-fail*. A too-big-to-fail financial institution is one whose size is so large that regulatory authorities would always come to its rescue, since its failure could cause the system to collapse. Since then, the notion has grown to encompass the concepts of *too-connected-to-fail* and *systemically important financial institutions* (SIFIs).[21]

When Lehman Brothers, a medium-sized global investment bank, was allowed to fail in the midst of the global financial crisis, worldwide financial panic and stresses threatened to cause a collapse in the financial system. With the benefit of hindsight, we can see that although Lehman Brothers was not necessarily the largest bank, its deep and extensive linkages to other financial institutions and markets around the world meant that the failure of this one medium-sized bank could threaten the survival of the whole system.

Recognizing now that *systemic* risk can be concentrated within certain systemically important, *core* financial institutions (whether termed "too big" or not), in the wake of the financial crisis researchers and authorities have been searching for ways to identify and assess financial institutions with systemic importance. In 2011 and 2012 the Basel Committee for Banking Supervision (BCBS) came up with guidelines to assess the systemic importance of individual institutions, both at the global level (i.e., *Global Systemically Important Banks*, or *G-SIBs*) and the domestic level (i.e., *Domestic Systemically Important Banks* or *D-SIBs*).[22]

To help identify G-SIBs, BCBS's 2011 report proposed five broad categories of indicators, including *size, interconnectedness, lack of readily available substitutes, cross-jurisdictional activity*, and *complexity*. Using these five categories of indicators, the report identified 25 financial institutions as G-SIBs. For D-SIBs, BCBS's 2012 report deemed that the actual identification was best be done by national authorities, since the classification would depend a lot on the country-specific context. The principles provided by BCBS for national authorities involved four categories of indicators, which mirrored those for G-SIBs except for cross-jurisdictional activity, which was subsumed into the *complexity* category.[23]

In identifying D-SIBs, central banks would learn more about how risks were concentrated in their domestic banking systems and therefore monitor and assess risk more effectively. The identification of G-SIBs, meanwhile, would help regulatory authorities become better at identifying and monitoring their banking systems' exposures to risks from global systemically important institutions.

CASE STUDY: Macro Stress Testing

Macro stress tests have been getting more and more attention since the middle of the first decade of the twentieth century. Macro stress tests are tests done to assess how financial institutions as a system would fare under adverse macroeconomic conditions. In conducting macro stress tests, regulatory authorities first make assumptions about plausible extreme adverse macroeconomic scenarios and corresponding movements of pertinent macroeconomic variables, such as GDP growth, inflation, and interest rates. Then assumptions about these macroeconomic variable movements are used in econometric or other types of relevant models to map how the movements would likely affect the institutions' financial positions; for example, through default rates, earnings, and the price of assets in the institutions' portfolios. Very importantly, *feedback loops* among the institutions such as counterparty credit risk and liquidity risk would also be taken into account before arriving at the final outcomes.[24]

Ideally, macro stress tests will be useful in helping regulatory authorities to determine the safety and soundness of financial institutions as a whole. However, the development of macro stress testing techniques was still in its infancy when the 2007–2010 crisis struck. There was still a lack of understanding of the interconnectedness among financial institutions, partly because of the growing complexities of banking activities but also because of the rise of shadow banking. Although ever-evolving activities in the financial sector could potentially dampen the success of macro stress tests in predicting an oncoming crisis, regulatory authorities have recently found the use of macro stress tests as a potent communication tool to alleviate panic after a crisis has actually occurred.

U.S. authorities used stress tests to determine the soundness of the largest U.S. banks right after the 2007–2010 global financial crisis. While results from the tests suggested that some banks had inadequate capital to deal with further shocks and would have required extra funding, they also suggested that most of the banks were in sound condition and that the extra funding that would have been required was at manageable levels. In this sense, apart from determining the ability of the banks to deal with further stress in the wake of the crisis, the tests were used as a tool to communicate with the public so that ungrounded fears would not turn into panics. Following the U.S. success, authorities in the euro area also used macro stress test results to shore up public confidence in European banks in the wake of Europe's sovereign debt crisis.

In a post-crisis world, U.S. authorities have also calibrated macro stress tests for use as a preemptive tool in sustaining financial stability. Banks that do not pass the macro stress tests given by the Federal Reserve will not be allowed to raise dividend payments or to do a stock buyback.[25] The aim is to encourage both the shareholders and the management of the bank to be more mindful of the risks they are taking.

Despite the growing profile of macro stress testing, Claudio Borio and Mathias Drehmann have warned central bankers not to let macro stress testing lull them into a false sense of security. According to their 2009 paper, potentially problematic issues of macro stress testing include the fact that (1) traditional macroeconomic models often do not well enough incorporate financial variables, (2) the source of shocks in macroeconomic models often come from macroeconomic variables, but shocks to the financial system would not necessarily come from macroeconomic factors, (3) the relationships between macroeconomic risk factors and credit risk are still often poorly modeled, and (4) important items that might be crucial to financial institutions sometimes are not included in the financial institutions' balance sheets (e.g., off-balance-sheet commitments).[26]

11.3 FINANCIAL MARKETS

Financial market indicators can provide useful information on the degree of *risk accumulation* as well as the degree of *stress and disruption* in the financial sector. Indicators of risks in the financial markets can often be extracted from transaction data in the financial markets, whether they are movements in prices and yields of financial products, or net positions of market players. Frequent transactions in financial markets mean that, in many cases, these indicators could reflect conditions in the financial system almost on a real-time basis. Figure 11.3 shows factors relating to financial markets that may affect financial stability not only in the markets themselves, but also in the macroeconomy and financial institutions through interrelated areas.

Prices and Yields

Despite the presence of information asymmetry in financial markets, prices and yields of financial products (such as stocks, bonds, currencies, and money market loans) and financial derivatives (such as credit default swaps) should reasonably reflect publicly available information on those products. Unusual movements in prices and yields of financial products would thus signal to the central bank threats to financial stability that might arise from financial markets.

Risk Accumulation   As discussed earlier in the chapter, fast-rising prices of equity, when taken together with credit growth, could reflect the risk accumulation that comes with speculative activities and asset price bubbles.[27] In general, fast increases in prices of financial products—whether stocks, bonds, or securities backed by subprime mortgages—can draw in more and more market player participation during the price run-up.

In bidding for even higher returns, market players often fund their purchases of financial products using leverage (i.e., borrowed money). As long as prices of the

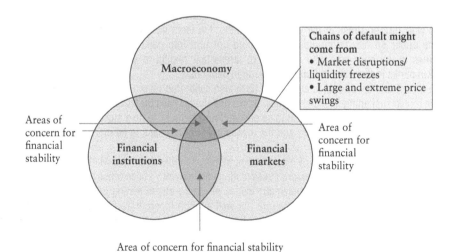

Area of concern for financial stability

FIGURE 11.3   Financial Stability Issues in Financial Markets

products keep rising, players are tempted to pile on even more leverage to buy more products, possibly by using the products themselves as collateral for more borrowing. The greater degree of leverage could expose market players and their lenders to tremendous losses once prices start to drop. In a speculative asset price bubble, prices of financial products can rise far beyond levels justified by their economic fundamentals, and thus the greater degree of leverage would lead to even more severe losses.

In practice, although it is difficult to determine *ex ante* if prices of financial products have risen beyond their economic fundamentals or not, it is crucial that the central bank examines unusually fast run-ups in prices of financial products very closely, even if the central bank itself does not trade in those products.

Stress and Disruption   While fast run-ups in prices of financial products could reflect a rising degree of risk accumulation in system, rising volatility in financial product prices could reflect a rising degree of stress and disruption in the financial markets. As financial market prices should reflect publicly available information relating to the markets, rising price volatility suggests that market players are not very certain about the quality of information that they have and are very sensitive to new information. With such uncertainty, market players might be willing to trade financial products only at extreme prices (to hedge for missing information) or simply stop trading. The stress and disruption in financial markets would affect not only market players, but are likely to have ripple effects through the financial system and the economy at large.

In practice, there are two key measures of price volatility: *historical* volatility, which is calculated from historical price data, and *option-implied* volatility, which is calculated from option prices of their underlying financial products when options on those products are available. For both measures, rising volatility of financial market prices would reflect a rising degree of uncertainty and the resulting stress and disruption in the financial markets.

Spreads

In financial market terms, a *spread* often refers to the difference in yields of two types of financial products. An example would be a spread between corporate and government bond yields of the same maturity, which means the difference in the yields of these two bonds.

Risk Accumulation   As a rule of thumb, yields of riskier products (such as corporate bonds) are supposed to be higher than those of less risky or risk-free products (such as government bonds), since buyers of riskier products demand higher yields as a premium to compensate for the extra risks that they take. The spread between the yields of riskier and less risky financial products is also known as *credit* spread (with reference to credit risk). When times are good, the spreads between the yields of risky and risk-free products are likely to be *narrow*. This is because in good times, even riskier projects have a lower chance of failure, and buyers of the riskier products would demand a smaller risk premium.

When the spread between the yields of riskier and risk-free products have become very narrow for a long period of time, however, risk accumulation in the economy might have also appreciably *risen*. With low credit spreads, funding of riskier projects would be easier than otherwise. The number of riskier projects undertaken in the economy might be more than optimal. This was what happened in the global financial markets prior to the global financial crisis of 2007–2010, when the credit spread remained compressed for a considerable period of time. Borio and Drehmann[28] termed a situation in which credit spreads are low, while credit growth and asset prices are increasing quickly, as the *paradox of financial stability*.

In practice, there is no established rule to determine if a spread is too narrow or too wide. The central bank often compares the existing levels of credit spread to their historical level and analyzes them together with other financial market indicators.

Stress and Disruption   In contrast to the situation just described, when times are bad, the spreads between yields of risky and risk-free financial products would likely *widen*. The chance of failure of a riskier project would thus also rise. Buyers of riskier products during such periods would demand a much higher risk premium if they were to take on extra risks. This raises funding costs for projects, and further raises the chance of actual project failures. In extreme conditions, such as during the European sovereign debt crisis in the early 2010s, the spreads of riskier Greek government bond yields and less risky German government bond yields had widened so much that the Greek government was unable to refinance its bonds and had to seek international assistance.

During the 2007–2010 crisis, the widening of the Libor-OIS spread was also a key important barometer of stress and disruption, as it could reflect credit risk in the banking system, the market's perception of risk endemic in the economy, as well as liquidity risk in financial markets (see "Case Study: Libor-OIS Spread as an Indicator of Stress and Disruption" in details).

CASE STUDY: Libor-OIS Spread as an Indicator of Stress and Disruption

During the 2007–2010 crisis, Libor-OIS spread became another important financial variable to monitor as it reflected *credit risk* of the banking system, as well as *liquidity risk* in financial markets.

Libor Rate

Libor, or London interbank offered rate, is the interest rate that major banks in London agree to lend among themselves, without collateral. Libor is calculated for 10 currencies, with fifteen maturities ranging from overnight to one year. Libor is a popular benchmark used in calculating short-term funding costs among banks as well as other financial market players.[29]

Overnight-Indexed-Swap (OIS)

OIS, or overnight-indexed-swap, is a fixed/float interest rate swap, whereby a counterparty agrees to receive a fixed rate of interest, called OIS rate, on a notional amount of money over a maturity (e.g., three months), in exchange for a compound interest payment to be determined by a reference floating rate on the notional amount at the maturity. The reference floating rate is often tied to an overnight interest rate such as the central bank's policy rate (e.g., the effective federal funds rate in the United States). As such, the OIS rate reflects the market's expectations of the average of the reference overnight interest rate over the maturity of the swap contract.[30]

Monitoring Libor-OIS to Gauge Risk

Libor-OIS spread is the difference between the Libor rate and the OIS rate. Libor rate typically includes credit risk since a Libor transaction is not secured by collateral and thus the lending bank is exposed to a default by the borrowing bank. OIS, on the other hand, involves only a minimal credit risk since the transaction does not involve any initial cash flow. The payments between the two counterparties in an OIS transaction would occur only when the contract reaches maturity.

Since the Libor rate includes credit risk, it is generally higher than the OIS rate of the same maturity. During times of stress, the Libor-OIS spread could be a useful indicator of credit risk within the banking system. The widening of the Libor-OIS spread reflects the perception of the banks with regards to the risk of default associated with lending to other banks. In early August 2007, the Libor-OIS spread stood at around 13 basis points (0.13%), before it widened to about 350 basis points (3.50 percent) for a period after Lehman Brothers went bankrupt on September 17, 2008. The one-month Libor-OIS spread subsequently narrowed down to around 28 basis points by April 6, 2009, although the three-month and six-month Libor-OIS spreads remained much higher than they were before the Lehman bankruptcy.[31]

Intuitively, while the Libor-OIS spread should reflect primarily *credit risk* in the banking system, it could also reflect the market's perception of risk endemic in the economy. Furthermore, it could also reflect *liquidity risk* in financial markets. A higher Libor-OIS spread suggests a decreased willingness to lend by major banks, which implies lower liquidity available.[32] In practice, however, it could be quite complicated to disentangle credit risk from liquidity risk from such a spread.[33]

Net Open Positions

A *net open position* in a financial product refers to a situation in which a player's total assets and liabilities in that particular product are unequal. If a player has an excess of assets over liabilities in that particular product, then the player is said to have a net *long* position in that product. If a player has an excess of liabilities over assets, then the player is said to have a net *short* position.

Risk Accumulation   In cases where data are available, the central bank might find it useful to monitor the aggregate net open positions for a key financial product, such as foreign currencies (see, for example, the 2011 work from Lim et al.[34]). A dramatic rise in net open positions (whether *long* or *short*) means that risk accumulation in the system is rising, since players are exposing themselves to adverse moves in foreign exchange rates.

Stress and Disruption   A net open position in a financial product, when taken together with movements in the price or yield of that product, could also reflect a degree of stress and disruption in a particular market segment. During the European sovereign debt crisis in the early 2010s, for example, the net open position of U.S. dollars as reflected by the International Monetary Market (IMM) data from the Chicago Mercantile Exchange was a useful indicator of how market participants responded to uncertainty and switched back and forth between the view favoring U.S. dollars against the euro and vice versa. In this particular case, such an indicator could be useful even for central banks outside Europe and the United States, because large movements in the U.S. dollar-euro exchange rate would have implications for their own currencies.

CONCEPT: AN INTEGRATED RISK MONITORING AND RISK IDENTIFICATION APPROACH: THE CONTINGENT CLAIMS ANALYSIS

While the separation of financial stability areas into the macroeconomy, financial institutions, and financial markets might make analysis more tractable, in practice, the inherent relationships among the three areas suggest that the central bank needs to take an integrated approach when monitoring and identifying risks to financial stability. At the most basic level, the central bank might construct a composite indicator or a heat map that takes account of developments in the macroeconomy, financial institutions, and financial markets.

Increasingly, however, many authorities are turning also to a more advanced approach known as contingent claims analysis (CCA), which has built-in forward-looking elements, and can also be applied to assess risk transmission between different economic sectors in a more integrated manner.[35]

Contingent Claims Analysis (CCA)

CCA can be thought of an approach that employs data from financial markets to estimate the *probability of default* for an economic entity. It is based on the option pricing theory pioneered by Black-Scholes, and Merton, in 1973.[36]

The use of a CCA approach to monitor and identify risks to financial stability has been proposed in the 2008 research of Gray, Merton, and Bodie[37] and Gray and Malone,[38] which provided a framework for assessing risk in the different sectors and linking them in an integrated manner.

The gist of the CCA approach is that it looks at the balance sheet of an entity (e.g., a household, a single firm, or an economic sector) and adjusts for the probability that its assets might be subject to random shocks, which could affect the entity's ability to repay its debt obligations, that is, the entity's probability of default. A positive shock to the value of assets will reduce the probability that the entity will be unable to repay its debt obligations. Conversely, a negative shock to the value of assets could raise the probability that the entity will be unable to repay its debt obligations and will default. If the entity defaults, owners of the entity's liabilities will be entitled to its assets.

Viewed this way, liabilities (which comprise *debt* and *equity*) of an entity can be seen as contingent claims on the assets of the entity. Given that the market price and volatility of market-traded securities—such as mortgage-backed securities (households' liabilities), pension fund and mutual funds (households' assets), corporate bonds and stocks (corporate liabilities), and government bonds (government liabilities)—can be observed directly, they could potentially be used to estimate the implied value and volatility of the underlying assets, and thus the probability of default in these sectors.

In practice, while there are currently data limitations in many cases, work such as that done in 2008 by Gray, Merton, and Bodie and Gray and Malone (cited above) suggests various ways to go forward. For the *corporate sector* (an aggregation of all nonfinancial firms) and *financial institutions* (banks and nonbanks), domestic equity markets could provide pricing and volatility information for the calculation of implied asset values, volatility, and *expected* default frequencies. For nonlisted firms and financial institutions, the relationship could be mapped using information from listed counterparties as a guide.

For the *government*, although the value of its assets cannot be observed directly, it could be inferred both from prices in international markets (including the foreign currency market) and information from domestic markets regarding the value and volatility of certain liabilities on the government's balance sheet.

For the *household* sector, since there is no traded equity for use in estimating assets, the 2008 research by Gray, Merton, and Bodie suggests that macroeconomic data and information from the households themselves could be used to construct measures of the portfolio of household assets directly. Household balance assets would include financial assets and estimated labor income. A subsidiary balance sheet of household real estate holdings might also be estimated from real estate prices and volatility, and pertinent debt obligations.

With balance sheets from the four sectors in place, the work from Gray, Merton, and Bodie and Gray and Malone suggests that regulatory authorities might then link the contingent claims balance sheets of the different sectors (possibly adding the external sector to represent foreign claims) to assess in a consistent manner how risk proliferates among the sectors. Furthermore, by linking models of CCA analysis to macroeconomic models used for monetary policy, potentially central banks would be able to assess the feedback loops between economic activity, financial activities, and the probability of default in the economy.

While it is still a work in progress, the use of CCA as a framework to monitor and assess financial stability has several promising features. First, it uses pricing and volatility from financial markets, which have built-in, forward-looking elements not afforded by the traditional balance sheet data. Gray showed in 2012 how the use of CCA on a real-time basis would have predicted the upcoming stresses leading to the 1997 Asian financial crisis, as well as the global financial crisis of 2007–2010.[39] Second, by linking the balance sheets of different economic sectors, CCA could be used to assess risk transmissions from one sector to the others. Third, CCA risk indicators could be linked to macroeconomic variables and to macroeconomic models, which would enable further testing and simulations of stress scenarios.

SUMMARY

In the macroeconomy, the central bank needs to monitor and identify the risk that economic agents might be unable to repay their debts. This might be done beforehand by identifying risks of overindebtedness among households, firms, and the government, as well as the overindebtedness of domestic economic agents to external lenders.

On the financial institutions front, risks to individual banks (whether in terms of credit risk, market risk, liquidity risk, or operational risk) must be examined by central banks that have a bank supervisory function. Risk distribution and risk concentration within the financial institutions system needs to also be identified and monitored.

In financial markets, prices and yields, spreads, and net open positions on financial instruments must be monitored in order to identify risk accumulation and stress and disruption in the markets.

The contingent claims analysis (CCA) approach has good potential as an integrated approach to monitoring and assessing risks in the different economic sectors and needs to be developed further. CCA uses observable real-time market data to assess the probability of default in the different sectors, whereby the probability of default of one sector could be linked to that of another sector in an integrated manner.

KEY TERMS

contingent claims analysis

contingent liabilities

credit default swaps (CDS)

currency mismatch

domestic systemically important banks (D-SIBs)

fallacy of composition

gap measure

global systemically important banks (G-SIBs)

historical volatility

household debt

implied volatility

Libor_OIS spread

macro stress test

maturity mismatch

net long position

net open position

net short position

paradox of financial stability

probability of default

public debt to GDP ratio

spread

systemically important financial institutions (SIFIs)

too-big-to-fail

too-connected-to-fail

QUESTIONS

1. What are examples of indicators that central banks might want to monitor with regard to *households* to ensure financial stability?
2. What are key indicators that central banks might want to monitor with regard to the *corporate sector* to ensure financial stability?
3. What are key indicators that central banks might want to monitor with regard to the *government* to ensure financial stability?
4. What are key indicators that central banks might want to monitor with regard to the *external sector* to ensure financial stability?
5. What are key indicators that central banks might want to monitor with regard to *asset prices* to ensure financial stability?

6. According to a 2002 paper by Borio and Lowe and a 2009 paper by Borio and Drehman, what might be good predictors of a banking crisis?

7. How might financial imbalances in the macroeconomy affect financial stability?

8. Please explain key types of risks that an individual financial institution normally faces.

9. In examining financial institution risks, one widely adopted framework is CAMELS; please explain what CAMELS is.

10. What might be a fallacy of composition problem in the context of a system of financial institutions?

11. How might network analysis help identify risk distribution within the financial system?

12. Give an example of the way in which risk concentration within the financial system might be identified and monitored.

13. Please explain the principle behind a macro stress test.

14. How can a macro stress test be used as a preemptive tool in sustaining financial stability?

15. How might prices and yields reflect risk accumulation in the financial system *ex ante*?

16. How might it be difficult to use prices and yields to identify risk accumulation ex ante?

17. How might prices and yields reflect stress and disruption in the financial system *ex post*?

18. Why might sustained tight credit spreads indicate risk accumulation? Why is this counterintuitive?

19. During periods of stress and disruption, why might the spreads between risk-free and risky assets widen?

20. Why might a rise in the net open position of a currency reflect risk accumulation, or stress and disruption, or both?

21. Please explain the idea behind Contingent Claim Analysis.

22. According to Contingent Claim Analysis, what can be valued as contingent claims on the assets of an entity?

CHAPTER 12

Financial Stability

Intervention Tools

Learning Objectives

1. Describe various tools that central banks can use to mitigate risks in the macroeconomy in order to sustain financial stability *ex ante* and *ex post*.
2. Describe various tools that central banks can use to mitigate risks in financial institutions in order to sustain financial stability *ex ante* and *ex post*.
3. Describe various tools that central banks can use to mitigate risks in financial markets in order to sustain financial stability *ex ante* and *ex post*.
4. Distinguish between Basel I, Basel II, and Basel III.

In Chapter 11 we reviewed some of the tools that can be used for monitoring and identifying financial stability risks. In this chapter we look at some of the tools that central banks might use to intervene, safeguard, and restore financial stability. Following the analytical framework used in the previous chapters, we review the tools in the context of three focus areas: (1) the *macroeconomy*, (2) *financial institutions*, and (3) *financial markets*. In each of the focus areas, we look at the tools that are meant to be used *ex ante* (i.e., sustaining financial stability by reducing the probability of a crisis happening, or reducing the severity of losses given a crisis), and those that are meant to be used *ex post* (i.e., managing a crisis that is unfolding, or providing a recovery resolution).

12.1 THE MACROECONOMY

The key tools that the central bank might use to intervene and maintain financial stability in the macroeconomy would be (1) monetary policy, and (2) macropruden-tial measures, especially those of a *credit-related* type.[1] Although monetary policy is normally used for the price stability objective, it can also be used to safeguard

TABLE 12.1 Possible Tools to Address Financial Instability

	Possible Tools	
Area of Focus	*Ex ante*	*Ex post*
Macroeconomy	▪ Monetary policy tightening ▪ Macroprudential measures	▪ Conventional monetary policy easing ▪ Unconventional easing ▪ Macroprudential measures
Financial institutions	▪ Supervisory actions ▪ Capital adequacy requirements ▪ Coordination with regulators of nonbank financial institutions	▪ Lender-of-last-resort facilities ▪ Special resolutions for troubled financial institutions
Financial markets	▪ Regulations on market players under central bank supervision ▪ Coordination with market regulators	▪ Lender-of-last-resort facilities ▪ Direct market interventions (e.g., asset purchases)

financial stability ex ante as well as ex post, since monetary policy has the potential to dampen amplification effects from the business cycle. Monetary policy, however, is a relatively blunt tool that affects all sectors of the macroeconomy. To address risk buildups or financial imbalances in specific areas of the macroeconomy ex ante, macroprudential measures, which are more akin to precision instruments, might be more appropriate. (See Table 12.1.)

The Debate on the Use of Monetary Policy for the Maintenance of Financial Stability

Even after the global financial crisis of 2007–2010, there was a continuing debate about how monetary policy should be used in the maintenance of financial stability.[2] Some argued that monetary policy should be used to help lean on asset price bubbles while they were still in the early forming stage so they would not grow excessively large. The proponents of the use of monetary policy to lean on asset price bubbles argued that it would help tame risk buildups in the economy, and possibly reduce the severity of a crisis, should one occur.

Others, however, suggested that monetary policy should be used instead to help clean up the aftereffects once the bubbles had burst. Those in this camp argued that monetary policy should only be used to stabilize the economy after asset price bubbles had actually burst. The arguments against the use of monetary policy in addressing the buildup of bubbles included (1) the belief, especially prior to the crisis, that in a market economy prices should reflect all relevant information, and thus the central bank would not know any better than the public if rising asset prices were beyond what was warranted by fundamentals and were actually bubbles, (2) that since monetary policy is a rather blunt tool, its use would affect the cost of money across the economy, not just in the sectors where bubbles were forming, and (3) that placing financial stability as an additional objective of monetary policy could place too much burden on monetary policy and compromise its credibility.[3]

According to those opposed to central banks' intervention during the period of bubble buildups, the central bank should intervene only when there were clear signs that financial stability was being impaired (i.e., when prices start falling and defaults are rising). Essentially, this latter approach argues that the use of monetary policy, a policy that affects all sectors of the economy, is appropriate only when financial instability has been manifested and becomes a threat to all sectors.

Learning from the experiences of the global financial crisis of 2007–2010, however, there has been a rethinking of the role of monetary policy in addressing the buildup of bubbles.[4] By not intervening early, overindebtedness in the economy could become a very large problem, and could ultimately overwhelm the ability of the central bank to maintain financial stability.[5] An alternative approach relies on using macroprudential tools as a complement to monetary policy in maintaining financial stability, rather than fully placing responsibility for maintaining financial stability on monetary policy tools.[6]

Sustaining Financial Stability: Dealing with Threats Against the Macroeconomy *Ex Ante*

To maintain financial stability, the central bank might want to deal with arising threats early, before they lead to a full-blown crisis. After the 2007–2010 crisis, it became increasingly recognized that the central bank could use *monetary policy* as well as *macroprudential measures* as the main instruments to address those threats *ex ante*. Monetary policy is a potent but blunt instrument that affects all sectors of the economy. Macroprudential measures are more precise, and can be used to address specific pockets of the economy. The central bank could also consider using both types of instruments in a complementary manner.

Since financial instability and price stability are intertwined, there are grounds for the central bank to take the possibility of excessive debt among economic agents (whether households or firms) into account when making monetary policy decisions. The Japanese experience of the late 1980s and early 1990s suggests that the inflation rate can remain low even when the economy is experiencing extreme forms of asset price bubbles and agents are taking on excessive debt.[7]

In Japan, once the bubbles burst, however, the excessive debt of economic agents sunk the economy into a debt-deflation spiral that it could not get out of, even after more than 20 years. To take financial stability into account in monetary policy decisions, policy makers might thus need to look beyond the usual two-year inflation outlook horizon. One possibility, practiced by the Bank of Canada, is to adjust the policy horizon to factor in risks such as supply shocks or asset prices when deciding on a monetary policy stance.[8] A slight variation of this approach is one used by the Reserve Bank of Australia, under which the horizon for monetary policy is described as "over the cycle," rather than as the typical two-year horizon.[9] In both cases it could be argued that looking out over a longer horizon is warranted, even for price stability, since over the long run financial instability could threaten price stability, the key objective of monetary policy.

In practice, if the central bank deems that agents are accumulating excessive debt in the economy, or that asset prices are rising too fast beyond levels supported by economic fundamentals (such that there might be too much speculative activity taking place), the central bank might choose to tighten its monetary policy, possibly through hikes in the policy interest rate. An advantage of tightening monetary policy early in this way is that it would prevent risks from building up to unsustainable levels, which could seriously worsen the situation and make it more difficult to deal with later on.

However, the use of monetary policy to discourage the taking on of excessive debt by economic agents, or to preempt asset price bubbles early on, requires caution on many fronts. Monetary policy normally affects all sectors of the economy, not just those sectors or agents that are in danger of being overindebted. For example, if the central bank chooses to hike the policy rate to temper a trend of fast-rising household debt, the rise in costs of funds is likely to also affect the corporate sector, even if the corporate sector was not the target of that hike. Another important concern is that, how could the central bank ever be certain that the debt level in any one sector is already too high, or that the rise in asset prices is excessive?

The Use of Macroprudential Measures   Acknowledging that monetary policy might be too blunt a tool to deal with risk buildups in specific pockets of the economy, authorities have increasingly turned to the use of so-called *macroprudential measures*, which are designed to address risk buildups in *specific* areas that, if remain unchecked, could affect *systemwide* stability. Although there is no single definitive set of macroprudential measures as yet, they can broadly be classified into those that are *credit-related*, *liquidity-related*, and *capital-related* (see the 2011 paper from Lim et al.[10]).

In addressing financial stability risks that might arise from the macroeconomy, key macroprudential measures would be those of the credit-related type, since they would address risk buildups that come with excessive borrowing by particular economic sectors.* Among the more prominent credit-related types of macroprudential measures are limits on the loan-to-value (LTV) ratio, limits on the debt-to-income (DTI) ratio, ceilings on credit or credit growth, and caps on foreign currency lending (again, see the 2011 paper from Lim et al.).

It should be noted, however, that the use of such measures for financial stability reasons are still in an early stage. There is no consensus on how the measures should be used in practice. The following discussion provides a glimpse into the fundamental concepts behind the tools, but the actual application would depend on individual contexts.

Limits on Loan-to-Value Ratios   Limits on LTV ratios are used to address risk buildups in the housing market.[11] LTV ratios limit households' borrowing capacity through the amount of the down payment required for a housing purchase. An LTV ratio of 80 percent in a particular segment of the housing market, for example, means that the buyer needs a down payment equivalent to 20 percent of the house's value, since banks would only be allowed to lend 80 percent of the value of the house in that particular market segment. If the LTV ratio is lowered to 70 percent, buyers will have to find more money for down payments, since they now need a 30 percent

---

*Liquidity-related and capital-related types of macroprudential measures are more relevant in addressing risks that might come from the financial institutions system, and are thus discussed later.

down payment. By lowering the LTV ratio, regulatory authorities can help reduce speculative activities in the housing market.

In practice, there are many variations on the use of limits of the LTV ratio. The central bank might lower the LTV directly as described above, or it could use other variations, such as imposing different risk weights for different LTV ratios, so that the banks will have to set aside higher reserves if they decide to lend to a client at a higher LTV ratio.

Debt-to-Income Ratio Debt-to-income (DTI) ratios can also be used to address risk buildups in the household sector. With limits on DTI ratios being imposed, lenders can extend a new loan to a household only if the level of pertinent household monthly debt repayments (mortgages, credit cards, auto loans, etc.) does not exceed a certain percentage of the household's income. By lowering limits on DTI ratios, the central bank would be constraining the households' capacity to borrow.[12]

In practice, limits on DTI ratios might be used in conjunction with LTV. They both can be lowered when households are deemed to be incurring more debt so fast that financial stability might be compromised.[13]

Ceilings on Credit Growth Ceilings on credit growth can be put on total bank lending as well as on lending to specific sectors.[14] Ceilings on credit growth for total bank lending could help reduce amplification effects from the business cycle in general. Banks would have to ration credits among different borrowers as they see fit. By putting ceilings on credit growth for specific sectors, on the other hand, regulatory authorities can address risk buildups in a more targeted way.

Caps on Unhedged Foreign Currency Lending Caps on unhedged foreign currency lending are placed on banks, which may borrow overseas to lend to domestic borrowers in a foreign currency.[15] Caps on foreign currency lending can be used to limit exposure to the unhedged foreign exchange rate risk that comes with external borrowing. When lending in a foreign currency to a domestic borrower, the banks might thus require the borrower to hedge the borrowing against foreign exchange rate risk, or they might simply limit their foreign currency lending.

With caps on unhedged foreign currency lending, borrowers' exposure to foreign exchange risk is limited, and thus their lenders are protected from credit risk. The caps are especially important in the case of emerging-market economies with a fixed exchange rate regime, since domestic interest rates that are higher than those overseas might prompt banks to borrow from abroad at low interest rates in order to lend to domestic borrowers at higher interest rates, without regard for the possibility that the central bank might be unable to keep the exchange rate at the fixed level if banks do this on a large scale.

Sustaining Financial Stability: Dealing with Risks within the Macroeconomy *Ex Post*

Once overindebtedness has started leading to chains of defaults, or when asset price bubbles start to burst, the central bank can also decide to intervene *ex post*, and deal with threats to financial stability that might arise from the macroeconomy.

Such intervention could be done through (1) the easing of monetary policy, and (2) the use of macroprudential measures.[16]

Monetary Policy Easing   The easing of monetary policy can be done *conventionally* through a cut in interest rates, and, in more severe cases, can be accompanied by *unconventional* measures, including the provision of credit to financial institutions, the provision of liquidity to financial markets, and the purchasing of long-term securities from the private sector (i.e., quantitative easing).[17]

Conventional Monetary Policy Easing   Conventional monetary policy easing through a cut in interest rates helps safeguard the macroeconomy and financial stability by reducing risk among the agents within the economy, particularly credit risk. In a situation in which financial stability is severely at risk, an easing of the monetary policy stance could help reduce credit risk in various sectors of the economy. Lowering of interest rates can help ease the interest burdens of borrowers, especially at a time when their income might also be falling, in line with the economic cycle. With a lighter interest burden, economic agents might be better able to cope with falling revenues and income, and may not resort to defaulting on their debts.

Unconventional Easing   In the case of an economic crisis, the central bank might choose to use additional measures in addition to the easing of monetary policy stance. In the wake of the 2007–2010 crisis, the U.S. central bank chose to do what had been previously considered an unconventional measure. As discussed in more extensive detail in Chapter 6, the unconventional monetary policy used to deal with the global financial crisis of 2007–2010 had three elements: (1) lending to financial institutions, (2) providing liquidity to key credit markets, and (3) purchasing of long-term securities.[18] As noted by Ben Bernanke, then chairman of the Federal Reserve, one common characteristic of the tools used for unconventional measures is that they rely on the central bank's authority to extend credit or to purchase securities.[19]

As discussed in Chapter 6, the first two elements (i.e., the lending to financial institutions and the provision of liquidity to key credit markets) were of the lender-of-last-resort type and were discontinued after the crisis had passed its peak. The last element, that is, the purchase of long-term securities (government bonds as well as asset-backed securities issued by the private sector), was aimed at providing liquidity to the private sector, taking out so-called toxic assets from the private sector's balance sheets (in the case of privately issued asset-backed securities), and bringing down long-term government bond yields. Given the fact that the last element is still on going in 2014 at the time that this book goes to press, the first two elements might fall into what Borio's 2012 paper described as *crisis management*, while the third element could be described as *crisis resolution*, as it was done to help the economy get back on a path to sustained recovery.[20]

Macroprudential measures   To help safeguard the macroeconomy and financial stability *ex post*, the central bank can also loosen *credit-related* macroprudential measures—such as caps on LTV, DTI, or credit growth—that had previously been tightened during the period of economic upturn.[21] The possibility of the countercyclical use of *credit-related* macroprudential measures has been given much attention in the wake of the recent financial crisis, but it remains to be seen if such measures can actually reverse a downward trend in a crisis. During a crisis, it is reasonable to expect that economic agents would be less willing to take out more loans, even if LTV and DTI are lower. Still, the unwinding of such measures might at least give some signals that are consistent with monetary policy easing.

12.2 FINANCIAL INSTITUTIONS

To help maintain stability of financial institutions, central banks with a bank supervisory role can use various tools on banks or other financial institutions under its supervision ex ante. The tools can be applied from a micro- or macroprudential perspective, depending on the particular context. Central banks that do not have a bank supervisory role still have the option of coordinating with regulatory authorities that do, to impose such rules and regulations. Ex post, however, whether the central bank has a bank supervisory role or not, it can intervene to safeguard financial stability through the provision of emergency liquidity or special resolutions for troubled financial institutions where necessary.

Sustaining Financial Stability: Dealing with Threats to Financial Institutions *Ex Ante*

To safeguard financial stability against risks that may come from financial institutions *ex ante*, it might be helpful for a central bank with bank supervisory role to take both a micro- and macroprudential perspective.[22] For example, the use of microprudential supervisory tools (such as those that come with onsite examinations) could be used to ensure that individual banks comply with regulatory requirements, and that their management is safe and sound, while macroprudential supervisory tools (such as time-varying capital requirements and dynamic provisioning) could be used to ensure the resiliency of the banking system against risks amplification by business cycles, as well as by cross-sectional risk concentration within the system.

Microprudential Supervision   For central banks that have a bank supervisory role, microprudential supervision would aim to ensure that individual banks do have enough capital and liquidity to cover any emerging shocks, and that the banks are managed in a safe and sound manner. Microprudential supervision is often associated with bank examinations and their associated actions, including enforcement of regulations and laws to ensure bank compliance. As mentioned in Chapter 3, bank examinations involve both *onsite* examination and *offsite* monitoring.

Through onsite examinations, the central bank would be aiming to ensure the general safety and soundness of each of the individual banks under its supervision. The use of the CAMELS rating in onsite examinations is one way that the central bank can assess and address individual banks' capital adequacy, asset quality, management, earnings, liquidity, and sensitivity to market risk. In the period that falls in between onsite examinations, the central bank would perform offsite monitoring to check if, where needed, corrective actions have been made. Analyses of current and projected conditions of the banks would also be made during this period, so that areas of focus on the next onsite examination could be determined.

With onsite examinations and offsite monitoring, the central bank would know the health of each of the individual banks in detail. Through its legal power and the use of "moral suasion," the central bank could ensure that banks comply with regulations and the law, and that suggested corrective actions are made by the banks when demanded. Since a serious breach of compliance could expose a bank to the risk of failure, the central bank always has the option to remove directors or management of the bank for negligence or misconduct, and install a temporary administration. In an extreme case, in which a bank has already been deemed insolvent or at great risk of insolvency, the central bank might recommend a forced sale or liquidation of the bank to prevent a bank run.

Macroprudential Supervision Unlike microprudential supervision, under which the focus is on the resiliency of individual banks, macroprudential supervision puts more emphasis on the resiliency of the banking system as a whole. Macroprudential measures, especially those that are capital-related and liquidity-related, are used to safeguard financial institutions against systemic risks. Capital-related macroprudential tools include *time-varying capital requirements*, *dynamic provisioning*, and *extra capital buffers for SIFIs*.[23] Liquidity-related macroprudential tools include *limits on net open positions* (especially of foreign currencies) and *limits on mismatches* (of currencies and maturities),[24] as well as the *liquidity coverage ratios* (LCR) and *net stable funding ratios* (NSFR) introduced in the wake of the 2007–2010 crisis by the Basel Committee for Banking Supervision.[25]

Capital-Related Macroprudential Measures Capital requirements are a key tool that the central bank can use to help ensure resiliency of the banking system against systemic risk, by requiring that banks hold enough capital to deal with multiple types of risks. Capital requirements can be used to guard against *systemic* risk that might arise from (1) risk amplification through the business cycle, and (2) risk concentration and distribution within the system.

CONCEPT: THE BASICS OF CAPITAL REQUIREMENTS: THE RELATIONSHIP BETWEEN ASSETS, LIABILITIES, AND CAPITAL

To comply with accounting rules, the total asset value of a bank must be equal to the value of that bank's liabilities. Bank liabilities can be categorized into debt (mostly in the form of deposits) and capital (owned by the bank's shareholders). Assets on the bank's balance sheet must be financed by either debt or capital. In practice, the major part of a bank's assets is often composed of loans made to firms and households. The major part of a bank's debt, on the other hand, is often deposits put in the bank by depositors.

If a bank's assets decline in value, possibly because borrowers cannot repay their loans, the value of the bank's total liabilities must also decline for the balance sheet to remain balanced. By law, to match the loss in total asset value, the value of the bank's capital must be completely written down before depositors absorb any loss. As discussed in Chapter 11, however, if depositors fear that

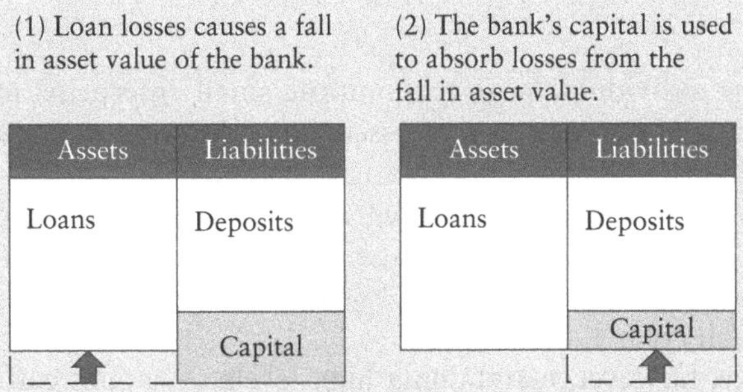

FIGURE 12.1 The Use of Bank Capital to Absorb Loan Losses
Source: Adapted from Jorge A. Chan-Lau, "Balance Sheet Network Analysis of Too-Connected-to-Fail Risk in Global and Domestic Banking Systems" (IMF Working Paper WP/10/107, April 2010).

their money might be affected then a run on the bank might occur even before the capital is depleted. To buffer any shock to the value of its assets, and to ensure the bank's resiliency, a high level of capital is often maintained. Figure 12.1 illustrates how a bank might need to use its capital to absorb its lending losses.

The Definition of Capital

In accounting terms, capital means the part of the business that actually belongs to shareholders (as opposed to creditors). For banks, capital would normally include common equity, preferred equity, retained earnings, and required reserves. Capital can be classified into two different tiers. Tier 1 capital reflects the banks' strength (or lack thereof), as it refers to the banks' *paid in capital*, and also takes account of retained earnings or losses. Tier 2 capital often refers to the part of capital that might temporary rise or might be transformed into Tier 1 capital under certain circumstances, such as debentures. Tier 2 capital also includes changes in valuation of fixed assets.

Capital Ratio

Determining whether an institution has enough capital or not is assessed by the ratio of the bank's capital to the value of the bank's risk-weighted assets (RWA).

$$\text{Capital ratio} = \text{Capital/RWA}$$

Since the value of different types of assets can behave differently when a crisis hits, the effects on capital should be different. Loans that the bank has made have different degree of riskiness, depending on (among other things) the type of loan (housing loan, corporate loan, etc.) and the type of borrower (high

(*Continued*)

(*Continued*)

or low income individual, large corporation, small enterprise, medium enterprise, etc.). Since different types of assets have different degrees of riskiness, the amount that the bank needs to hold as a capital buffer against a particular type of asset will also depend on the degree of asset riskiness. In aggregate, how much capital the bank should hold against their assets should thus be determined by how many different types of assets are being held and the degree of riskiness of each type.

In practice, however, maintaining high levels of capital can be costly for banks. Funds that are maintained as capital normally do not earn high returns when compared to funds that are lent out as loans. Higher capital requirements imply not only higher opportunity costs for banks, but also impose higher handicaps on them, since the banks still need to pay interest to depositors as well as overhead costs for their own operations, whether the deposits are lent out or not.

Capital Adequacy Requirements in the Macroprudential Context   In the macroprudential context, it is recognized that capital adequacy should be adjusted to take account of risk accumulation and risk-taking behavior by both banks and borrowers over the business cycle. As such, new regulations—such as Basel II and III—recommend that capital requirements vary over time. A proposal made by Goodhart in a 2013 paper also suggested the use of capital requirements as an active tool to prevent financial instability.[26]

TIME-VARYING CAPITAL REQUIREMENTS   The gist of time-varying capital requirements is that capital requirements should be raised during good times and lowered during bad times to safeguard the stability of the banking system from the vagaries of the business cycle. During good times, economic and business projections often focus on the upside, which make risky projects often appear viable. An increase in capital adequacy requirements would automatically reduce the likelihood that banks would take on excessive exposures to risks. Apart from reducing risky exposures, higher capital accumulated during good times will help banks better deal with adverse shocks to their portfolios when bad times eventually arise.

As bad times arise, the lowering of capital adequacy requirements will help alleviate pressure on banks. Banks would not be required to keep their capital levels high, and would thus be able to run down some of their capital to absorb shocks that occur to their portfolios. With better ability to absorb shocks on their portfolios, there will be less pressure for the banks to call back their loans, an action that not only affects their immediate customers but also could appreciably worsen macroeconomic prospects, which could lead to more pressure on their portfolios.

By raising capital requirements during good times and lowering capital requirements during bad times, it is expected that the banking system will be more robust against the vagaries of business cycles. In practice, however, the actual application of the concept of time-varying capital requirements is still very much in the early stages.

Research is still being done on what measures should be used to assess what constitutes good times, when capital requirements should be raised, and what constitutes bad times, when capital requirements should be lowered.

In 2011, Borio, Drehmann, and Tsatsaronis suggested that the gap between the credit-to-GDP ratio and its long-term backward-looking trend might be a good indicator to signal the need for capital requirements to be raised, as it could capture the buildup of systemic vulnerabilities. To signal the need for capital requirements to be lowered, however, they found other indicators (such as credit spreads) to be better, as they provide more timely signals of the banking sector distress that can precede a credit crunch.[27]

CAPITAL REQUIREMENTS AS AN ACTIVE TOOL TO SUSTAIN FINANCIAL STABILITY
According to Goodhart's 2013 paper, there should also be "an increasing ladder of penal sanctions" as a bank's equity capital falls. As the bank's capital adequacy falls towards a "minimum intervention point," official action should be taken to remove management and shareholders, and to move to a resolution.[28] Such an approach would make capital adequacy requirements more potent as a macroprudential tool. According to this view, rather than passively monitoring banks to ensure that they comply with capital adequacy requirements, capital adequacy requirements could be used by regulatory authorities as an *active* tool to maintain financial stability *ex ante*.

CONCEPT: INTRODUCTION TO BASEL I, II, AND III

The international framework for capital adequacy requirements that central banks often adopt is the one recommended by the Basel Committee on Banking Supervision, an international committee of central banks and experts based in Basel, Switzerland. As mentioned in Chapter 3, the first version of the recommended framework was issued in 1988 and was known as the *Basel Accord* (or later, *Basel I*). An updated version, known as *Basel II*, was introduced in 2004 but had not been fully or widely implemented by the time the 2007–2010 crisis hit the global financial system. Incorporating lessons learned from the crisis, the Basel Committee released *Basel III* as the latest version of the framework in 2010.[29]

The Basel Accord (Basel I)

Under the original Basel Accord (or Basel I), issued in 1988, assets of financial institutions were classified into five categories according to their perceived riskiness. Banks were required to hold capital as reserves against the assets at 0, 10, 20, 50, or 100 percent, depending on their perceived riskiness. The safest assets (such as domestic government bonds, which are supposedly risk-free, since the government is unlikely to default on debts denominated in domestic currency) were assigned a risk-weight of 0 percent. Zero risk-weight means that banks do not have to hold any capital as reserves against this type of asset on their

(Continued)

(*Continued*)

balance sheets. At the other extreme, Basel I deemed corporate bonds to be very risky and assigned them a risk-weight of 100 percent. This meant that for corporate bonds held as assets on their balance sheets, the banks would have had to hold capital as reserves equivalent to the full amount.

In total, Basel I specified that a bank had to hold capital of at least 8 percent of risk-weighted assets. Basel I can thus be expressed as

$$\text{Capital Adequacy Ratio} = \text{Capital/RWA} \geq 8\,\%$$

where Capital is the value of the bank's capital and RWA is the value of the bank's risk-weighted assets. In setting the minimum capital adequacy ratio at 8 percent of risk-weighted assets, the Basel Committee did not clearly specify economic reasons why it chose 8 percent as the minimum. It was believed, however, that 8 percent would ensure that there was enough room for safety and allow international banks from different jurisdictions to compete on a level playing field.

In the 1990s the Basel Committee revised the Basel Accord to cover market risk, which comes with changes in financial asset prices and could affect financial institutions' balance sheets along with credit risk. After its introduction in 1988, more than 100 countries adopted the guidelines of Basel I for the supervision of their financial institutions, with the specifics adjusted according to the countries' specific needs and circumstances.[30]

Basel II

In 2004, the Basel Committee published new guidelines for capital requirements known as Basel II. Basel II was an attempt to make improvements upon Basel I through the use of the *three pillars* approach. Pillar 1 put emphasis on making *capital requirements* more comprehensive and responsive with respect to risks that financial institutions might be facing. Pillar 2, known as *supervisory review*, stressed the importance of a banking supervisor making risk-weight adjustments to truly reflect what the supervisor sees as the underlying risks faced by a bank. Pillar 3, *market discipline*, emphasized the ability of market forces to discipline the bank's management to be vigilant about risks that the bank might take.

Under Pillar 1, capital requirements were made more comprehensive and responsive to risk. *Operational* risk and *market* risk were covered, in addition to *credit* risk and all three were required to be quantified. For small financial institutions with simple transactions, ratings from external rating agencies such as Standard & Poor's and Moody's could be used to determine the risk-weights to be assigned to different assets. For larger financial institutions or those with complex transactions, Basel II allowed the use of in-house risk models to determine the risk-weights of assets on their own balance sheets. Basel II also emphasized that different types of assets might have risk characteristics that offset each other (e.g., certain derivatives on the bank's balance sheets could mitigate risk for other assets in the bank's portfolio).

Under Pillar 2, the Basel Committee stressed the importance of regulatory authorities examining banks with regard to the calculation of risk-weights and ascertaining whether the weights came from external credit rating agencies or were based on the banks' internal risk models. The bank supervisory agency would then require a bank to adjust its risk-weights to truly reflect underlying risks if it saw fit.

Under Pillar 3, Basel II focused on having private investors validating banks' risk management practices to augment regulatory authorities' assessment of risk-weight calculation made by the banks. The transparency of financial institutions was emphasized so that market players themselves could better assess whether the institutions were sound and had good prospects. Since investors typically want to hold more shares of those financial institutions that are sound with good prospects, they would be willing to bid up share prices of those institutions. Accordingly, it was believed that share prices of financial institutions would reflect the effectiveness of the management and help discipline the institutions' risk-management process in tandem with the supervisory review carried out by regulatory authorities.[31]

Basel III

Although the Basel Committee published Basel II in 2004, its adoption took time, as both regulatory authorities and banks needed to do a lot of preparation. By the time the global crisis became full-blown in 2008, however, it became apparent that Basel II itself needed revision in many areas. The revisions ultimately led to the issuance of Basel III in late 2010, which improved upon Basel II with respect to the *three pillars* and laid out *minimum global liquidity standard* as well as *additional capital buffers for SIFIs*.[32]

Improvements to the Three Pillars

In learning from the 2007–2010 crisis, the Basel Committee made considerable adjustments in Basel III that improved upon the three pillars of Basel II.

Pillar I Under Pillar I, Basel III aimed to improve the *quality* and *quantity* of capital, as well as the *coverage of risk* and limits on the banks' *leverage*.

With respect to capital quality, Basel III focused on having common equity as capital. During the global financial crisis, despite the existence of capital requirements, financial institutions did not have enough of a capital buffer to absorb losses on their balance sheets. Partly this was due to the fact that Tier 2 capital, such as debentures and changes in the valuation of fixed assets, could not actually be counted on to absorb the losses of the bank. Owners of debentures of a bank are unlikely to convert the debentures into common equity during a period of stress, since they would lose seniority in claims on the bank's assets. Fixed assets, such as the bank's own real estate, can also fall in value during the period of stress.

(Continued)

(*Continued*)

By focusing on having common equity as a key ingredient in capital requirements, Basel III raised the quality of capital, since common equity can be written down directly against losses during a period of crisis. Under Basel III, common equity must be 4.5 percent of risk-weighted assets. The relevant authorities also have the discretion to demand the write-off or conversion of other capital instruments (such as debentures) into common equity to absorb bank losses.

With respect to capital quantity, Basel III also required that banks have a *capital conservation buffer* in the form of common equity equivalent to 2.5 percent of risk-weighted assets. This requirement, together with the one just described, brought the total common equity standard to 7 percent. The conservation buffer was meant to help with a dilemma that became apparent during the financial crisis: when losses actually occurred, financial institutions were unable to write down their capital to absorb the losses, since a write-down would have reduced their capital to below the minimum capital requirements.

Basel III also required a *countercyclical (or time-varying) capital buffer* in the form of common equity, to be imposed in the range of 0–2.5 percent of risk-weighted assets when the relevant authorities deemed that credit growth would lead to excessive buildups of systemic risk.

With respect to *risk coverage*, in light of the 2007–2010 crisis, which was partly precipitated by the growth in securitization and derivatives trading among different types of counterparties, Basel III required stricter treatment for securitized assets, for trading and derivatives activities and counterparty credit risk, as well as for exposure to central counterparties who were responsible for clearing financial market transactions.

As a backstop to risk-based capital requirements, Basel III also introduced a nonrisk-based *leverage ratio*, under which a bank would not be allowed to have assets (including off-balance sheet assets) in excess of capital beyond a certain ratio. The leverage ratio was meant to limit the temptation and the ability of bankers to make an excessive number of loans or take on excessive off-balance sheet exposure, both of which could jeopardize the soundness of the bank.

Pillar 2 Under Pillar 2, Basel III introduced *supplemental requirements for supervisory review* by addressing issues relating to (1) bankwide governance and risk management practices, (2) off-balance sheet exposures and securitization activities (3) the management of risk concentration within the bank, (4) compensation and valuation practices, (5) accounting standards for financial instruments, and (6) supervisory colleges, which are multilateral working groups of relevant supervisors that are formed specifically to do consolidated supervision of an international banking group on an ongoing basis.

Pillar 3 Under Pillar 3, Basel III suggested revisions to disclosure requirements for all banks. The banks' securitization exposures and sponsorship of off-balance sheet vehicles would have to be disclosed, along with specifics of the components of the banks' regulatory capital and calculations of regulatory capital ratios.

Global Liquidity Standard for All Banks and Additional Loss Absorbency Capacity for SIFIs

In addition to improvements in the three pillars, Basel III also introduced a global liquidity standard and corresponding supervisory monitoring for all banks, as well as higher loss absorbency capacity for SIFIs.

Global Liquidity Standard The global liquidity standard introduced a *liquidity coverage ratio* (*LCR*) that requires all banks to have liquid assets sufficient to withstand a 30-day stress funding scenario as conducted by supervisors. A *net stable funding ratio* (*NSFR*) was also introduced to incentivize banks to use stable sources of funding (e.g., term deposits instead of money market borrowing) and address liquidity mismatches. In addition, Basel III set out a regulatory framework that includes a common set of monitoring metrics to assist supervisors in identifying and analyzing trends in liquidity risk, both at the level of individual banks and systemwide.

Additional Loss Absorbency Capacity for SIFIs For SIFIs, Basel III required additional loss absorbency capacity through progressive common equity Tier 1 capital requirements ranging from 1 percent to 2.5 percent, depending on a bank's systemic importance. Basel III also suggested a 1 percent additional loss absorbency for banks that are already facing the highest SIB surcharge, to discourage those banks from materially increasing their global systemic importance in the future.

DYNAMIC LOAN LOSS PROVISIONING   Another concept that has many similarities to time-varying capital requirements is dynamic loan loss provisioning. Simply put, dynamic provisioning suggests that banks *raise* their provisions for expected losses for the loans they make during good times and *lower* their provisions for expected losses during bad times.[33] The key differences between dynamic provisioning and time-varying capital requirements are that (1) dynamic provisioning affects the banks' income statements directly, while time-varying capital requirements do not, and (2) dynamic provisioning deals with *expected* losses from lending, while time-varying capital requirements deal with *unexpected* losses that might come through the business cycle.

During good times, the quantity of loans will increase but the quality of loans may decrease as banks compete to extend credit. Accordingly, expected losses from loans made during good times should rise, and banks should be expected to make more provisions for lending during good times. As bad times come, with greater provisions already made for the expected losses, the banks' will not be affected as much as otherwise. Moreover, during bad times, as banks become more cautious, and economic conditions are conducive only to the safest projects, loan quantities are likely to decline, while the quality of loans is likely to rise. Expected losses from lending during bad times are likely to be lower, and banks should be required to make less provision.

The use of dynamic provisioning was pioneered by the Bank of Spain in 2000 and has since increasingly been adopted by many other central banks. A 2012 paper from Wezel, Chan-lau, and Columba suggested that dynamic loan loss provisioning can be used as a complementary tool to time-varying capital requirements.[34] Dynamic loan loss provisioning could act as a first line of defense, whereby banks will have dynamic loan loss provision funds to run down during bad times, protecting their profits and capital unless it ultimately becomes necessary to tap into their capital. To point out the complementarity between these two tools, it might be worth repeating that dynamic loan loss provisioning will help safeguard banks against *expected* losses, while time-varying capital requirements will help safeguard the banks against *unexpected* losses.

Liquidity-Related Macroprudential Measures   *Limits on banks' net open positions* (e.g., on foreign currencies) ensure that banks are not overexposed to liquidity and market risks. If many banks have large net open positions on a foreign currency at the same time (e.g., in the case of a carry trade, where banks borrow in a foreign currency that has low interest rates, in order to lend to domestic borrowers at higher interest rates) and the exchange rate moves against the banks, for example, the banks might suffer losses and need to raise funds quickly to meet those losses. If banks have to raise funds at the same time, they might have to conduct a fire sale of their assets, exacerbating the situation. By having limits placed on banks' net open positions, the banks will need to hedge their positions and the banking system might be less exposed to liquidity and market risks.

Limits on currency and maturity mismatches also reduce the banking system's exposure to liquidity and market risks. A large currency mismatch suggests that a bank has assets (e.g., loans) denominated largely in one currency, and liabilities (e.g., its deposit base) largely in another currency. When the exchange rate moves against the bank's assets, but in favor of the bank's liabilities, the bank will incur losses, and might need to raise funds quickly. A maturity mismatch suggests a bank is depending too much on short-term loans to finance long-term loans, which will result in liquidity problems if the bank cannot roll over the short-term loans when they become due.

Liquidity coverage ratios (LCR) and *net stable funding ratios (NSFR)* are also among the global liquidity standard introduced by Basel III to strengthen banks' liquidity positions. (See Concept: Introduction to Basel I, I, and III for specifics.)

Sustaining Financial Stability: Dealing with Threats to Financial Institutions *Ex Post*

Micro- and macroprudential measures and capital adequacy requirements such as those proposed in Basel I, II, and III are used to ensure that financial institutions are generally in a safe and sound conditions ex ante. In practice, however, financial institutions often borrow short-term and lend long-term, meaning that it is very possible that they could experience unexpected liquidity shortages, whether from internal or external factors, despite being very well capitalized.

The Discount Window To prevent liquidity shortages from creating undue strain on financial institutions and causing systemic failures, the central bank can provide access to backup liquidity for eligible financial institutions through a facility that is often known as the discount window. In the early days of central banking, the discount window was the principal instrument of central banking operations where the central bank provided funds to financial institutions that needed them. Later on, with market operations becoming the dominant instrument of monetary policy, the discount window was relegated to a complementary role, and was used primarily as a safety valve to help alleviate unexpected liquidity pressures on financial institutions.[35]

As a provider of liquidity, the discount window can be used as another channel to either inject liquidity into financial institutions that are under extreme liquidity pressures, or to redistribute liquidity—through the borrowing financial institutions—to other parts of the economy where it is needed.

To borrow from the discount window, eligible financial institutions normally have to post eligible assets at a discount as collateral for the central bank. The interest rate charged on discount window lending is often a little higher than the policy interest rate, to discourage financial institutions from overreliance on the discount window. By charging a higher interest rate on discount window lending, the central bank is expecting financial institutions to manage their liquidity more prudently and come to the discount window for backup liquidity only when necessary. In the course of normal operations, financial institutions thus often try to access other sources of liquidity first, since they are likely to be charged lower interest rates.

While the central bank might generally want to discourage banks from relying on the discount window as their main source of liquidity, however, it has become increasingly recognized that excessive stigma should *not* be placed on those that are truly in need of temporary liquidity.[36] Even well run banks might run into emergency liquidity needs in times of general crisis, and the excessive stigma placed on discount window borrowing might unduly deter them from tapping that much needed liquidity.

To resolve this dilemma, the central bank now often distinguishes between different tiers of liquidity provision, and accordingly charges different interest rates at the discount window. The first tier is for provision of very short-term liquidity backup to generally sound financial institutions, and the interest rate charged might be only a little higher than the policy interest rate. Liquidity would be provided on a no-questions-asked basis, and that liquidity could be used for any purpose. Financial institutions that are not qualified to access the first tier of liquidity at the discount window might still be allowed to access liquidity, but they would be charged a higher interest rate, and the central bank might require confirmation that the loan is consistent with regulatory requirements.

Special Resolutions for Troubled Financial Institutions and *Living Wills* Despite various measures put in place, there is always a possibility that a bank might still fail. To ensure financial stability, the central bank and related authorities might need special resolutions to ensure that a troubled bank does not fail in a disorderly manner.

According to 2012 work from Claire McQuire, there are four key types of special resolutions that regulatory authorities might resort to when they want to ensure an orderly resolution for a troubled bank: (1) liquidation, or closing of the bank; (2) conservatorship, or temporary administration of the bank; (3) purchase and assumption; and (4) nationalization.[37]

Liquidation: Closing of a Bank   Liquidation is often the preferred option in cases in which regulatory authorities feel that the closure of the bank would not lead to contagion effects. Under the liquidation option, regulatory authorities might simply order the bank closed, withdraw the bank's license, and follow procedures laid out in either the country's bankruptcy laws, commercial laws, or special resolution regimes for banks. The bank's assets would be sold over time to repay its liabilities to depositors and other creditors. If the country has a deposit insurance program, the insurance agency would pay depositors up to an agreed amount and the payments would be substituted for depositors' claims during the recovery process. Bank shareholders would only receive residual claims after all other bank creditors have been paid.

Conservatorship: Temporary Administration   If regulatory authorities feel that closing the troubled bank immediately would create unnecessary disruption, regulatory authorities might appoint a temporary administration team who would take over from the bank's own senior executives. In a conservatorship, preexisting shareholders may be removed from ownership of the bank or their rights might be temporarily constrained. The administration team would reform the bank's operations to improve its financial health, with the goal of possibly selling or merging the bank with another financial institution at a later date.

Purchase and Assumption: Facilitating an Acquisition by Another Party   To prevent unnecessary disruptions, another alternative is for regulatory authorities to pursue what is known as purchase and assumption (P&A). This approach essentially aims to transfer the troubled bank's operations to another healthy bank. Regulatory authorities withdraw or cancel the license of the troubled bank, terminate shareholders' rights, facilitate the assumption of the troubled bank's good assets and deposits by the other bank, and take over the troubled bank's problem assets so they can be managed and sold afterward. One form of P&A is for regulatory authorities to create a *bridge bank*, which takes over all or part of the troubled bank with the goal of selling it to a private party at some later date.

Nationalization: Assumption of Ownership by the Government   In the environment in which the system is already under a lot of stress and a more market-based resolution might not be timely or effective, regulatory authorities might need to assume ownership of the troubled bank. In such a case, all assets and liabilities of the troubled bank are transferred to the government in exchange for cash injection and ownership. The government might appoint new management or it might let current management continue to improve the bank's financial health, such that the government would either be repaid over time or would sell the bank to a private party at a future date.

Living Wills   In the wake of the 2007–2010 crisis, it has been recognized that modern financial institutions can be very large with very complex ownership structures and contractual obligations. Unless the banks' structures are well-known to regulatory authorities in advance, regulatory authorities' efforts to provide a bank resolution at the time of the crisis might not be efficient or effective. Consequently, financial reforms after the 2007–2010 crisis, such as the Dodd-Frank Act in the United States, now require that the largest banks file *living wills* with regulatory authorities that detail the banks' existing ownership structures, assets, liabilities, and contractual obligations plan for resolutions, in case the banks go bankrupt and need to be wound down.[38]

Apart from helping regulatory authorities know in advance about the existing structures and resolution plans of banks, the exercise of creating living wills forces the banks' management to know more about their own bank operations and plan for emergencies. Among living wills of the 11 largest banks that filed living wills with U.S. authorities in 2013, plans include recapitalizing of subsidiaries while putting the parent company into bankruptcy, selling off assets and businesses, and closing of business units.[39] Given that the plans are done before the banks actually run into trouble, living wills could also be considered an *ex ante* tool.

12.3 FINANCIAL MARKETS

Since the central bank is normally not the direct regulator of financial markets,* it is often the case that the central bank will take a hands-off or a very selective and very cautious approach in dealing with those markets. As it is not a direct regulator of financial markets, the central bank might not have adequate regulatory tools to mitigate risk buildup among financial market players, except possibly in cases in which players are banks under its supervision (and that only applies if the central bank is a bank supervisor).

Although the central bank is normally not a direct regulator of financial markets, there are at least three key reasons that the central bank might need to take an active role in reducing risk in the financial markets.

First is the growing importance of financial markets. The 2007–2010 crisis highlighted the need to rethink the role of the central bank in maintaining financial market stability. In the United States, financial intermediation was increasingly being conducted in the financial markets, outside of the traditional depository institutions that were under central bank supervision. At the same time commercial bank assets, as a proportion of total financial intermediary assets, has declined, while the proportion attributable to securities broker-dealers, hedge funds, and mutual funds has grown in importance.

What came along with the growing importance of these nonbank institutions was the securitization of financial institutions' assets (such as mortgages, auto loans, and credit card loans) into tradable securities. Trading of these securitized assets became an important activity among financial institutions all by itself. If developments in the United States are any guide, it is likely that financial markets in other countries will also grow in importance relative to traditional banking.

---

*Depending on the country, the role of financial market regulation is either assigned to a single regulator (such as the Financial Services Authority) or to different regulators for different markets (such as the Securities and Exchange Commission and the Commodity Futures Trading Commission).

Second, severe disruptions in the financial markets can result in shortages of liquidity, which could cause chains of settlement failures to spread across the financial system and the economy. This is especially true for the many countries where financial markets have grown in significance to become an important source of funding for economic activity. The central bank, with its financial stability mandate, cannot thus stay idle, especially if market disruptions threaten the stability of the financial system and the economy.

As the ultimate creator of money, it is the central bank that has ultimate liquidity provision power, and thus the ability needed to offset systemic liquidity shortages in financial markets. The growing importance of financial markets and the intertwining nature of financial markets, financial institutions, and ultimately, the macroeconomy, make it inevitable that central banks will have to take a more proactive role in dealing with risk buildup in financial markets.

Third, through its day-to-day monetary policy operations in the financial markets, the central bank already has in place the network of contacts, tools, and facilities that can readily be used to help sustain the smooth functioning of markets. For its day-to-day monetary policy operations, the central bank normally is at the center of a network of primary dealers, which may include institutions not under its direct supervision but are key players in different segments of financial markets. In terms of gathering information, in being connected to a network of primary dealers, the central bank is more likely to be aware of disruptions outside the market segments in which the central bank normally operates. In operational terms, the central bank can also use the primary dealers as conduits to redistribute liquidity to where it is needed in the financial markets.

Sustaining Financial Stability: Dealing with Threats to Financial Markets *Ex Ante*

A central bank is normally not the lead regulator of financial markets. Still, with its monetary policy fundamentally affecting prices and cost of funds in financial markets, its extensive operations in the financial markets, and its regulatory power over banks that are key financial market players (in cases in which the central bank is also a bank supervisor), a central bank has the ability to deal with threats to financial markets *ex ante*.

Using Monetary Policy to Address Risk Buildups in the Financial Markets   In theory, *ex ante*, a central bank could choose to tighten monetary policy in order to prevent the buildup of risk in financial markets. A tightened monetary policy stance raises the cost of funds among players in financial markets, which discourages them from undertaking more speculative activities. In practice, however, this is rarely done, unless it is also clear that the buildup of risk in any particular segment of the market is already a serious risk to financial stability and ultimately price stability. The central bank would be very hesitant to tighten its monetary policy stance simply in response to fast-rising prices of stocks, for example, since the tightening would affect all sectors of the economy, and it can never be sure whether the fast-rising stock prices are justified by economic fundamentals.

Regulations on Market Players   Rather than simply tighten monetary policy stance, the central bank might target regulations to financial market players under their supervision (i.e., banks). Examples of such regulations include limits on net *currency* positions, limits on *currency* mismatches, and limits on *maturity* mismatches of banks under the central bank's supervision. (See the previous section on liquidity-related macroprudential tools.)

For market players that are not directly under the central bank's supervision, the central bank might need to coordinate with the relevant regulators to ensure that there is a *level playing field* among the different types of market players (i.e., market activities are equivalently regulated among different types of market players). Otherwise, risk-taking activities might simply migrate from players that are tightly regulated to those that are lightly, or not adequately, regulated.

Sustaining Financial Stability: Dealing with Threats to Financial Markets *Ex Post*

Given the central banks' control of monetary policy, and their lender-of-last-resort status, the central banks also are in a good position to deal with threats to financial markets *ex post*.

Monetary Policy and Liquidity Risk   As overindebtedness or bubbles start to materially affect financial stability, it becomes more likely that players in the financial markets would be wary of lending to each other, as they become unsure of each other's ability to fulfill their transaction obligations. If those with excess liquidity become very worried and refuse to lend or demand excessively high interest rates for loans, even those players who are solvent (the value of their assets exceeds their debt) but need liquidity urgently (possibly to pay for their own transaction obligations, for example), might also fall into trouble, which could create a trail of liquidity shortages that runs through the whole system.

In the case where liquidity shortages spread widely, such that system's stability might be affected, the central bank might decide to use monetary policy to reduce the system's liquidity risk. This could be done through cuts in the policy interest rate, as well as cuts in rates charged on emergency lending. The cuts in interest rates would help lower the costs of funding in the financial markets, and ease liquidity shortages.

Liquidity Provision to Institutions Not Supervised by the Central Bank   Once financial markets are experiencing stress and disruption, the central bank might also decide to intervene *ex post* by providing liquidity to financial market players (even those that are not directly under its supervision), if not doing so would aggravate system instability. Traditionally, central banks often refrain from providing liquidity to financial market players not under their supervision for fear of moral hazard. As financial markets have grown in importance, however, it could be hazardous for the central bank to ignore liquidity shortages of systemically important players just because they are outside its direct supervision.

On this note, it is good to draw from the U.S. central bank's experiences in alleviating pressure in the financial markets during the 2007–2010 crisis. Notably, the Federal Reserve intervened in the financial markets ex post in three nontraditional ways: (1) the provision of liquidity to institutions and firms not supervised by the central bank, (2) the expansion of types of collateral taken *in lieu* of liquidity provisions, and (3) the provision of nonrecourse loans of longer maturities in certain cases normally outside traditional liquidity provision.[40]

Notable among firms and institutions that the U.S. central bank provided liquidity to during the crisis although they were not necessarily under its supervision were (1) *primary dealers*, consisting banks that are under the Federal Reserve's supervision as well as nonbanks that are not;[41] (2) *money market mutual funds*, which are, strictly speaking, outside the Federal Reserve's supervision but which have gained in importance as people have started to treat the money in money market accounts as a substitute for bank deposits (details of money market mutual funds will be discussed in Chapter 13);[42] (3) *commercial paper issuers*, which includes many nonfinancial corporations that issued paper in the financial markets to raise funds for their operational activities, including payroll payments; (4) *investors in the asset-backed securities market*, which included banks and various other types of financial institutions that invested in asset-backed securities; and (5) *foreign central banks*, which might have needed to meet a demand for U.S. dollars from domestic and foreign corporations in their own jurisdictions.[43]

SUMMARY

If risks to financial stability become apparent, the central bank can intervene to sustain financial stability both ex ante and ex post. *Ex ante* means that the central bank intervenes to preempt a crisis from occurring. *Ex post* means that the central bank intervenes to restore stability after a crisis has occurred.

To deal with threats to financial stability in the macroeconomy, the central bank might tighten monetary policy and use macroprudential tools to tame overindebtedness among economic sectors *ex ante*. The central bank might also loosen monetary policy and macroprudential tools to less the effects of the crisis on economic agents in the macroeconomy *ex post*.

To deal with threats to financial stability in the financial institutions system, the central bank could rely on *capital* and *liquidity-related* measures. Time-varying capital requirements, dynamic loan loss provisioning, Basel II and III, are measures to help strengthen banks' capital, while limits on net open positions, limits on mismatches of currencies and maturities, as well as liquidity coverage ratio, and net stable funding ratio are examples of liquidity-related measures. *Ex post*, the central bank might provide liquidity to financial institutions through the discount window, as well as to resort to special resolutions for troubled banks. In addition, regulatory authorities might also require largest banks to submit their living wills.

Although the central bank is often not the lead regulator in financial markets, it could deal with threats to financial stability in financial markets ex ante through the use of monetary policy and regulations on banks under its supervision. *Ex post*, the central bank might restore stability in the financial markets through the use of monetary policy as well as liquidity provision to institutions not supervised by the central bank.

KEY TERMS

Basel I	currency mismatch
Basel II	dynamic loan loss provisioning
Basel III	liquidity coverage ratio
commercial paper issuer	macroprudential measure

maturity mismatch	net stable funding ratio
money market mutual fund	primary dealer
net open position	time-varying capital requirement

QUESTIONS

1. Given experiences from the 2007–2010 crisis, why might a central bank use monetary policy to lean on asset price bubbles in addition to cleaning up after the bubbles have burst?
2. How can monetary policy be used to lean on asset price bubbles?
3. Why might the central bank hesitate to use monetary policy to lean on asset price bubbles?
4. How can monetary policy be used to clean up after asset price bubbles have burst?
5. Give four examples of macroprudential tools.
6. What are the key differences between dynamic loan loss provisioning and time-varying capital requirements?
7. How can macroprudential measures be used to help sustain financial stability ex post (i.e., after a crisis has occurred)? Should we expect these measures to help reverse the crisis or just alleviate the effect of the crisis?
8. Give examples of how *capital-related* macroprudential tools could be used to safeguard financial institutions against systemic risks.
9. Give examples of how *liquidity-related* macroprudential tools could be used to safeguard financial institutions against systemic risks.
10. When the value of loans are written down, which component on a commercial bank's balance sheet would first be used to absorb losses?
11. What is a *capital ratio*?
12. What does Basel I say regarding the capital ratio of commercial banks?
13. What are the three pillars of Basel II and Basel III?
14. What are the key improvements of Basel II over Basel I?
15. What are the key improvements of Basel III over Basel II?
16. Give examples of special resolutions for troubled financial institutions.
17. Why might the central bank be hesitant to use monetary policy to address risk buildups in financial markets?
18. Why is a level playing field necessary in financial markets?
19. Why might the central bank be hesitant to provide liquidity to firms that are not under its supervision?
20. In the wake of the global financial crisis of 2007–2010, what kind of extra measures did the Federal Reserve embark on with respect to liquidity provision in financial markets?
21. Give four examples of entities that were not under the Federal Reserve's supervision, but which were given access to liquidity by the Federal Reserve.
22. How could a macro stress test be used as a tool to help restore financial stability ex post?
23. Why might we consider quantitative easing as a tool to help restore financial stability?

Four

Sustaining Monetary and Financial Stability for the Next Era

Part IV looks at the future challenges of central banking and how central banks might prepare themselves to meet those challenges.

Chapter 13 reviews three major forces that will likely shape the economic and financial landscape that central banks will be operating in, in the near future: the intensification of the globalization process, the continued evolution of financial activities, and unfinished business from the global financial crisis.

Chapter 14 discusses how central banks might prepare themselves to meet future challenges and deliver value to society using a public policy analysis framework that involves improving the analytical capacity, operational capacity, and political capacity of central banks.

CHAPTER 13

Future Challenges for Central Banking

Learning Objectives

1. Explain how the intensification of globalization might pose challenges to central banking in the future.
2. Explain how the recent evolution in financial activities might pose challenges to central banking in the future.
3. Describe key features of financial reforms instituted after the 2007–2010 global financial crisis.

Part I of this book discusses how central banking has evolved over the centuries to meet the challenges that have arisen with changes in political, economic, and financial circumstances. Parts II and III of this book discusses how the practice of modern central banking is shaped by theoretical developments and practical experience. Specifically, Part II focuses on the central banks' use of monetary policy to achieve their monetary stability mandate. Part III, meanwhile, focuses on the central banks' use of macroprudential tools in addition to monetary policy to help attain their financial stability mandate, given the lessons learned from the 2007–2010 financial crisis.

In this chapter we look into the future and discuss three major forces that are likely to continue to shape the economic and financial landscape that central banks operate in. These three forces are (1) the intensification of globalization, (2) the evolution in financial activities, and (3) unfinished business from the 2007–2010 financial crisis. (See Figures 13.1 and 13.2.)

13.1 THE INTENSIFICATION OF GLOBALIZATION

In economic terms, globalization involves the process of reduction and removal of cross-border barriers to international trade, production, investment, and labor.[1] Such reduction and removal of barriers often arise through liberalization, privatization, and deregulation of markets and economies, as well as advances in transportation, information, and communications technology.

The intensification of the globalization process has gathered strong momentum since the late 1970s, through changes in geopolitics, technological advances, and the

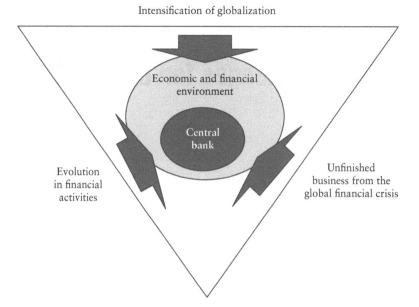

FIGURE 13.1   Three Future Challenges for Central Banks

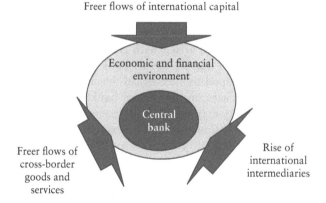

FIGURE 13.2   The Intensification of Globalization

belief in market mechanisms. Despite various hiccups in the form of financial crises, including the global financial crisis of 2007–2010, it is likely that the intensification of globalization will continue. Through globalization, countries have become so dependent on each other through international trade and investment that any attempt to disentangle such interdependence would be too disruptive and costly.

The intensification of globalization will affect central banking through at least three key dimensions: (1) *freer flows of international capital*, (2) *freer cross-border flows of goods and services and factor inputs*, and (3) *the rise of international intermediaries*. One important implication from the intensification of globalization through these three dimensions is that *external* factors will have an increasing influence on domestic monetary and financial stability.

Freer Flows of International Capital

As discussed in Chapters 4 and 9, freer flows of international capital could put pressures on the exchange rate and domestic inflation, as well as trigger asset price bubbles. If left unchecked, large inflows of capital into a small open economy could easily lead to a sharp appreciation of the exchange rate. Once these inflows work their way into the economy, they could also lead to a pickup in economic activity as well as general price inflation. Often, the inflows could also trigger speculative bubbles in domestic asset prices.

A sudden reversal of the capital inflows, in contrast, could lead to a sharp fall in the exchange rate, a slowdown in economic activity and inflation, as well as sharp falls in domestic asset prices. Accordingly, through freer flows of international capital, the intensification of globalization has the potential to destabilize both monetary stability and financial stability.

CASE STUDY: The Growing Challenges from International Capital Flows

The challenges of freer flows of international capital for central banks have been felt at least since the gold standard era, when outflows of gold could threaten the value of the currency. Speculative attacks on European currencies in the 1960s and 1970s, financial crises in Latin America in the 1980s and 1990s, and the Asian financial crisis in the late 1990s were all also partly by-products of freer flows of international capital.

Whereas the speculative attacks and financial crises of earlier eras had been largely confined to particular countries or regions, as the globalization process has intensified, the effects of volatile international capital flows now tend to be more global in nature. This was witnessed in the effects of quantitative easing (used to fight the 2007–2010 crisis) in advanced economies, which led to large capital outflows from advanced economies into emerging economies across the globe.[2]

Despite heavy intervention in the foreign exchange market by emerging-market central banks, the large inflows of international capital led to a sharp appreciation in exchange rates, a pickup in domestic economic activity and domestic inflation, as well as a pickup in asset prices in emerging-market economies across different regions from 2009 until early 2013.

Subsequently, in mid-2013, as the Federal Reserve announced the possibility of a tapering of the quantitative easing program, the sharp outflows of international capital were felt across emerging-market economies. The exchange rates of many emerging-market economies fell along with prices of stocks, bonds, and in many cases, real estate.[3]

Going forward, in a world of freer capital flows, it will be a challenge for central banks of small, open economies to temper the volatility of asset prices that the sharp reversal of international capital flows brings about.

Freer Cross-Border Flows of Goods and Services and Factor Inputs

Freer cross-border flows of goods and services and factor inputs also imply that external factors can have a great influence on domestic economic activity and domestic inflation, at least in the short run. While globalization allows countries to reap the benefits of comparative advantage, the greater reliance on imports and exports of goods and services and global supply chains means that events occurring outside their borders could affect the domestic economy more readily.[4]

On the *import side*, changes in international price levels have the potential to affect domestic inflation through the import prices of factor inputs, for example.

This is especially noticeable in the case of energy imports, which for many countries are essential *factor inputs* to economic activity. For countries that rely heavily on energy imports, fluctuations in oil prices can affect not only domestic energy prices, but also the general price level, through cost-push inflation as well as the expectations effect. Outsourcing of production to foreign countries with cheaper production costs, on the other hand, could also help hold down inflationary pressures in the domestic economy.

On the *export* side, changes in global demand also have the potential to affect both domestic economic activity and domestic inflation. A boom in global demand for natural resources, for example, will likely lead to a boom in domestic economic activity of a resource-producing country, as well as an uptick in inflationary pressure.

On the other hand, as countries are integrated more and more into a global supply chain, a glitch in that chain has the potential to affect economic activity in other countries. For example, the major flood that disrupted car part and hard-disk drive manufacturers in Thailand in 2011 did disrupt car and computer production, as well as related activities, in other countries in these global supply chains.

CASE STUDY: The Growing Challenge of International Pressure on Domestic Economic Activity and Domestic Inflation

In the past decade, through the intensification of globalization, many events seem to have had a great impact on economic activity and inflation beyond their borders. In the early part of the first decade of the twenty-first century, the burst of the dot-com bubble and terrorist attacks in the United States helped slow down global demand and global economic activity for some time. Meanwhile, the accession of China into the WTO in 2001 and the entry of many low-cost emerging Asian economies into the global trading system might have also contributed to a slowdown in global inflation through the floods of their exports.[5] In response to low inflation, many central banks, including the Federal Reserve, cut their interest rates during this period.

In the middle of that same decade, as China and other emerging economies grew rapidly, they started to demand more natural resources. Speculation that the demand for energy from China and other emerging economies would keep going up helped push the price of crude oil from around USD 30 per barrel in 2000 to a peak of more than USD 140 in July 2008. The fear of a disinflation period that had existed earlier in the decade started to dissipate.

To counter this pickup in inflation, by 2007 many central banks, including the Federal Reserve, had started to raise their interest rates, only to find that as Lehman Brothers collapsed the following year, they had to cut interest rates to near 0 percent to counter deflation.

While oil prices fluctuated wildly between USD 35 and USD 82 per barrel in 2009, by 2011 they had again risen above USD 100 per barrel on concerns over the political uprising in Egypt. Although this later spike in oil prices did not raise many inflation concerns in the advanced economies that were still reeling from the financial crisis, it did raise concerns in many emerging economies, which were booming from capital inflows. In 2011, many emerging-market economy central banks in Asia started to raise their interest rates to preempt inflationary pressures that were building from oil prices as well as capital flows.

Going forward, it is easy to see that as countries integrate more and more into the global economy, their central banks will have to contend more and more with the ability of external factors to affect domestic activities and domestic inflation.

The Rise of International Intermediaries

In the past three decades, as financial liberalization has taken place around the world, financial intermediaries have started to expand their operations internationally. The increasing importance of international banks and the implications for global financial stability has been recognized partly by the Basel Committee's guidelines for the supervision of global systemically important banks (G-SIBs), as discussed in Chapter 11.

During the most critical phase of the financial crisis of 2007–2010, it became recognized that the existence of international banks could have profound implications for financial stability, not only in the *home countries* where these banks based their headquarters and the *host countries* where these banks operate their branches and subsidiaries, but also in *other countries* through the interlinkages of financial transactions and contagion effects.

Going forward, the rise of G-SIBs and other international intermediaries will likely add more complexity to supervisory work for central banks. International cooperation among central banks, whether bilaterally or through multilateral channels such as the Basel Committee or the Financial Stability Board, will also be very important.

13.2 THE CONTINUED EVOLUTION IN FINANCIAL ACTIVITIES

Along with the increasing degree of globalization, the continued evolution of financial services will likely also shape the future of central banking, since they both will change the landscape in which central banks operate. Two key features of the continued evolution in financial activities include (1) *the rise of market-based financial activities* and (2) *the rise of electronic payments*.

The Rise of Market-Based Financial Activities

In the past three decades, liberalization and attainment of higher development stages have resulted in the rising importance of market-based financial activities. Unlike in a bank-based system—where banks play a leading role in mobilizing savings, allocating capital, overseeing the investment decisions of corporate managers, providing risk management vehicles, and lending funds out to borrowers—in a market-based system, securities markets share a leading role with banks in channeling savings to firms, exerting corporate control, and facilitating risk management.[6] (See Figure 13.3.)

The proliferation of market-based financial activities is partly reflected by (1) the *rise of nonbank financial entities* in the mobilization of savings and the allocation of

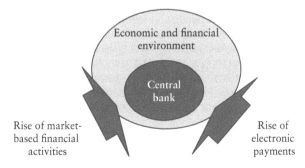

FIGURE 13.3   The Continued Evolution in Financial Activities

funds in the economy, and (2) the *embracing of market-based financial activities by banks* in their operations.

The Rise of Nonbank Financial Market Entities   Nonbank financial market entities are those entities that are involved in investment, risk pooling, or contractual saving of funds, yet are not operating under a banking license.[7] Prominent among such entities is a category called *institutional investors*, which includes mutual funds, pension funds, insurance companies, and hedge funds.[*] Broadly speaking, institutional investors are collective investment vehicles that pool large sums of money and invest those sums in securities and other investment assets including real estate.

Institutional investors specialize in investing on behalf of others. An individual who buys a share in a mutual fund, for example, is effectively putting money in the pool of money managed by the mutual fund, and is entitled to a proportion of the assets held by the mutual fund as well as a proportion of the income or profits that those assets generate. By pooling large sums of money, institutional investors can spread their investments across many securities or assets, and thereby diversify away some of the risks that are associated with investment in only a single security or asset.

Money Market Mutual Funds   The rise of institutional investors potentially poses challenges to central banks in terms of financial stability. By pooling money from retail investors and investing the pooled money on the retail investors' behalf, institutional investors perform functions quite similar to banks, yet they are not supervised or regulated by central banks. The problem became apparent with the run on money market mutual funds in the United States in the wake of the collapse of Lehman Brothers (see Case Study: Money Market Mutual Funds for details).

CASE STUDY: Money Market Mutual Funds

Prior to the collapse of Lehman Brothers, money market mutual funds that invested money in short-term debt securities (such as U.S. Treasury bills and commercial paper) were considered and accordingly treated as near substitutes for bank deposit accounts by individuals in the United States. By maintaining a stable net value of 1 U.S. dollar per share, and paying out steady dividends, money market mutual funds allowed individuals to preserve their capital and earn yields that were slightly higher than traditional bank deposits.

With large amounts of money being placed in money market mutual funds, the money market mutual funds themselves became increasingly important as lenders of short-term liquidity to companies in the wholesale money market in the years leading up to the crisis. Companies and investment banks (such as Lehman Brothers) borrowed short-term money in the wholesale money market by issuing commercial paper that money market mutual funds would buy and hold.

When Lehman Brothers collapsed, however, the commercial paper issued by Lehman Brothers became worthless and money market mutual funds that held Lehman Brothers' commercial paper had to absorb the loss and write down their assets. In the process of writing down the loss from Lehman Brothers' commercial paper, Reserve Primary Fund, which had been founded in the 1970s and was the oldest money market fund, found that its shares fell below 1 dollar, to 97 cents per share.[8] The fact

---

[*]Some smaller operators such as pawnshops are also considered nonbank financial market entities, but they operate at a much smaller scale and their systemic impact is rather limited.

that Reserve Primary Fund fell below 1 dollar per share caused panic among investors, since they had deemed the investment in these funds to be almost as safe as bank deposits, and thought that they would never lose their capital.

The run on Reserve Primary Fund and other money market mutual funds threatened not only investors in the funds, but also companies and banks that relied on the funds as a key source of short-term funding. In response to the run, the U.S. Department of the Treasury announced an optional program (akin to a deposit insurance program) to guarantee that if a covered fund's share price fell below 1 dollar, it would be restored back to 1 dollar.

Hedge Funds   Aside from the possibility of runs on mutual funds, the proliferation of hedge funds also poses another challenge for central banks in terms of financial stability. Hedge funds (unlike mutual funds, which aim to pool money from retail investors and invest using relatively conservative styles) aim to pool money from sophisticated or accredited investors and invest using relatively faster and riskier styles, including *short selling** and *leveraging,*† in order to achieve higher returns.

Since hedge funds need to be quick in exploiting good investment opportunities, sometimes they can rush into similar kind of trades at the same time, which can tip a market's balance and financial stability. Examples include speculative attacks on the British pound in 1992 and the Thai baht in 1997; in these instances, short selling of the currency by a hoard of large hedge funds inflicted large losses on the central banks of these countries and forced them out of their *de facto* fixed exchange rate regimes.

Not all hedge fund operations are successful, however, and a failure of a highly leveraged hedge fund could lead to systemic risk. The collapse in 1998 of Long Term Capital Management (LTCM), a highly leveraged hedge fund, threatened to affect many global banks and global financial markets, such that the Federal Reserve Bank of New York had to step in and orchestrate a rescue despite the fact that it did not regulate LTCM.

Insurance Companies   In the wake of the 2007–2010 crisis, the U.S. central bank also had to rescue AIG, a large insurance company that it did not regulate. Traditionally, insurance companies diversify their investments in relatively safe assets (e.g., stocks and bonds) to match their liabilities (i.e., insurance payouts). By the middle of the first decade of the twenty-first century, however, AIG had branched out into insuring the credit risk of companies and financial securities via the selling of *credit default swaps* to a large number of counterparties, including large banks.

In a credit default swap, an entity insures its holding of, say, Company X's bonds by regularly paying the insurer a premium. If Company X's bonds get down-graded, then the insurer has to post cash collateral to the entity. If Company X then defaults on its bonds, the insurer pays the entity to cover the loss on the

---

*Short selling involves selling borrowed securities in the hope that the prices of the securities will fall so that they can be bought back more cheaply. If the prices do fall, sellers make a profit on the difference between the price they sold them at and the price they bought them back at, before returning the securities to the rightful owner.

†Leveraging involves borrowing funds beyond one's own capital to invest. It can also be done through the short selling of securities to raise funds to invest in other securities.

entity's bond holdings. Using this logic, AIG also expanded to provide insurance on complex financial securities, including mortgage-backed securities and subprime mortgages.[9]

As the subprime crisis raged on, banks, firms, and mortgage-backed securities were downgraded. AIG started to take on heavy losses from its credit default swap deals. When Lehman Brother filed for bankruptcy in September 2008, AIG itself was downgraded, and was on the verge of collapsing as demands for large amounts of cash collateral came in from their counterparties.[10]

Finally the Federal Reserve had to step in and rescue AIG, since if AIG were also to go bankrupt, its counterparties (including many large banks) would have faced large losses that could have brought the whole system down. The fact that the Federal Reserve had to step in to orchestrate the rescue of a hedge fund like LTCM, and had to actually bail out AIG, an insurance company, reflects how market-based activities and nonbank financial institutions have become so important that they can pose systemic risk.

The Embracing of Market-Based Activities by Banks   In the past three decades, not only have market-based activities become plausible alternatives for bank-based activities, but nonbank financial institutions have become very important as well. In many countries banks themselves have embraced market-based activities in their own operations. Among the important market-based activities that banks have embraced are *securitization* and *proprietary trading* and in many cases banks have set up *market-based subsidiaries* to handle these activities.

Securitization   Securitization involves the issuance of securities that entitle the holder of the securities to a claim on future cash flows or income derived from prescribed underlying assets. An entity (e.g., a bank) issues and sells the securities to investors who then earn income from the underlying assets (e.g., mortgages). By purchasing the securities, the investors have the rights to income derived from the underlying assets, as well as a claim on the underlying assets in case of a default on income payment.

For banks, securitization involves pooling contractual debts that often are traditional bank assets such as residential mortgages, commercial mortgages, auto loans, and credit card debt obligations into *packages*, and selling those packages to outside investors. With securitization, banks could drastically transform their traditional banking business models into an *originate-to-distribute* model.

With the advent of securitization, rather than originating loans and holding them on their books for the long haul as they traditionally had done, banks started to originate the loans and distribute them out in packages. Banks took in money from the sale of these securitized assets, money that could be lent out again to borrowers. By repeating the process, a bank with an originate-to-distribute model could earn high fees from both packaging and distributing the securitized assets.

Through securitization, traditional bank assets (such as loans) that are normally illiquid, become liquid and more readily tradable. Often investors bought these securitized debts because they offered better returns than bank deposits, and (at least prior to the 2007–2010 financial crisis) were deemed to be rather safe, since the pooling of debts would have diversified away the risk of default by any one individual bank borrower.

Proprietary Trading *Proprietary trading* refers to an arrangement under which banks trade securities in financial markets using their own capital in the hope of generating profits. Prior to the crisis banks had started to do a lot of proprietary trading, including trading in financial securities (such as government and corporate debt) as well as in derivative contracts (such as collateralized debt obligations, or CDOs). The rise in proprietary trade occurred partly because there was a lot of liquidity in the system and interest rates were low (which kept the cost of funds used in such trading low), and banks had to seek ways other than giving out simple loans to generate profits from the extra liquidity.

Given the need for profits, many banks decided to set up units devoted purely to proprietary trading, that is, the so-called *prop desks*. Through proprietary trading, banks themselves became heavily involved in financial market activities as active traders who took on risks in order to generate profits. In the wake of the 2007–2010 financial crisis, however, it became clearer that proprietary trading could create great risks for bank depositors. If the trading generates losses rather than profits, the bank's capital base is reduced, jeopardizing not only the bank's shareholders but also bank depositors.

CONCEPT: PROPRIETARY TRADING, MARKET-MAKING, AND THE VOLCKER RULE

The recognition that proprietary trading might bring unnecessary risks to banks and losses to depositors led to the proposal of a ban on proprietary trading by commercial banks. This proposal was advocated by Paul A. Volcker, the former chairman of the Federal Reserve who brought U.S. inflation down in the early 1980s, and who later became the chair of President Obama's Economic Recovery Advisory Board in 2009. The proposal subsequently became known as the *Volcker rule*.[11]

The Volcker rule aimed to make sure that banks would go back to their traditional banking services and not get sidetracked by an excessive focus on speculative activities in financial markets, as those activities might bring unnecessary risks to the banks and create conflicts of interest among the banks' management, shareholders, and depositors.[12] While the Volcker rule was being proposed in the 2010 Dodd-Frank Act, however, there was some resistance from the banks, as they believed that it was difficult to distinguish between a bank's *proprietary trading* activities and *market-making* activities.

Market-making activities in financial markets are warehousing of financial securities for future resale to customers. A market-maker buys securities from customers who want to get rid of the securities, and sells them to customers who want to get hold of the securities. Since a bank normally has a large number of customers, some of whom might want to buy and some of whom might want to sell securities, the bank might attempt to *make market* by committing its own capital to buy securities from customers who want to sell and then reselling those securities to customers who want to buy.

(Continued)

(*Continued*)

At first glance, the line between market-making and proprietary trading activities might look very thin. In a market-making activity, a bank might need to commit its capital to buy securities from customers, similarly to proprietary trading. In practice, however, given the opportunity costs involved in warehousing the securities, it could be argued that in a market-making activity, a bank would want to keep as little inventory on hand as possible for the shortest period of time possible. In a proprietary trading activity, however, a bank would want keep a large position of securities for quite a longer period of time, in order to generate the biggest possible profits.[13]

Despite quibbles on the definitions of market-making and proprietary trading, many large banks officially started to dismantle their proprietary trading units in the early 2010s, partly in anticipation of the Volcker rule.[14]

The Proliferation of Market-Based Bank Subsidiaries   Aside from securitization and proprietary trading, another trend that indicated that banks had embraced market-based activities was the setting up of bank subsidiaries to engage in market-based financial activities. This trend came about partly because banks saw wealth management for their clients as an activity that could generate good fee-based income.

In many countries, banks are allowed to have mutual fund subsidiaries or to set up affiliations with *third party* mutual funds with whom they can advise their own clients to invest, as part of the financial products being offered to them. Although these mutual fund subsidiaries are considered legally separate entities from the parent bank, they also reflect the wider trend toward more market-based activities that is occurring among banks.

With the proliferation of such subsidiaries, one may ask (1) how much responsibility does the parent bank have to its mutual fund subsidiaries if the mutual fund subsidiaries of a bank does face a crisis, and (2) what about bank clients who invested in those funds based on the bank's advice.

Although the fund affiliates and the banks are often legally separated, in cases where the fund subsidiaries use names that imply ownership by the bank, it could lead to contagion effects between the fund subsidiaries and the parent bank. The question could become very poignant in cases where the assets of mutual subsidiaries have grown to match or exceed the bank's total assets.

On this note, in 2007 Bear Stearns, a U.S. investment bank, decided to rescue and absorb the losses of its two hedge fund subsidiaries that invested primarily in subprime mortgages, for fear that the failures of those funds would affect the bank's reputation, despite the bank's initial small investments in these two funds.[15] While Bear Stearns initially survived this episode, the losses undermined confidence in the bank and helped contribute to its fall in 2008. Through the assistance of the Federal Reserve Bank of New York, Bear Stearns was bought by JPMorgan Chase, another large U.S. bank. To prevent a similar problem from happening in the United States in the future, Paul Volcker, with the backing of President Obama, sought to put an explicit ban on banks, or institutions that own a bank, from owning or investing in a hedge fund or private equity fund.[16]

The Rise of Electronic Payments

The evolution of payment technology has had profound implication for central banking since the start of central banking history, as shown by the rise of paper money to replace coins in the early history of central banking, which later gave rise to fractional reserve banking. In the past four decades the rise of information and communications technology (ICT) has led to new electronic payments systems, as evidenced by the proliferation of ATMs, credit cards, debit cards, mobile payments, and e-money at the retail level, and real-time gross settlement systems (RTGS) at the wholesale level.

The Rise of E-Payments Has Much Potential, but the Complete Picture Is Unclear At the moment, we are still in the initial stages of the ICT revolution, and it is still not clear where the revolution will ultimately take us. What can be safely deduced from recent ICT developments, however, is that electronic payments of various forms will proliferate.

Competition with Paper Money: Debit Cards, Credit Cards, Online E-Payments, Mobile Payments, E-Money At the most basic level, the increase in electronic payments in retail transactions will compete with the use of paper money. The use of debit cards, credit cards, online e-payments, mobile payments, and e-money will potentially compete with the use of cash and checks. While this might potentially reduce demands on central banks' resources for money printing and handling, it also implies that central banks will need to put more resources into understanding the unintended consequences from the increase in these electronic forms of payment.

Unintended Consequences: Credit Card Promotion and Household Debt in South Korea Excessive promotion and use of *credit cards* have led to an unintended rise in household debt in South Korea, which has implications for financial stability. In 2012, household debt in South Korea rose to 164 percent of income, partly helped by the use of multiple credit cards in households; the government subsequently had to set up a fund to relieve the poorest and most indebted households from their debt burdens.[17]

Increasing Financial Access for the Poor: Mobile Payments The rise of electronic payments in the form of *mobile payments* has shown great benefits in increasing financial access in remote places where there is little access to physical banks, but where there is mobile phone coverage (e.g., in rural villages of developing countries).[18] Some forms of mobile payment transactions can be made through mobile phone services and charged through phone bills. This gives rise to the issue of appropriate regulation to ensure consumer protection, that will not be stifling to innovation.

Another Unknown: E-Money At a more fundamental level, certain forms of electronic payments (such as e-money) issued by private firms have the theoretical potential to supplant sovereign currencies, which unless properly regulated has the potential to affect both monetary and financial stability.* In practice, however, despite its introduction over a decade ago, the success of e-money is still very limited. Furthermore, regulations and guidelines have already been put in place in many jurisdictions that require issuers of e-money be monitored by regulatory authorities.[19] (See Concept: Overview of Retail E-Payments for details on various types of retail e-payments.)

CONCEPT: OVERVIEW OF RETAIL E-PAYMENTS

With the progress in information and communications technology, new electronic payments methods have become more common and, to an extent, have replaced coins, banknotes, and even checks. Here we look at some of the more popular retail e-payments that have become quite common in our daily lives: credit cards, debit cards, online payments, mobile payments, and e-money.

Credit Cards and Debit Cards

A *credit card* is issued by the issuer to the holder so that the holder can use the card for payments to merchants who are in the credit card network. The issuer of the card pays the merchants up front and the holder of the card repays the issuer, probably with interest if the repayment is not made in full within a specified period.

A *debit card* is also issued by the issuer to the holder so that the holder can use the card for payments to merchants who are in the card network. Unlike a credit card, however, a debit card allows merchants within the network to deduct money from the holder's account at the time he presents the card for payment of goods and services.

Online Payments

One area in which the use of credit cards and debit cards has become dominant is *online payments*. Online payments, where the holder uses his credit or debit card to pay for online transactions, has grown steadily over the years. In the immediate future, new innovations such as *Square*, a device attached to a mobile phone that allows small businesses and individuals to take credit card payments, will likely also encourage more use of credit cards in lieu of cash.

---

*Theoretically, the buyer of e-money could buy a certain amount of e-money from a private issuer by depositing an equivalent amount of, say, paper money with the issuer. The buyer of e-money could then use the e-money to buy goods and services from merchants that accept it. If the number of these merchants is large enough, the issuer of e-money is effectively issuing money that potentially could be used across the economy, just like paper money issued by the central bank.

Mobile Payments

Mobile payments refer to regulated payment services that allow payment for goods and services to be made from or via a mobile phone, in lieu of cash, credit cards, or debit cards. Mobile payments can take many forms. In certain forms, the user needs to be preregistered with payment service operators such as PayPal or a credit card company. In other forms, users of mobile payment can be charged through their mobile phone accounts, bypassing banks and credit card companies altogether. Mobile payments not only allow convenient transactions in the advanced economies, but also are widely used in developing countries where access to physical banks might be limited.

E-Money

E-money involves an electronic store of monetary value on a device that could be used to trade for goods and services, possibly also bypassing the use of bank accounts (and thus is different from a debit card).

An example of e-money is a multipurpose card, on which monetary value is electronically stored, and which can be used to pay for small daily items as well as public transportation services (these cards are used in countries such as Belgium, the Netherlands, Hong Kong, and Singapore, although the rate of success and the extent of use vary among countries).

13.3 UNFINISHED BUSINESS FROM THE GLOBAL FINANCIAL CRISIS

Although half a decade has passed since the bleakest periods of the 2007–2010 global financial crisis, the aftereffects are still being felt. Among the aftereffects of the financial crisis that are still being played out and are likely to help shape the financial landscape that central banks will operate in include (1) the *heavy fiscal debt burden* in advanced economies, (2) the *normalization of monetary policy* in advanced economies, and (3) the *push for regulatory reforms*.

The Heavy Fiscal Debt Burdens in Advanced Economies

The heavy fiscal debt burdens in the advanced economies will have implications for the global economic landscape and global financial markets through the *creditworthiness* of government securities issued by the advanced economies. Government securities issued by major advanced economies such as the United States, Germany, and Japan are deemed virtually riskless by investors and central banks across the world. These securities are used as benchmarks in pricing other financial assets, as well as in international reserves maintained by central banks of other countries.

The heavy fiscal debt burdens of many of the advanced economies, particularly the United States, however, have raised growing concerns among investors globally, as reflected by the uncertainty in global financial markets surrounding the U.S. government shutdown in October 2013. Although the shutdown was due to the

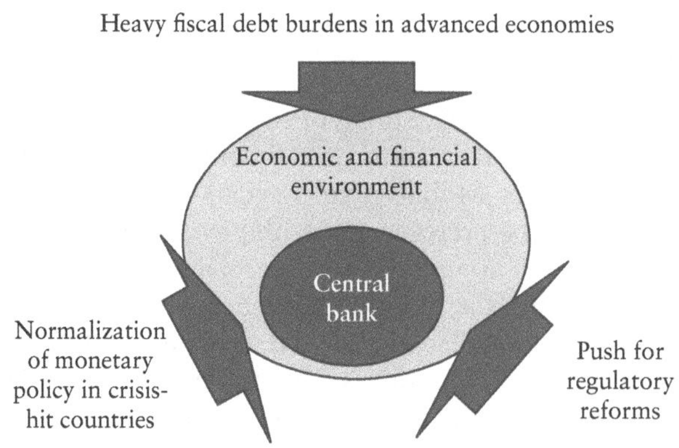

Heavy fiscal debt burdens in advanced economies

FIGURE 13.4 Unfinished Business from the Global Financial Crisis

Congress's failure to enact legislation appropriating funds for fiscal year 2014, financial market players as well as President Obama saw the shutdown as being linked to the debate on the raising of the U.S. government debt ceiling later that month.[20]

CASE STUDY: Heavy Fiscal Debt Burdens in Advanced Economies

Even before the financial crisis of 2007–2010, it had already been well recognized that for many advanced economies, unfunded liabilities of the government, such as healthcare and pensions liabilities, could likely pose heavy costs on these economies in the medium term. On top of these unfunded liabilities, however, the financial crisis of 2007–2010 brought about large jumps in fiscal burden that pushed the public debt-to-GDP ratio of the major advanced economies (G7 countries*) from 83.2 percent of GDP to 124.8 percent of GDP in 2012.[21]

To deal with the financial crisis, the governments of the advanced economies had to step in not only to provide financial assistance to rescue the financial system, but also to provide large fiscal stimuli to prevent their economies from falling into deflationary traps. The interventions by these governments were funded largely by issuance of government securities, which resulted in a fast rise in public debt for these advanced economies.

In the United States, the ballooning government debt helped prompt a downgrade of U.S. government securities, the safest financial asset in the world, from AAA to AA+ by Standard & Poor's, one of the three key rating agencies, in 2011.[22] In the euro area, a combination of the banking crisis and a sharp economic contraction resulted in many governments being unable to refinance their own public debt, which threatened a breakup of the euro area in 2010–2012. In Japan, the legacy from its own financial crisis in the early 1990s still lingered. With the economy battling deflation for more than 20 years, despite massive injections of fiscal stimulus, Japanese government debt reached 237.9 percent of GDP in 2012.[23]

Unless the situation is corrected in a timely manner, the vast amounts of public debt in advanced economies are likely to continue to pose challenges for central banks globally. Any marked deterioration in fiscal prospects of the advanced

---

*The Group of Seven (G7) countries include Canada, France, Germany, Italy, Japan, the United Kingdom, and the United States.

economies would mean that seemingly risk-free assets will no longer be perceived as risk-free. This would cause not only turmoil in the global financial markets, but also hurt the ability of many emerging-market central banks to intervene and protect their domestic financial markets. This is because many emerging-market central banks hold a large part of their international reserves in the form of government securities issued by the advanced economies.

The Normalization of Monetary Policy in the Advanced Economies

For the advanced economy central banks, one of the short-term challenges that is a legacy from the 2007–2010 global financial crisis is the timing of their *exit* from their quantitative easing strategies (i.e., stopping the purchase of their own government debt and starting the sale of government debt back into the financial system).

On the one hand, an early exit from the quantitative easing policy could trigger panics in the financial markets. In 2013 the Federal Reserve's mere announcement of an intent to taper its purchases of government securities prompted panics in the financial markets worldwide, before the Federal Reserve subsequently decided to delay the taper owing to the weak economy.[24] On the other hand, a late exit from the quantitative easing could lead to asset price bubbles, and possibly inflation, since the quantitative easing would keep interest rates artificially low, leading to speculation in asset price booms.

For emerging-market central banks, the short-term challenges will be to deal with the spillover effects from the existence of, and the exit from, the quantitative easing policies of advanced economy central banks. On the one hand, a late exit from quantitative easing in the advanced economies will pressure emerging-market economies with capital inflows, which could lead to speculation in asset prices in these economies. On the other hand, an early exit of quantitative easing in the advanced economies may cause emerging-market central banks to have to deal with the abrupt cutoff of flows of capital, which could be destabilizing to their economies.

The Push for Regulatory Reforms

The 2007–2010 financial crisis has revealed structural weaknesses in the increasingly complex global financial systems. Such weaknesses partly reflected the fact that existing regulations in place at the time had not kept up adequately with changes in the global financial environment, and that regulatory reforms were needed. As of the end of 2013, at the time that this book was being written, while many regulatory reforms had been proposed at both national and international levels, only some had been approved, while many were still being debated.

Whether all the reforms proposed will be approved or not will have a profound impact on the future economic and financial landscapes that the central banks will be operating in. The reforms, as well as the lack of reforms, are likely to affect the behavior of banks, nonbank financial market players, as well as the regulators themselves. In any case, it must be recognized that although any regulatory reform is likely to address problems that have become apparent, the reform itself might also lead to growing activities in less regulated areas, or unperceived new loopholes that might arise with the reforms. Consequently, even regulatory reforms could pose new challenges for central banks.

Using a framework proposed by R. Glen Hubbard in 2009,[25] here we will review the regulatory reforms that came in the wake of the 2007–2010 crisis on three fronts: (1) the *reduction of systemic risk*, (2) the *increase in transparency*, and (3) a *change in the financial regulatory structure*, both at the national and global levels.

The Reduction of Systemic Risk   The effort to reduce systemic risk, at least at the international level, can partly be seen through the following initiatives.

1. The introduction of Basel III in 2010 by the Basel Committee on Banking Supervision to make sure that banks have capital levels that are more responsive to risk, and that the capital has a better ability to absorb loss. Basel III provides guidance on bank supervision that is more sensitive to risk in all banks, and thus should make the system as a whole more resilient. (See Concept: Introduction to Basel I, II, and III in Chapter 12 for more details.)
2. The identification and publication of the list of *global systemically important financial institutions* (*G-SIFIs*) by the Financial Stability Board* in 2011 (the list was updated in 2012).[26] The publication and the list of G-SIFIs made central banks and national regulators more aware of the operations of these institutions, as well as the international coordination required to supervise them.
3. The introduction of guidelines for the assessment of and additional loss absorbency requirements for *globally systemically important banks* (*G-SIBs*) by the Basel Committee on Banking Supervision in 2011, followed by a corollary framework for *domestically systemically important banks* in 2012.[27] These guidelines and the framework provided will help provide guidance for central banks and other regulators in supervising these systemically important banks.[†]

The *Volcker rule* against proprietary trading by banks that was discussed earlier in the chapter was another effort that aimed to reduce systemic risk. Since the United States is the leading financial center, where many international banks operate, the adoption of the Volcker rule is likely to have an impact far beyond U.S. borders.

The Increase in Transparency   To increase transparency (as discussed in Chapter 12), Basel III enhanced Pillar III (market discipline) through additional requirements on the disclosure of a bank's securitization exposures and sponsorship of off-balance sheet vehicles, as well as on the details of the components of the bank's regulatory capital and calculations of its regulatory capital ratios.

In addition to Basel III requirements, another key example of a postcrisis reform is the effort to put over-the-counter‡ (OTC) derivatives trades onto organized exchanges.[28]

---

*The Financial Stability Board was established in 2009 at the G20 London Summit, to act as an international body that monitors and makes recommendations on financial regulations and supervision. It is hosted by the Bank for International Settlements in Basel, Switzerland.

†It must be noted, however, that the Financial Stability Board and the Basel Committee are not direct regulatory bodies, and while their recommendations might be helpful, it still depends on regulatory agencies at the national level to adopt their recommendations.

‡*Over-the-counter* refers to an arrangement in which two parties (e.g., two banks, or a bank and a nonbank counterparty) agree to execute a derivative contract (such as a credit default swap) privately between themselves, rather than through an organized exchange.

CASE STUDY: Putting Over-the-Counter Derivatives Trades onto Organized Exchanges

---

Prior to the crisis, many derivative deals were done privately between financial institutions or players and dealers in the financial markets. No one kept track of the total number of deals in the market, or how the different financial institutions might be exposed to risk through their counterparties. When a counterparty failed, there would be panic as to who was exposed and the degree of exposure.

Furthermore, while in normal times OTC derivative trades might function properly, with sufficient liquidity to establish (or discover) the prices of derivatives, during a financial crisis that might not be the case.[29] Lack of transparency could reduce liquidity and make the valuation of one's own portfolio holdings very difficult, which could lead to panic selling with no buyers.

In an OTC market during normal times, there would be dealers willing to make markets by maintaining inventories of derivatives and selling them to those who wanted them, or buying derivatives from those who wanted to sell them. During a financial crisis, however, OTC dealers might be less willing to take the risk of maintaining inventories of derivatives that could fluctuate wildly in value and actually stop making markets for derivatives altogether. With no dealers willing to step in to buy and sell derivatives, market players cannot easily sell securities. Furthermore, one would find it difficult to determine what market prices are, or what market value should be assigned to derivative holdings.

The OTC arrangement is different from the arrangement in an organized exchange, where financial market players make bids and offers through a central platform, not through separate dealers. In an organized exchange, players can post bids and offers for assets to the platform, so that everyone else can see the prices and trade with them if they find the prices of those bids and offers to be attractive enough. During a financial crisis, if market players really want to unload their holdings, they can post a low offer price for their holdings to the exchange. If another party feels that the price offered is attractive enough, that party can buy it.

Better transparency of prices in an organized exchange helps make the market more resilient during times of crisis. Also, with the central clearing system that comes with an organized exchange, it is easier to keep track of trading activities. Through the use of margin requirements, a standard for organized exchanges, counterparty risk is reduced, as the parties to a derivative contract will either be constantly paying in or receiving payments to keep the value of the contract whole, or the contract will be canceled before any one party is overly exposed to loss from the failure of its counterparty.

While leaders of the G20 (the Group of Twenty finance ministers and central bank governors) agreed in London in 2009 about the importance of putting derivatives onto organized exchanges, the task will likely take some time.[30] Given the interconnectedness of financial markets across the globe, moving derivatives onto an organized exchange in one country will only yield a good result if the same is done in other countries. Otherwise the playing field will not be level, especially since some financial market players will want to avoid the transparency that comes with organized exchanges.

As a follow-up to the G20 London meeting, currently regulators from various countries are working together to set international guidelines for rules on putting derivatives onto organized exchanges. Rules will eventually address which products to put onto exchanges, timing for adoption, and compliance and regulatory measures.[31]

A Change in the Regulatory Structure   In addition to the efforts to reduce systemic risk and increase transparency, the push for regulatory reforms has also focused on needed changes in regulatory structures. The rise of *shadow banking*—that is, intermediation and financial activities done by nonbank financial intermediaries or market players—has meant that many market-based financial activities are being done by different types of financial institutions, which themselves are supervised by different regulatory agencies. Such complexities make it harder to pinpoint responsibility and coordinate efforts to prevent a financial crisis or to rescue the financial system.

In the United States, a key example of changes in regulatory structure was the creation of the Financial Stability Oversight Council (FSOC), which has regulatory authority to identify risks that might be a threat to financial stability across the entire financial system. FSOC was proposed as part of the Dodd-Frank Wall Street Reform and Consumer Protection Act, is chaired by the secretary of the Treasury, and is composed of the heads of various U.S. financial regulatory agencies, such as the Federal Reserve, the Securities and Exchange Commission, and the Commodity Futures Trading Commission.

In the United Kingdom, it became apparent during the time of the global financial crisis that there had been difficulties in the coordination among the three key agencies responsible for sustaining financial stability, that is, the Treasury, the Bank of England, and the Financial Services Authority. The newly elected Conservative Party thus decided to dissolve the Financial Services Authority, which previously had been a super regulator overseeing various types of financial institutions, and create two new regulators in its place: (1) the *Financial Conduct Authority*, with the focus on consumer protection and ensuring healthy competition among financial institutions, and (2) the *Prudential Regulation Authority*, with the task of regulating various types of financial institutions, including banks, credit unions, insurers, and major investment firms. The Prudential Regulation Authority is now part of the Bank of England, while the Financial Conduct Authority is an independent agency.

In Europe, partly as a response to the European sovereign debt crisis, the European Commission in 2012 proposed the Single Supervisory Mechanism, under which the ECB would assume responsibility for the supervision of the largest banks in the euro area and coordinate with euro area national central banks in the supervision of smaller banks.[32] The proposal was a step toward a banking union within the euro area, which the European Commission believed would help make it easier should a decision be made to use European resources to recapitalize banks.[33] The ECB was to start assuming regulatory authority in 2014 and was to be accountable to the European Parliament for supervisory decisions.[34]

It's important to note that while a change in the financial regulatory structure might help address problems that had already become apparent, by definition it may lead to new, unanticipated problems. Financial players often move their activities to where there is less regulation. Any change in regulatory structure creates new avenues that are less regulated, and risk can build up in areas with less regulatory oversight, or where new loopholes are created.

13.4 PIECING THEM TOGETHER

From the discussion above, we can see that the global financial and economic landscape that central banks will be facing will continue to evolve. The three major forces that we discussed in this chapter can interact in numerous ways, and we can never know the *exact* ways in which the global financial and economic landscape might evolve.

Consequently, given that in the future central banks' main mandates will still be monetary and financial stability (notwithstanding the attention given to the full employment mandate in the United States), there are three implications from our analysis that central banks might focus on.

First, the intensification of the globalization process (*external forces*)—whether in terms of freer flows of international capital, freer flows of cross-border goods and services, or the rise of international intermediaries—will have increasing influence on *domestic* monetary and financial conditions. Risks to domestic monetary and financial stability might originate from events outside the control of central banks.

Second, *financial activities* are likely to keep evolving, and market-based activities of banks as well as nonbank financial institutions will play a greater role than before. Given the revolution in information and telecommunications technology, existing and new forms of electronic payments will gain more prominence.

Third, *unfinished business from the global financial crisis*—whether the heavy debt burdens of major advanced economies, normalization of monetary policy in crisis-hit countries, or the push for regulatory reforms—has the potential to alter the financial and economic landscape that central banks operate in.

In Chapter 14, we will discuss how central banks might prepare themselves to meet these future challenges.

SUMMARY

Looking forward, three major forces are likely to interact and shape the economic and financial landscape that central banks will be operating in. The intensification of the globalization process, the evolution in financial activities, and the unfinished business from the 2007–2010 crisis are likely to raise the complexity of the landscape and pose challenges for central banks in their pursuit of monetary and financial stability.

KEY TERMS

credit card

credit default swap

cross-border flows of goods and services

debit card

the Dodd-Frank Act

domestic systemically important bank (D-SIB)

e-money

Financial Conduct Authority

Financial Stability Oversight Council

global systemically important bank (G-SIB)

globalization

hedge fund

home countries

host countries

international capital

international intermediary

leveraging

market-making

mobile payment

money market mutual fund

online payment

organized exchanges

over-the-counter derivatives

proprietary trading

Prudential Regulation Authority

securitization

shadow banking

short selling

single supervisory mechanism

the Volcker rule

QUESTIONS

1. How might globalization affect the future of central banking through freer flows of international capital?
2. How might globalization affect the future of central banking through freer cross-border flows of goods and services and factor inputs?
3. How might globalization affect the future of central banking through the rise of international intermediaries?
4. How might the rise of money market mutual funds affect financial stability?
5. How might the rise of hedge funds affect financial stability?
6. Why should a central bank worry if banks have nonbank financial intermediaries, such as mutual funds, as their subsidiaries?
7. In the promotion of the use of credit cards as a means of payment, what implications on financial stability might we want to look out for?
8. What is e-money in terms of multipurpose card?
9. Why might the heavy fiscal debt burdens in advanced economies be detrimental to stability of the financial markets in general, and emerging-market central banks in particular?
10. How have quantitative easing measures in advanced economies affected emerging-market central banks in the wake of the 2007–2010 global financial crisis?
11. What are examples of regulatory reforms that would help reduce systemic risk in the global financial system in the wake of the 2007–2010 global financial crisis?
12. What are the similarities and differences between proprietary trading and market-making activities?
13. What are the goals of the Volcker rule?
14. What are examples of regulatory reforms that would help increase transparency in the global financial system in the wake of the 2007–2010 global financial crisis? How are these reforms supposed to work?
15. What are examples of changes in the financial regulatory structure in the United States in the wake of the 2007–2010 global financial crisis?
16. What are examples of changes in the financial regulatory structure in the United Kingdom in the wake of the 2007–2010 global financial crisis?
17. What are examples of changes in the financial regulatory structure in the euro area in response to the European sovereign debt crisis?

CHAPTER 14

Future Central Banking Strategy and Its Execution

Learning Objectives

1. Describe the concept of central banking strategy.
2. Identify what might have proven to be bad central banking strategies.
3. Identify how central banking strategies might have changed in the wake of the 2007–2010 global financial crisis.
4. Explain how a central bank might better meet future challenges by improving its analytical capacity.
5. Explain how a central bank might better meet future challenges by improving its organizational capacity.
6. Explain how a central bank might better meet future challenges by improving its political capacity.

In Chapter 13, we discussed three major forces that might shape the future economic and financial landscape that central banks operate in. Since these forces could interact in ways that are unpredictable, if central banks are to succeed in the ever-changing landscape, they will have to be flexible, nimble, and adapt their operations to a fluid environment. In Chapter 14 we propose using a framework based on public policy literature, which central banks could adopt to enhance their capacity to effectively navigate changes in the environment and successfully deliver value to society.

14.1 CENTRAL BANKING STRATEGY

To successfully deal with the future challenges described in Chapter 13, central banks will need to carefully consider their strategies in pursuing their mandates. As a public sector entity, however, a central bank will consider strategy differently than a private sector entity. Unlike a private sector entity (say, a commercial bank), a central bank does not have a competitor or profit motive to consider, as would have been assumed for the kind of business strategy analysis pioneered by Michael Porter in 1980.[1]

In this section we will look the concept of strategy at both a basic and an advanced level, and examine various strategies that have been proposed or adopted by central banks.

Strategy and the Central Bank

According to Richard Rumelt, author of the 2011 book *Good Strategy, Bad Strategy: The Difference and Why It Matters*, at the most basic level we can think of strategy as "the application of strength against weakness," or "strength applied to the most promising opportunity."[2] As we have learned from hard experience—including various episodes of hyperinflation, the Great Depression, the Great Inflation, speculative attacks in both emerging-market and advanced economies, and the recent global financial crisis—for modern central banks the most promising opportunity seems to be the delivery of monetary stability and financial stability, as opposed to short-term economic growth.

At a more advanced level, Rumelt suggests that the two most important natural sources of strength include (1) "having a coherent strategy" (i.e., one that coordinates policies and actions) and (2) "the creation of new strength through subtle shifts in viewpoint." In Rumelt's view, "a good strategy doesn't just draw on existing strength, but through the coherence of its design," and "an insightful reframing of the competitive situation can create whole new patterns of advantage and weakness."[3]

At this more advanced level, a central bank would thus need to (1) make sure that its monetary policy framework, its conduct of monetary policy, its financial stability framework, and its conduct of policies to sustain financial stability (e.g., macroprudential policy as well as monetary policy) are well coordinated, and (2) regularly reflect on and rethink ways to use its strengths.

Proven Bad Strategies

Given that the environment that central banks operate in will continue to change, and that the context might differ from one central bank to another, there might not be one absolute best strategy for all central banks. Lessons from history suggest, however, that there are certain strategies that central banks should not pursue. Examples of bad central banking strategies include (1) directly financing government spending or pursuing excessively easy monetary policy to stimulate short-term growth, which could lead to rising inflation, and ultimately the hyperinflation problem; (2) allowing a financial crisis to deepen without adequate early intervention efforts, which ultimately could lead to the deflation problem as in the case of the Great Depression in the 1930s; (3) pursuing excessively accommodative monetary policy in the face of supply shocks, which can lead to rising inflation expectations and wage-price spirals, as during the Great Inflation period in the 1970s; (4) pursuing the impossible trinity (i.e., trying to maintain free flows of international capital, a fixed exchange rate regime, and independent monetary policy concurrently), which could ultimately lead to speculative attacks on the currency as in the case of the Asian financial crisis in the 1990s; and (5) narrowly focusing on securing low inflation in the short run, while ignoring the possibility that a low interest rate policy during the time of low inflation might also encourage the buildup of asset price bubbles, which might result in financial instability, as in the case of the global financial crisis of 2007–2010.

THE SEARCH FOR NEW CENTRAL BANKING STRATEGY

The recent global financial crisis of 2007–2010, like many crises before it, has prompted a reexamination of central banking strategy by central bankers, policy makers, and academic economists. Work by Borio in 2011, Posner in 2009, and Taylor in 2009, among others, suggest that central banks need to be aware that monetary stability and financial stability are *intertwined* in the long run.[4] If anything, low interest rates prior to the 2007–2010 crisis might have contributed to its emergence.[5] As the depth of the 2007–2010 crisis has shown, financial instability can lead to the threat of debt deflation, which in turn will come back to haunt monetary stability.

Monetary Policy Strategy

On the monetary policy front, lessons from the recent global financial crisis and Japan in the 1980s suggest that in the conduct of its monetary policy, central banks might follow the lead of the Bank of Canada and the Reserve Bank of Australia and explicitly look beyond their normal two-year horizon, since low inflation and low interest rates might lead to asset price speculation, which could ultimately lead to financial instability. Also, a central bank might consider using macroprudential tools to address specific pockets of financial imbalances *ex ante* in case it finds the use of monetary policy to be too blunt for addressing such imbalances.

In terms of using monetary policy to ensure financial stability *ex post* (i.e., as a tool for crisis resolution), there is more widespread agreement that massive purchases of long-term securities might be needed, especially once interest rates have reached the zero lower bound. By 2014 the central banks of four advanced economies, including the Federal Reserve, the ECB, the Bank of Japan, and the Bank of England, had adopted various forms of such purchases, which were previously deemed as constituting unconventional monetary policy. For emerging-market economies, the use of capital controls now seems to be more acceptable, since massive flows of capital from the advanced economies can create excess volatilities that affect the stability of financial markets.

Supervisory Strategy

On the supervision front, the use of macroprudential measures in addition to traditional microprudential supervision is now being emphasized, as reflected partly by the introduction of Basel III. Since the 2007–2010 global financial crisis, there has been great interest in creating and refining macroprudential tools that would deal with risk buildups *over time* (e.g., time-varying capital requirements and dynamic loan loss provisioning), as well as *across institutions* (e.g., macro stress testing, the global liquidity standard, and additional loss absorbency capacity for systemically important institutions). The use of macroprudential measures should also help alleviate the burden placed on monetary policy with regard to sustaining financial stability.

Closer coordination among supervisors seems to be another popular strategy adopted after the 2007–2010 crisis, as it has become clear that the line between different types of financial institutions (e.g., banks, asset management firms, and insurance companies) has become rather blurred. The creation of the Financial Stability Oversight Council in the United States, the absorption of the Prudential Regulation

Authority into the Bank of England in the United Kingdom, and the introduction of the Single Supervisory Mechanism (SSM) in the euro area seems to point in that direction (although in the case of SSM, the main key driver was the blurring national boundary lines among euro area members).

In addition to the above strategies, the recent crisis has also led to a fresh reexamination of the role of central banking in the future. One of the more radical ideas came from Goodhart's 2010 paper that examined historical roles of central banks. In it he asked whether it might be better to spin off the interest rate setting function from central banks and put it into a separate, independent entity, while (since the essence of central banking is liquidity provision) central banks retain the liquidity management function and adopt the financial stability role.[6] (See Case Study: A Radical Rethinking of the Future Role of Central Banking.)

CASE STUDY: A Radical Rethinking of the Future Role of Central Banking

A 2010 paper by economist Charles Goodhart argued that the essence of central banking is its power to create liquidity by manipulating its own balance sheet, and thus the key role of central banking should be liquidity management for the financial system (e.g., through open market operations), not the actual setting of interest rates, which could be done by some other entity.[7] In the paper, Goodhart quotes a former governor of the Bank of England who is reputed to have once said that a central bank is a bank, not a "study group."[8]

Following this line of argument, Goodhart suggested that the interest setting role (i.e., the conduct of monetary policy) could be spun off from central banks, possibly to a politically independent study group. Central banks, meanwhile, would concentrate on liquidity management and other tasks that might be related to a central bank's balance sheet (e.g., the lender-of-last-resort role and the implementation of quantitative easing when interest rates hit the zero lower bound). In normal times, a central bank would do open market operations (OMOs) to ensure that short-term interest rates would remain close to the interest rates set by the so-called study group.[9]

Although Goodhart argued in favor of spinning off the interest rate setting function (since liquidity management and crisis resolution and prevention might need to be closely coordinated with the government while the interest rate setting function requires political independence), he also acknowledged that in practice, setting interest rates and OMOs are two closely connected facets of monetary policy. If the interest rate setting body is outside the central bank, then which entity would decide on the size of quantitative easing measures? Or, if interest rates have risen beyond the zero lower bound, which entity would set the width of the interest rate corridor, or the terms on the discount window, for example?[10]

14.2 EFFECTIVE EXECUTION OF CENTRAL BANKING STRATEGY

Whatever strategy a central bank ultimately chooses to adopt, the success of a central bank in achieving its mandates also relies heavily on effective execution of its adopted strategy. In this section, we will use a public policy analysis framework to examine ways that a central bank might enhance its capacity to effectively execute its chosen strategy.

Here is should be noted that while a central bank is a bank, in the modern context it is essentially a public entity. The modern central bank's role in society is to deliver monetary stability and financial stability, which are essentially public goods that cannot be efficiently provided by the private sector, since markets are not able to correctly price public goods. As such, a public policy framework is used here for the analysis of how to enhance a central bank's capacity to execute its strategies.

A Public Policy Analysis Framework for Enhancing a Central Bank's Capacity to Execute Its Chosen Strategy

In successfully formulating a strategy to meet future challenges, a central bank first needs to assess its likely future environment. As discussed in the previous chapter, the *intensification of globalization*, the *continued evolution in financial activities*, and *unfinished business from the global financial crisis* could all bring fundamental changes that affect the global financial and economic landscape that a central bank operates in, although the actual context might differ from one central bank to another.

To successfully operate in the new environment, which is likely to be very complex and full of uncertainty, and deliver *value* to its society,* a central bank will need to (1) understand and adequately prepare for changes in the environment it is operating in, (2) be flexible and inventive in the use of its policy instruments, and (3) be able to gain public support when implementing necessary policies that might also create winners and losers. (See Figure 14.1.)

To meet such future challenges, one might find it useful to adopt the framework proposed by Wu, Ramesh, Howlett, and Fritzen in their 2010 book, which argues that for a public entity to effectively conduct its policy, the institution will need (1) *analytical capacity*, (2) *organizational capacity*, and (3) *political capacity*.[11]

Such a framework is advocated here because it recognizes that to succeed in an uncertain environment, a central bank needs not only analytical capacity (something that is well recognized within central banks' circles), but also the capacity to effectively *execute* and *coordinate* policies in order to deliver value to its society.

A central bank does not operate in a vacuum, and it does indeed have stakeholders to tend to or to work with. Consequently, along with analytical capacity, organizational capacity and political capacity are also essential ingredients if a central bank is to be able to effectively deliver value to society (e.g., by sustaining monetary and

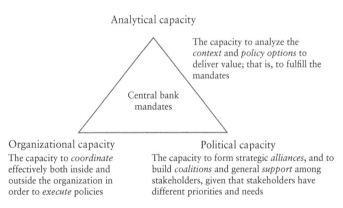

Analytical capacity

The capacity to analyze the *context* and *policy options* to deliver value; that is, to fulfill the mandates

Central bank mandates

Organizational capacity
The capacity to *coordinate* effectively both inside and outside the organization in order to *execute* policies

Political capacity
The capacity to form strategic *alliances*, and to build *coalitions* and general *support* among stakeholders, given that stakeholders have different priorities and needs

FIGURE 14.1   A Public Policy Analysis Framework for Central Banks
Source: Adapted from X. Wu, M. Ramesh, M. Howlett, and S. A. Fritzen, *The Public Policy Primer: Managing the Policy Process* (New York: Routledge, 2010).

---

*In the modern context, the value that a central bank delivers to society is reflected in its mandates, whether those mandates are monetary stability, financial stability, or, in the case of the United States, full employment.

financial stability, or by achieving their other mandates, such as full employment in the case of the United States).

Analytical Capacity

Analytical capacity in our context refers to a central bank's capacity to effectively analyze how changes in the economic and financial environment might affect their mandates, and what policy options might be available to address those changes. This capacity depends on *cognitive ability*, *expertise*, and the *experience* of central bank staff, as well as the availability of data to be used in the analysis.

Greater Emphasis on Cross-Discipline Institutional Knowledge   In the past 40 years, with the emphasis on maintaining monetary stability, a lot of focus has been given to analytical capacity in the field of *macroeconomics*. However, given emerging challenges such as the intensification of globalization, and the rise of financial markets and international intermediaries, it is easy to see that analytical capacity as related to financial stability will become very important. To achieve monetary and financial stability in the next era, central bankers will not only need deep technical knowledge in macroeconomics, but also in *finance*, *law*, *accounting*, and *financial risk management*.

To effectively increase analytical capacity, deep technical knowledge will need to be augmented by a practical understanding of the actual inner workings of three key overlapping areas: the *macroeconomy*, *financial markets*, and *financial institutions*, as well as how risk factors in each of the three areas might interact. To top it off, information needed for pertinent economic and financial analyses will also need to be systemically gathered, organized, stored, and used. Central banks will need to invest in IT capability.

Academic and Professional Training, Hands-On Experience, Job Rotation, Data Collection and Dissemination   For central bankers, such an enhancement in analytical capacity might be gained from *academic training* and *professional training* and augmented by *hands-on experience* and *job rotations*. Such training and rotation might take place within the central bank or with outside agencies, domestic as well as international.

In addition, to effectively raise analytical capacity, the availability and capability of a central bank's IT system for *data collection* and *dissemination*, and the ability of central bankers to utilize such a system, will also be vital.

This need for analytical capacity in the key areas of macroeconomics, finance, and risk management is reflected in the recent selections of the heads of the Bank of England, the Federal Reserve, the ECB, and the Bank of Japan in the period immediately after the 2007–2010 crisis. Each of the heads of these major central banks have advanced degrees in economics, as well as extensive experience in dealing with international financial markets and financial institutions.[*]

---

[*]Mario Draghi (an Italian) became the head of the ECB in 2011; Mark Carney (a Canadian) became the governor of the Bank of England in 2013; Haruhiko Kuroda became the governor of the Bank of Japan in 2013; and Janet Yellen became chair of the Federal Reserve in 2014.

Organizational Capacity

Organizational capacity refers to the capacity to coordinate effectively, both internally within the organization and externally with outside stakeholders. Given that risks to stability can manifest themselves differently in each of the three key areas—the macroeconomy, financial markets, and financial institutions—and that such manifestations can also interact across these three areas, a central bank will need to organize itself to be nimble and flexible enough to deal with emerging risks. Effective coordination will be required, not only *internally* but also *externally* (for example, with other regulatory agencies at home and abroad). A central bank's ability to coordinate effectively both inside and outside the organization will be beneficial to its decision making and policy implementation.

Internal Coordination   *Internal coordination* includes data sharing and joint problem solving across the organization. For example, data from banks showing a fast rise in credit card and mortgage debt might be shared by the bank supervision unit with the unit that is responsible for monetary policy and monetary stability, which itself is monitoring the rise in household debt. Another example could be data sharing between the unit that does foreign exchange market interventions, the unit that monitors banks' foreign currency exposures, and the unit that is monitoring the effects of the exchange rate on the macroeconomy.

In cases in which internal data sharing and joint problem solving needs to be improved, a central bank might set up an internal committee to coordinate and facilitate these activities across units, or even to make relevant decisions. The key, however, is to make sure that the committee is flexible and nimble enough to identify risks as they emerge. If the context or the situation permits, such a committee might also be given the responsibility to deal with the risks identified.

External Coordination: *Domestic* **as Well as** *International*   As risks to stability can also come from areas outside a central bank's full jurisdiction (e.g., money market funds and insurance companies), a central bank's ability to effectively coordinate with outside agencies will be essential in terms of both identification and management of risks. A central bank might proactively try to reach out to agencies on its own, or it could participate through an interagency forum if there is one. In the United States, the Financial Stability Oversight Council, composed of the heads of various regulatory agencies and the Federal Reserve and chaired by the Treasury secretary, was set up in 2010 in response to the lessons learned from the collapse of Lehman Brothers in 2008.

In addition to external coordination with other domestic regulatory agencies, given that external factors are having an increasing influence on domestic stability, a central bank will also need to coordinate effectively with its foreign counterparts and foreign agencies, including multilateral financial institutions such as the IMF and the BIS (Bank for International Settlements). During the height of the 2008–2010 financial crisis, the ability of many central banks to open reciprocal currency swap lines with the Federal Reserve helped ensure that there would not be a shortage of U.S. dollars in international markets, avoiding the potential for global panics.

Political Capacity

Political capacity in this context means the ability of a central bank to form strategic alliances and build coalitions and support among its key *stakeholders* and the *public*, so that it can effectively and efficiently achieve its mandates and create value for society.* This capacity is important since many of the policies conducted by a central bank can create winners and losers within the society, drawing political resistance from the losers. Yet such policies might be necessary for the greater good of the public in the long run.

Ability to Create Consensus and Legitimacy for Policies   Given the intensification of globalization, the rise of financial markets, and the rise of international financial intermediaries, the environment that a central bank operates in is likely to grow more complex. In such a situation, a central bank will need to deal with the fact that different *stakeholders* might have conflicting interests and conflicting perceptions of situations. To effectively implement its policy in a complex environment, a central bank will need to generate trust among its stakeholders so that they are confident that the bank has the best interests of the public in mind.

To do this, a central bank will first need to identify the key stakeholders and their interests. The bank will then need to communicate clearly to the stakeholders what the ultimate goals of its policies are and what the short-term and long-term effects of such policies might be.

For example, to ensure both long-term monetary stability and long-term financial stability, a central bank might find itself needing to raise interest rates to cool down overheated economic and financial activities. The decision to raise interest rates, however, might draw criticism and political resistance from the government, which inherently wants more growth in the economy, as well as from businesses, which want to keep the cost of capital low.

If a central bank does not have enough political capacity, then it might need to spend excessive energy defending its position. Worse, without adequate political capacity a central bank might be pressured to back away from its decision, a decision that had been made based on improving the welfare of the public as a whole.

CASE STUDY: Political Capacity in the Context of Exchange Rate Policy in a Small, Open Economy

A rush of capital inflows can affect different stakeholders in a small, open economy differently, which means that different stakeholders might react to the situation in conflicting ways. In such a situation, the central bank of that small, open economy might need to rely on its political capacity to ensure that its policy decision is effective.

In this example, the rush of capital inflows could quickly push up the exchange rate of that small, open economy. The fast appreciation of the exchange rate, however, could affect importers, consumers, exporters, and local producers that compete with imports rather differently, or even in opposite ways. On the one hand, *importers* and *consumers* might gain additional purchasing power from a

---

*The term *politics* can be a charged word in central bank circles. Here we employ the term *political capacity* used in the 2010 book from Wu, Ramesh, Howlett, and Fritzen.

stronger exchange rate. On the other hand, *exporters* and *local producers that compete with imports* might lose from such a situation, since their products will have a cost disadvantage.

While importers and consumers might keep relatively quiet about the gains that they have gotten—partly because the gains are dispersed widely across many individuals and firms—exporters and local producers that compete with imports might be more vocal about the situation—partly because they feel that they are bearing the brunt of the burden of the fast appreciating exchange rate.

The *government*, meanwhile, might see the situation as an opportunity to pressure the central bank to lower interest rates (at least through the media), using the argument that having domestic interest rates that are higher than those in the advanced economies is actually attracting capital inflows. Many businesses might agree with the government's push for lower interest rates, since they might want the cost of funds to be lower.

Against this backdrop, the central bank's own *internal* analysis might suggest that interest rates actually need to be *raised* to maintain monetary and financial stability in the face of such capital inflows. Its internal analysis might suggest that capital inflows are the result of an external factor (quantitative easing in this case), since all countries in the region have similar levels of interest rates and all are on the receiving end of the capital inflows.

In such a complex situation, in order to carry out its policy as effectively and as efficiently as possible, a central bank will need to deal effectively with pressures coming from the different stakeholders. A central bank will need to communicate its assessment of the situation to the different stakeholders in the clearest manner possible to generate trust among them. Furthermore, the central bank might need to engage with the media and the academic community to form a *strategic alliance* that can communicate the situation to the public and build public support. (This example reflects a situation faced by the Bank of Thailand between 2010 and mid-2013.[12])

Forming Strategic Alliances with Key Stakeholders and Communicating with the Public To ensure consensus and that its policy is seen as legitimate, a central bank might need to form *strategic alliances* with influential actors, including the media, academics, think tanks, and other stakeholders who can help communicate its position to the public. One key example of the use of political capacity is the decision of the chairman of the Federal Reserve, Ben Bernanke, to give an unprecedented exclusive interview to *60 Minutes*, a popular television investigative news program, in 2009 at the height of the crisis.[13]

In the interview, Chairman Bernanke led the interviewer to the inside of the Federal Reserve building in Washington, DC, and then into the room where the Federal Open Market Committee (FOMC) meets to deliberate on monetary policy decisions. He also brought him to his childhood home in South Carolina. Bernanke was able to answer the questions about the Federal Reserve's policies that had been on the minds of many Americans, explaining his answers in simple terms.[14] By opening up and humanizing the Federal Reserve, and clearly articulating the Federal Reserve's positions, Ben Bernanke was able to generate public trust that many believed greatly helped the Federal Reserve in subsequently dealing with the financial crisis.

14.3 EPILOGUE: FROM THE PAST TO THE PRESENT AND BEYOND

The central bank has evolved greatly during its nearly 400 years of history. From its humble origins as an institution set up to simply help sort metal coins, the central bank is now at the center of modern economic and financial life. While the actual operations and structures of different central banks differ, it is widely accepted at this time in history that central banks' key mandates include the maintenance of monetary stability and financial stability (and perhaps full employment, at least in the United States).

The current state of central banking has been shaped by both theoretical developments and hard experience learned through episodes of instability and crisis. With respect to monetary stability, it is now widely agreed that a central bank can best use monetary policy to support long-run economic growth by ensuring that inflation remains low and stable. With the central bank delivering low and stable inflation, agents in the economy will be able to make their investment and consumption decisions more effectively. A push by a central bank to stimulate growth in the short run through easy monetary policy is likely to be futile and could lead to detrimental effects, since it can feed inflation.

With respect to financial stability, the crisis in Japan in the 1990s and the 2007–2010 global financial crisis have shown that monetary stability cannot exist without financial stability. Financial imbalances can and do build up during periods of low and stable inflation. Once such imbalances tip into a full-blown financial crisis, the economy can face a deflationary spiral. Given such a threat, a central bank's focus on delivering low and stable inflation will not be enough. A central bank will need to be mindful of how a monetary policy of low interest rates during a time of low inflation might also bring about financial imbalances.

The lessons from the 2007–2010 global financial crisis, however, also highlighted the fact that monetary policy is not a cure-all. For one thing, monetary policy is too blunt an instrument to deal with financial imbalances, as it affects everyone in the economy. Lessons from the 2007–2010 financial crisis suggest a greater role for macroprudential tools, which could be used to address financial imbalances in specific sectors of the economy. Many of these macroprudential tools are currently in an early developmental stage and are constantly being refined; examples are discussed in Chapter 12.

Going forward, the intensification of globalization, the rise of financial markets, and unfinished business from the recent crisis could add complexity to the economic and financial landscape that central banks have to operate in. To successfully maintain monetary and financial stability and deliver value to society, central bankers will need to understand the inner workings of and be able to operate across three key overlapping domains: the macroeconomy, financial markets, and financial institutions. The public policy analysis framework discussed earlier in this chapter can be used by central banks to improve their ability to execute their policies; the framework's emphasis on enhancing analytical capacity, organizational capacity, and political capacity will allow central banks to be better able to meet future challenges and effectively deliver value to society.

SUMMARY

According to Rumelt, strategy can be thought of as "strength against weakness." Two natural sources of strength include (1) having a coherent strategy, that is, one that coordinates policies and actions, and (2) the creation of new strength through subtle shifts in viewpoint.

For central banks, experience has shown that the pursuit of short-term economic growth (whether through the direct financing of the government's budget or excessively easy monetary policy), the interventions that come too late in preventing a financial crisis from deepening, the pursuit of overly accommodative monetary policy in the face of a supply shock, the pursuit of the impossible trinity, and a narrow focus on inflation without regard to the possibility of asset price bubbles are bad central banking strategies.

In the wake of the 2007–2010 crisis there has been a rethinking of central banking strategy, whether in terms of monetary policy or supervisory functions. It is now recognized that monetary stability and financial stability are inherently intertwined, and that monetary policy and macroprudential tools might be used together.

In order to meet future challenges and deliver value to society, a central bank, as a public entity, needs to consider enhancing its ability to execute policies. This can be done by the enhancement of *analytical capacity*, *organizational capacity*, and *political capacity* as defined in the public policy framework proposed by Wu, Ramesh, Howlett, and Fritzen in 2010.

To enhance analytical capacity, a central bank might want to ensure that (1) its staff is well versed in technical and practical knowledge of the macroeconomy, financial institutions, and financial markets; and (2) it has access to appropriate data and tools to be used to analyze the macroeconomy, financial institutions, and financial markets.

To enhance organizational capacity a central bank will want to ensure effective coordination, both internally (within the central bank) and externally (with other regulatory agencies and stakeholders).

To enhance political capacity, a central bank will need to be able to articulate clearly to stakeholders the tradeoffs and synergies that might occur in the pursuit of its mandates, so that it can gain support for the effective conduct of its policies.

KEY TERMS

analytical capacity

organizational capacity

political capacity

public entity

strategic alliances

strategy

study group

QUESTIONS

1. According to Rumelt, what is the basic concept of strategy?
2. What have proven to be bad strategies for central banks?
3. How might central banking strategy change in the wake of the 2007–2010 crisis?
4. What impact will its role as a public sector entity have on a modern central bank?
5. What aspects of a central bank's analytical capacity might be crucial in the face of future challenges such as the intensification of the globalization process, the rapid evolution of financial services, and unfinished business from the 2007–2010 crisis?

6. How might a central bank improve its analytical capacity?

7. What aspects of a central bank's organizational capacity might be crucial in the face of future challenges such as the intensification of the globalization process, the rapid evolution of financial services, and unfinished business from the 2007–2010 crisis?

8. How might a central bank improve its organizational capacity?

9. What aspects of a central bank's political capacity might be crucial in the face of future challenges such as the intensification of the globalization process, the rapid evolution of financial services, and unfinished business from the 2007–2010 crisis?

10. How might a central bank improve its political capacity?

Notes

CHAPTER 1   A Brief Look at Central Banking History

1. Majorie Deane and Robert Pringle, *The Central Banks* (New York: Viking Penguin, 1995).
2. Ibid.
3. Deane and Pringle, *Central Banks*; Stephen Quinn and William Roberds, "The Big Problem of Large Bills: The Bank of Amsterdam and the Origins of Central Banking," Federal Reserve Bank of Atlanta, 2005.
4. Deane and Pringle, *Central Banks*.
5. Ibid.
6. Ibid.
7. Ibid.
8. Michael D. Bordo, "A Brief History of Central Banks," Economic Commentary, Federal Reserve Bank of Cleveland, December 2007.
9. Deane and Pringle, *Central Banks*.
10. Ibid.
11. Ibid.
12. Ibid.
13. Ibid.
14. Ibid.
15. Ibid.
16. Charles Goodhart and Dirk Schoenmaker, "Should the Functions of Monetary Policy and Banking Supervision Be Separated?," Oxford Economic Papers, New Series vol. 47, no. 4 (October 1995): 539–560.
17. Ibid.
18. Goodhart, "The Organisational Structure of Banking Supervision," Financial Stability Institute Occasional Papers no. 1, October 25, 2000.
19. Ibid.
20. Goodhart and Schoenmaker, "Should the Functions of Monetary Policy."
21. Goodhart, "Organizational Structure of Banking Supervision."
22. Maurice Obstfeld and Paul Krugman, *International Economics: Theory and Policy*, 8th ed. (Upper Saddle River, NJ: Pearson Addison-Wesley, 2009).
23. Bordo, "A Brief History of Central Banks."
24. Obstfeld and Krugman, *International Economics*.
25. Charles Goodhart, *Money Information and Uncertainty*, 2nd ed. (London: Macmillan Press, 1989).
26. Ibid.
27. Goodhart, *Money Information and Uncertainty*; Frederic S. Mishkin, "International Experiences with Different Monetary Policy Regimes" (NBER Working Paper 6965, National Bureau of Economic Research, 1999).
28. Lars E. O. Svensson, "Inflation Targeting," in *The New Palgrave Dictionary of Economics*, 2nd ed., ed. Larry Blum and Steven Durlauf.
29. Mishkin, "International Experiences with Different Monetary Policy Regimes."
30. Obstfeld and Krugman, *International Economics*.

31. European Central Bank, "Banking Supervision," 2013, www.ecb.europa.eu/ssm/html/index.en.html, accessed February 13, 2014.

CHAPTER 2   A Brief Overview of the International Monetary System

1. Maurice Obstfeld and Paul Krugman, *International Economics: Theory and Policy*, 8th ed. (Upper Saddle River, NJ: Pearson Addison-Wesley, 2009).
2. Ibid.
3. Majorie Deane and Robert Pringle, *The Central Banks* (New York: Viking Penguin, 1995); Obstfeld and Krugman, *International Economics*.
4. Obstfeld and Krugman, *International Economics*.
5. Ibid.
6. Obstfeld and Krugman, *International Economics*; Deane and Pringle, *Central Banks*.
7. Ibid.
8. Obstfeld and Krugman, *International Economics*.
9. Ibid.
10. Obstfeld and Krugman, *International Economics*; James M. Boughton, "The IMF and the Forces of History: Ten Events and Ten Ideas that Have Shaped the Institution" (IMF Working Paper 04/75, May 2004).
11. Ibid.
12. Obstfeld and Krugman, *International Economics*.
13. Ibid.
14. Ibid.
15. Ibid.
16. Ibid.
17. Ibid.
18. Obstfeld and Krugman, *International Economics*; William L. Silber, *Volcker: The Triumph of Persistence* (New York: Bloomsbury Press, 2012).
19. Obstfeld and Krugman, *International Economics*.
20. Ibid.
21. Edward Nelson, "The Great Inflation of the Seventies: What Really Happened?" (The Federal Reserve Bank of St. Louis, Working Paper Series 2004-001, January 2004).
22. C. A. E. Goodhart, *Money Information and Uncertainty*, 2nd ed. (London: Macmillan Press, 1989).
23. Obstfeld and Krugman, *International Economics*.
24. Ibid.
25. Ibid.
26. Sebastian Mallaby, *More Money than God* (New York: Penguin Press, 2010).
27. B. S. Bernanke, T. Laubach, F. S. Mishkin, and A. S. Posen, *Inflation Targeting: Lessons from the International Experience* (Princeton, NJ: Princeton University Press, 1999); Guillermo A. Calvo and Carmen M. Reinhart, "Fear of Floating," *Quarterly Journal of Economics* 107, no. 2 (May 2002): 379–408.
28. Mallaby, *More Money than God*.
29. Hanspeter K. Scheller, *The European Central Bank: History, Role, and Functions* (Frankfurt, Germany: European Central Bank, 2004).
30. Ibid.
31. Ibid.
32. Obstfeld and Krugman, *International Economics*.
33. Richard A. Posner, "Underlying Causes of the Financial Crisis of 2008–2009," in *New Directions in Financial Services Regulation*, ed. Roger B. Porter, Robert R. Glauber, and Thomas J. Healey (Cambridge, MA: MIT Press, 2009).
34. Ibid.

35. Ibid.

36. Ibid.

37. James R. Barth, Gerard Caprio Jr., and Ross Levine, *Guardians of Finance: Making Regulators Work for Us* (Cambridge, MA: MIT Press, 2012).

38. Randall S. Kroszner, "Making Markets More Robust," in *Reforming US Financial Markets: Reflections and Beyond Dodd-Frank*, ed. Benjamin Friedman (Cambridge, MA: MIT Press, 2011).

39. Barth, Caprio, and Levine, *Guardians of Finance*.

40. Ibid.

41. Gregory Viscusi, "EU Nations Commit 1.3 Trillion Euros to Bank Bailouts (Update3)," Bloomberg, October 13, 2008, www.bloomberg.com/apps/news?pid=newsarchive&sid=aAAqUi9CW.h4.

42. Maria Woods and Siobhan O'Connell, "Ireland's Financial Crisis: A Comparative Context," *Quarterly Bulletin*, October 2012, Central Bank of Ireland.

43. Reuters, "Spain's Public Debt to Approach 100 Percent of GDP End-2014," September 30, 2013, http://uk.reuters.com/article/2013/09/30/uk-spain-debt-economy-idUKBRE98T0G320130930.

CHAPTER 3   Modern Central Banking Roles and Functions

1. F. S. Mishkin, *The Economics of Money, Banking, and Financial Markets*, 6th ed. (Reading, MA: Addison Wesley, 2001).

2. Majorie Deane and Robert Pringle, *The Central Banks*, (New York: Viking Penguin, 1995).

3. Anthony M. Santomero, "A United States Perspective on the Changing Pattern of Payments," Central Banks in the 21st Century, Banco de España Conference, Madrid, 2006; Curzio Giannini, *The Age of Central Banks* (Cheltenham, UK: Edward Elgar, 2011).

4. Maxwell J. Fry, Isaack Kilato, Sandra Roger, Krzysztof Senderowicz, David Sheppard, Francisco Solis, and John Trundle, "Payment Systems in Global Perspective," Routledge International Studies in Money and Banking, London, 1999; Gertrude Tumpel-Gugerell, "Driver for Change in Payment and Securities Settlement System," Central Banks in the 21st Century, Banco de España, Madrid, 2006.

5. Ibid.

6. Ibid.

7. Fry, Kilato, Roger, Senderowicz, Sheppard, Solis, and Trundle, "Payment Systems in Global Perspective."

8. Deane and Pringle, *The Central Banks*.

9. Xavier Freixas, Curzio Giannini, Glenn Hogarth, and Farouk Soussa, "Lender of Last Resort: A Review of the Literature," *Financial Stability Review*, November 1999.

10. Ibid.

11. Ibid.

12. Tobias Adrian, Christopher R. Burke, and James J. McAndrews, "The Federal Reserve's Primary Dealer Credit Facility," *Current Issues in Economics and Finance* 14, no. 4 (2009).

13. Tobias Adrian, Karin Kimbrough, and Dina Marchioni, "The Federal Reserve's Commercial Paper Funding Facility," *Federal Reserve Bank of New York Economic Policy Review*, May 2011.

14. Deane and Pringle, *The Central Banks*.

15. Glenn Tasky, "Introduction to Banking Supervision," United States Agency for International Development, June 25, 2008.

16. Ibid.

17. Tasky, "Introduction to Banking Supervision"; J. Beverly Hirtle and Jose A. Lopez, "Supervisory Information and the Frequency of Bank Examinations," *FRBNY Economic Policy Review*, April 1999.

18. Tasky, "Introduction to Banking Supervision"; Board of Governors of the Federal Reserve System, *The Federal Reserve System: Purposes and Functions* (Washington, DC: Board of Governors of the Federal Reserve System, 2005).

19. Tasky, "Introduction to Banking Supervision."

20. Hirtle and Lopez, "Supervisory Information and the Frequency of Bank Examinations."

21. Simon Gray, "Central Bank Balances and Reserve Requirements" (IMF Working Paper WP11/36, February 2011).

22. Ibid.

23. Ibid.

24. Tasky, "Introduction to Banking Supervision."

25. Ibid.

26. Claire L. McGuire, *Simple Tools to Assist in the Resolution of Troubled Banks* (Washington, DC: World Bank, 2012).

CHAPTER 4   A Brief Review of Modern Central Banking Mandates

1. Bank of England, "Core Purposes," accessed November 28, 2013, www.bankofengland .co.uk/about/Pages/corepurposes/default.aspx.

2. Daniel L. Thornton, "The Dual Mandate: Has the Fed Changed Its Objectives?," *Federal Reserve Bank of St. Louis Review* 94, no. 2 (2012).

3. The European Central Bank, "Tasks," accessed November 28, 2013, www.ecb.europa.eu/ ecb/tasks/html/index.en.html; Bank of Japan, "Outline of the Bank," accessed November 28, 2013, www.boj.or.jp/en/about/outline/index.htm/.

4. Thomas Baxter Jr., "Financial Stability: The Role of the Federal Reserve System," Remarks at the Future of Banking Regulation and Supervision in the EU Conference, Frankfurt, Germany, November 15, 2013, www.newyorkfed.org/newsevents/speeches/2013/bax 131120.html; Frederic S. Mishkin, Frederic S. (2007), "Monetary and the Dual Mandate," speech given at Bridgewater College, Bridgewater, Virginia, April 10, 2007, www .federalreserve.gov/newsevents/speech/mishkin20070410a.htm.

5. Baxter, "Financial Stability."

6. Aaron Steelman, "The Federal Reserve's 'Dual Mandate': The Evolution of an Idea," Economic Brief, The Federal Reserve Bank of Richmond, December 2011; Thornton, "The Dual Mandate."

7. Ibid.

8. Claudio Borio and Philip Lowe, "Asset Prices, Financial and Monetary Stability: Exploring the Nexus" (BIS Working Paper no. 114, July 2002).

9. Richard A. Posner, "Underlying Causes of the Financial Crisis of 2008–2009," in *New Directions in Financial Services Regulation*, ed. Roger B. Porter, Robert R. Glauber, and Thomas J. Healey (Cambridge, MA: MIT Press, 2009).

10. Thornton, "The Dual Mandate."

11. Ibid.

12. Ibid.

13. Ibid.

14. Bank of England, "Core Purposes."

15. Claudio Borio, and Mathias Drehmann, "Towards an Operational Framework for Financial Stability: 'Fuzzy' Measurement and Its Consequences" (BIS Working Paper no. 284, June 2009); Garry Schinasi, "Defining Financial Stability" (IMF Working Paper, WP/04/187, International Monetary Fund, Washington, DC, October 2004).

16. Ibid.

17. Borio and Lowe, "Asset Prices"; Schinasi, "Defining Financial Stability."

18. Borio and Lowe, "Asset Prices"; Claudio Borio, "Rediscovering the Macroeconomic Roots of Financial Stability Policy: Journey, Challenges and a Way Forward" (BIS Working Paper no. 354, September 2011); Claudio Borio and William White, "Whither Monetary and Financial Stability? The Implications of Evolving Policy Regimes" (BIS Working Paper no. 147, February 2004).

19. Borio, "Rediscovering the Macroeconomic Roots"; Frederic S. Mishkin, "How Should Central Banks Respond to Asset-Price Bubbles? The 'Lean' versus 'Clean' Debate After the GFC," Bulletin, Reserve Bank of Australia, June Quarter, 2011.

20. Ibid.

21. Borio, "Rediscovering the Macroeconomic Roots"; Mishkin, "How Should Central Banks Respond?"

22. Borio and White, "Whither Monetary and Financial Stability?"

23. Shigenori Shiratsuka, "The Asset Price Bubble in Japan in the 1980s: Lessons for Financial and Macroeconomic Stability" (paper prepared for the IMF-BIS Conference on Real Estate Indicators and Financial Stability, International Monetary Fund, Washington, DC, October 27–28, 2003), www.bis.org/publ/bppdf/bispap21e.pdf; Borio and Lowe, "Asset Prices."

24. Ibid.

25. Shiratsuka, "The Asset Price Bubble"; Borio and Lowe, "Asset Prices."

26. Posner, "Underlying Causes of the Financial Crisis of 2008–2009"; John B. Taylor, "Origins and Policy Implications of the Crisis," in *New Directions in Financial Services Regulation*, ed. Roger B. Porter, Robert R. Glauber, and Thomas J. Healey (Cambridge, MA: MIT Press, 2009).

27. Stefan Ingves (2011), "Central Bank Governance and Financial Stability: A Study Group Report," Bank for International Settlements, Basel, Switzerland, May 2011.

28. Steelman, "The Federal Reserve's 'Dual Mandate.'"

29. Ibid.

30. Steelman, "The Federal Reserve's 'Dual Mandate'"; Thornton, "The Dual Mandate."

31. Ibid.

32. Ibid.

33. Ibid.

34. Board of Governors of the Federal Reserve System, "How Does Forward Guidance about the Federal Reserve's Target for the Federal Funds Rate Support the Economic Recovery?, Current FAQs," 2013, www.federalreserve.gov/faqs/money_19277.htm.

35. Ibid.

36. John B. Taylor, "Discretion versus Policy Rules in Practice," Carnegie-Rochester Conference Series on Public Policy, 39 (1993), 195–214.

37. Richard Clarida, Mark Gertler, and Jordi Galí, "Monetary Policy Rules in Practice: Some International Evidence," *European Economic Review* 42, no. 6 (1998): 1033–1067.

38. Committee on International Economic Policy and Reform, "Rethinking Central Banking," Brookings Institution, Washington, DC, September 2011.

39. Thornton, "The Dual Mandate."

40. Stefan Ingves, "Central Bank Governance and Financial Stability: A Study Group Report," Bank for International Settlements, Basel, Switzerland, May 2011; Committee on International Economic Policy and Reform, "Rethinking Central Banking."

41. Ingves, "Central Bank Governance;" Committee on International Economic Policy and Reform, "Rethinking Central Banking."

42. Ibid.

43. Borio and Drehmann, "Towards an Operational Framework for Financial Stability"; Committee on International Economic Policy and Reform, "Rethinking Central Banking."

44. Committee on International Economic Policy and Reform, "Rethinking Central Banking"; Posner, "Underlying Causes of the Financial Crisis of 2008–2009."

45. Borio and Drehmann, "Towards an Operational Framework for Financial Stability"; Ingves, "Central Bank Governance and Financial Stability."

46. Thornton, "The Dual Mandate"; Board of Governors of the Federal Reserve System, "How Does Forward Guidance?"

47. Posner, "Underlying Causes of the Financial Crisis of 2008–2009."

48. Borio and Lowe, "Asset Prices."

49. Ibid.

50. Borio, "Rediscovering the Macroeconomic Roots."

51. Ibid.

52. Thornton, "The Dual Mandate."

53. Thornton, "The Dual Mandate"; Clarida, Gertler, and Galí, "Monetary Policy Rules in Practice."

54. Thornton, "The Dual Mandate."

CHAPTER 5 Theoretical Foundations of the Practice of Modern Monetary Policy

1. Charles Goodhart, *Money Information and Uncertainty*, 2nd ed. (London: Macmillan Press, 1989).

2. Daniel L. Thornton, "Why Does Velocity Matter?," *Federal Reserve Bank of St. Louis Review*, December 1983.

3. Goodhart, *Money Information and Uncertainty*; N. Gregory Mankiw, *Principles of Economics*, 6th ed. (Mason, OH: South-Western Cengage Learning, 2012).

4. Goodhart, *Money Information and Uncertainty*.

5. Majorie Deane and Robert Pringle, *The Central Banks* (New York: Viking Penguin, 1995).

6. Paul A. Samuelson and William N. Nordhaus, *Economics*, 16th ed. (New York: McGraw-Hill, 1998).

7. Goodhart, *Money Information and Uncertainty*; Marco A. Espinoza-Vega and Steven Russel, "History and Theory of the NAIRU: A Critical Review," *Federal Reserve Bank of Atlanta Economic Review*, Second Quarter (1997).

8. Ibid.

9. Edmund S. Phelps, "Phillips Curves, Expectations of Inflation and Optimal Unemployment Over Time," *Economica* 34, no. 3 (1967): 254–281.

10. Milton Friedman, "The Role of Monetary Policy: Presidential Address to the American Economic Association," *American Economic Review*, 1968.

11. Goodhart, *Money Information and Uncertainty*.

12. Friedman, "The Role of Monetary Policy."

13. Joseph Stiglitz, "Reflections on the Natural Rate Hypothesis," *Journal of Economic Perspectives* 11, no. 1 (1997): 3–10.

14. Lawrence Ball and N. Gregory Mankiw, "The NAIRU in Theory and Practice," *Journal of Economic Perspectives* 16, no. 4 (2002): 115–136.

15. Robert J. Gordon, "The Phillips Curve Is Alive and Well: Inflation and the NAIRU During the Slow Recovery" (NBER Working Paper no. 19390, August 2013).

16. Edward S. Knotek II, "How Useful Is Okun's Law?," *Federal Reserve Bank of Kansas City Economic Review*, Fourth Quarter (2007); Arthur M. Okun, "Potential GDP, Its Measures and Significance," Cowles Foundation Paper No. 190, 1962. Reprinted from the 1962 Proceedings of the Business and Economic Statistics Sections of the American Statistical Association.

17. Knotek, "How Useful Is Okun's Law?"; Okun, "Potential GDP."

18. Ibid.

19. Michael T. Kiley, "Output Gaps," Finance and Economics Discussion Series (2010-27), Divisions of Research & Statistics and Monetary Affairs, Federal Reserve Board, Washington, DC., 2007.

20. Kiley, "Output Gaps"; S. Beveridge and C. R. Nelson, "A New Approach to the Decomposition of Economic Time Series into Permanent and Transitory Components with Particular Attention to Measurement of the Business Cycle," *Journal of Monetary Economics* 7 (1981): 151–174.

21. Okun, "Potential GDP."

22. Robert Lucas, "Economic Policy Evaluation: A Critique," in *The Phillips Curve and Labor Markets*, Carnegie-Rochester Conference Series on Public Policy, 1, ed. K. Brunner and A. Meltzer (New York: American Elsevier, 1976), 19–46.

23. Thomas Sargent and Neil Wallace, "Rational Expectations and the Theory of Economic Policy," *Journal of Monetary Economics*, no. 2 (April 1976): 169–183.

24. Charles A. Goodhart, *Monetary Theory and Practice: The UK Experience* (London: Macmillan, 1984).

25. Bennett T. McCullum, "Rational Expectations and Macroeconomic Stabilization Policy: An Overview," *Journal of Money, Credit, and Banking* 2, no. 4 (1980).

26. Ibid.

27. Finn E. Kydland and Edward C. Prescott, "Rules Rather than Discretion: The Inconsistency of Optimal Plans," *Journal of Political Economy* 85: 473–490.

CHAPTER 6   Monetary Policy Regimes

1. Frederick S. Mishkin, "International Experiences with Different Monetary Policy Regimes" (NBER Working Paper 6965, National Bureau of Economic Research, February 1999); Vladimir Kyuev, Phil de Imus, and Krishna Srinivasan, "Unconventional Choices for Unconventional Times: Credit and Quantitative Easing in Advanced Economies," IMF Staff Position Note, SPN/09/27, International Monetary Fund, November 4, 2009.

2. B. S. Bernanke, T. Laubach, F. S. Mishkin, and A. S. Posen, *Inflation Targeting: Lessons from the International Experience* (Princeton, NJ: Princeton University Press, 1999).

3. Bernanke, Laubach, Mishkin, and Posen, *Inflation Targeting;* Frederic S. Mishkin, "Monetary Policy," *NBER Reporter*, Winter 2001/2002, www.nber.org/reporter /winter02/mishkin.html.

4. Mishkin, "International Experiences."

5. Ibid.

6. Ibid.

7. William H. Branson and Louka T. Katseli, "Currency Baskets and Real Exchange Rates" (NBER Working Paper No. 666, National Bureau of Economic Research, April 1981).

8. Branson and Katseli, "Currency Baskets and Real Exchange Rates."

9. Christopher J. Neely, "Realignments of Target Zone Exchange Rate Systems: What Do We Know?," *Federal Reserve Bank of St. Louis Review*, September/October 1994; Mishkin, "International Experiences."

10. Hong Kong Monetary Authority, "An Introduction to the Hong Kong Monetary Authority," 2013, www.hkma.gov.hk/media/eng/publication-and-research/reference-materials/intro_to_hkma.pdf.

11. Mishkin, "International Experiences."

12. Frederic S. Mishkin, "From Monetary Targeting to Inflation Targeting: Lessons from the Industrialized Countries" (Bank of Mexico Conference, "Stabilization and Monetary Policy: The International Experience," Mexico City, November 14–15, 2000).

13. Ibid.

14. Ibid.

15. William L. Silber, *Volcker: The Triumph of Persistence* (New York: Bloomsbury Press, 2012).

16. Mishkin, "From Monetary Targeting."

17. Ibid.

18. Ibid.

19. Ibid.

20. Ibid.

21. Mishkin, "From Monetary Targeting"; Silber, *Volcker.*

22. Mishkin, "From Monetary Targeting."

23. Ibid.

24. Mishkin, "From Monetary Targeting"; Alan Greenspan, "Monetary Policy under Uncertainty." (Remarks at a symposium sponsored by the Federal Reserve Bank of Kansas City, Jackson Hole, Wyoming, August 29, 2003).

25. Mishkin, "From Monetary Targeting."

26. Ibid.

27. Ibid.

28. Ibid.

29. Ibid.

30. Charles Goodhart, *Money Information and Uncertainty*, 2nd ed. (London: Macmillan Press, 1989); Mishkin, "From Monetary Targeting."

31. Daniel L. Thornton, "Why Does Velocity Matter?," *Federal Reserve Bank of St. Louis Review*, December 1983, http://research.stlouisfed.org/publications/review/83/12/Velocity_Dec1983.pdf.

32. Ibid.

33. Daniel L. Thornton, "Why Does Velocity Matter?"; Goodhart, *Money Information and Uncertainty*; Mishkin, "From Monetary Targeting."

34. Goodhart, *Money Information and Uncertainty.*

35. Charles A. Goodhart, *Monetary Theory and Practice: The UK Experience* (London: Macmillan, 1984).

36. Goodhart, *Money Information and Uncertainty.*

37. Ibid.

38. Bernanke, Laubach, Mishkin, and Posen, *Inflation Targeting*; Mishkin, "International Experiences;" Greenspan, "Monetary Policy under Uncertainty."

39. Mishkin, "International Experiences"; Greenspan, "Monetary Policy under Uncertainty."

40. Alan Greenspan, "The Challenge of Central Banking in a Democratic Society." (Remarks at the Annual Dinner and Francis Boyer Lecture of The American Enterprise Institute for Public Policy Research, Washington, DC, December 5, 1996), www.federalreserve.gov/boarddocs/speeches/1996/19961205.htm.

41. John B. Taylor, "Discretion versus Policy Rules in Practice," Carnegie-Rochester Conference Series on Public Policy 39 (1993): 195–214.

42. Mishkin, "International Experiences"; Greenspan, "Monetary Policy under Uncertainty."

43. John B. Taylor, "Origins and Policy Implications of the Crisis," in *New Directions in Financial Services Regulation*, ed. Roger B. Porter, Robert R. Glauber, and Thomas J. Healey (Cambridge, MA: MIT Press, 2009).

44. Bernanke, Laubach, Mishkin, and Posen, *Inflation Targeting*; Lars E. O. Svensson, "Inflation Targeting after the Financial Crisis" (Challenges to Central Banking in the Context of Financial Crisis, International Research Conference, Mumbai, February 12, 2010), www.bis.org/review/r100216d.pdf?frames=0.

45. Charles Freedmand and Douglas Laxton, "Inflation Targeting Pillars: Transparency and Accountability" (IMF Working Paper WP/09/262, 2009).

46. Bernanke, Laubach, Mishkin, and Posen, *Inflation Targeting;* Freedmand and Laxton, "Inflation Targeting Pillars."

47. Bernanke, Laubach, Mishkinand, and Posen, *Inflation Targeting.*

48. Mervyn King, "Changes in UK Monetary Policy: Rules and Discretion in Practice," *Journal of Monetary Economics 39* (1997): 81–97; Svensson, "Inflation Targeting."

49. Mishkin, "International Experiences"; Ben S. Bernanke and Mark Gertler, "Inside the Black Box: The Credit Channel of Monetary Policy Transmission," *Journal of Economic Perspectives* 9, no. 4 (1995): 27–48; Lawrence J. Christiano, Martin Eichenbaum, and

Charles L. Evans, "Nominal Rigidities and the Dynamic Effects of a Shock to Monetary Policy," *Journal of Political Economy* 113, no. 1 (2005): 1–45.

50. Mishkin, "International Experiences"; Christopher Ragan, "Monetary Policy: How It Works, and What It Takes," in *Why Monetary Policy Matters: A Canadian Perspective*, 2005, www.bankofcanada.ca/monetary-policy-introduction/why-monetary-policy-matters/4-monetary-policy/; Bernanke and Gertler "Inside the Black Box"; Christiano, Eichenbaum, and Evans, "Nominal Rigidities."

51. Svensson, "Inflation Targeting."

52. Bernanke, Laubach, Mishkin, and Posen, *Inflation Targeting*.

53. Jonathan Spicer, "In Historic Shift, Fed Sets Inflation Target," *Reuters*, January 25, 2012, www.reuters.com/article/2012/01/25/us-usa-fed-inflation-target-idUSTRE80O25C20120125.

54. Federal Reserve Open Market Committee, Press Release, January 25, 2012, www.federalreserve.gov/newsevents/press/monetary/20120125c.htm; Spicer, "In Historic Shift."

55. Svensson, "Inflation Targeting."

56. Ibid.

57. Bank of Canada, "Monetary Policy," Backgrounders, 2012, www.bankofcanada.ca/wp-content/uploads/2010/11/monetary_policy.pdf.

58. Svensson, "Optimal Inflation Targets, 'Conservative' Central Banks, and Linear Inflation Contracts" (NBER Working Paper no. 5251, September 1995).

59. Claudio Borio and Philip Lowe, "Asset Prices, Financial and Monetary Stability: Exploring the Nexus" (BIS Working Paper no. 114, July 2002).

60. Masaaki Shirakawa, "One Year under 'Quantitative Easing,'" Institute for Monetary and Economic Studies, Bank of Japan, Discussion Paper No. 2002-E-3, 2002; Richard A. Posner, "Underlying Causes of the Financial Crisis 2008–2009," *in New Directions in Financial Services Regulation*, ed. Roger B. Porter, Robert R. Glauber, and Thomas J. Healey (Cambridge, MA: MIT Press, 2009).

61. Shirakawa, "One Year under 'Quantitative Easing'"; Borio and Lowe, "Asset Prices."

62. Claudio Borio, "Rediscovering the Macroeconomic Roots of Financial Stability Policy: Journey, Challenges and a Way Forward" (BIS Working Paper no. 354, September 2011).

63. Ibid.

64. Reserve Bank of Australia, "Inflation Target," in *Monetary Policy*, 2013, www.rba.gov.au/monetary-policy/inflation-target.html

65. Stefan Ingves, "Central Bank Governance and Financial Stability: A Study Group Report," Bank for International Settlements, May 2011.

66. Kyuev, de Imus, and Srinivasan, "Unconventional Choices"; Shirakawa, "One Year under 'Quantitative Easing.'"

67. Ben S. Bernanke, "The Crisis and the Policy Response" (speech given at the Stamp Lecture, London School of Economics, January 13, 2009), www.federalreserve.gov/newsevents/speech/bernanke20090113a.htm; Kyuev, de Imus, and Srinivasan, "Unconventional Choices."

68. Bernanke, "The Crisis and the Policy Response."

69. Bernanke, "The Crisis and the Policy Response"; Kyuev, de Imus, and Srinivasan, "Unconventional Choices."

70. Bernanke, "The Crisis and the Policy Response."

71. Bernanke, "The Crisis and the Policy Response"; Kyuev, de Imus, and Srinivasan, "Unconventional Choices."

72. Ibid.

73. Federal Open Market Committee, Press Release, Board of Governors of the Federal Reserve System, September 13, 2012, www.federalreserve.gov/newsevents/press/monetary/20120913a.htm.

74. Kyuev, de Imus, and Srinivasan, "Unconventional Choices."

75. Louise Armidstead, "Debt Crisis: Draghi Presents 'Unlimited' Bond Buying Plan to ECB Council," *The Telegraph*, September 5, 2012, www.telegraph.co.uk/finance/financialcrisis/9523871/Debt-crisis-Draghi-presents-unlimited-bond-buying-plan-to-ECB-council.html.

76. Ibid.

CHAPTER 7   Monetary Policy Implementation

1. Corrine Ho, "Implementing Monetary Policy in the 2000s: Operating Procedures in Asia and Beyond" (BIS Working Paper no. 253, June 2008).

2. The Monetary Policy Committee, "The Transmission Mechanism of Monetary Policy," Bank of England, 1999, www.bankofengland.co.uk/publications/Documents/other/monetary/montrans.pdf.

3. Robert N. McCauley, "Developing Financial Markets and Operating Monetary Policy in Asia" (Financial Market Development and Their Implications for Monetary Policy: BNM-BIS Conference, August 13, 2007).

4. Bernanke, "The Crisis and the Policy Response."

5. Zvi Bodie, Alex Kane, and Alan Marcus, *Essentials of Investments*, 9th ed. (New York: McGraw-Hill/Irwin, 2013).

6. Frank J. Fabozzi, Steve V. Mann, and Moorad Choudhry, *The Global Money Markets* (New York: John Wiley & Sons, 2002).

7. Board of Governors of the Federal Reserve System, *The Federal Reserve System: Purposes and Functions* (Washington, DC: Board of Governors of the Federal Reserve System, 2005), www.federalreserve.gov/pf/pdf/pf_complete.pdf; Ho, "Implementing Monetary Policy."

8. Ho, "Implementing Monetary Policy."

9. Ho, "Implementing Monetary Policy"; Board of Governors of the Federal Reserve System, *The Federal Reserve System*.

10. Posner, "Underlying Causes."

11. Ibid.

12. Board of Governors of the Federal Reserve System, *The Federal Reserve System*.

13. Ibid.

14. Ho, "Implementing Monetary Policy"; Board of Governors of the Federal Reserve System, *The Federal Reserve System*.

15. Ho, "Implementing Monetary Policy."

16. Piti Disyatat, "Monetary Policy Implementation: Misconceptions and Their Consequences" (BIS Working Paper no. 269, December 2008).

17. Ibid.

18. Ho, "Implementing Monetary Policy"; Board of Governors of the Federal Reserve System, *The Federal Reserve System*; David E. W. Laidler and William B. P. Robson, *Two Percent Target: Canadian Monetary Policy Since 1991* (Toronto: C.D. Howe Institute, 2004).

19. Ho, "Implementing Monetary Policy"; Board of Governors of the Federal Reserve System, *The Federal Reserve System*.

20. Board of Governors of the Federal Reserve System, *The Federal Reserve System*; Ho, "Implementing Monetary Policy."

21. Ho, "Implementing Monetary Policy."

22. Ibid.

23. George A. Kahn, "Monetary Policy under a Corridor Operating Framework," *Economic Review* 95, no. 4 (2010): 5; Ho, "Implementing Monetary Policy."

24. Ho, "Implementing Monetary Policy"; Board of Governors of the Federal Reserve System, *The Federal Reserve System*.

25. Board of Governors of the Federal Reserve System, *The Federal Reserve System*.

26. Bodie, Kane, and Marcus, *Essentials of Investments.*
27. Ibid.

CHAPTER 8   The Monetary Policy Transmission Mechanism

1. The Monetary Policy Committee, "The Transmission Mechanism of Monetary Policy," Bank of England, 1999, www.bankofengland.co.uk/publications/Documents/other/monetary/montrans.pdf; Bank of Canada, "How Monetary Policy Works: The Transmission of Monetary Policy," Backgrounders, 2012, www.bankofcanada.ca/wp-content/uploads/2010/11/how_monetary_policy_works.pdf; Ben S. Bernanke and Mark Gertler, "Inside the Black Box: The Credit Channel of Monetary Policy Transmission," *Journal of Economic Perspectives* 9, no. 4 (1995): 27–48.
2. The Monetary Policy Committee, "The Transmission Mechanism"; Bank of Canada, "How Monetary Policy Works"; Bernanke and Gertler, "Inside the Black Box."
3. Treasury Direct, "Treasury Inflation-Protected Securities (TIPS)," Bureau of Fiscal Service, U.S. Department of the Treasury, 2013, https://www.treasurydirect.gov/indiv/products/prod_tips_glance.htm.
4. Joseph G. Haubrich, George Pennacchi, and Peter Ritchken, "Estimating Real and Nominal Term Structures Using Treasury Yields, Inflation, Inflation Forecasts, and Inflation Swap Rates" (Federal Reserve Bank of Cleveland Working Paper no. 0810, 2008), www.clevelandfed.org/research/workpaper/2008/wp0810.pdf.
5. The Monetary Policy Committee, "The Transmission Mechanism"; Christopher Ragan, "Monetary Policy: How It Works, and What It Takes," in *Why Monetary Policy Matters: A Canadian Perspective*, 2005, Bank of Canada, www.bankofcanada.ca/monetary-policy-introduction/why-monetary-policy-matters/4-monetary-policy/.
6. The Monetary Policy Committee, "The Transmission Mechanism."
7. The Monetary Policy Committee, "The Transmission Mechanism"; Ragan, "Monetary Policy."
8. The Monetary Policy Committee, "The Transmission Mechanism."
9. Ibid.
10. Ibid.
11. The Monetary Policy Committee, "The Transmission Mechanism"; Bank of Canada, "How Monetary Policy Works"; Bernanke and Gertler, "Inside the Black Box."
12. The Monetary Policy Committee, "The Transmission Mechanism."
13. Ibid.
14. The Monetary Policy Committee, "The Transmission Mechanism"; Bank of Canada, "How Monetary Policy Works."
15. The Monetary Policy Committee, "The Transmission Mechanism"; Ragan, "Monetary Policy"; Bernanke and Gertler, "Inside the Black Box."
16. The Monetary Policy Committee, "The Transmission Mechanism."
17. Ibid.
18. Ibid.
19. The Monetary Policy Committee, "The Transmission Mechanism"; Bernanke and Gertler, "Inside the Black Box."
20. The Monetary Policy Committee, "The Transmission Mechanism."
21. Ibid.
22. Ibid.
23. Ibid.
24. Ibid.
25. Laidler and Robson, *Two Percent Target*; Bernanke and Gertler, "Inside the Black Box."
26. Ibid.
27. Ibid.

28. Laidler and Robson, *Two Percent Target*; Bernanke and Gertler, "Inside the Black Box."
29. Ibid.
30. The Monetary Policy Committee, "The Transmission Mechanism."
31. The Monetary Policy Committee, "The Transmission Mechanism"; Bank of Canada, "How Monetary Policy Works."
32. The Monetary Policy Committee, "The Transmission Mechanism"; Ragan, "Monetary Policy."

CHAPTER 9   The Exchange Rate and Central Banking

1. Jeffery Amato, Andrew Filardo, Grabriele Galati, Goetz von Peter, and Feng Zhu, "Research on Exchange Rates and Monetary Policy: An Overview" (BIS Working Paper no. 178, June 2005).
2. Ibid.
3. Ibid.
4. Ibid.
5. Ibid.
6. Barry Eichengreen and Raul Razo-Garcia, "The International Monetary System in the Last and Next 20 Years," *Economic Policy* 21, no. 47 (2006): 393–442; Maurice Obstfeld and Paul Krugman, *International Economics: Theory and Policy*, 8th ed. (Upper Saddle River, NJ: Pearson Addison-Wesley, 2009).
7. Ibid.
8. International Monetary Fund, "De Facto Classification of Exchange Rate Arrangements and Monetary Policy Frameworks," Appendix Table II.9, Annual Report, April 30, 2013, www.imf.org/external/pubs/ft/ar/2013/eng/pdf/a2.pdf; Tony Latter, *The Choice of Exchange Rate Regime*, Handbooks in Central Banking No. 2 (London: Centre for Central Banking Studies, Bank of England, May 1996); Stanley Fischer, "Exchange Rate Regimes: Is the Bipolar View Correct?" (Distinguished Lecture on Economics in Government, jointly sponsored by the American Economic Association and the Society of Government Economists, at the meetings of the American Economic Association, New Orleans, January 6, 2001).
9. Latter, *Choice of Exchange Rate Regime*; Fischer, "Exchange Rate Regimes."
10. Latter, *Choice of Exchange Rate Regime*.
11. Ibid.
12. International Monetary Fund, "De Facto Classification."
13. Hong Kong Monetary Authority, *An Introduction to the Hong Kong Monetary Authority*, accessed December 14, 2013, www.hkma.gov.hk/media/eng/publication-and-research/reference-materials/intro_to_hkma.pdf.
14. Latter, *Choice of Exchange Rate Regime*.
15. International Monetary Fund, "De Facto Classification."
16. Latter, *Choice of Exchange Rate Regime*.
17. Ibid.
18. International Monetary Fund, "De Facto Classification."
19. Latter, *Choice of Exchange Rate Regime*.
20. Ignatius Low, Fiona Chan, Gabriel Chen, et al., *Sustaining Stability, Serving Singapore—40th Anniversary 1971–2011* (Singapore: Monetary Authority of Singapore, 2011).
21. Amato, Filardo, Galati, von Peter, and Zhu, "Research on Exchange Rates."
22. K. Pilbeam, *International Finance* (London: Macmillan, 1992).
23. Jeffrey Frankel, "Monetary and Portfolio Balance Models of Exchange Rate Determination," in *Economic Interdependence and Flexible Exchange Rates*, ed. Jagdeep Bhandari and Bluford Putnam (Cambridge: MIT Press, 1983), reprinted with 1987 Addendum in Jeffrey Frankel, *On Exchange Rates* (Cambridge, MA: MIT Press, 1993), www.hks.harvard.edu/fs/jfrankel/Monetary&PB%20Models%20ExRateDetermtn.pdf; Pilbeam, *International Finance*.

24. Frankel, "Monetary and Portfolio Balance Models"; Pilbeam, *International Finance*.
25. Ibid.
26. Frankel, "Monetary and Portfolio Balance Models."
27. Pilbeam, *International Finance*; Frankel, "Monetary and Portfolio Balance Models."
28. T. Anderse, T. Bollerslev, F. Diebold, and C. Vega, "Micro Effects of Macro Announcements: Real-Time Price Discovery in Foreign Exchange," *American Economic Review* 93, no. 1 (2003): 38–62; J. Zettlemeyer, "The Impact of Monetary Policy on the Exchange Rate: Evidence from Three Small Open Economies," *Journal of Monetary Economics*, 51, no. 3 (2004): 635–652; Jonathan Kearns and Phil Manners, "The Impact of Monetary Policy on the Exchange Rate: A Study Using Intraday Data," 2, no. 4 (2006).
29. Latter, *Choice of Exchange Rate Regime*.
30. Ibid.
31. Ibid.
32. Ibid.
33. Ibid.
34. Ibid.
35. Ibid.
36. Ibid.
37. Ibid.
38. Garry Schinasi, "Defining Financial Stability" (IMF Working Paper, WP/04/187, International Monetary Fund, Washington, DC, October 2004).

CHAPTER 10 Financial Stability: Definition, Analytical Framework, and Theoretical Foundation

1. Claudio Borio and William White, "Whither Monetary and Financial Stability? The Implications of Evolving Policy Regimes" (BIS Working Paper no. 147, February 2004).
2. Claudio Borio and Mathias Drehmann, "Towards an Operational Framework for Financial Stability: 'Fuzzy' Measurement and Its Consequences" (BIS Working Paper no. 284, June 2009); Claudio Borio, "Rediscovering the Macroeconomic Roots of Financial Stability: Journey, Challenges and a Way Forward" (BIS Working Paper no. 354, September 2011).
3. Borio and Drehmann, "Towards an Operational Framework"; Borio, "Rediscovering the Macroeconomic Roots"; O. Aspachs, C. Goodhart, M. Segoviano, D. Tsomocos, and L. Zicchino, "Searching for a Metric for Financial Stability," in *Financial Stability in Practice*, ed. C. Goodhart and D. Tsomocos (Cheltenham, UK: Edward Elgar, 2006).
4. Ben S. Bernanke and Mark Gertler, "Financial Fragility and Economic Performance," *Quarterly Journal of Economics* 105 (February, 1990): 87–114.
5. Aspachs, Goodhart, Segoviano, Tsomocos, and L. Zicchino, "Searching for a Metric."
6. Charles Goodhart, "What Can Academics Contribute to the Study of Financial Stability?," *The Economic and Social Review* 36, no. 3 (2005): 189–203.
7. Borio and Drehmann, "Towards an Operational Framework."
8. Gary J. Schinasi, "Defining Financial Stability" (IMF Working Paper WP/04/187, October 2004).
9. Mark Gertler, "Financial Structure and Aggregate Economic Activity: An Overview," *Journal of Money, Credit, and Banking* 20, no. 3 (1988).
10. Claudio Borio and Philip Lowe, "Asset Prices, Financial and Monetary Stability: Exploring the Nexus" (BIS Working Paper no. 114, July 2002); Thammarak Moenjak, Warangkana Imudom, and Siripim Vimolchalao, "Monetary and Financial Stability: Finding the Right Balance under Inflation Targeting" (Bank of Thailand Symposium, September 2004).
11. Irving Fisher, "The Debt-Deflation Theory of Great Depressions," *Econometrica* 1(October 1933): 337–357.
12. John G. Gurley and E. S. Shaw, "Financial Aspects of Economic Development," *The American Economic Review* XLV, no. 4 (1955).

13. Hyman P. Minsky, *Stabilizing an Unstable Economy* (New Haven, CT: Yale University Press, 1986).

14. Charles P. Kindleberger, *Manias, Panics and Crashes: A History of Financial Crises* (New York: John Wiley & Sons, 1978).

15. Bernanke and Gertler, "Financial Fragility."

16. Borio and White, "Whither Monetary and Financial Stability?"

17. Claudio Borio and Philip Lowe, "Assessing the Risk of Banking Crises, "*BIS Quarterly Review*, December 2002.

18. Ibid.

19. Douglas W. Diamond and Philip H. Dybvig, "Bank Runs, Deposit Insurance, and Liquidity," *Journal of Political Economy* 91, no. 3 (1983): 401–419.

20. J. C. Rochet and J. Tirole, "Interbank Lending and Systemic Risk," *Journal of Money, Credit and Banking* 28, no. 4 (1996): 733–762.

21. F. Allen and D. Gale, "Financial Contagion," *Journal of Political Economy* 108, no. 1 (2000): 1–33.

22. X. Freixas, B. Parigi, and J. C. Rochet, "Systemic Risk, Interbank Relations and Liquidity Provision by the Central Bank," *Journal of Money, Credit and Banking* 32, no. 3 (2000): 611–638.

23. Andrew Haldane, "Rethinking the Financial Network" (speech delivered at the Financial Student Association, Amsterdam, April 2009).

24. George G. Akerloff, "The Market for 'Lemons': Quality Uncertainty and the Market Mechanism," *The Quarterly Journal of Economics* 84, no. 3 (1970).

25. Joseph E. Stiglitz and Andrew Weiss, "Credit Rationing in Markets with Imperfection," *The American Economic Review* 71, no. 3 (981).

26. Irving Fisher, "The Debt-Deflation Theory of Great Depressions," *Econometrica* 1 (October 1933): 337–357.

27. Gertler, "Financial Structure and Aggregate Economic Activity."

28. Gurley and Shaw, "Financial Aspects of Economic Development."

29. Kindleberger, *Manias, Panics and Crashes.*

30. Hyman P. Minsky, *Stabilizing an Unstable Economy* (New Haven, CT: Yale University Press, 1986).

31. Bernanke and Gertler, "Financial Fragility and Economic Performance."

32. Borio and Lowe, "Asset Prices, Financial and Monetary Stability."

33. Borio and White, "Whither Monetary and Financial Stability?"

34. Borio and Drehmann, "Towards an Operational Framework."

35. Borio, "Rediscovering the Macroeconomic Roots."

36. Claudio Borio, "The Financial Cycle and Macroeconomics: What Have We Learnt?" (BIS Working Paper no. 395, December 2012).

37. Carmen Reinhart and Kenneth Rogoff, "Growth in a Time of Debt" (NBER Working Paper no. 15639, January 2010).

38. Hyman P. Minsky, *Stabilizing an Unstable Economy.*

39. Gurley and Shaw, "Financial Aspects of Economic Development."

40. Kindleberger, *Manias, Panics and Crashes.*

41. Ibid.

42. Hyman P. Minsky, *Stabilizing an Unstable Economy.*

43. Ben S. Bernanke, "Nonmonetary Effects of Financial Crisis on the Propagation of the Great Depression," *The American Economic Review* 73, no. 3 (1983): 257–276.

44. Gertler, "Financial Structure and Aggregate Economic Activity"; Borio, "The Financial Cycle and Macroeconomics."

45. Gertler, "Financial Structure and Aggregate Economic Activity."

46. Franco Modigliani and Merton Miller, "The Cost of Capital, Corporation Finance, and the Theory of Investment," *The American Economic Review* 48 (June, 1958): 261–297.

47. Milton Friedman and Anna J. Schwartz, *A Monetary History of the United States: 1867–1960* (Princeton, NJ: Princeton University Press, 1963).

48. Borio, "Rediscovering the Macroeconomic Roots."
49. Diamond and Dybvig, "Bank Runs, Deposit Insurance, and Liquidity."
50. Allen and Gale, "Financial Contagion."
51. Freixas, Parigi, and Rochet, "Systemic Risk, Interbank Relations and Liquidity Provision by the Central Bank."
52. Diamond and Dybvig, "Bank Runs, Deposit Insurance, and Liquidity."
53. Ibid.
54. J. C. Rochet and J. Tirole, "Interbank Lending and Systemic Risk," *Journal of Money, Credit and Banking* 28, no. 4 (1996): 733–762.
55. Allen and Gale, "Financial Contagion."
56. Freixas, Parigi, and Rochet, "Systemic Risk, Interbank Relations and Liquidity Provision by the Central Bank."
57. Haldane, "Rethinking the Financial Network."
58. Allen and Gale, "Financial Contagion."
59. Haldane, "Rethinking the Financial Network."
60. Ibid.
61. Gertler, "Financial Structure and Aggregate Economic Activity."
62. Hyman P. Minsky, *Stabilizing an Unstable Economy*.

CHAPTER 11   Financial Stability: Monitoring and Identifying Risks

1. Claudio Borio and Mathias Drehmann, "Towards an Operational Framework for Financial Stability: 'Fuzzy' Measurement and Its Consequences" (BIS Working Paper no. 284, June 2009); C. Lim, F. Columba, A. Costa, P. Kongsamut, A. Otani, M. Saiyid, T. Wezel, and X. Wu, "Macroprudential Policy: What Instruments and How to Use Them? Lessons from Country Experiences" (IMF Working Paper WP/11/238, 2011); Christian Weisstroffer, "Macroprudential Supervision: In Search of an Appropriate Response to Systemic Risk," Current Issues: Global Financial Markets, Deutsche Bank, May 24, 2012.
2. Claudio Borio and Philip Lowe, "Asset Prices, Financial and Monetary Stability: Exploring the Nexus" (BIS Working Paper no. 114, July 2002); Claudio Borio and Philip Lowe, "Assessing the Risk of Banking Crises," *BIS Quarterly Review*, December 2002.
3. Borio and Lowe, "Assessing the Risk of Banking Crises."
4. Borio and Drehmann, "Towards an Operational Framework for Financial Stability."
5. Borio and Lowe, "Asset Prices, Financial and Monetary Stability"; Borio and Lowe, "Assessing the Risk of Banking Crises."
6. Borio and Drehmann, "Towards an Operational Framework for Financial Stability."
7. Lim et al., "Macroprudential Policy."
8. Borio and Lowe, "Asset Prices, Financial and Monetary Stability"; Borio and Lowe, "Assessing the Risk of Banking Crises."
9. Borio and Drehmann, "Towards an Operational Framework for Financial Stability."
10. Borio and Lowe, "Assessing the Risk of Banking Crises."
11. Borio and Drehmann, "Towards an Operational Framework for Financial Stability."
12. Mark Carey and Rene M. Stultz, "The Risks of Financial Institutions" (NBER Working Paper no. 11442, National Bureau of Economic Research, June 2005).
13. Lim et al., "Macroprudential Policy"; Weisstroffer, "Macroprudential Supervision."
14. Miguel A. Segoviano and Charles Goodhart, "Banking Stability Measures" (IMF Working Paper WP/09/4, 2009).
15. Camelia Minoiu and Javier A. Reyes, "A Network Analysis of Global Banking: 1978–2009" (IMF Working Paper WP/11/74, April 2011).
16. Jorge A. Chan-Lau, "Balance Sheet Network Analysis of Too-Connected-to-Fail Risk in Global and Domestic Banking Systems" (IMF Working Paper WP/10/107, April 2010).
17. Basel Committee on Banking Supervision, "Global Systemically Important Banks: Assessment Methodology and the Additional Loss Absorbency Requirement," Bank for International Settlements, November 2011; Basel Committee on Banking Supervision,

"A Framework for Dealing with Domestic Systemically Important Banks," Bank for International Settlements, October 2012.

18. Franklin Allen and Ana Babus, "Networks in Finance," in *The Network Challenge, Strategy, Profit, and Risk in an Interlinked World*, ed. Paul R. Kleindorfer and Yorram Wind with Robert E. Gunther (Upper Saddle River, NJ: Pearson Education, 2009).

19. Franklin Allen and Ana Babus, "Networks in Finance"; Haldane, "Rethinking the Financial Network."

20. Segoviano and Goodhart, "Banking Stability Measures."

21. Chan-Lau, "Balance Sheet Network Analysis"; Basel Committee on Banking Supervision, "A Framework."

22. Basel Committee on Banking Supervision, "Global Systemically Important Banks"; Basel Committee on Banking Supervision, "A Framework."

23. Ibid.

24. Borio and Drehmann, "Towards an Operational Framework."

25. Douwe Miedeman, "U.S. Fed Sets Tough Tests in Annual Bank Health War Games," *Reuters*, November 1, 2013, www.reuters.com/article/2013/11/01/us-banks-fed-tests-idUSBRE9A00W120131101.

26. Borio and Drehmann, "Towards an Operational Framework."

27. Borio and Lowe, "Asset Prices."

28. Borio and Drehmann, "Towards an Operational Framework."

29. British Bankers' Association, "BBA Libor," http://www.bbalibor.com/.

30. Rajdeep Sengupta and Yu Man Tam, "The Libor-OIS Spread as a Summary Indicator" (Economic Synopses, Federal Reserve Bank of St. Louis, 2008). http://research.stlouisfed.org/publications/es/08/ES0825.pdf, Retrieved March 10, 2014.

31. Daniel L. Thornton, "What the Libor-OIS Spread Says" (Economic Synopses, Federal Reserve Bank of St. Louis, May 2009). http://research.stlouisfed.org/publications/es/09/ES0924.pdf, Retrieved March 10, 2014.

32. Steven Drobny, *The Invisible Hands: Hedge Funds Off the Record—Rethinking Real Money*, (Hoboken, NJ: John Wiley & Sons, 2010).

33. Rajdeep Sengupta and Yu Man Tam, "The Libor-OIS Spread as a Summary Indicator" (Economic Synopses, Federal Reserve Bank of St. Louis), http://research.stlouisfed.org/publications/es/08/ES0825.pdf, Retrieved March 10, 2014.

34. Lim et al., "Macroprudential Policy."

35. Dale Gray, Robert C. Merton, and Zvi Bodie, "A New Framework for Analyzing and Managing Macrofinancial Risks and Financial Stability" (NBER Working Paper No. 13607, National Bureau of Economic Research, November 2007).

36. Fischer Black and Myron Scholes, "The Pricing of Options and Corporate Liabilities" *Journal of Political Economy* 81, no. 3: 637–654, 1973; Robert C. Merton, "Theory of Rational Option Pricing," *Bell Journal of Economics and Management Science*, The Rand Corporation 4, no. 1: 141–183, 1973).

37. Dale F. Gray, Robert C. Merton, and Zvi Bodie, "New Framework for Measuring and Managing Macrofinancial Risk and Financial Stability" (Working Paper, August 2008).

38. Dale Gray and Samuel W. Malone, *Macrofinancial Risk Analysis* (Hoboken, NJ: John Wiley & Sons, 2008).

39. Dale F. Gray, "Using Contingent Claims Analysis (CCA) to Measure and Analyze Systemic Risk, Sovereign and Macro Risk" (presentation to Macro Financial Modeling Conference, International Monetary Fund, September 13, 2012).

CHAPTER 12   Financial Stability: Intervention Tools

1. Claudio Borio and Mathias Drehmann, "Towards an Operational Framework for Financial Stability: 'Fuzzy' Measurement and Its Consequences" (BIS Working Paper no. 284, June 2009); C. Lim, F. Columba, A. Costa, P. Kongsamut, A. Otani, M. Saiyid,

T. Wezel, and X. Wu, "Macroprudential Policy: What Instruments and How to Use Them? Lessons from Country Experiences" (IMF Working Paper WP/11/238, 2011).

2. Claudio Borio, "Rediscovering the Macroeconomic Roots of Financial Stability Policy: Journey, Challenges and a Way Forward" (BIS Working Paper no. 354, September 2011).

3. J. Patrick Raines, J. Ashley McLeod, and Charles G. Leathers, "Theories of Stock Prices and the Greenspan-Bernanke Doctrine on Stock Market Bubbles," *Journal of Post Keynesian Economics* 29, no. 3 (2007): 393–408; Borio, "Rediscovering the Macroeconomic Roots"; Lim et al., "Macroprudential Policy"; Christian Weisstroffer, "Macroprudential Supervision: In Search of an Appropriate Response to Systemic Risk," Current Issues: Global Financial Markets, Deutsche Bank, May 24, 2012; International Monetary Fund, "Macroprudential Policy: An Organizing Framework," March 14, 2011, www.imf.org/external/np/pp/eng/2011/031411.pdf; Financial Stability Board, "Macroprudential Policy Tools and Frameworks—Progress Progress Report to G20," October 27, 2011, www.financialstabilityboard.org/publications/r_111027b.htm.

4. Borio, "Rediscovering the Macroeconomic Roots."

5. Richard A. Posner, "Underlying Causes of the Financial Crisis 2008–2009," in *New Directions in Financial Services Regulation*, ed. Roger B. Porter, Robert R. Glauber, and Thomas J. Healey (Cambridge, MA: MIT Press, 2009); John B. Taylor, "Origins and Policy Implications of the Crisis," in *New Directions in Financial Services Regulation*, ed. Roger B. Porter, Robert R. Glauber, and Thomas J. Healey (Cambridge, MA: MIT Press, 2009).

6. Borio, "Rediscovering the Macroeconomic Roots."

7. Claudio Borio and Philip Lowe, "Asset Prices, Financial and Monetary Stability: Exploring the Nexus" (BIS Working Paper no. 114, July 2002).

8. Bank of Canada, "Monetary Policy," Backgrounders, 2012, www.bankofcanada.ca/wp-content/uploads/2010/11/monetary_policy.pdf.

9. Reserve Bank of Australia, "Inflation Target," in *Monetary Policy*, 2013, www.rba.gov.au/monetary-policy/inflation-target.html.

10. Lim et al., "Macroprudential Policy."

11. Ibid.

12. Ibid.

13. Ibid.

14. Ibid.

15. Ibid.

16. Ben S. Bernanke, "The Crisis and the Policy Response" (speech given at the Stamp Lecture, London School of Economics, January 13, 2009), www.federalreserve.gov/newsevents/speech/bernanke20090113a.htm; Vladimir Kyuev, Phil de Imus, and Krishna Srinivasan, "Unconventional Choices for Unconventional Times: Credit and Quantitative Easing in Advanced Economics" (IMF Staff Position Note SPN/09/27, November 4, 2009).

17. Bernanke, "The Crisis and the Policy Response"; Kyuev, de Imus, and Srinivasan, "Unconventional Choices."

18. Ibid.

19. Bernanke, "The Crisis and the Policy Response."

20. Claudio Borio, "The Financial Cycle and Macroeconomics: What Have We Learnt?" (BIS Working Paper no. 395, December 2012).

21. Lim et al., "Macroprudential Policy."

22. Borio, "Rediscovering the Macroeconomic Roots."

23. Lim et al., "Macroprudential Policy."

24. Ibid.

25. Basel Committee on Banking Supervision Reforms, Basel III Summary Table, accessed May 11, 2013, www.bis.org/bcbs/basel3/b3summarytable.pdf.

26. Charles Goodhart, "Ratio Controls Need Reconsideration," *Journal of Financial Stability* 9, no. 3 (2013): 445–450.

27. Mathias Drehman, Claudio Borio, and Kostas Tsatsaronis, "Anchoring Capital Buffers: The Role of Credit Aggregates" (BIS Working Paper no. 355, November 2011.)
28. Ibid.
29. Basel Committee on Banking Supervision, Report to G20 Finance Ministers and Central Bank Governors on Basel III implementation, October 2012.
30. Basel Committee on Banking Supervision, "International Convergence on Capital Measurement and Capital Standards," Bank for International Settlements, July 1988, www.bis.org/publ/bcbs04a.pdf.
31. Basel Committee on Banking Supervision, "International Convergence on Capital Measurement and Capital Standards: A Revised Framework," Bank for International Settlements, November 2005, https://www.bis.org/publ/bcbs118.pdf.
32. Basel Committee on Banking Supervision Reforms, Basel III Summary Table.
33. Lim et al., "Macroprudential Policy."
34. Torsten Wezel, Jorge A. Chan-Lau, and Francesco Columba, "Dynamic Loan Loss Provisioning: Simulations on Effectiveness and Guide to Implementation" (Working Paper 12/110, 2012).
35. Committee on the Global Financial System, "Central Bank Operations in Response to the Financial Turmoil" CGFS Paper no. 31, Bank for International Settlements, July 2008); Corrine Ho, "Implementing Monetary Policy in the 2000s: Operating Procedures in Asia and Beyond" (BIS Working Paper no. 253, June 2008).
36. Committee on the Global Financial System, "Central Bank Operations."
37. Claire L. McGuire, *Simple Tools to Assist in the Resolution of Troubled Banks* (Washington, DC: World Bank, 2012).
38. Jesse Hamilton, "Banks File Living Wills Outlining Plans to Dismantle," Bloomberg .com, October 4, 2013, www.bloomberg.com/news/2013-10-03/banks-file-living-wills-outlining-plans-to-dismantle.html.
39. Ibid.
40. Tobias Adrian, Christopher R. Burke, and James J. McAndrews, "The Federal Reserve's Primary Dealer Credit Facility," *Current Issues in Economics and Finance* 15, no. 4 (2009), www.newyorkfed.org/research/current_issues; Tobias Adrian, Karin Kimbrough, and Dina Marchioni, "The Federal Reserve's Commercial Paper Funding Facility," *FRBNY Economic Policy Review*, May 2011.
41. Adrian, Burke, and McAndrews, "The Federal Reserve's Primary Dealer Credit Facility."
42. Adrian, Kimbrough, and Marchioni, "The Federal Reserve's Commercial Paper Funding Facility."
43. Ibid.

CHAPTER 13 Future Challenges for Central Banking

1. International Monetary Fund, "Globalization: Threat or Opportunity?," 2000, www.imf .org/external/np/exr/ib/2000/041200to.htm#II.
2. Peter J. Morgan, "Impact of US Quantitative Easing Policy on Emerging Asia" (ADBI Working Paper Series no. 321, Asian Development Bank Institute, November 2011); *The Economist*, "Electronic Payments in Africa: Cash Be Cowed," September 14, 2013.
3. *The Economist*, "Electronic Payments in Africa: Cash Be Cowed," September 14, 2013.
4. International Monetary Fund, "How Has Globalization Affected Inflation?," *World Economic Outlook*, Chapter III, April 2006, www.imf.org/external/pubs/ft/weo/2006/01/pdf/c3.pdf.
5. Haruhiko Kuroda and Masahiro Kawai, "Time for a Switch to Global Reflation," FT.com, December 1, 2002.
6. Asli Demirguc-Kunt and Ross Levine, "Bank-Based and Market-Based Financial Systems: Cross-Country Comparisons" (Policy Research Working Paper 2143, The World Bank, July 1999).

7. Jeffrey Carmichael and Michael Pomerleano, *Development and Regulation of Non-Bank Financial Institutions* (Washington, DC: The World Bank, 2002), 12.

8. Christopher Condon, "Reserve Primary Money Fund Falls Below $1 a Share," Bloomberg, September 16, 2008, www.bloomberg.com/apps/news?pid=newsarchive&sid=a5O2y1go 1GRU.

9. Satyajit Das, *Extreme Money: Masters of the Universe and the Cult of Risk* (Hoboken, NJ: John Wiley & Sons, 2011).

10. Ibid.

11. William L. Silber, *Volcker: The Triumph of Persistence* (New York: Bloomsbury Press, 2012).

12. Paul Volcker, "The Financial Crisis in Perspective" (keynote address at Harvard's Kennedy School of Government), in *New Directions in Financial Service Regulation*, ed. Roger B. Porter, Robert R. Glauber, and Thomas J. Healey (Cambridge, MA: MIT Press, 2009).

13. Silber, *Volcker*.

14. Ibid.

15. Julie Creswell, and Vikas Bajaj, "$3.2 Billion Move by Bear Stearns to Rescue Fund," *New York Times*, June 23, 2007, www.nytimes.com/2007/06/23/business/23bond.html.

16. The White House (2010), "President Obama Calls for New Restrictions on Size and Scope of Financial Institutions to Rein in Excesses and Protect Taxpayers," January 31, 2010, www.whitehouse.gov/the-press-office/president-obama-calls-new-restrictions-size-and-scope-financial-institutions-rein-e.

17. Lucy Williamson, "South Korea's Growing Credit Problem," BBC, September 16, 2013, www.bbc.co.uk/news/world-asia-24059038.

18. The Economist, "Electronic Payments in Africa."

19. European Central Bank, "Report on Electronic Money," August 31, 1998, www.ecb .europa.eu/press/pr/date/1998/html/pr980831.en.html.

20. British Broadcasting Service, "US Shutdown: Barack Obama Warns of Default Danger," October 2, 2013, www.bbc.co.uk/news/world-us-canada-24375591.

21. International Monetary Fund, World Economic Outlook Database, April 2013, https:// www.imf.org/external/pubs/ft/weo/2013/01/weodata/index.aspx.

22. Standard & Poors, "United States of America Long-Term Rating Lowered to 'AA+' Due to Political Risks, Rising Debt Burden; Outlook Negative," Press Release, August 5, 2011, www.standardandpoors.com/ratings/articles/en/us/?assetID=1245316529563.

23. International Monetary Fund, World Economic Outlook Database.

24. "The Fed and Emerging Markets: The End of the Affair: The Prospect of Less Quantitative Easing in America Has Rocked Currency and Bond Markets in the Emerging World," *The Economist*, June 15, 2013; Martin Crutsinger, "Fed Delays Bond Tapering, Wants to See More Data," Associated Press, September 18, 2013, http://finance.yahoo.com/news/fed-delays-bond-tapering-wants-180106376.html.

25. R. Glen Hubbard, "The Morning After: A Road Map for Financial Regulatory Reform," in *New Directions in Financial Service Regulation*, ed. Roger B. Porter, Robert R. Glauber, and Thomas J. Healey (Cambridge, MA: MIT Press, 2009).

26. Financial Stability Board, "Policy Measures to Address Systemically Important Financial Institutions," November 2011, www.financialstabilityboard.org/publications/ r_111104bb.pdf; Financial Stability Board, "Update of Group of Global Systemically Important Banks," November 2012, www.financialstabilityboard.org/publications/ r_121031ac.pdf.

27. Basel Committee on Banking Supervision, "Global Systemically Important Banks: Assessment Methodology and the Additional Loss Absorbency Requirement: Rules Text," Bank for International Settlements, November 2011.

28. Hubbard, "The Morning After"; Volcker, "The Financial Crisis in Perspective"; Randall Dodd, "Markets: Exchange or Over-the-Counter," Finance & Development, International Monetary Fund, March 2012, www.imf.org/external/pubs/ft/fandd/basics/markets

.htm; U.S. Securities and Exchange Commission, Joint Press Statement of Leaders on Operating Principles and Areas of Exploration in the Regulation of the Cross-Border OTC Derivatives Market, December 2012.

29. Dodd, "Markets: Exchange or Over-the-Counter."

30. U.S. Securities and Exchange Commission, Joint Press Statement of Leaders.

31. Ibid.

32. European Commission, "Commission Proposes New ECB Powers for Banking Supervision as a Part of Banking Union" (press release, September 12, 2012), http://europa.eu/rapid/press-release_IP-12-953_en.htm; European Central Bank, "Banking Supervision: What Is It?," accessed February 20, 2014, www.ecb.europa.eu/ssm/html/index.en.html.

33. European Commission, "Commission Proposes New ECB Powers."

34. European Commission, "Commission Proposes New ECB Powers"; European Central Bank, "Banking Supervision."

CHAPTER 14 Future Central Banking Strategy and Its Execution

1. Michael E. Porter, *Competitive Strategy* (New York: Free Press, 1980).

2. Richard P. Rumelt, *Good Strategy, Bad Strategy: The Difference and Why It Matters* (New York: Crown Business, 2011).

3. Ibid.

4. Claudio Borio, "Rediscovering the Macroeconomic Roots of Financial Stability Policy: Journey, Challenges and a Way Forward" (BIS Working Paper no. 354, September 2011); Claudio Borio, "Central Banking Post-Crisis: What Compass for Uncharted Waters?," in *The Future of Central Banking*, ed. Robert Pringle and Claire Jones (London: Central Banking Publications, 2011); Richard A. Posner, "Underlying Causes of the Financial Crisis 2008–2009," in *New Directions in Financial Services Regulation*, ed. Roger B. Porter, Robert R. Glauber, and Thomas J. Healey (Cambridge, MA: MIT Press, 2009); John B. Taylor, "Origins and Policy Implications of the Crisis," in *New Directions in Financial Services Regulation*, ed. Roger B. Porter, Robert R. Glauber, and Thomas J. Healey (Cambridge, MA: MIT Press, 2009).

5. Posner, "Underlying Causes"; Taylor, "Origins and Policy Implications."

6. Charles Goodhart, "The Changing Role of Central Banks" (BIS Working Paper no. 326, Bank of International Settlements, 2010).

7. Ibid.

8. Ibid.

9. Ibid.

10. Ibid.

11. X. Wu, M. Ramesh, M. Howlett, and S. A. Fritzen, *The Public Policy Primer: Managing the Policy Process* (New York: Routledge, 2010).

12. Suttinee Yuvejwattana and Yumi Teso, "Kittiratt Cites Rift With Bank of Thailand Chief as Baht Rises," Bloomberg, April 19, 2013, www.bloomberg.com/news/2013-04–19/kittiratt-cites-rift-with-bank-of-thailand-chief-as-baht-rises.html; Yumi Teso, "Thai Baht Climbs to 16-Year High on Capital Inflows Into Bonds," Bloomberg, April 22, 2013, www.bloomberg.com/news/2013-04–22/thai-baht-climbs-to-16-year-high-on-capital-inflows-into-bonds.html; Daniel Ten Kate and Suttinee Yuvejwattana, "Kittiratt Urges Thai Rate Cut Exceeding Quarter Percentage Point," Bloomberg, May 10, 2013, www.bloomberg.com/news/2013-05–10/kittiratt-urges-thai-rate-cut-exceeding-quarter-percentage-point.html; Suttinee Yuvejwattana, "Thailand Holds Rate as BOT Resists Government Call for Cut," BloombergBusinessweek, May 2, 2013, www.businessweek.com/news/2012-05–02/thailand-holds-key-rate-as-bot-resists-government-call-for-cut.

13. CBS News, "Fed Chairman Bernanke On The Economy," *60 Minutes*, December 4, 2010, www.cbsnews.com/video/watch/?id=7120553n.

14. Ibid.

Printed in the USA/Agawam, MA
February 4, 2022

787718.105